Dance played a fundamental role in French Baroque theatrical entertainments. *Le Mariage de la Grosse Cathos*, a comic mascarade composed by André Danican Philidor in 1688, is of major importance, because it is the only theatrical work from the court of Louis XIV to have survived complete in all its components – choreography, music, and text, both spoken and sung. It provides a concrete model not only of how dance was integrated into the musical theatre, but of how ballets – or even operas – were staged. Moreover, it uses a previously unknown dance notation system developed around the same time as Feuillet notation by choreographer Jean Favier *l'aîné*. This book reproduces the entire manuscript of the mascarade and provides a comprehensive study of the work itself and of the circumstances in which it was created and performed. Chapters devoted to the music, the dance, and the performers provide a framework for understanding the performance context not only of this work, but of other court entertainments of the period. A study and evaluation of the notation system in which the dances are recorded, together with detailed analyses of the dances and of the movement indications for the musicians, complete the monograph.

Musical Theatre at the Court of Louis XIV

CAMBRIDGE MUSICAL TEXTS AND MONOGRAPHS

This series has as its centers of interest the history of performance and the history of instruments. It includes annotated translations of authentic historical texts on music and monographs on various aspects of historical performance.

Published titles

Rebecca Harris-Warrick (trans. and ed.)
Principles of the Harpsichord by Monsieur de Saint Lambert

Ian Woodfield
The Early History of the Viol

Robin Stowell
Violin Technique and Performance Practice in the late Eighteenth and early Nineteenth Centuries

Vincent J. Panetta (trans. and ed.)
Treatise on Harpsichord Tuning by Jean Denis

John Butt
Bach Interpretation: Articulation Marks in Primary Sources of J. S. Bach

Grant O'Brien
Ruckers: A Harpsichord and Virginal Building Tradition

Christopher Page (trans. and ed.)
Summa musice: A Thirteenth-Century Manual for Singers

Ardal Powell (trans. and ed.)
The Virtuoso Flute Player by Johann George Tromlitz

Keith Polk
German Instrumental Music in the Late Middle Ages

Beth Bullard (trans. and ed.)
Musica getutscht: A Treatise on Musical Instruments by Sebastian Virdung

David Rowland
A History of Pianoforte Pedalling

John Butt
Music Education and the Art of Performance in the German Baroque

William E. Hettrick (trans. and ed.)
The "Musica instrumentalis deudsch" of Martin Agricola

Musical Theatre at the Court of Louis XIV

Le Mariage de la Grosse Cathos

Rebecca Harris-Warrick
Department of Music
Cornell University

Carol G. Marsh
School of Music
University of North Carolina at Greensboro

CAMBRIDGE UNIVERSITY PRESS
Cambridge, New York, Melbourne, Madrid, Cape Town, Singapore, São Paulo

Cambridge University Press
The Edinburgh Building, Cambridge CB2 2RU, UK

Published in the United States of America by Cambridge University Press, New York

www.cambridge.org
Information on this title: www.cambridge.org/9780521380126

© Cambridge University Press 1994

© Bibliothèque Nationale de France – Paris 1994
for the manuscript *Le Mariage de la Grosse Cathos*.
Pho. Bibl. Nat. de Fr. – Paris.

This publication is in copyright. Subject to statutory exception
and to the provisions of relevant collective licensing agreements,
no reproduction of any part may take place without
the written permission of Cambridge University Press.

First published 1994
This digitally printed first paperback version 2005

A catalogue record for this publication is available from the British Library

Library of Congress Cataloguing in Publication data
Harris-Warrick, Rebecca.
Musical theatre at the court of Louis XIV /
by Rebecca Harris-Warrick and Carol G. Marsh.
p. cm. – (Cambridge musical texts and monographs)
Includes bibliographical references and index.
ISBN 0 521 38012 X (hardback)
1. Ballet – France – History. 2 *Mariage de la Grosse Cathos* (Ballet)
3. Court dances – France – History. 4. Louis XIV, King of France, 1638–1715.
5. Musical theatre – France – History. I. Marsh, Carol G.
II. Title. III. Series.
GV1649.H37 1994
792.8'0944 – dc20 93–31380 CIP

ISBN-13 978-0-521-38012-6 hardback
ISBN-10 0-521-38012-X hardback

ISBN-13 978-0-521-02022-0 paperback
ISBN-10 0-521-02022-0 paperback

Contents

List of plates   page ix
Preface   xi
Acknowledgments   xv
List of abbreviations   xvii

1 The performance context   1
    The genres   1
    The king's musical establishment   4
    The musicians of the *écurie*   5
    The musicians of the *chambre*   7
    Instrumentalists on stage   8
    The dancers   9
    The actors   10

2 The creators and the performers   14
    André Danican Philidor   14
       Stage works by André Danican Philidor   18
    Jean Favier   21
       Works by Jean Favier   27
    The singers   29
    The dancers   32
    The Italian comedians   33

3 *Le Mariage de la Grosse Cathos* in performance   35
    The performance circumstances   35
    The work   40
    The work on stage   48
    The performance practices   59

4 The music   67
    Vocal scoring   67
    Instrumental scoring   68
    Vocal forms   74
    Instrumental forms   78

5 The dance notation   82
    The invention of dance notation   83
    The key to Favier's notational system: the *Encyclopédie*   87
    The issue of terminology   92
    Feuillet notation in brief   94
    Favier notation: an overview   97
    Favier notation: a detailed study   99
    An assessment of the two systems   121

6 The dances		123
Introduction		123
I.	Marche pour neuf hautbois, huit danseurs, et neuf musiciens	126
II.	Chœur "Allons, accourons tous"	132
III.	Entrée de deux garçons de la noce	135
IV.	Entrée de deux filles de la noce [Gigue]	140
V.	Entrée des deux garçons et des deux filles de la noce [Menuet]	144
VI.	Air des ivrognes	149
VII.	Rigaudon	153
VIII.	Passepied	161
IX.	Chœur "Passons toujours la vie"	171
X.	La Pavane	177
7 The sources		184
Facsimile of *Le Mariage de la Grosse Cathos* (F-Pn Rés. F. 534^{a-b})		189
Appendix A: Libretto		311
Appendix B: Facsimile of the article "Chorégraphie" from the *Encyclopédie ou dictionnaire raisonné des sciences, des arts et des métiers* (1753)		320
Bibliography		330
Index		337

Plates

1 Floor plan of the apartment of the Princesse de Conti at Versailles *page* 38
2 Mascarade in the apartment of Monsieur le Duc, March 1683   39
3 Mascarade of a village wedding performed at Versailles, March 1683   42
4 Dame Ragonde   44
5 Dumoulin costumed as a peasant   45
6 Example of Feuillet notation   95

Preface

One of the many diversions presented during the 1688 carnival season at the château of Versailles was a mascarade with the comic title of *Le Mariage de la Grosse Cathos*. At the time it was probably regarded as but another of the music and dance spectacles that Louis XIV provided in abundance for the entertainment of his courtiers. It probably should have suffered the same fate as so many of its fellows, preserved only as an entry in a diary or in a list of that season's divertissements. Perhaps the melody lines of some of the dance pieces might have found their way into a collection of favorite tunes, or a copy of the libretto might have ended up in a library. Yet for reasons that can only provide food for speculation, this particular mascarade was beautifully copied in full score by its composer and the choreographies of its ten dances were painstakingly notated. The volume was deposited in the royal library, where it fortuitously escaped the destruction wrought in the nineteenth century when a number of its companions in the music collection either disappeared or were plundered for their bindings. Today this manuscript provides us with our only known example of an essentially complete theatrical entertainment from the court whose dancing set the standard for the rest of Europe.

The work contained in this manuscript is a small-scale mascarade that was probably performed in a private apartment within the château. Its comic subject is the wedding of a gargantuan servant girl, whose main interest in life is food, to her country-bumpkin swain; the "plot" opens with the astounding announcement that fat Kate has snagged a husband and proceeds through the wedding festivities to the traditional raucous serenade that interrupts the wedding night. The village wedding was a familiar theme in seventeenth- and eighteenth-century entertainments and in this one the familiar stock characters are present: the self-important bourgeois couple, the drunk peasant, the pompous priest, and so on. The sense of burlesque was heightened by the fact that the entire cast was male, even the bride, who sings in the baritone range. All the principal actors have singing roles; the dancers represent guests at the wedding. The one exception is the bridegroom, La Couture, who in true musical comedy fashion is required to act, sing, and dance.

One of the most extraordinary aspects of the document in which this mascarade is preserved is its completeness. The first section includes a full score of the music, that is, all of the instrumental and vocal parts for the entire work, plus the spoken dialogue for a scene in the manner of the *comédie italienne*.[1] The second part contains the choreographic notation for the ten dances, and also notates movement for the nine on-stage instrumentalists and for the singers. The fact that the entire work is choreographed already makes it unique in the corpus of Baroque dance; in Beauchamps/Feuillet notation[2] the most that survives from any given theatrical work are a few dances that may not even have come from the same production. In addition, the movement indications for the musicians

---

[1] There is a second, partially reduced score, also in Philidor's hand, in the Bibliothèque de l'Arsenal in Paris; it contains the music and the spoken scene, but not the choreographic notation. See chapter 7, p. 186.
[2] This notational system, invented by Pierre Beauchamps but commonly known as "Feuillet notation" after the man who first commercially exploited it, is discussed in chapter 5.

and singers show how the instrumentalists were integrated into the visual aspect of the performance and provide a basis for establishing the staging of the work as a whole.

The choreographic notation itself comprises another extremely important aspect of the manuscript. The notational system found here is completely different from that of Beauchamps and Feuillet, yet equally capable of communicating complex types of movement. The source dates from 1688, that is, twelve years before Feuillet's first publications, and thus is of very great significance historically and choreographically. It provides a perspective from a different angle on already known physical gestures, introduces hitherto unknown steps, and makes use of symbols capable of notating certain aspects of the dances with much greater precision than does Feuillet's system. The existence of this source adds an entirely new dimension to the inquiry into the invention of dance notation, and pushes our knowledge of Baroque dance back twelve years during a period in which dance technique was developing rapidly.

The manuscript provides a wealth of new information in regard to Baroque dance. Of the more than 335 known dances recorded from the period in Feuillet notation, all the theatrical choreographies, with a single exception, are for either one or two dancers. As a result, most of our understanding of Baroque theatrical dance is based on solo or couple dances and very little is known of how Baroque choreographers treated dancers in groups. *Le Mariage de la Grosse Cathos* contains dances not only for two, but for four, five, eight, and nine dancers. In addition, some of these choreographies exhibit a different use of space and different relationships among the performers than do the dances preserved in Feuillet notation; whereas the latter operate according to strict principles of symmetry, the dances in this manuscript show greater freedom in the positioning of the dancers. They also introduce patterns such as the hey and the line dance familiar from other types of dance but not heretofore seen in Baroque theatrical choreographies. Moreover, in all previously known choreographies the dancers perform the steps in unison (with the exception of some ornamental versions of the basic step for the male dancer in certain couple dances); in contrast one of the dances in this mascarade sets the steps of one dancer against those of a group of four. All ten of the dances enlarge our previous understanding of what constitutes Baroque dance style.

Since the subject of this mascarade is both rustic and humorous, the dances here help fill in another area of the Baroque repertoire in which our understanding is limited, that is, character and comic dances. Very few such dances exist in Feuillet notation – the three choreographies for Harlequin are notable examples – so the dances from this mascarade represent welcome expansions of the repertoire. All of the dancing characters in the mascarade are peasants and several of the dances they perform are quite different from any previously known, either incorporating hitherto unknown steps or making use of known steps in unfamiliar combinations.

This mascarade also includes the only known notated choreographies set to choruses rather than to purely instrumental music. Although it is clear from the librettos and scores of Lully's operas that dance often accompanied choral pieces, none of the choreographies in Feuillet notation is set to choral music. In *Le Mariage de la Grosse Cathos* two of the choruses are choreographed, one of them in a way that is clearly responsive to the text. Both cases provide models for the ways in which the singing chorus and the dance troupe may have related to each other in other theatrical entertainments. Moreover, the relationship between the dance pieces and the sung texts in the mascarade, both choral and solo, makes it possible to see how fundamental dance was to French musical theatre – not as a decorative element, but as a basic mode of expression.

Le Mariage de la Grosse Cathos requires a cast of twenty-eight performers: nine singers, eight dancers, two actors from the Italian theatre, and nine musicians. All of the performers, including the musicians, remain on stage throughout the performance. The presence of instrumentalists on stage was not at all unusual for court productions, as librettos of both ballets and operas reveal. In this case, however, it is possible to establish how the musicians entered, when and where they moved around the stage, how they interacted with the dancers, and what kind of impact they had on the visual spectacle.

Because the choreographic notation includes information regarding all the performers, it is also possible to get a sense of how transitions between numbers were accomplished and hence how the work as a whole was put together.

The combined information of both score and dance notation helps establish with greater precision than is generally possible for music of this period the scoring of the ensemble that provided the music. This mascarade used a nine-member oboe band playing primarily as a four-part ensemble to provide the instrumental accompaniment. The choice of woodwind instruments was undoubtedly due to the rustic subject of the mascarade, but it is striking that there seem to have been no other instruments involved, not even to accompany the recitatives. Both the scoring of the work and the staging information open up new lines of inquiry regarding the functioning of instrumentalists in the seventeenth-century theatre.

Although the existence of this manuscript has been known for some time to a number of musicologists working in the field of French Baroque music, its full significance went unrecognized until it became possible to decipher the unfamiliar choreographic notation. Our early struggles to read the notation were fortuitously brought to an end by our recognition of its Rosetta Stone – the article entitled "Chorégraphie" in the *Encyclopédie* of Diderot. In it Feuillet notation is explained in detail and then compared with another system that is also described at some length. Not only is the second notational system the same one used in *Le Mariage de la Grosse Cathos*, but the notation is attributed to a "sieur Favier," a name that figures prominently among the dancers who performed in the mascarade. Thus the article in the *Encyclopédie* provided us with the key to our investigations into both the content and the history of this work.

The two creators of the mascarade were both members of the royal musical establishment. André Danican Philidor, its composer, played oboe and other wind instruments in several different ensembles, but it is as the king's music librarian and copyist that he is best known today. Jean Favier *l'aîné*, one of the leading professional dancers at the court and dancing master to the Dauphine, composed, performed, and probably also notated, the dances of the mascarade.[3] The librettist's name is unknown, but the names of the performers appear in many other court entertainments. It is clear that this work built upon the talents of a group of musicians and dancers who had worked together on many prior occasions. The very centrality of the performance tradition of which this work was a part makes the new information about music and dance at the French court that it contains of very great importance for the study of French Baroque performance practices.

Against the incomplete performance records provided by other documents from the period, this mascarade stands out in bold relief. In its two parts the manuscript contains information about the number and the identity of the performers; the full score of the music; the full verbal text, both spoken and sung; choreographic notation of the dances; some staging indications for all of the performers; and scoring indications for the instrumental accompaniment. Although the manuscript does not answer all of the questions it raises, it nonetheless makes it possible to reconstruct an entire late seventeenth-century entertainment with a degree of confidence hitherto unimaginable.

This book about *Le Mariage de la Grosse Cathos* is in two parts. The second part provides a facsimile of the entire manuscript containing the mascarade, slightly reduced from its

---

[3] Philidor's name appears on the title page of the mascarade, but nowhere in the manuscript of *Le Mariage de la Grosse Cathos* is Jean Favier identified as the choreographer of the work. It must be noted, however, that choreographers are never named in music scores of the period, and the dance notation portion of the manuscript has no separate title page where his name might have appeared. The case for his authorship of the dances is a circumstantial one: the name of Favier *l'aîné* appears among the dancers in this mascarade and the notational system used to record its dances is attributed in the article "Chorégraphie" of the *Encyclopédie* to the "sieur Favier." Based on the congruence of the name, supplemented by research into Favier's career (see chapter 2), we have concluded that Jean Favier was the person who both developed this particular notational system and choreographed this mascarade. The manuscript reproduced here is the only known example of dances notated using Favier's system.

actual size. The first part constitutes a study of the work that examines it from several angles and places it in the context of other theatrical works at the French court. We have aimed to make this study accessible to a broad audience from the fields of music, dance, and theatre history who come to this book with varying degrees of knowledge about the subject and the period. The seven chapters – devoted successively to the historical context in which works such as this were created, biographical information about the authors and performers, a performance study of the mascarade itself, the music, the dance notation, the dances, and a description of the manuscript – are supplemented by two appendices: the libretto of the mascarade in both French and English and a facsimile of Goussier's "Chorégraphie" article from the *Encyclopédie*. The chapters are largely self-contained, and readers may let their own interests guide them through the book. In the interests of speaking to people from different fields, we have tried to avoid jargon and technical language whenever possible. Even chapter 5, which because it deals with the dance notation contains of necessity a number of dance-specific terms, is arranged to accommodate different levels of interest and experience. The opening and closing sections of the chapter deal with historical and conceptual questions, while the central section explains Favier notation on both a general and a detailed level. Thus most of the chapter should be accessible to all readers, including those who are inexperienced in dance. Unless otherwise attributed, all translations are our own.

In the course of working on this book, we found ourselves frequently forced to reevaluate a number of our earlier ideas, particularly those pertaining to dance, staging, and instrumentation. We found that working intensely on a single mascarade did not impose an ever-narrowing focus on us, but that on the contrary it engaged us in a process that continually opened outwards. It became clear that *Le Mariage de la Grosse Cathos* was not only interesting on its own merits, but that it provided a lens through which to examine many aspects of Louis XIV's musical theatre. We hope that as this mascarade and the notation that preserves it become known to a wider public, other dancers, musicians, and scholars will make use of the information presented here to help them further their own explorations of the repertoire of French Baroque theatre.

Acknowledgments

To the large number of people on both sides of the Atlantic who helped us with our work on the mascarade we offer our grateful thanks. Catherine Massip, Conservateur-en-chef of the Music Department at the Bibliothèque Nationale, gave us her encouragement from the start and graciously made all the necessary arrangements for us to publish this remarkable manuscript. Patricia Ranum guided our first tentative steps into the labyrinthine Minutier Central in search of Favier documents, and Marcelle Benoit lent us her vast experience in interpreting archival materials once we had found them. Régine Astier called our attention to still other documents about the extended Favier family and helped us decipher some of the scribblings and abbreviations of seventeenth-century French notaries. Lois Rosow, Carl Schmidt, and James Anthony generously allowed us access to some of their recent writings prior to publication. Eugénia Kougioumtzoglou-Roucher made information from her doctoral dissertation available to us before it was completed and engaged us in many stimulating conversations about dance notation and terminology. Barbara Coeyman shared ideas with us about the court ballets of the 1680s and about theatrical spaces at the French court. Jérôme de La Gorce provided many insights into the workings of the Paris Opéra and graciously gave us a photograph of a Dame Ragonde from an engraving in his private collection. Bruce Haynes and Marc Ecochard willingly served as sounding boards for ideas about French oboes and oboe bands and provided many stimulating ideas of their own. Marian Smith and Linda Tomko read our entire manuscript and offered many valuable suggestions. W. Sheridan Warrick and Richard N. Schwab provided bibliographic assistance. Michèle Reynier, Danièle Tritsch, and Sylvie Mioche helped on points of translation. John Foster assisted with the computer graphics. Ron Harris-Warrick kept the home fires burning during research trips and late nights at the office. We thank Penny Souster, our editor at Cambridge University Press, for her support and patience. We also gratefully acknowledge the support offered for this project by George Dorris and by the late Howard Mayer Brown.

In the summer of 1991 we had the opportunity to mount a fully-staged production of *Le Mariage de la Grosse Cathos* as part of the Amherst Early Music Festival. We are extremely grateful to Valerie Horst, director of the Amherst Early Music Workshop, for bringing this production to the stage and helping us show how well the mascarade works for a modern audience. Its success would not have been possible without the dedication and hard work of a large number of faculty, staff, and students – more than we can name here. In particular we would like to thank Peter Becker, Marilyn Boenau, Sand Dalton, David Klausner, James Middleton, Lawrence Rosenwald, and Mitchell Sandler.

Our greatest debt is to Ken Pierce, who has been involved in this project ever since the thrilling evening we all spent hopping around a tiny kitchen in Paris as we struggled through the unfamiliar dance notation. Ken brought to this project his superb skills as a Baroque dancer and his insights as a reconstructor and choreographer. Perhaps his most valuable contribution was the reconstruction of all the dances in the mascarade for the performance at Amherst, bringing them to life for the first time since 1688. But even before then he reconstructed two of the dances and trained other dancers for presentations we made in 1988 at the annual meetings of the Society of Dance History Scholars and the American Musicological Society. On the basis of his own experience of working with Favier's notation Ken has pointed things out or sometimes argued with us, but at every stage in the writing of this book his ideas have helped us clarify our own.

Abbreviations

LMC   Little–Marsh Catalogue: Meredith Ellis Little and Carol G. Marsh, *La Danse Noble: An Inventory of Dances and Sources* (Williamstown, New York, Nabburg: Broude Brothers Ltd., 1992).

LWV   Lully Werke Verzeichnis: Herbert Schneider, *Chronologisch-Thematisches Verzeichnis Sämtlicher Werke von Jean-Baptiste Lully* (Tutzing: Hans Schneider Verlag, 1981).

Library sigla

F: France

A	Avignon, Bibliothèque du Musée Calvet
Pa	Paris, Bibliothèque de l'Arsenal
Pan	Paris, Archives Nationales
Pan MC	Paris, Archives Nationales, Minutier Central
Ph	Paris, Bibliothèque Historique de la Ville de Paris
Pn	Paris, Bibliothèque Nationale
Po	Paris, Bibliothèque de l'Opéra
V	Versailles, Bibliothèque Municipale

D: Germany

W	Wolfenbüttel, Herzog August Bibliothek

GB: Great Britain

Lbl	London, British Library
Lad	London, Royal Academy of Dance

NL: The Netherlands

DHgm	The Hague, Gemeentemuseum

US: United States of America

BE	Berkeley, University of California, Music Library
CA	Cambridge, Harvard University

1

The performance context

In 1688, the year in which *Le Mariage de la Grosse Cathos* was performed, Louis XIV was fifty years old and had already been on the throne for forty-five years. France's wealth and power were ostentatiously displayed at the newly expanded château of Versailles to which the king had moved the seat of his government six years earlier. For both political and artistic reasons the king supported a large musical establishment that performed at a myriad of ceremonial and private events – from military parades and theatrical spectacles to religious ceremonies and quiet evenings of chamber music.[1] A sizable proportion of court entertainments – operas, ballets, plays, balls – involved dancing; although by 1688 Louis XIV himself no longer danced, he continued to promote the cultivation of dance as both a professional and a social activity. *Le Mariage de la Grosse Cathos* is but one small example of the kind of balletic events that made the French style of dancing the model for the rest of Europe. This mascarade belonged to a performing tradition with roots in the masked ball, the *ballet de cour*, the opera, and the spoken theatre. The following discussion examines the genres that helped shape *Le Mariage de la Grosse Cathos* as well as the court institutions that supported such performances.

THE GENRES

The year preceding the performance had marked a momentous change in France's musical life: on 22 March 1687 Jean-Baptiste Lully, the dominant figure in French music for thirty years, had died. From his humble origins as a miller's son in Florence, Lully had risen to a role of musical absolutism that paralleled his master's position in the political sphere. Not only did Lully control both the king's musical operations and the most important public musical establishment, the Académie Royale de Musique, or Opéra, his compositions defined the French style. His greatest impact was on the musical theatre – ballet, comedy-ballet, and opera – but even genres in which he himself did not compose – the solo suite, for example – felt his influence. So complete was his domination of French music, both administratively and stylistically, that any discussion of late seventeenth-century music in France is impossible without reference to him and his compositions.

During Louis XIV's youth the dominant form of danced entertainment had been the *ballet de cour*.[2] As it developed in the hands of Lully and his principal librettist, Isaac de Benserade, the ballet consisted of a series of danced entrées organized around a theme, often an allegorical one with an overt political message. The ostensible subject of the *Ballet des Saisons* of 1661, for example, was the succession of pleasures throughout the four seasons taken by the court at the royal château of Fontainebleau, but its true purpose was to set up the young king, who played the role of Spring, as representing the rebirth of

---

[1] For a study of the ceremonial and political roles of music at the French court, see Isherwood, *Music in the Service of the King*.
[2] For studies of the *ballet de cour* during this period, see Fournel, "Théâtre de la cour," pp. 171ff.; Silin, *Benserade*; and Christout, *Le ballet de cour*.

France: the hated Cardinal Mazarin had just died and Louis XIV had now decided to take control of the government himself. This encoding of politics within entertainment already had a long history and was to remain a constant element throughout Louis's reign.

In its structure the ballet was built primarily on instrumental dance pieces. A *ballet à entrées* usually opened with a vocal air, or *récit*, that introduced the subject of the ballet, and then proceeded through a series of dances, each performed by a different set of characters. In the *Ballet des Saisons*, the *récit* by the Nymph of Fontainebleau was followed by separate entrées for fauns, Diana and her nymphs, Flora and her gardeners, Ceres and her harvesters, and so forth. Longer ballets included more vocal numbers, sometimes even choruses. Although a work as a whole might be very substantial, sometimes lasting several hours, the music for individual dances was often very short and must have been repeated several times, particularly in entrées for which the libretto called for some kind of action. The ballet generally culminated in a large group dance, called the *grand ballet*, in which most, if not all, of the characters appeared on stage together. No choreographies survive for any dances from the *ballets de cour*, but the librettos list the names of the participants for each entrée and sometimes offer tantalizing tidbits about the dances, particularly when they were of a pantomimic nature.[3]

A sub-genre of the *ballet de cour* was the mascarade, of which *Le Mariage de la Grosse Cathos* is a late example. By the middle of the seventeenth century the term already had a long history; originally deriving from the Italian word *mascherata*, it applied both to a type of ballet and to a group of people costumed according to a theme who circulated together at a masked ball, with or without participating in the dancing. Dictionaries from the period tend to focus on the second use of the term; to understand the first it is necessary to examine those works that were called mascarades. (Because the English term "masquerade" primarily connotes a costume ball, we have chosen to retain the French spelling "mascarade" in order to indicate the balletic genre.) The distinguishing features of the mid-seventeenth-century mascarade are its subject and its length. Mascarades all have light subjects, usually of a humorous or even burlesque nature, and often have rustic settings. The danced entrées are performed by such characters as village officials, peasants, old ladies, drunks, and gypsies. Social satire is often an important element. Mascarades do not require machinery or other elaborate staging and are generally quite short. They have the same form as the longer ballets, that is, an opening *récit* followed by a series of dances, occasionally augmented by other vocal pieces, but there are fewer numbers in all.[4] In some mascarades the conventions of the ballet form itself are parodied: in Lully's *Nopces de Village*, for example, the closing *grand ballet* degenerates into a brawl when a troupe of gypsies tries to cut the purses of the wedding guests. As will be seen below, late seventeenth-century mascarades such as *Le Mariage de la Grosse Cathos* retained the basic character of these earlier types, but underwent structural changes under the influence of opera.

Still another seventeenth-century use of the term "mascarade" falls between the two given above. Written accounts of the annual carnival season at court often mention mascarades performed during the course of masked balls; these might consist of one or two dances organized around a theme or have some kind of story line and a longer series of dances. A group of costumed dancers might perform a series of Spanish entrées, for

---

[3] See, for example, the sixth entrée from the *Ballet des Arts* (1661), "La Chirugie," which involved a surgeon, four doctors, and eight cripples: "Plusieurs Estropiez de toutes les manieres, dansent une fort ridicule Entrée, qu'un Chirugien sçavant & adroit ayant veuë, il les met en estat, par leur guerison entiere, d'en danser une autre avec beaucoup de disposition." ("Several cripples of all types dance a ridiculous entrée, which a knowledgeable and skillful surgeon having seen, he completely cures them and makes them capable of dancing another [entrée] with a good deal of skill.") *Ballet des Arts* [libretto], (Paris: Robert Ballard, 1663), pp. 18–19. The role of the surgeon was danced by Lully.

[4] Some mascarades from the period, all of them performed at court, include *Cassandre*, mascarade en forme de ballet (1651); *La Galanterie du Temps*, mascarade (1656); *Les Nopces de Village*, mascarade ridicule (1663); *La Mascarade du Capitaine* (1654 or 1664); and *Le Carnaval*, mascarade royale (1668).

example; another might poke fun at a village schoolmaster and his pupils. Such mascarades provided a break in the normal succession of social dances done at balls.[5]

Although most ballets, and probably mascarades as well, were set to music throughout, some, like *Le Mariage de la Grosse Cathos*, incorporated spoken scenes. In the second part of the *Ballet des Plaisirs* (1655), the series of entrées depicting the diversions of the city (the first part of the ballet had evoked the delights of the countryside) includes two little plays: in the first, "four French comedians announce and perform a short comic play"; next "three Italian comedians put on a short ridiculous play in their turn."[6]

The inverse of the ballet that incorporated a play was the much more common phenomenon of the play that incorporated ballet. Both the French and Italian troupes of actors were frequently called in from Paris to put on plays at court; in many of their performances "entrées de ballet" were inserted between the acts. The dancers might be professional, as was the case for an Italian comedy performed in October of 1684 with chaconnes in the entr'actes by Pécour, Favier, and an English dancer; or they could be amateur, as when Racine's play *Mithridate* was performed a few days later by the French troupe with dancing by the Princesse de Conti and other nobles between the acts.[7] Since in such cases the play and the ballet had nothing to do with each other, the same ballet was sometimes repeated for a run of several different plays.

One genre, the comedy-ballet as developed by Molière and Lully, used dances not merely as entr'actes, but integrated them to some extent into the plot of the spoken play. In *Le Bourgeois Gentilhomme* (1670), the best-known example of this genre, the sung and danced *intermèdes* reflect the various ways in which Monsieur Jourdain apes the accomplishments of his social superiors in his vain attempt to become a gentleman.[8] Unlike the *ballets de cour*, which generally had only a single run of performances, comedy-ballets were frequently revived, both at public performances in Paris and at court. As with other plays put on at court, the performances involved actors who were professional, but sometimes drew upon dancers from among the courtiers for the *intermèdes*; this was the case in the fall of 1687 when Louis XIV's son, the Dauphin, arranged a performance of *Le Bourgeois Gentilhomme* in which the noble dancers were supplemented by Pécour and Favier (Dangeau, *Journal* II, p. 67). Yet despite the greater integrity of the genre, the music and dance sections of the comedy-ballets were often excerpted and performed separately or else used in pastiches such as the *Ballet des Ballets* (1671) or *Le Carnaval Mascarade* (1675).

In 1672 Lully took over the operation of the Académie Royale de Musique that Perrin had founded three years earlier. Under his leadership opera was at last permanently established in France, three-quarters of a century after its birth in Italy. Until his death in 1687, Lully composed approximately one opera a year for the Académie Royale de Musique, most of which were performed at court as well as at the Académie's public theatre in Paris in the Palais Royal. During Lully's lifetime, no other composers were permitted to write opera. The establishment of the Paris Opéra brought about the founding of a permanent, fully professional troupe of singers, dancers, and musicians; some of its members came from the ranks of the king's music. One of them, Pierre Beauchamps, who had been choreographing the ballets at court for many years, was put in charge of the newly formed dance troupe. It was his responsibility to provide the choreography for the divertissements that were carefully structured into the prologue and into each of the five acts of Lully's *tragédies en musique*. Although the word "divertissement" implies that the dancing provided a diversion from the storyline of the opera, most of the divertissements created by Lully and his librettist Quinault were well integrated into the plot. In Act III of *Atys* (1676), for example, the goddess Cybèle sends

---

[5] For further discussion of the mascarade within a ball, see Harris-Warrick, "Ballroom dancing."
[6] "II. ENTREE. Quatre Comediens François, affichent & joüent une Piece courte & Comique. Comedie. III. ENTREE. Trois Comediens Italiens representent à leur tour une Piece courte & ridicule." *Ballet des Plaisirs* [libretto] (Paris: Robert Ballard, 1655), p. 19. The text of the plays does not appear in the libretto.
[7] See Dangeau, *Journal* I, pp. 63 and 67, entries of 24 October and 5 November 1684.
[8] For more extended discussion of the integration of ballet into Molière's theatre, see McBride, "Ballet."

a series of dreams, performed by both singers and dancers, to the sleeping Atys to tell him of her love. The celebratory dances and choruses that end Act I of the same opera do not forward the plot, but serve to emphasize the rejoicing of the populace at the arrival of the goddess. Even though dancing occupied a subordinate role to the sung drama and the dancers represented minor characters, dance was viewed as an indispensable element of every act of every opera, one that was particularly appreciated by French audiences.

Even before Lully began composing operas, his ballet and comedy-ballet scores had been evolving toward a more operatic structure. As the 1660s progressed, Lully incorporated more and more vocal music into his ballets, breaking up the sequence of entrées and organizing scenes around larger complexes of vocal and instrumental material. During the 1670s he turned his abilities wholly toward the opera and composed no ballets, but when he returned to the genre again in 1680 with the composition of *Le Triomphe de l'Amour* (first performed at court in January of 1681), his approach to ballet structure had been significantly altered by his experience with opera. In this work, the action within the entrées is carried by the singers, while the dances have more of the character of divertissements inside an essentially vocal framework. This new type of work confused the writer for the *Mercure galant*, who was uncertain as to how to classify it, although he finally settled on "ballet" by default. "I say 'ballet,'" he wrote in one report, "because it isn't an opera. There won't be any *comédie* [i.e., spoken drama]. It will consist of entrées mixed with *récits*, and the whole thing will be called *Le Triomphe de l'Amour*." The next month he reported that "It is neither an opera, nor a *ballet en machines*, but only a mascarade." Thereafter, however, he always referred to the work as a ballet.[9]

Le Mariage de la Grosse Cathos, although on a much smaller scale than *Le Triomphe de l'Amour*, bears more resemblance to it in structure than it does to the ballets of the 1660s. Both this work and Philidor's mascarades for the 1700 carnival season bear witness to the transforming power of the Lullian operatic model on even this modest genre. Rather than making use of dances to depict a sequence of events or to highlight a theme, this mascarade has a plot that is expressed through the sung text and even relies on that most operatic of vocal styles, recitative, in addition to the solo airs, duets, and choruses. Most of the dances in the work are found in one long sequence that functions in the manner of a divertissement within an act of an opera. A higher proportion of the music in the mascarade is vocal rather than instrumental; the dances, as well as the dancing characters, thus occupy a subordinate role in the overall structure.

THE KING'S MUSICAL ESTABLISHMENT

The royal musical establishment was organized into three units according to function: *chapelle*, *chambre*, and *écurie* (stables).[10] Although administratively the units were separate, in practice musicians sometimes held appointments in more than one unit, or musicians from one of the three might participate in events that were theoretically in the jurisdiction of another. Ballet performances at court often drew upon the resources of all three branches of the king's music.

The chapel musicians were primarily singers, supplemented by a few instrumentalists,

---

[9] "La convalescence de ce jeune Prince [the Dauphin] fait qu'on prépare à la Cour avec plus d'empressement & de plaisir, un Balet, qui doit y estre dancé aussitost apres Noel. Je dis Balet parce que ce n'est point un Opéra. Il n'y aura point de Comédie. Ce seront des Entrées mêlées de Recits, & le tout sera nommé, *Le Triomphe de l'Amour*." (*Mercure galant*, October 1680, pp. 279–81); "Je vous ay déja mandé qu'on faisoit de grands appresps pour un Balet magnifique, qui a pour Sujet, *Le Triomphe de l'Amour*. Ce n'est ny un Opéra, ny un Balet en Machines, mais seulement une Mascarade, qui devoit estre dancée à Versailles le jour de la Feste de S. Hubert." (*Mercure galant*, December 1680, pp. 317–18).

[10] The indispensable works regarding Louis XIV's musicians are the two companion volumes by Marcelle Benoit, *Musiques de cour: chapelle, chambre, écurie, 1661–1733* (a 533-page book of documents regarding the royal musicians and their employment) and *Versailles et les musiciens du roi* (the accompanying interpretive study, with a bibliography of almost 400 items). Much of the information in the following discussion has been derived from one or the other of the two books.

who supplied the music for the daily religious services at court. Singers from the chapel, some of whom served simultaneously in the chamber, also participated in theatrical productions, as the inclusion of their names in librettos shows. Such was the case for the cast of *Le Mariage de la Grosse Cathos*, several of whom were members of the chapel.

As the names suggest, the division between the chamber and the stables rested on the differences between indoor and outdoor performances. The musicians of the chamber – singers and instrumentalists alike – performed for concerts, plays, operas, ballets, and balls. The instruments they played were relatively quiet ones such as violin, viol, flute and recorder, harpsichord, and lute. The *grande écurie*, or "large stable," on the other hand, not only housed the king's horses, but administered that part of the royal musical establishment concerned with outdoor performances such as parades, military salutes, outdoor fêtes, and other ceremonial occasions.[11] Since such performances required substantial volume, the instruments of the *écurie* were primarily loud wind and percussion instruments – trumpets, crumhorns, oboes, fifes, drums, and the like. Both the *chambre* and the *écurie* contained several ensembles whose names remained fixed over the years even as their composition changed. Only those ensembles that participated in theatrical productions in the late seventeenth century will be discussed here. Some of these groups not only supplied the performers for *Le Mariage de la Grosse Cathos*, they served as the cradle for the two creators of the work, Philidor and Favier.

THE MUSICIANS OF THE *ÉCURIE*

The *grande écurie*, that part of the king's musical establishment to which most of his wind players were attached, probably provided the instrumentalists who played for *Le Mariage de la Grosse Cathos*. Many of the members of the *écurie* came from large families of musicians who played either together or successively in the different groups. Such was the case for the Roddes family, which in 1661 accounted for eight of the twelve trumpet players (Benoit, *Musiques de cour*, p. 3); such was also the case for the Philidors, several generations of whom found employment as wind players for the king. Some musicians held appointments in more than one ensemble.

In 1688 there were five ensembles in the *grande écurie*: the twelve trumpets; the twelve *joueurs de violons, hautbois, sacquebouttes et cornets*; the six *hautbois et musettes de Poitou*; the eight *joueurs de fifres et tambour*; and the five *cromornes et trompettes marines*.[12] The titles of the ensembles were established by tradition and did not necessarily indicate the actual instrumentation of the groups in the late seventeenth century. The familiar name by which the *joueurs de violons, hautbois, sacquebouttes et cornets* were known, the *douze grands hautbois du roi*, probably reflected more accurately the makeup of the ensemble than did the official appellation. The fact that many of these musicians were capable of playing several instruments further complicates the task of determining the instrumentation practices of the period.

Two of these groups, the trumpets and the fifes and drums, provided musicians only for the occasional theatrical performances that required special, usually military, effects. A third ensemble, the *cromornes et trompettes marines*, in which André Danican Philidor played when he first entered the king's service, also seems to have been involved in theatrical productions only on an occasional basis. The function of the group remains somewhat mysterious: it is rarely mentioned except in records of salaries. According to the

---

[11] The king's two stables at Versailles, the *grande* and the *petite*, still face the château across its expansive front courtyard. The musicians were entirely attached to the *grande écurie*; hence in a musical context the words "écurie" and "grande écurie" are often used interchangeably.

[12] These numbers are taken from membership lists for the ensembles of the *grande écurie* in F-Pan O¹ 872 for the year 1689, as reproduced in Benoit, *Musiques de cour*, pp. 121–2. In 1680 and in 1695, the closest years for which comparable lists are available, the numbers are the same, with the exception of six *cromornes et trompettes marines* in 1680. The *Etat de la France* for 1692 (Paris: chez Jean Guignard, 1692), p. 335, mentions four *hautbois de Poitou* rather than six.

official designations, each of its five members had to be able to play both marine trumpet and one of the four sizes of crumhorn. The latter, a wooden instrument shaped in a curve with a double reed enclosed by a cap, had reached the height of its popularity in the late sixteenth century, when it was generally played in a consort of like instruments of different sizes. Although it seems to have faded from use in other parts of Europe, in France it existed on into the eighteenth century. As late as 1700, Philidor himself scored for the bass crumhorn in his mascarade *Le Roy de la Chine*. The marine trumpet, despite its name, was actually a large bowed instrument with a single string and no verifiable connections to the sea. When played it rested on the floor, and its tone was considered to resemble that of a trumpet. Whatever the origin of the marine portion of the name, the instrument came to be used in France in association with nautical subjects. At least one of Lully's ballet librettos seems to call for participation by members of this ensemble: the fourth entrée of the ballet added to Cavalli's opera *Xerxès* (1660) requires sailors playing marine trumpets; three of the six performers listed are known to have been members of this group. Philidor also scored for the marine trumpet in his mascarade *Le Vaisseau Marchand* (*The Merchant Ship*) of 1700.

The remaining two ensembles of the *grande écurie* had the greatest involvement with indoor performances: these were the *hautbois et musettes de Poitou* and the *joueurs de violons, hautbois, sacquebouttes et cornets*. In both cases the immutable official names of the ensembles hid a flexible and evolving performance tradition. Although for decades the official documents of the latter group list each member as playing both a wind and a string instrument (in 1689, for example, André Danican Philidor is listed as playing both *haute-contre de hautbois* and *dessus de violon*, his brother Jacques the *dessus de cornet* and *haute-contre de violon* [Benoit, *Musiques de cour*, p. 121]), less formal references to the group or its members suggest that by the late seventeenth century the ensemble played primarily, if not exclusively, double-reed instruments of the oboe family. Similarly the members of the *hautbois et musettes de Poitou* played not only the capped double-reed instruments qualified as "de Poitou," but the standard woodwind instruments such as oboe, bassoon, recorder, flute, and musette.[13] During the 1650s and 1660s members of this group frequently participated in performances of Lully's ballets, as a comparison between the casting information in some of the librettos and membership lists for the ensemble reveals.

Still another group of double-reed players was active at court, the *hautbois des mousquetaires*. There were two companies of musketeers, each of which had an ensemble of six drums and four oboes, the eight winds of which often seem to have played together as a single group (see Benoit, *Versailles*, pp. 235–6). Although administratively attached to the king's military establishment, these musicians also performed for ballets, plays, and balls.[14] Membership lists for these ensembles are unfortunately not available for the late seventeenth century.

Since the names of the instrumentalists are not given in *Le Mariage de la Grosse Cathos*, it is not possible to establish firmly which of the wind ensembles might have supplied the nine *hautbois* called for in the mascarade, or whether the performers might have been drawn from more than one group. However, it seems inconceivable that Philidor himself

---

[13] The *hautbois de Poitou* was a shawm with a windcap somewhat similar to that of the crumhorn (for further information see Haynes, "Lully and the rise of the oboe," pp. 333–4), but it is clear that the members of this group did not confine themselves to that instrument. In fact, the ensemble appears to have had two posts reserved for players who were primarily flutists, although they too played other instruments (see Benoit, *Versailles*, pp. 221–3). Even when some performance indications survive, it is often very difficult to determine what instruments the musicians were playing in a given work. Near the end of the *Ballet des Nations* that concludes *Le Bourgeois Gentilhomme*, for example, there is a piece entitled "Second menuet pour les hautbois des Poitevins" [LWV 43/38]. Whether this piece was intended for *hautbois de Poitou* or normal oboes is a subject of some dispute (see Eppelsheim, *Das Orchester*, p. 105).

[14] Records for 1685, for example, include expenses for lodging some of the members of the group at Chambord and Fontainebleau for the entertainments of that season (Benoit, *Musiques de cour*, p. 101). In 1700 the eight *hautbois des mousquetaires* were paid for playing at balls given by the king and by the Dauphin, as well as for the rehearsals for the balls (*ibid.*, p. 175).

would not have played, probably along with members of his family and other colleagues from the court. Whoever the musicians were, they must have belonged to a tight circle of performers, familiar to each other from years of working together in similar circumstances.

THE MUSICIANS OF THE *CHAMBRE*

The largest ensemble of the king's chamber was known as the *vingt-quatre violons du roi* (the twenty-four violins of the king), sometimes called the *grande bande* or the *grands violons*. It consisted of a five-part ensemble of instruments in the violin family: violins on the highest part, with three sizes of violas on the three inner parts (known collectively as the *parties de remplissage*, or simply *parties*), and the *basse de violon*, a cello-like instrument tuned a step lower, on the bass line. Surviving membership lists for the ensemble mention all the performers under the generic term "violon"; thus although it is possible to establish who participated in the ensemble, it is not possible to tell from these lists which instrument or instruments any given member played. Nonetheless, documents from both the beginning and the end of the century show that the two outer parts were heavily reinforced, while the three inner ones were more lightly voiced.[15] This group was widely admired for the precision of its playing, and its five-part framework ultimately became the model for the orchestra Lully created at the Paris Opéra in 1672. It was to this ensemble that Jean Favier's family was attached.

The *petits violons*, or *violons du cabinet*,[16] formed a smaller version of the same kind of five-part string ensemble; in 1692, for example, it had eighteen members. By 1690, if not before, the strings were supplemented by four wind players, two oboes and two bassoons.[17] It was from his position as leader of this ensemble during the 1650s that Lully began his meteoric ascent in the musical establishment at court. According to contemporary documents, both string ensembles performed for balls, ballets, plays, and social gatherings. The true nature of their respective roles in the ballets Lully composed during the 1650s and 1660s is difficult to determine; the librettos from these productions mention only those instrumentalists who appeared on stage, not those who may have played in a pit, while the scores generally transmit the instrumental music without further indications as to instrumentation. Given the respective annual salaries for the two groups – 600 *livres tournois* apiece for the *petits violons*, 365 lt each for the *grande bande* in 1684 (Benoit, *Versailles*, p. 233) – it appears that the smaller group performed more often. It is only for a few productions, such as *Le Carnaval* of 1668 and *Le Triomphe de l'Amour* of 1681 that the participation of both ensembles together can be documented,[18] although they must have combined forces for other performances as well.

The remaining instrumentalists attached to the chamber did not form an ensemble, but consisted of several individuals who played together in whatever combination the occasion demanded, be it for chamber music or theatrical productions. Many of them played instruments that could function in either a solo or continuo capacity, for example harpsichord, lute, theorbo, guitar, and viol. In the late seventeenth century this group included such eminent musicians as Marin Marais (viol), Jacques Champion de Chambonnières and Jean-Henry d'Anglebert (harpsichord), and the flutists Descouteaux

---

[15] In 1636 there were six players on each of the two outer parts and four on each of the three inner parts. By 1692 the balance had shifted still farther in favor of the outer voices, with a distribution of 7-4-4-2-8 on the five parts from top to bottom. For information regarding the distribution of parts in both the *grands* and the *petits violons*, see La Gorce, "Some notes," p. 111.

[16] The *petits violons* were officially attached to the *cabinet*, in essence an annex of the *chambre*, which was administered separately for financial reasons (see Benoit, *Versailles*, pp. 232–4).

[17] The *Etat de la France* for 1692, pp. 226–7, provides the names of the members as well as the date they joined the ensemble: for all four wind players, one of whom was Philidor, the year of entry was 1690.

[18] For the former see the libretto published in Paris by Robert Ballard in 1668, pp. 4–5; for a discussion of the latter, see La Gorce, "Some notes," pp. 107–10.

and Philbert. This last also had talents as a singer; it was he who played the role of the bridegroom in *Le Mariage de la Grosse Cathos*.

The musicians of the chamber included a substantial number of singers in addition to the instrumentalists. Several of the singers who performed in *Le Mariage de la Grosse Cathos* belonged to this group.

INSTRUMENTALISTS ON STAGE

By placing instrumentalists on stage in *Le Mariage de la Grosse Cathos*, Philidor was adhering to a well-established performance tradition. The spatial relationship between performers that prevails in a modern theatre – the orchestra in the pit, the actors, singers, and dancers on a raised stage – was by no means the only operative model for theatrical performances at the court of Louis XIV. There was no single theatrical space that was always used for ballets or operas; instead such works were performed in a variety of different places ranging from outdoor spaces such as courtyards or gardens to rooms or genuine theatres indoors. Of the several available spaces in the different châteaux among which the court circulated, some were simply large rooms which were set up to accommodate theatrical performances on an ad hoc basis. If no pit or other established place for the musicians existed, the court carpenters might be called upon to construct boxes or tiered benches for them; thus the arrangements for the musicians varied considerably depending on both the location and the nature of the performance. In many court spectacles, the musicians were not discreetly located in unobtrusive spots where they would be heard but not seen; rather they were often costumed and incorporated into the visual spectacle.

One of the ways in which musicians appeared on stage in both ballet and opera performances was as participants in a single entrée or scene. The last entrée of the ballet *Xerxès* (1660) involves Bacchus, the god of wine, accompanied by dancing sylvans, bacchantes, and satyrs plus a group of eighteen followers "playing several instruments."[19] Similarly, a number of Lully's operas call for on-stage musicians in such roles as blessed spirits in the underworld (*Proserpine* IV, 1), followers of the *grand sacrificateur* (*Bellérophon* I, 5), and flute-playing satyrs and shepherds (*Isis*, III, 4).[20] In other instances, particularly in ballets and mascarades, the brief descriptions offered by the librettos sometimes suggest that the musicians may have been located on stage throughout the performance. *Le Carnaval* (1668) opens with a singer personifying the carnival season seated on a throne surrounded by a group of singers and instrumentalists, all of whom wear his livery. These musicians are all named in the libretto: they consist of a group of twenty-one singers and continuo players, twenty-two *grands violons*, eighteen *petits violons*, and eight flutes, all led by Lully himself. Their participation in the music-making is specifically mentioned in the first and last entrées; in the interim they presumably remained on stage while accompanying the dances. In *Les Nopces de Village* (1663), performed at the château of Vincennes (probably in a large room since there was no fixed theatre in the château), the opening *récit* is accompanied by a "rustic harmony" (i.e., a wind band) consisting of eight musicians, and in the following entrée the bride and groom make their appearance, "led by the violins and the oboes."[21] As in *Le Carnaval*, the libretto shows that the opening

---

[19] See the libretto published in Paris in 1660 by Robert Ballard, p. 40. Ballet librettos and librettos for those operas that were performed at court list the names of the instrumentalists who appeared on stage, although only occasionally say what instruments they played. Judging from the names of the performers in this scene, the instruments appear to be both winds and strings.

[20] For the names of the instrumentalists involved in operatic performances at court and the instruments they played, although not their roles, see La Gorce, "Some notes." This article also includes costume designs by Jean Berain for instrumentalists in *Thésée* and *Isis*.

[21] See the respective librettos published by Robert Ballard in the year of the performance. In *Les Nopces de Village*, the *hautbois et musettes de Poitou* seem to have supplied the musicians for the *harmonie rustique*; five of the eight performers listed in the libretto also appear on a membership list for that ensemble dating from 1661 (see Benoit, *Musiques de cour*, p. 4).

of the work set up a mechanism for bringing the musicians on stage and into the visual landscape of the ballet; whether they withdrew to a special location thereafter or remained on stage, they presumably still participated as visible as well as audible elements of the spectacle.

The sketchy descriptions in Lully's librettos offer only the vaguest of hints as to how the musicians functioned while they were on stage with the singers or dancers. In the example from *Les Nopces de Village* just cited, the instrumentalists appear to have moved onto the stage with the bride and groom, presumably while playing, but no further details are supplied. The dance notation for *Le Mariage de la Grosse Cathos*, however, provides concrete information regarding the movements of the instrumentalists for a particular work. The changing patterns made by the musicians shape the space available to the dancers or even enter directly into the choreography; it is clear that their movements were carefully worked out as part of the overall scenario of the work. The model of *Le Mariage de la Grosse Cathos* opens avenues toward interpreting the functioning of similar groups in other works.

THE DANCERS

The professional dancers who performed at court generally came from another small circle of performers, that is, from the ranks of the violinists. This was the case for Jean Favier, whose grandfather, father, and uncle all played the violin and who himself was accorded the succession of a post among the *grands violons*. Before Lully assumed control of the king's musical establishment, there had often been a division of labor in the composition of ballet music: singers composed the vocal airs, while the dancing master/violinists both composed and choreographed the dance pieces.[22] Pierre Beauchamps, the principal choreographer for both the king's ballets and the Opéra, who also came from a family of violinists, composed the music for Molière's first comedy-ballet, *Les Facheux*, in 1661, as well as that for a number of ballets performed at the Jesuit college of Louis le Grand.[23] Archetypical images of the dancing master from this period always depict a man offering instruction with violin in hand.

By the second half of the seventeenth century, however, this relationship between violinists and dancers had begun to change. The creation of the Académie Royale de Danse in 1661 lent royal support to the state of independence declared by the dancing masters at that time. The bitter polemics on both sides of the issue mask the fact that the separation of the two groups was a gradual, not an abrupt process.[24] The increasing professionalization of the dancers was accelerated by the creation of a permanent dance troupe for the Opéra in 1672 under the direction of Pierre Beauchamps. This period also witnessed a great expansion in dance technique that laid the foundations for what was to become classical ballet.[25] More and more as time went on dancers perceived themselves as a group separate from the musicians.

The professional dancers at court performed in ballets, mascarades, plays, and masked balls. Some of them also served as dancing masters to the young pages attached to the court, and all of them undoubtedly supplemented their incomes by taking private pupils.

---

[22] For further discussion regarding the dual role of dancing master and violinist, see Ward, "Newly devis'd measures."

[23] Astier, "Beauchamps and the ballets de collège" and the same author's "When fiddlers danced to their own tunes."

[24] Many of the documents regarding the split between the dancing masters and the musicians' guild are included in the history of the guild by Loubet de Sceaury, *Musiciens*, pp. 67ff. A brief discussion of the issues raised by the two sides may be found in Kunzle, "In search of L'Académie Royale de Danse."

[25] Pierre Beauchamps is often given responsibility both for the new developments in dance and for codifying its basic precepts (see, for example, Rameau, *Le maître à danser*, preface and chapter 3). This may well be the case, but in the absence of surviving examples of his works either for the court or the Opéra (beyond two choreographies in Feuillet notation of unknown origin), it is impossible to define his precise contributions.

Most, including Favier, lived in Paris rather than Versailles (Du Pradel, *Livre commode*), which suggests that more of their livelihood derived from teaching done in the city than from performances at court. In terms of their training, seventeenth-century dancers were expected to be adept at pantomime, to dance in both serious and comic styles, and to be capable of performing both male and female roles.[26] They often started performing at a tender age – Jean Favier made his debut at the age of twelve – and had long careers: Pierre Beauchamps was still performing as late as 1702 when he was sixty-six (*Mercure galant*, December 1702, pp. 300–2).

One of the most noteworthy features of theatrical productions at court was that they often involved both professional and amateur dancers. The *ballet de cour* was the most visible vehicle for noble dancers, both male and female. The king himself danced in ballets for almost twenty years from *Cassandre* in 1651 to *Les Amants Magnifiques* in 1670, and his children, most notably the Dauphin, the Princesse de Conti, and Madame la Duchesse [de Bourbon], upheld the family tradition into the next generation.[27] In the court ballets some entrées were danced exclusively by either noble or professional dancers, but the two groups often shared the stage. In the court performance of *Le Triomphe de l'Amour*, for example, the thirteenth and fourteenth entrées involved the Princesse de Conti as Ariadne with six noble ladies as her followers, and the Comte de Brionne as Bacchus with three noble and three professional dancers in his entourage. The addition of danced entr'actes, performed by both professionals and amateurs, to plays at court has already been mentioned (see p. 3). In addition, noble ladies sometimes even danced with professionals at court balls. During the course of a masked ball given for the king during the carnival season of 1683 by Monsieur le Duc, the Princesse de Conti and Mademoiselle de Laval danced a chaconne with Pécour and Létang *le cadet*.[28] This frequent mingling of professional dancers in performances by members of the court meant that when the Dauphin and the Princesse de Conti sat in the audience for *Le Mariage de la Grosse Cathos*, they were watching people whom they had not only applauded for years, but with whom they themselves had shared the stage on numerous occasions.

THE ACTORS

During the 1680s there were two troupes of actors that performed regularly at court, one French, the other Italian. The Comédie Française, which had been directed by Molière until his death in 1673, performed both serious and comic plays in French. The Comédie Italienne was an offspring of the *commedia dell'arte* and was performed by Italian actors who had established themselves in France in the middle of the seventeenth century.[29] Both troupes had public theatres in Paris – the French troupe used the Théâtre

---

[26] Contrary to many writings on the subject, there were indeed professional female dancers active at court before the oft-cited performance of *Le Triomphe de l'Amour* (1681); in this work professional female dancers performed not for the first time ever, but for the first time on the stage of the Opéra. Their numbers, however, were few, and most female roles in the court ballets were performed either by noble ladies or by men, professional or noble.

[27] Louis XIV's eldest son Louis (1661–1711), the Dauphin, was commonly known as *Monseigneur* at court; Marie Anne de Bourbon (1666–1739), the Princesse de Conti, was his legitimized half-sister, daughter of the king and Louise de La Vallière. Madame la Duchesse (1673–1743), daughter of the king and Madame de Montespan, was known before her marriage to the Duc de Bourbon as Mademoiselle de Nantes. She created a stir when she danced in *Le Triomphe de l'Amour* at the age of seven and a half.

[28] *Mercure galant*, March 1683, p. 325. The *Mercure* also reveals that the music for this chaconne was composed by Lully. The piece in question may well be the "Chaconne pour Madame la Princesse de Conty" (LWV 70/5) published in a brief collection of music by Lully entitled *Plusieurs pièces de symphonie* that was attached to the ballets *L'Idylle sur la Paix* and *La Grotte de Versailles* (Paris: Ballard, 1685). Other pieces in this collection also appear to date from the carnival season of 1683.

[29] The best guide to the vast amount of material available regarding the *commedia dell'arte* and its descendants is Thomas F. Heck's annotated bibliography, *Commedia dell'Arte: A Guide to the Primary and Secondary Literature*. In this context, see especially section IV, pp. 111ff. The most complete treatment of the early history of the Comédie Italienne is found in Virginia Scott, *The Commedia dell'Arte in Paris, 1644–1697*.

Guénégaud, the Italians the Hôtel de Bourgogne – while at Versailles they shared the use of the small *salle de comédie* in the south wing of the château or occasionally adapted themselves to other performance surroundings as circumstances required.[30]

The Comédie Italienne was built around a number of stock characters such as Harlequin, Colombine, Scaramouche, and Mezzetin, each of whom had a well-defined personality and wore a characteristic costume that made him instantly recognizable to the audience. Harlequin's familiar suit was covered in multi-colored diamond-shaped patches; he wore a mask and often carried a bat. Mezzetin played unmasked and wore a suit of vertical red and white stripes. Each character was portrayed by a single actor who was thus identified with his role to the extent of being known by his stage name even when not in costume. In general the actors performed from pre-planned scenarios on the basis of which they improvised their lines. Their social satire, slapstick humor, and free, even licentious, use of language brought them a large and enthusiastic following. The leader of the troupe at this time was its Harlequin, Giuseppe Domenico Biancolelli.

As a largely improvisatory art, the Comédie Italienne was very responsive to its surroundings and absorbed a number of French comic traditions into its own well-established framework. Thus during the 1680s the Italian comedians began presenting more and more of their scenes in French, as well as developing new roles that appealed to French audiences. The character of Mezzetin, though based on Italian models, made his debut on the French stage, having been developed by Angelo Constantini after he arrived in Paris in 1682.[31] The comedians also mocked local people and events; one of their favorite targets was the Opéra.[32] Eventually their irreverence brought about their downfall: in 1697 the king ordered them to close their theatre.[33] It was not until 1716, several months after Louis XIV's death, that the Comédie Italienne was allowed to reopen its doors.

In a late seventeenth-century collection of plays put on by the Comédie Italienne, the troupe's style of performance is explained:

> the Italian comedians don't learn anything by heart and all they need to perform a play is to have seen the subject of it a moment before they go on stage. Thus the greatest beauty of their plays is inseparable from the action, and the success of their comedies depends completely on the actors who embellish them to a greater or lesser degree depending on their level of wit . . . It is the necessity of inventing on the spot that makes it so difficult to replace a good Italian comedian if something happens to him . . . Whoever speaks of a "good Italian comedian" means a man who is resourceful, who acts more from his imagination than from his memory; who invents, while acting, everything he says; who knows how to react to the person with whom he finds himself on stage; that is, he unites his words and actions so well with those of his comrade, that he enters immediately into the spirit and into all the movements that the other asks of him in such a way as to make everyone believe that they had already worked things out in advance.[34]

---

[30] Regarding the *salle de comédie*, see Lagrave, *Le théâtre et le public*, pp. 132–5 and Coeyman, "Theaters." Regarding performance spaces at Fontainebleau, another of the royal châteaux, see Rice, *The Performing Arts*.

[31] According to Moureau, "Les comédiens italiens," p. 66, Constantini first performed in Paris in 1683. His debut at court as Mezzetin was in 1686.

[32] For a discussion of seventeenth-century parodies of Lully's operas, including those by the Comédie Italienne, see Grout, "Seventeenth-century parodies."

[33] Louis XIV offered no explanation for his decision to close the theatre, but it is widely accepted that he did so in order to prevent the performance of a play called *La Fausse Prude* in which his morganatic wife, the pious Madame de Maintenon, was depicted in an unflattering light. F. Moureau, however, believes that the expulsion of the Italians was the final step in a slow process of deterioration in their standing in the king's eyes that had begun at the beginning of the decade (see Moureau, "Les comédiens italiens," pp. 75–7).

[34] "les Comediens Italiens n'apprennent rien par cœur, & qu'il leur suffit, pour jouer une Comedie, d'en avoir vu le sujet un moment avant que d'entrer sur le Théâtre. Ainsi la plus grande beauté de leurs Piéces est inséparable de l'action, le succés de leurs Comedies dépendant absolument des Acteurs, qui leur donnent plus ou moins d'agrémens, selon qu'ils ont plus ou moins d'esprit . . . C'est cette nécessité de jouer sur le champ qui fait qu'on a tant de peine à remplacer un bon Comedien Italien, lorsque malheureusement il vient à manquer . . . Qui dit bon Comedien Italien dit un homme qui a du fond, qui joue plus

Although the Italian troupe was fairly large – royal regulations of 1684 fixed the number of actors at twelve[35] – the titles alone of the plays suggest to what extent the plots revolved around Harlequin, whose roles often involved him in disguises: *Arlequin cabaretier, turc et capitaine espagnol* (1682), *Arlequin lingère du palais* (1683), *Arlequin empereur dans la lune* (1684). In Biancolelli's hands, Harlequin's character was defined as a glutton and a coward, conniving yet stupid. The verbal play, often scatological or involving sexual innuendo, was accompanied by physical buffoonery that included comic beatings, pratfalls, and acrobatics. Certain stereotypical comic routines, called *lazzi*, recurred in many of the plays. A set of notes left by Biancolelli describing a number of the scenes in which he played Harlequin paints a vivid picture of the Italians on stage; the following excerpt describes a scene near the end of *Arlequin dogue d'Angleterre et médecin du temps* of 1679.

> In this scene I enter as a doctor accompanied by Flautin. I carry a shield on my arm and a covered basket full of vials of urine and I have a sword in hand. The drums and trumpets sound, I do my lazzi of fear. Flautin mounts the hill and gives me courage, I also mount the hill as Flautin plants the flag; then Spezzafer appears on horseback followed by surgeons, apothecaries, and charlatans with their cannons, which are large syringes; they challenge me, I answer that I will defend myself to the last drop of urine. I take off my doctor's gown and make a sortie, I hit Spezzafer several times with a bladder . . . then retire into the fortress, which Spezzafer says he will set on fire.[36]

The role of Mezzetin was still relatively new on the stage of the Comédie Italienne when *Le Mariage de la Grosse Cathos* was performed, but already by then Constantini had defined Mezzetin as second *zanni* or clown to Biancolelli's Harlequin. The scene the two of them play in the mascarade, in which they disguise themselves in an attempt to use La Couture's wedding to their own advantage, is typical of the situations in which their roles placed them. It was around the time of Mezzetin's arrival that the troupe began to perform scenes or even entire plays in French, written by French playwrights, in addition to their traditional Italian repertoire. The collections of the troupe's French scenes and plays, published in 1694 and 1700 by Evaristo Gherardi,[37] may well include translations of works that were originally improvised in Italian. For this transitional period it is difficult to determine how much of the troupe's repertoire was performed in Italian, how much in French, and to what extent improvisation had an impact on those scripts that have been preserved. The scene for Mezzetin and Harlequin in *Le Mariage de Grosse Cathos* appears complete and fully worked out, but it would surely have been within the traditions of the troupe for the two performers to have taken liberties with the script or to have embellished it on the spot.[38]

Although the cast list for *Le Mariage de la Grosse Cathos* does not identify the performers who played the roles of Harlequin and Mezzetin in the spoken scene, there

---

d'imagination que de mémoire; qui compose, en jouant, tout ce qu'il dit; qui sçait seconder celuy avec qui il se trouve sur le Theâtre; c'est à dire, qu'il marie si bien ses paroles & ses actions avec celles de son camarade, qu'il entre sur le champ dans tout le jeu & dans tous les mouvemens que l'autre luy demande, d'une maniere à faire croire à tout le monde qu'ils estoient déja concertez." "Avertissement," *Le theatre italien de Gherardi*, pp. 3–4.

[35] Moureau, "Les comédiens italiens," p. 65.
[36] Quoted in Scott, *Commedia dell'arte*, p. 217.
[37] In 1694 Gherardi, the troupe's Harlequin after Biancolelli's death in August of 1688, published a single-volume collection of scenes from seventeen plays dating between 1681 and 1694, *Le théâtre italien, ou le recueil de toutes les scènes françoises qui ont esté jouée sur le théâtre italien de l'Hostel de Bourgogne*. In 1700 he published a second and considerably expanded edition of the collection, this one in six volumes. (The six-volume collection was reprinted in Amsterdam in 1701; it is this edition that we have consulted.) Although both collections include works performed before Gherardi himself joined the troupe, they are much more complete for the period following his arrival. See Scott, *Commedia dell'arte*, pp. 275ff.
[38] Scott points out (p. 279) that "Gherardi's 1700 texts may be more complete than any others, but they are not necessarily authoritative. In fact, the idea of an authoritative text is meaningless in this context. The Italian theatre in Paris remained a commedia dell'arte troupe, always ready to cut its cloth to suit the circumstances. The existence of written texts does not imply any particular consistency in the actual performances . . ."

seems no reason to suspect that anyone other than Biancolelli and Constantini, the creators of those roles in the Italian troupe, took their parts. Certainly this would not have been the only occasion in which Italian players participated in spectacles other than those of their own devising: in the 1670 premiere of *Le Bourgeois Gentilhomme* at Chambord, "Le Seigneur Dominique," the name by which Biancolelli was familiarly known, performed as Harlequin in the *Ballet des Nations* that closed the work.

As this brief survey has shown, entertainments at court involved a restricted circle of composers, musicians, dancers, and actors, many of whom had been working together for years. As early as 1670 at least seven of the performers who were later involved in *Le Mariage de la Grosse Cathos* appeared together in the premiere just mentioned of *Le Bourgeois Gentilhomme*: these included both Philidor and Favier, the singers Philbert, Le Roy, Morel, and Gingant, and the actor Biancolelli. Even the briefest of glances at the librettos of court entertainments turns up lists of familiar names, merely reshuffled for the different occasions. Moreover, the genres of the entertainments – ballets, operas, plays, and balls – convenient as it is to separate them in historical analyses, had many points in common and drew on many of the same conventions. *Le Mariage de la Grosse Cathos* is but one small work within a well-established performance tradition. If it is exceptional in the survival of so many of its components, in the circumstances of its performance it is utterly typical.

2

The creators and the performers

Of the twenty-eight members of the cast of *Le Mariage de la Grosse Cathos*, fifteen are identified in the manuscript: the composer, Philidor *l'aîné*, is named on the title page of the musical score; the cast list which immediately follows provides the names of seven of the nine singers; five of the eight dancers are named on p. 43 of the dance notation; and the mention of the roles of the Italian comedians is tantamount to an identification of the actors playing them. None of the players in the nine-member oboe band is identified, but Philidor himself must have served as one of the instrumentalists, as he did in the mascarades he composed for the 1700 carnival season. All fifteen of the named performers were in the employ of the king, as were undoubtedly the remaining thirteen. This chapter presents a summary of the biographical information about these fifteen that may be gleaned from court documents and performance records, with emphasis on those aspects of their lives that bear on their participation in court entertainments.[1]

The two creators of the mascarade, André Danican Philidor and Jean Favier, may well have known each other since childhood. They were exact contemporaries, spent most of their professional lives in the the service of Louis XIV, and had performed in the same works on numerous occasions. Both came from well-established families of musicians.

ANDRÉ DANICAN PHILIDOR

André Danican Philidor was born into a family of wind players. The family name had originally been Danican; tradition attributes the acquisition of the surname Philidor to a gesture on the part of Louis XIII, who, supposedly enchanted by the oboe playing of one Michel Danican, recently arrived in Paris, compared him favorably to a famous Italian oboist named Filidori. Although the details of this story, if not the general tenor of it, were called into question over a hundred years ago by Ernest Thoinan, documents from 1659 onward do often refer to members of the family by the name of "Danican dit Philidor" ("Danican known as Philidor"), or eventually just "Danican Philidor."[2]

---

[1] The documentary information found in studies such as Benoit, *Musiques de cour* and *Versailles*, Massip, *Vie des musiciens*, Jurgens, *Documents*, and Brossard, *Musiciens* has been supplemented by an examination of librettos of ballets, comedy-ballets, operas, and other divertissements from the court. Published in Paris by Ballard at the time of the performance, the librettos for court performances often included the names of those performers who appeared on stage, which in a number of cases meant that at least some of the instrumentalists were mentioned in addition to the singers and dancers. Starting around the turn of the century the librettos for works performed by the Académie Royale de Musique at their public theatre in Paris also began to list the performers' names. Unless otherwise noted, information presented in this chapter regarding participation in theatrical entertainments has been derived from the printed librettos. Sources that provide access to at least some of the information regarding the performers found in the librettos are Silin, *Benserade* and Christout, *Le ballet de cour* for the *ballets de cour*; Powell, "Music" for the *comédies-ballets*; La Gorce, "Some notes" and Schmidt, *Catalogue* for Lully's *tragédies lyriques*.

[2] Most of the biographical information presented here regarding the Philidor family has been drawn from Thoinan, "Les Philidor" and "Philidor (Danican-)," Benoit, *Musiques de cour* and *Versailles*, and Waquet, "Philidor l'aîné," all of whom base their findings on seventeenth- and eighteenth-century documents.

Both André's uncle Michel (?–1659) and his father Jean (?–1679) were employed in the *grande écurie*. Judging from the titles of their positions, they were capable of playing a variety of wind and percussion instruments: crumhorn, marine trumpet, fife, drum, and oboe. No documentation establishing the date of André's birth has been located, but he was probably born in 1646 or 1647: when he married for the second time in 1719 his grandson reported that he was seventy-three years old. He must have acquired proficiency as a wind player at a tender age, for when his uncle died in 1659, young André was appointed to replace him.

The ensemble to which he was named, the *cromornes et trompettes marines*, consisted of five members, one of whom was his father Jean. Until 1678 this was André's only known official appointment, but librettos from court theatrical performances make it clear that he was capable of playing more than these two instruments and that his musical duties were not limited to performing as a part of this group. In 1670, for example, he appeared as one of eight flutes and oboes in the *Ballet des Nations* that concludes *Le Bourgeois Gentilhomme*, and the following year he played the bassoon in the last scene of *Psyché*. By 1675, if not before, he was appearing in costume and on stage in court performances of Lully's operas. Scores and librettos from these and later stage works show that he knew how to play a variety of wind and percussion instruments: oboes, flutes (recorders), and crumhorns, each in varying sizes, as well as bassoon, musette, and various types of drum. The impressive list of the instruments he had in his possession in 1714 confirms the versatility that was a necessary condition of his employment: two pairs of timpani with their sticks, one side drum, four bassoons, a musette, three flutes (probably recorders), four other little ebony [flutes] trimmed with ivory, a bass flute and a *quinte*, nine recorders (*flûtes à bec*), two German (transverse) flutes, four *quintes* and an oboe, for a total of thirty-three instruments.[3] His younger brother Jacques (1657–1708), who was also a musician in the *grande écurie* as well as an instrument maker, left at his death a collection of no fewer than forty-four instruments, among them flutes (recorders) in four sizes, oboes in three sizes, two bassoons, one violin, a pair of timpani, and a side drum.[4] (It was to distinguish the two brothers from each other that librettos from the period generally referred to André as Philidor *l'aîné* [the elder], and Jacques as Philidor *le cadet* [the younger].) The reputation of the Philidor family as players of woodwinds was so well established that the *Mercure galant*, in reporting an outdoor musical entertainment offered to the Duchesse de Bourgogne by the Princesse d'Harcourt in July of 1700, stated that, "The oboists were the Philidors and their comrades who without any doubt are the best in France."[5]

During the late 1670s the number of Philidor's official appointments at court began to increase. He was first named a drummer in the *fifres et tambours* in 1678,[6] and in 1681 was

---

According to Waquet, p. 204, the story regarding the change in the family name goes back to J.-B. de La Borde, who reported it as hearsay in 1780. Noting that all known documents referring to Michel Danican use only his birth name, and that the name Philidor first appears in conjunction with a member of the family in 1659 when it refers to Jean Danican on a document naming him "fifre du roi," Ernest Thoinan suggested in 1881 that the story, if it had any truth at all, probably applied to Louis XIV and Jean Danican, not to Louis XIII and Michel Danican (see Thoinan, "Philidor [Danican-]," p. 333). There are many variant spellings of both names found in the documents, Danicamp, d'Anicamp, and Filidor being the most common.

[3] Inventory made after the death of Philidor's first wife, Marguerite Mouginot, of the couple's joint property, F-Pan MC CXVII-268, 12 Nov. 1714, cited in Waquet, "Philidor l'aîné," p. 213.

[4] The inventory of Jacques's possessions made after his death also included "outils servans à faire des instruments de simphonie" ("tools used to make musical instruments"). The musical portions of the inventory are quoted in Dufourcq and Benoit, "Musiciens de Versailles" (1963), p. 195.

[5] *Mercure galant*, July 1700, pp. 242–52: "Les Hautbois étoient les Philidors & leurs camarades, qui sans contredit sont les meilleurs qu'il y ait en France." The music for this event was composed by Philidor *l'aîné* (see *La Fête d'Arcueil* in the Philidor work list below).

[6] This post required the musicians to follow the king on his military excursions. Documents cited in Benoit, *Musiques de cour*, record various orders to the *fifres et tambours* to prepare to go to the front, but on at least one occasion in 1692 Philidor was singled out from the group in being allowed to come and go as he pleased, on the condition that he provide a suitable substitute for himself: "Permettons audit André Danican dit Philidor, comme l'un des plus anciens, d'agir en ses affaires, aller, venir, passer et repasser pendant lad[ite]

appointed to the prestigious *grands hautbois du roi*. It was undoubtedly this marked rise in Philidor's fortunes that led him to resign his post in the *cromornes et trompettes marines* at around this same time.[7] Participation in these two new ensembles probably involved Philidor in a greater number of performances than before. The *fifres et tambours* played frequently for occasions of state, and the *grands hautbois* not only participated in outdoor musical events, but were often called upon to join with the king's string orchestras, the *grands* and *petits violons*, in providing music for balls, ballets, and other divertissements. In 1690 Philidor and three other wind players officially became members of the *petits violons*, and he seems also to have played on a regular basis for services in the royal chapel.[8] Thus Philidor participated in all three branches of the royal musical establishment: chamber, chapel, and stable.

It was probably during the 1680s that Philidor was appointed to the position by which he is best remembered today, that of librarian of the king's music collection.[9] Until at least 1697 he shared the post with François Fossard, one of the king's violinists, but by 1702 he was acting alone.[10] Judging from the number of copies of music that came from his pen, Philidor's role in this enterprise was much larger than Fossard's. Philidor presided over an enormous effort instituted by Louis XIV to collect the music that had been performed in the earlier part of his reign and in the reigns of his father and grandfather. He not only oversaw the operation, but personally copied dozens of volumes of music.[11] Philidor collected music from as far back as the reign of Henri III, more than a century earlier, then copied it into large folio scores, many of which are now located in the Bibliothèque Nationale in Paris. The dedications to the king in the series of Lully ballets he copied as part of this effort reveal Philidor's consciousness of the historical value of his work, particularly in preserving the early works of the "incomparable genius" who had recently died. (Most of Philidor's copies of the Lully ballets date from 1690, three years after the composer's death.) In addition to full scores of complete sacred and secular works, Philidor and his assistants copied many volumes of chamber suites drawn from the works of Lully and other composers, plus collections preserving the repertoire which Philidor himself performed at court: dances for the ballroom and music for the ensembles of the

---

campagne, [à] conditions toutesfois de fournir en sa place une personne capable pour remplir le service. Et à l'effet des voyages que lesd[its] Tambours et Fifres feront de l'armée du Roy a Paris, et de Paris a l'armée, le present ordre leur servira de passeport . . . " (p. 133).

[7] Philidor's name still appeared on the membership list of the *cromornes et trompettes marines* in 1677, but in 1680, the next year for which records are available, his name was crossed out and replaced by that of Dumont, the man to whom Philidor officially sold his position in 1685 (Benoit, *Musiques de cour*, pp. 56, 74, 95; and Benoit, *Versailles*, pp. 109–10).

[8] The *Etat de la France* for 1692 lists 1690 as the year of entry into the *petits violons* for all four wind players, two *dessus de cromorne* (of whom Philidor was one) and two bassoons. The after-death inventory in 1714 of Philidor's first wife (see n. 3 above) contains records of Philidor's wages as *grand hautbois*, *hautbois de la chapelle*, and *petit violon*.

[9] The date of 1684 for Philidor's appointment, repeated in a number of writings about him, is nowhere documented. The earliest known score he copied for the royal library, a volume of ballets, is dated 1681, but most of the other volumes in the same series of Lully ballets were not copied until 1690, by which time it is clear that his position in the library was an official one. In the preface to an anthology of Italian airs he selected from the library's collection and published with Ballard in 1694, he said he had been working as music librarian for thirty years.

[10] Waquet, "Philidor l'aîné," p. 205. For reasons unknown, Philidor seems to have tried to destroy the evidence of his association with Fossard. In the dedications to the king that preface many of the volumes of Lully ballets Philidor copied, the name of Fossard was carefully scratched out, leaving only that of Philidor.

[11] To date no inventory has been made of the extant music copied by Philidor and his assistants. The so-called Philidor Collection at the Bibliothèque Nationale in Paris (see chapter 7, p. 185) includes only a portion of that library's Philidor holdings. Another large collection of Philidor materials is in the Bibliothèque Municipale de la Ville de Versailles. A third body of Philidor copies was owned by St. Michael's College in Tenbury (see Fellowes, "The Philidor manuscripts") until 1978 when the collection was put up for sale. A number of volumes returned to France, either to the Bibliothèque Nationale or to Versailles (see Massip, "La collection Toulouse-Philidor"), while others were bought by research libraries or collectors. Many more volumes of music copied by Philidor are to be found in libraries throughout Europe and North America or are in private hands.

grande écurie. Sometimes Philidor even composed bass lines or inner parts for tunes written by other people, as annotations in some of these anthologies reveal (e.g. "Menuet de Monsieur le Prince de Fustemberg. La Basse par Monsieur Philidor l'aîné"). Payment records show that Philidor was also called upon to copy out parts for many of the musical entertainments performed at court. Anyone who studies French music of this period owes a debt of gratitude to Philidor, without whose copies a substantial amount of music from the court would no longer exist.

In 1672 Philidor married Marguerite Mouginot, daughter of a cloth merchant. Over the next twenty-five years, the couple had sixteen children, of whom three sons – Anne (1681–1728), Michel (b. 1683, still alive in 1720), and François (1689–1717) – continued the family profession of wind and percussion players in the king's music. Anne also composed both stage and chamber music, and in 1725 founded the Concert Spirituel, an important public concert series that ran in Paris until 1790. He was destined by his father to succeed him both among the *grands hautbois* and as royal music librarian, and his may well be one of the unidentified hands that helped Philidor *l'aîné* produce so many copies of music. But owing to Anne's death in 1728, it was the husband of his sister Hélène (1686–1716), the wind player Jean-Louis Schwartzenberg, known as Le Noble, who eventually took over the responsibilities of the royal music library. André's brother Jacques (Philidor *le cadet*) also produced numerous musical progeny. Four of his twelve children became musicians in the *grande écurie*, one of whom, Pierre Danican Philidor (1681–1731), also composed.

In 1719, five years after his first wife died, Philidor remarried at the age of seventy-three. The six children born of this union testify to the vigor of their father's old age. One of them, François-André (1726–95), brought the greatest renown to the family name, both as a chess champion and as a composer of *opéras comiques*. Around the time of his second marriage, Philidor moved to the village of Dreux in Normandy. He may have worked there for the Duchesse de Vendôme;[12] despite his ostensible retirement from the court, he seems to have kept up at least some of his activities as librarian, at least to the extent of drawing up a catalogue of ballets and operas by Lully and other composers in 1729 when he was eighty-three.[13] Only in December of 1729 did he officially resign his position among the *grands hautbois*, although as early as 1717 his name had appeared in a list of "veteran" musicians.[14] Philidor died in Dreux on 11 August 1730.

Philidor's activities as a composer were undoubtedly restricted by the iron control Jean-Baptiste Lully exercised over musical life at the court. It was not until after Lully's death in 1687 that Philidor began to compose theatrical music; whether the three productions he mounted over eight months in 1687 and 1688 represent work merely intended to fill in the gap left by the *surintendant*'s death, or an attempt to offer himself as a possible replacement is unknown. In the event it was not Philidor, but Michel Richard de Lalande who was appointed *surintendant de la musique de la chambre du roi* in 1689.

As with his performing, Philidor's composing seems to have been restricted to court circles. Philidor provided the music for a number of ballets and mascarades (see list below), composed pieces for the ensembles of the *grande écurie*, and wrote a large number of dance tunes for court balls. Some of his music has been lost; much of it is contained in anthologies of music from the court that Philidor and his assistants copied. (To date no complete listing of Philidor's works has been made, nor has there been a study of his compositions.) Like so many other composers, Lully included, Philidor was not averse to reusing some of his pieces in later works. He borrowed, for example, the rigaudon and passepied from *Le Mariage de la Grosse Cathos* for use in his 1700 mascarade, *La Noce de Village*.

---

[12] Waquet, "Philidor l'aîné," p. 212, n. 46.
[13] F-A Ms. 1201, *Catalogue general de tous les vieux ballets du roy et operas tant de Mr de Lully que de plusieurs autres compositeurs modernes*.
[14] Benoit, *Musiques de cour*, pp. 290, 394, and 397.

The following list includes only those compositions of Philidor *l'aîné* that were intended for theatrical performance, presented in chronological order. The number of members of the Philidor family who composed music for the court has led to a considerable amount of confusion in secondary sources as to the authorship of some of the works listed below. As a result, a second list mentions those works by other members of his family that have sometimes been erroneously attributed to Philidor *l'aîné*. (The subsidiary list does not purport to provide a complete listing of the theatrical works of the two younger Philidors.)

The attributions in both lists have been taken from the scores and librettos of the works in question.[15] In only one instance is there a discrepancy in attribution between the two; in this case we lend more credence to the manuscript score, copied by Philidor himself, than to the printed libretto. The sources for each attribution are noted below. Information regarding date and place of performance is taken from the libretto or score when possible, or from contemporary secondary sources listed for each work under "Bibliography." (Some of these accounts merely mention the work, others provide some measure of description.) Almost all of the librettos were published by Ballard, while with one exception all of the music is in manuscript, much of it copied by Philidor himself.

Many of the dances from Philidor's stage works also appear in contemporary anthologies of instrumental music, some of them prepared by Philidor himself. Two such manuscript anthologies are F-Pn Rés. F. 533 (dating from 1695) and F-V Ms. mus. 139–143 (after 1719), a set of partbooks for one or two treble instruments and bass. The dances within these collections are generally arranged by key and are not always identified as to source or title; for example, only one of the three dances from *Le Mariage de la Grosse Cathos* found in F-V Ms. mus. 139–143 identifies the mascarade as its source. With the exception of works for which the anthologized excerpts represent the only surviving music, we list only scores that contain the entire work, not the numerous concordances for individual pieces from collections such as these.

Costume designs by Jean Berain for four of the 1700 mascarades by Philidor and his son may be seen in a catalogue of the Parisian auction house Nouveau Drouot, *Maquettes de costumes de théâtre de Jean I et Jean II Berain*, for an auction held on 26 April 1982. These works are: *Le Roy de la Chine* (five designs); *Le Vaisseau Marchand* (two designs); *La Noce de Village* (one design); and *Le Lendemain de la Noce de Village* (two designs, including one for Philbert).

Stage works by André Danican Philidor
(Philidor *l'aîné*, Philidor *le père*)

LE CANAL DE VERSAILLES, BALLET
Versailles, 16 July 1687
Score: F-Pn (Musique) Rés. F. 522
Libretto: F-Pn (Musique) ThB 4508; US-CA (Theatre) TS C17 vol. 2 (7)
Comments: attribution in libretto. In four acts.

LA PRINCESSE DE CRETE, COMÉDIE HEROÏQUE MESLÉ D'ENTRÉES DE BALLET
Marly, January 1688
Score: complete score lost from Philidor Collection (vol. 52); however, there are twelve instrumental pieces from this work in F-V Ms. mus. 139–143, and five instrumental pieces in F-Pn (Musique) Rés. F. 533, pp. 148–9.

---

[15] Philidor's name is given in these sources either as Philidor *l'aîné* or as Philidor *le père*, the latter to distinguish him from his son, Anne, called Philidor *le fils*. Both surnames for the elder Philidor appear in various anthologies containing his works. The distinction has led some researchers to conclude that compositions attributed to Philidor *le père* were actually composed by André's father, Jean Danican Philidor. The musical sources for the 1700 mascarades, however, give the composer's name as "Philidor *le père*, ordinaire de la Musique du Roy et Garde des Livres de Musique de Sa Majesté," thus making it clear that Philidor *le père* refers to André, not Jean.

Libretto: F-Po Liv. 17 [R7 (2); US-CA (Theatre) TS C43 (1)
Bibl.: possibly Dangeau II, 106, 9 Feb. 1688 (see ch. 3, p. 36)
Comments: attribution in libretto. Prologue and three acts.

LE MARIAGE DE LA GROSSE CATHOS
1688 (probably at Versailles, apartment of Princesse de Conti, 17 February)
Scores: F-Pn (Musique) Rés. F. 534ª; F-Pa Ms. 3239
Libretto: not located
Bibl.: possibly Dangeau II, 109, 17 Feb. 1688 (see ch. 3, p. 36)
Comments: attribution in score

LA MASCARADE DU ROY DE LA CHINE
Marly, 7 and 8 January 1700
Score: US-BE Ms. 455, fols. 1ʳ–14ᵛ
Libretto: F-Po Liv. 17 [R7 (13); US-CA (Theatre) TS C43 (21)
Bibl.: *Mercure galant*, Feb. 1700, 154; Dangeau VII, 226 & 227
Comments: attribution in score and libretto

LA MASCARADE DES SAVOYARDS
Marly, 22 January 1700
Score: US-BE Ms. 455, fols. 32ʳ–42ʳ
Libretto: F-Po Liv. 17 [R7 (16); F-Pn (Imprimés) 8º Z Le Senne 14539; US-CA (Theatre) TS C43 (20)
Bibl.: *Mercure galant*, Feb. 1700, 158–60; Sources VI, 222; Dangeau VII, 237
Comments: attribution in score and libretto

LA MASCARADE DE LA NOCE DE VILLAGE
Marly, 4 February 1700
Score: US-BE Ms. 455, fols. 43ʳ–56ᵛ
Libretto: F-Po Liv. 17 [R7 (10); F-Pn (Imprimés) 8º Z Le Senne 14538; US-CA (Theatre) TS C43 (10)
Bibl.: *Mercure galant*, Feb. 1700, 166; Sources VI, 227–8; Dangeau VII, 244
Comments: attribution in score and libretto

LA MASCARADE DU VAISSEAU MARCHAND
Marly, 18 February 1700
Score: US-BE Ms. 455, fols. 70ʳ–88ᵛ
Libretto: F-Po Liv. 17 [R7 (14); F-Pn (Imprimés) Yf Rés. 2270; F-Pn (Imprimés) 8º Z Le Senne 14537; US-CA (Theatre) TS C43 (17)
Bibl.: *Mercure galant*, Feb. 1700, 224–6; Sources VI, 232–3; Dangeau VII, 259
Comments: attribution in score and libretto. The *Mercure* gives the date of the performance as 17 February, but the score, the libretto, Sources, and Dangeau say the 18th.

LA FÊTE D'ARCUEIL
Arcueil, 1 July 1700
Score: US-BE Ms. 455, fols. 103ʳ–112ʳ
Libretto: not located[16]
Bibl.: Dangeau VII, 334; *Mercure galant*, July 1700, 242–52
Comments: given by the Princesse d'Harcourt in honor of the Duchesse de Bourgogne. Attribution to Philidor in score.

LES TRAVAUX D'HERCULE OU L'AMANT GUÉRI
Date of performance unknown
Score: lost from Philidor collection (vol. 53)

---

[16] Brenner, *Bibliographical List*, reports a copy of this and of other Philidor librettos in F-Ph, but none of them can be located among the library's holdings.

Libretto: not located

Comments: another ballet by the title *Les Travaux d'Hercule*, probably not the same work, was performed at Jesuit college Louis le Grand on 7 August 1686. Although the libretto (F-Pn [Imprimés] Yf Rés. 2855) does not mention composer or choreographer, vol. 18 of the Philidor Collection attributes the music to Beauchamps (see Astier, "When fiddlers danced to their own tunes," pp. 3–4).

LE CERCLE D'ANET
1717, for the Duchesse de Vendôme
Score: 25 pieces in F-V Ms. mus. 139–143
Libretto: not located
Comments: attribution to Philidor on p. 105, to Philidor *le père* on p. 135 of the treble part

Works by other members of the Philidor family sometimes attributed to André Danican Philidor

By his nephew, Pierre Danican Philidor (1681-1731)

PASTORALE
Marly, 3 August 1697; Versailles, 3 September 1697
Score: F-V Ms. mus. 144
Libretto: not located
Comments: attribution in the score

LA MASCARADE DU JEU D'ECHECS
Marly, 19 February 1700
Score: US-BE Ms. 455, fols. 89r–102v
Libretto: F-Pn (Imprimés) 8º Z Le Senne 14541; GB-Lbl 11740.g.49 (1); US-CA (Theatre) TS C43 (18)
Bibl.: *Mercure galant*, Feb. 1700, 228–9; Sourches VI, 233; Dangeau VII, 260
Comments: attributed to Philidor *l'aîné* in the published libretto, but to Pierre Philidor in the score copied by Philidor *l'aîné*

L'EGLOGUE DE MARLY, DIVERTISSEMENT
Marly, 4 January 1702; Versailles, 8 January 1702
Score: not located
Libretto: F-Pn (Imprimés) Yf Rés. 2023
Comments: attributed to Pierre Philidor in the published libretto, which also attributes the text to Guérin (Nicolas-Armand-Martial Guérin d'Estrich)

By his son, Anne Danican Philidor (1681–1728)

L'AMOUR VAINQUEUR, PASTORALE
Marly, 9 August 1697
Score: published by Roger (Amsterdam, [1698]), copy in NL-DHgm; manuscript score missing from Philidor Collection (vol. 45)
Libretto: F-Pn (Musique) ThB 4511; F-Pn (Manuscrits) Ms. fr. 24.352, fol. 129–134; US-CA (Theatre) TS C43 (5)
Comments: attribution in libretto and in published score

DIANE ET ENDYMION, PASTORALE HÉROÏQUE
Marly, 1698
Score: F-Pa M. 897; F-Pn (Musique) Rés. 922
Libretto: F-Pn (Imprimés) Yf Rés. 1983; F-Pn (Manuscrits) Ms. fr. 24.353, fol. 117; US-CA (Theatre) TS C43 (8)
Comments: attribution in score and libretto. According to the F-Pa score, the text was by Morel.

LA MASCARADE DES AMAZONES
Marly, 21 January 1700
Score: US-BE Ms. 455, fols. 15r–31v
Libretto: F-Po Liv. 17 [R 7 (9); US-CA (Theatre) TS C43 (19)
Bibl.: *Mercure galant*, Feb. 1700, 157–8; Dangeau VII, 236
Comments: attribution in score and libretto

LE LENDEMAIN DE LA NOCE DE VILLAGE
Marly, 5 February 1700
Score: US-BE Ms. 455, fols. 57r–69v
Libretto: F-Po Liv. 17 [R7 (15); F-Pn (Imprimés) 8º Z Le Senne 14540; US-CA (Theatre) TS C43 (24)
Bibl: *Mercure galant*, Feb. 1700, 167–8; Sourches VI, 228–9; Dangeau VII, 244–5
Comments: attribution in score and libretto

DANAË, OPÉRA
Marly, 1701, performed by the king's musicians
Score: F-Pn Vm² 168
Libretto: F-V Ms. mus. 130; F-Pn (Manuscrits) Ms. fr. n.a. 4676
Comments: attribution in score and libretto, which also say text by Mr Lenoble

JEAN FAVIER

Jean Favier came from a family of violinists. His grandfather Jehan (d. 1615), had been a *maître joueur d'instruments*; his father Jacques (1605?–91), and his uncle Jean (b. 1583?, still living 1644) were both *violons de la chambre du roi*.[17] Jacques had bought his post among the *grands violons* in 1633 from the widow of Jean Mazuel (Jurgens, *Documents* I, p. 168) and retained it until his death in 1691. In addition to his court activities, Jacques was a member of an association of violinists that joined together in 1642 for the purpose of giving concerts in the Louvre. He was almost certainly a dancing master as well as a violinist; not only were the two roles inseparable at the time, one document from 1634 refers to a Jacques Favier as *maître à danser* (Jurgens, *Documents* II, p. 213). Around 1630 he married Gillette Bourdonné, a seamstress who rapidly increased the size of the household both through her numerous pregnancies (the couple had eight children in eleven years) and by taking in a number of young girls as apprentices. After Gillette died in 1643, Jacques married one of the apprentices, Marguerite Voiture, with whom he had five more children. The family lived in Paris, which meant that Jacques was obliged to travel to the various châteaux used by the court in order to fulfill the functions of his employment.

Jean Favier, Jacques's first child by his second wife, was baptized at the church of Saint-Germain-l'Auxerrois in Paris on 25 March 1648.[18] He undoubtedly learned to play the

---

[17] The family relationships among the numerous Faviers are difficult to establish given the similarity of names used over several generations. Jehan Favier had three sons named Jehan (or Jean), born in 1583, 1603, and 1608 and two named Jacques, born 1592 and 1605. Mercifully the second Jean only named one of his sons after himself, but Jacques produced two Jeans, one Jacques, and one Jean Jacques. The information given here about the earlier generations of Faviers is derived from documents of baptisms, deaths, marriages and financial transactions of seventeenth-century musicians listed in Jurgens, *Documents* (vol. I, pp. 123–6, 168, 347ff.; vol. II, pp. 212–15) and Brossard, *Musiciens*, pp. 118–20. Conclusions about relationships are based on comparisons of dates, occupations, addresses, etc. For example, our Jean Favier's uncle by the same name, who was one of the king's violinists, was married in 1613 and had his first child two years later. Therefore he could not have been either of the Jean Faviers born to Jehan in 1603 and 1608.

[18] Except when other sources are cited, biographical information about Jean Favier is derived from a comparison of the documents cited in Jurgens, *Documents* and Brossard, *Musiciens* with other documents discovered in the course of this study relating to his marriage in 1690: F-Pan MC CII-150: *Constitution de rente viagère* for Genevieve Rassicod, 6 March 1690, and *Constitution de rente viagère* for Jean Favier, 14 March 1690 (which included a copy of portions of Favier's baptismal certificate); CII-151: Wedding contract, 29 April 1690; and *Declaration et reconnoissance*, also dated 29 April 1690 (another copy of the wedding contract may be found in F-Pan, Y256, fols. 151r–152v). Other documents concerning Favier's

violin and to dance at a young age, either taught at home by his father or perhaps apprenticed to another family of dancing master/violinists.[19] By the age of twelve he was deemed ready to dance before the court; his first role was as a monkey in the ballet Lully set between the acts of Cavalli's opera *Xerxès*, performed in November of 1660 in honor of the marriage of Louis XIV to Maria Theresa, Infanta of Spain. During the next few years, the youthful Favier was cast in roles befitting a young dancer: a small child and a duck in the *Ballet de l'Impatience* (1661); a *petit Amour* in the *Ballet des Amours Déguisés* (1664); and as Cupid, his first solo role, in *La Naissance de Vénus* (1665). It is clear that by the time he was eighteen when he performed a number of roles in the *Ballet des Muses* and its accompanying comedy-ballets (1666–67), he was a fully accomplished professional dancer: he could play the castanets, dance both male and female parts, and perform in serious, comic, pastoral, or exotic styles. The roles he played in virtually all of Lully's ballets and comedy-ballets on into the 1670s reveal his ever-growing versatility.

In 1669 another member of the Favier family began appearing as a dancer in court productions. From this time on the librettos generally distinguish between Favier *l'aîné* (the elder) and Favier *le cadet* (the younger). The latter was probably Jean's younger brother Bernard Henri (b. 1651): a payment record from 1671 (F-Pn [Manuscrits] Ms. fr. 28.624) identifies Jean Favier as "Favier *l'aîné*" and Bernard Henri Favier as "Favier *le cadet*." Their father Jacques was still performing in the *grande bande* – his name appears on the lists of musicians occasionally included in ballet librettos – and the three Faviers often participated in the same productions. Yet another brother, Jean Jacques (b. 1649), gave dancing lessons and presumably also performed; perhaps he is the dancer identified in a 1677 libretto for Lully's *Isis* as "Favier de Zell," an appellation suggesting that he might have been employed at the German court of Celle and therefore only in France temporarily.[20]

In 1672 when Lully assumed control of the fledgling Académie Royale de Musique, Jean Favier, along with a number of other professional dancers from the court, may have joined the dance troupe. The lack of surviving records from the Opéra during Lully's tenure as director makes it difficult to establish his personnel, but the librettos published for performances of Lully's operas at court show that Favier appeared regularly among the dancers there. That he also performed at the Opéra's public theatre in the Palais Royal in Paris cannot be established but seems likely.[21] The man put in charge of the ballet troupe at the new Opéra was one under whom Favier had already danced for many years at court,

---

financial dealings are cited in Jurgens and Fleury, *Documents*, pp. 141 and 146–7. Information about his performing career comes from the cast lists in the published librettos for court performances of ballets and operas.

[19] Regarding the training of young dancers in the seventeenth century, see Astier, "La vie quotidienne."

[20] In addition to Jean Jacques and Bernard Henri, there was yet another younger son in the family, Christophe (b. 1650), but as his name does not appear in any subsequent family documents, he probably died young. If Jean Jacques Favier did find employment abroad, he did not stay away permanently. Two documents show that Jean Jacques was working in Paris as a dancing master at least in 1691 and 1719 (F-Pan MC I-193 and MC XXVII-119). His address was given as the Rue du Petit Lion (F-Pan MC I-193), the same street listed for Favier *le cadet* in the *Livre commode des adresses de Paris* for 1692. With the exception of *Isis*, however, there do not seem to have been more than two Faviers dancing at any one time in court performances; only the qualifiers *l'aîné* and *le cadet* appear in librettos. (By way of contrast, in the early eighteenth century when there were four Dumoulin brothers dancing at the Opéra, they were distinguished in the librettos by first initial.) Similarly, only two Faviers appear in the 1695 lists of Parisian dancing masters (see n. 29 below): they are once listed as Favier *l'aîné* and *cadet*, in another place as Favier *cadet* and Favier J (presumably meaning "Jean," as appears to be the case with other names on the list), a third time as Favier *cadet* and Favier *le jeune*. Since the three listings largely duplicate each other, the "le jeune" appellation is probably an error, perhaps due to extrapolation from "Favier J" on the previous list; on the other hand, it might be a reference to the third brother. Bernard Henri lived until at least 1691, when he, Jean, and Jean Jacques were all present at the burial of their father (Brossard, *Musiciens*, p. 118).

It is often impossible to establish who danced which role with complete certainty because the librettos never give the performers' first names. In the *Ballet de Flore* (1669), for example, Favier is listed in one dancing role, Favier *l'aîné* in four, Favier *le cadet* in one, and there is a Favier among the *grands violons*.

[21] The librettos published during this period for the Parisian performances do not list the names of the performers.

Pierre Beauchamps. In 1677 the *Mercure galant* praised Beauchamps and his dancers following a particularly brilliant series of performances at court which included Lully's operas *Alceste*, *Thésée*, and *Atys*:

> The dancers who were admired [in these operas] provided extraordinary satisfaction in their entrées; the proof is that Favier, Letang, Faure, Magny, and five others received large bonuses beyond their usual salaries. Pupils such as these, to whom Mr Beauchamp has given and still gives daily lessons, despite the fact that they are already masters, show that he is one of the most skillful men in the world in his art.[22]

It was around this time, Beauchamps was to declare in 1704, that the king charged him with the task of inventing a system of dance notation in order to preserve dances from the court ballets and the Opéra. What impact this request may have had on the dancers working under his tutelage can only be a matter of speculation, but as one of Beauchamps's leading dancers, Favier probably would have been aware of Beauchamps's work in this direction. Further testimonials to Favier's dancing abilities come from La Bruyère, who singled him out as an unambiguous example of a "beau danseur," and from Pierre Rameau, who included the elder Favier among "the most skillful executants in Paris and at the court."[23]

During the early 1670s Favier, like many French dancers before and after him, crossed the English Channel. In 1673 Robert Cambert, the composer who had lost the battle for control of the Paris Opéra to Lully, had gone to London, taking with him several French dancers, among them Pécour, Lestang, and Dumirail. There he attempted to establish a Royal Academy of Music on the French model and succeeded in mounting two operas, *Ariane* and *Pomone*. Whether Favier was also involved in these productions is unknown, but in January or February of 1674 Cambert and Favier presented a *divertissement* of ballet and music for King Charles II. The music has been lost, but this work provides the first indication of Favier's activities as a choreographer. Cambert's English enterprise failed and by January of 1675 Favier was back at the French court, performing in Lully's new opera *Thésée*.

In 1676 Jacques Favier legally named his son Jean to be his successor as one of the twenty-four violins of the king (Benoit, *Musiques de cour*, p. 49). Although Jean must have been qualified for the position, it seems unlikely that he ever filled it. Not only would his dancing activities have made such a job difficult to manage – Favier often danced in court entertainments for which the *grands violons* played – but as soon as his father died in 1691, Favier sold the position to another violinist (Benoit, *Musiques de cour*, p. 127). The records of payment in the interim period are to "Jacques Favier et Jean son fils en survivance," so it is not impossible that Jacques himself continued to play; but given that he was probably seventy-one at the time he named his successor, it seems more likely that an unknown violinist was hired to fill in. Nonetheless, Jean Favier's skills as a violinist probably extended to the composition of dance music: there are a number of tunes bearing his name in various collections from the period, and an undated libretto for a pastorale called *Le Triomphe de Bacchus* attributes the music to Favier.[24]

---

[22] "Les Danseurs qui s'y sont fait admirer, ont extraordinairement satisfait dans leurs Entrées; & ce qui n'en laisse pas douter, c'est que les Sieurs Favier, Letang, Faure, Magny, et cinq autres, ont eu de grandes gratifications, outre leurs pensions ordinaires. De Pareils Ecoliers à qui Mr de Beauchamp a donné et donne encor tous les jours des Leçons, quoy qu'ils soient déjà grands Maistres, font voir qu'il est dans son Art un des plus habiles Hommes du monde." (*Mercure galant*, October 1677, pp. 205–6).

[23] Jean La Bruyère, "De la mode" in *Les caractères ou les mœurs de ce siècle* (Paris, 1688–1694) and Rameau, *Le maître à danser*, Préface (trans. Beaumont), p. xiii.

[24] In the absence of any information beyond the name Favier, this work might be by another member of the family, possibly Jacques.

The presence of Favier's name in collections of dance music does not necessarily mean that he himself was a composer. The "rigaudon de Mr Favier," for example, may have been choreographed and/or performed rather than composed by him. On the other hand, dancing masters of the seventeenth century were generally violinists and were expected to be capable of composing dance tunes. Pierre Beauchamps composed the music for a number of ballets including *Les Facheux* of 1661 (see Astier, "Beauchamps and the ballets de collège"). Anthologies of seventeenth-century dance music as well as collections of

In 1680 the Dauphin, heir to the throne, married the princess Marie-Anne Christine-Victoire of Bavaria. Favier was appointed dancing master to her pages, and Guillaume Raynal was given the prestigious position of dancing master to the Dauphine herself.[25] Nonetheless, despite the arrangements on paper, it seems to have been Favier who actually gave the Dauphine her dancing lessons. Not only did Favier style himself "dancing master to Madame la Dauphine" in various legal documents during her lifetime, he clearly considered this appointment the pinnacle of his career and continued to use that title after her untimely death in 1690. Even his son, also a dancer, used his father's eminent position to reflect glory on himself when he wrote his memoirs in the middle of the eighteenth century.

In her early days at the court, the Dauphine danced frequently in ballets and balls. She was given two prominent roles in *Le Triomphe de l'Amour* which had its premiere at court in January of 1681. Perhaps it was Favier who coached her when she learned in less than two hours a difficult entrée in order to replace her ailing sister-in-law, the Princesse de Conti (*Mercure galant*, January 1681, pp. 288–90). Perhaps he was also involved in setting her dances in carnival mascarades, such as the village wedding, arranged by her husband, in which the Dauphine participated in 1683 (*Mercure galant*, March 1683, pp. 335–9; see the engraving of the cast in plate 3). Favier almost certainly composed and choreographed ball dances for her: three dance tunes found in collections of ballroom music from the court – a pavane, a courante, and a rigaudon – bear titles indicating that they were created by Favier for the Dauphine.[26] But the Dauphine's poor health, undoubtedly aggravated by her pregnancies, restricted her participation in many of the social activities of the court. Although she danced at a court ball as late as 1687 (Dangeau, *Journal* II, p. 9), contemporary reports indicate that she was more often a spectator than a participant in court entertainments. One even wonders how much of her early display of enthusiasm for the dance represented a desire to please both her husband and her father-in-law. Even in the 1683 mascarade, the Dauphine played only the role of the sister of the bride, despite her status as the highest-ranking woman at court – the very accomplished Princesse de Conti was the bride, the Comte de Brionne, another enthusiastic dancer, the bridegroom – and she did not appear in the *Temple de la Paix*, Lully's last court ballet, in 1685. Nonetheless Favier's services for the Dauphine were not unappreciated: at the time of her death in 1690, the king was paying Favier 1,000 *livres tournois* a year for her instruction.

The Dauphine was not Favier's only pupil. A document from 1690 listing Favier's

---

choreographies in Feuillet notation contain large numbers of tunes for which the composer has not been identified; many of these were probably composed by dancing masters.

Regarding Favier's presumed skills as a violinist, it is curious to note that the list of his possessions drawn up in 1690 at the time of his marriage (see n. 28 below) includes an organ and a harpsichord, but no violin.

[25] F-Pan Z^{1A}514. Favier is listed among the staff of the *écurie* of the Dauphine as a *baladin* for the years 1680, 1681, and 1690 (the only years for which records are preserved). This title meant that its holder was one of the instructors of the Dauphine's pages, the adolescent sons of country gentry, sent to court to finish their educations and to train them for service to king and country. For further information regarding the instruction of the pages, see Benoit, *Versailles*, pp. 228–9.

Guillaume Raynal (?–1706) was one of the original members of the Académie Royale de Danse, founded by the king in 1661 (Loubet de Sceaury, *Musiciens*, p. 78). He was already well established at the time, having appeared in court ballets since at least 1648. He was named dancing master to the Dauphin in 1662 when his pupil was only one year old, and was later appointed to teach both the Dauphin's eldest son, the Duc de Bourgogne (1682–1712), and his wife (Benoit, *Versailles*, pp. 30–2). In the last case at least, his appointment may have been more honorific than real: Louis Pécour, choreographer at the Opéra from 1687 to 1729, was the one who appears to have given the Duchesse de Bourgogne her lessons (Harris-Warrick, "The dancing Duchess of Burgundy," paper presented to the Society of Dance History Scholars, February 1989 and La Gorce, "Pecour").

[26] The full titles of all three tunes are listed below. The pavane is particularly interesting in that it changes meter eight times over the space of only fifty-two measures. Such a piece was probably designed to demonstrate the dancer's skill in performing in different dance types, and as such would also serve as a demonstration of the dancing master's skill as a teacher. A similar piece is *La Bourgogne*, a choreography by Pécour published in 1700, which includes a few measures each of a courante, bourrée, sarabande, and passepied. The title suggests that it was composed for the Duchesse de Bourgogne, the wife of the Dauphine's oldest son, who, like the mother-in-law she never knew, was required by her elevated social position to show off her dancing abilities in front of the court.

assets, including sums owed to him by people who were in arrears for their dancing lessons, reveals how important his teaching must have been to his financial well-being. How much Favier earned for his performances is not known, but his basic salary in the Dauphine's *écurie* was only 180 lt per year;[27] the amounts paid him by his pupils, whose debts to him ranged from 110 lt to 1,800 lt for unspecified periods of instruction, must have represented a substantial portion of his income.[28] In the 1695 records of the dancing masters' guild, Favier *l'aîné* was classified as a master "of the first class";[29] his abilities coupled with his favorable position at court enabled him to attract students from the highest aristocratic families. (Either that, or any less illustrious pupils he may have had kept up with the payments for their lessons!) Of the seventeen students on his list, several were accorded the honor two years later of dancing at the wedding ball for the Duc de Chartres (Duc d'Orléans after 1701), the king's nephew and future regent of France. These included the Princesse d'Espinay, the Comte de Guiche, the Chevalier de Sully, the Marquis de Grignon, the Prince d'Enrichemont, and the Vidame de Chartres. This last was shortly to inherit his father's title and as the Duc de Saint-Simon to paint a vivid picture in his memoirs of life at the court. Alas for dance historians, he wrote not one word about his dancing master.

In 1690, at the relatively advanced age of forty-two, Favier married for the first time. The documents drawn up on this occasion provide our only glimpse into Favier's private life. They reveal that Favier and his wife, Genevieve Rassicod, daughter of an apothecary to the king, already had a seven-year-old daughter at the time of their marriage. They had had the intention to marry for a number of years, they declared, but various unnamed considerations had prevented them from doing so. Now that they were in a position to solemnize their union, they wished to recognize their daughter, Jeanne Genevieve, as their own. The couple took up residence in the Rue Dauphine (Favier may already have been living there), the street that descends into the Left Bank of Paris from the Pont Neuf. They had at least three more children, a son Jean, born in 1694, and two daughters, Marie and Marie-Anne.[30]

Favier's marriage documents also reveal that he and his wife had both social and financial connections to the French comedians, the troupe of actors that had formerly been headed by Molière. One of the witnesses at their wedding was Charles Chevillet, Sieur de Champmeslé (1642–1701), husband of the famous dramatic actress Marie Champmeslé, from whose declamation Lully is reputed to have derived ideas about recitative. The Champmeslé couple were infamous for their scandalous behavior:

---

[27] Amount listed in F-Pan Z^{1A}514 (see n. 25 above). Philidor received the same amount for his position among the *grands hautbois* (see Benoit, *Musiques*, pp. 121 et passim). Court musicians' and dancers' official salaries represented only a small portion of their income: they also received sums for food, transportation, lodging, and when appropriate, clothing. In addition the king accorded extra payments, or gratifications, for special performances beyond the normal duties, and pensions for services of long duration. See Benoit, *Versailles*, pp. 146–74.

[28] The list of Favier's material assets was drawn up as part of his wedding contract (F-Pan MC CII-151, 29 April 1690). In addition to his household possessions, from spoons to furniture, it includes his investments and the sums owed him "par les personnes cy apres nommez pour pensions, gages et sallaires pour avoir appris a dancer auxdites personnes" – in other words, it supplies a partial list of his students. At the head of the list of debtors was the king, who owed Favier for two years of instruction for the Dauphine. Unfortunately there is no breakdown of cost per lesson or per period of instruction. Favier's net worth was figured at 21,993 lt, his bride's at 4,739 lt.

[29] F-Pan Z^{1H} 657. In these documents, drawn up in 1695 in order to facilitate collection of the *capitation* on the *Compagnons qui montrent à dancer et à jouer des instruments dans la ville de Paris*, dancing masters are classified in four groups: members of the Royal Academy of Dance, of whom there were thirteen, then *maîtres à danser de première, deuxième, et troisième classe*, each group being charged progressively lower fees. Favier *le cadet* was also listed among the first class.

[30] The names of these four children appear in a document from 1740 relating the sale of a house that Favier and his wife had bought in 1696, and which the children had inherited following the deaths of their parents (Favier is said to have predeceased his wife, but no date is given for either death). By 1740, when the house was sold, both Jeanne Genevieve and her sister Marie had also died (F-Pan MC XXI-341). Marie Anne Favier and her husband Jean Baptiste Robert Adam appear to have retained the family home in Paris: their address is listed in several documents as being in the Rue Dauphine.

according to du Tralage, "there would be enough material to write a large book about their amorous adventures."[31] The extent to which the Faviers were a part of this social circle can only be a matter of speculation, but it is clear that both Favier and his wife had financial dealings with members of the troupe.[32] Favier's professional connections with both the French and Italian troupes were already of long duration. Favier had performed on the same stage with the French comedians during the 1660s and early 1670s in productions of Lully's and Molière's comedy-ballets at court; during the 1680s his name appears several times in accounts of performances of plays at court, by both the French and the Italian comedians, that incorporated dances between the acts.[33] Perhaps Favier also danced in their Parisian performances, during the entrées the actors regularly incorporated into their plays. Be that as it may, Favier's long associations with both the French and Italian troupes in court performances may well have facilitated the presence of two Italian comedians in the cast of *Le Mariage de la Grosse Cathos* in 1688.

It is not known when Favier stopped dancing. The absence of performers' names from the operatic librettos of the late 1680s and 1690s makes it impossible to follow whatever performing he may have done at the Opéra, but he was still performing at court at least until he was fifty-one in 1699, when both he and his brother appeared in the *Intermèdes de la Comédie des Fées* of de Lalande. He did not, however, perform in any of Philidor's mascarades in the following year. At some time after 1695 one of the Faviers was elected a member of the Académie Royale de Danse – Jean, the most eminent member of the family, seems the likeliest candidate for this honor – and this same person died in 1719. If this was indeed Favier *l'aîné*, he would have been seventy-one.[34]

Favier's son, born in 1694 and also named Jean, followed in his father's footsteps. The name "Favier" without further qualification reappears in a few librettos from the 1711 and 1712 seasons at the Paris Opéra (by this time the singers' and dancers' names were always listed); the late date suggests that the dancer in question was the son, who would have been seventeen at the time. Toward the end of the decade the young Jean Favier entered the

---

[31] "Il y aurait de quoi faire un gros livre de leurs aventures amoureuses." Cited in Mongrédien, *Dictionnaire*, pp. 52–3.

[32] In addition to the two *constitutions* among the Faviers' marriage documents (see n. 18), *constitutions* between Favier and members of the French troupe were drawn up in 1692 and 1695 (F-Pan MC XLIV-116 [*Constitution* 14 April 1692] and XLIV-128 [*Constitution* 17 January 1695]). Besides Chevillet, other *comédiens français* whose names appear in these documents include Nicolas Dorné, Sieur d'Auvilliers and his wife, Françoise Victoire Poisson; and Charles Varlet, Sieur de La Grange and his wife, Marie Raguenau. La Grange, whose daily register of the troupe's performances is an invaluable source for study of the Comédie Française, was classified by du Tralage as among those comedians who led Christian lives. Not only do the documents themselves suggest that Genevieve Rassicod may have known the French comedians independently of her husband's professional connections, she was connected to them by marriage, her brother Pierre having married Marguerite Béjart, cousin of Molière's wife Armande Béjart, in 1680 (document cited in Jurgens and Maxfield-Miller, *Cent ans*, p. 667).

[33] Two examples from the diary of Dangeau: "Le soir il y eut comédie française; entre la comédie et la farce Favier et Pécourt dansèrent la chaconne du dernier opéra." (22 October 1684, Dangeau, *Journal* I, p. 62); "Monseigneur . . . fit répéter des entrées de ballet qu'on dansera au premier voyage [de Marly], et qui seront les intermèdes du *Bourgeois gentilhomme*, que le roi y fera jouer. Mesdames les Princesses et madame de Seignelay apprirent leur entrée avec le comte de Brionne, Pécourt et Favier." (19 November 1687, Dangeau, *Journal* II, p. 67). In the November issue of 1684, the *Mercure galant* reported the performance of an Italian comedy, a synopsis of which is given on pp. 228–41, which was interspersed with danced entrées, most of them performed by courtiers. "Messieurs Favier & Pecour firent aussi une Entrée, déguisez en Magiciens, & il y eut ensuite un Balet général, composé de tous ceux qui avoient déja dancé . . . Les Entrées avoient été faites par Mr Favier & Pecour, tous deux Danceurs du Roy." ("Favier and Pécour also danced an entrée, costumed as magicians, followed by a general dance made up of all those who had already danced . . . The entrées had been choreographed by Favier and Pécour, both dancers of the king.")

[34] The name Favier does not figure on the 1695 list of members of the Académie Royale de Danse (see n. 29 above), but another document in the Archives Nationales (cited in Benoit, *Musiques de cour*, p. 306) reports a meeting of the members of the Academy in September 1719 to elect a replacement for Favier who had recently died. Since no first name or other identifying indication is given in the document, it is possible that the reference is to Favier *le cadet*. (Although nothing is known of Bernard Henri Favier at this time, Jean Jacques was still alive in March of 1719 when he acknowledged payment of money owed him for dancing lessons [see n. 20].) This is the only known record of the death of any of the three brothers, although a document from 1740 (cited in n. 30 above) makes it clear that Jean Favier had been dead for some time.

employ of Stanislas Lesczinski, deposed King of Poland, and gave dancing lessons to his daughter Maria, who was to become Queen of France upon her marriage to Louis XV in 1725. In 1719 he went to Dresden where he established himself as *premier danseur* and ballet master at the court first of Augustus II, then of Augustus III, both of whom held the two titles of Elector of Saxony and King of Poland. He seems to have remained for most of his professional career in Saxony, although he made periodic visits to Paris. His wife, Marie Barbéry, was the daughter of a Parisian merchant. Toward the end of his life he wrote a few pages of anecdotes about his life which he deposited in the royal library in Paris.[35] Unfortunately these brief memoirs focus almost entirely on his dealings with important persons – most notably the Maréchal de Saxe, natural son of Augustus II – and have nothing to say about his dancing. Later generations of Faviers continued in the family profession: there were at least three other Faviers working in Dresden during Jean Favier's tenure as ballet master – François, Jeanne, and Marie – and at the end of the eighteenth century Giovanni Favier and Carlo Augusto Favier were established in northern Italy, choreographing for operas and ballets.[36]

Works by Jean Favier (Favier *l'aîné*)

The following list contains both musical and choreographic works that may be attributable to Jean Favier. It includes only those works for which some kind of written evidence survives; Favier's actual work list must have been much longer. In those instances where the source gives only the name "Favier" without qualification, the person intended may have been another member of the family. Category A includes complete works for which Favier presumably either choreographed the dances or composed the music; for two of them only the text remains. Category B lists tunes found in anthologies of music to which Favier's name is attached. Titles in parentheses are found in the concordant sources listed. It is not always clear whether the preposition "de" means "music composed by," "choreography by," "performed by," or some combination of the three. No attempt has been made to search all seventeenth- and eighteenth-century anthologies of music, nor are all known concordances of the tunes given here; the anthologies cited below were included because of their connections with the repertoire of the French court. Category C includes choreographies preserved in Feuillet notation that bear Favier's name. It is followed by an annotated listing of the musical anthologies cited.

A. Theatrical works

1. *Le Mariage de la Grosse Cathos*. Music by Philidor *l'aîné*, [choreography by Favier *l'aîné*]. 1688. Score, spoken text and choreography in F-Pn (Musique) Rés. F. 534^{a-b}; score and spoken text in F-Pa Ms. 3239.

2. *Le Triomphe de Bacchus*. Pastorale. Mise en musique par Favier. Manuscript libretto in F-Pn (Manuscrits) Ms. fr. 24.352, fols. 309–14.

---

[35] F-Pn (Manuscrits) Ms. fr. 12.763, fols. 260–4: "Anecdotes données à la Bibliothèque du Roy par Favier, maître à danser de la reine de France lorsque cette princesse était à Deux-Ponts, et depuis maître de ballet et premier danseur du roi de Pologne Auguste II et d'Auguste III." These pages were transcribed and published by Léon G. Pélissier as "Souvenirs du danseur Favier" in the *Journal de la Société d'Archéologie Lorraine* (1897). The younger Favier's birthdate is recorded in a *constitution viagère* established for him by his sister in 1751 (F-Pan MC LXXXII-519, doc. 27), his wife's name and family connections in documents relating to her mother's death in 1747 (F-Pan MC XXX-305 and XXIV-568). Information about some of the works for which he provided the choreography may be found in Fürstenau, *Geschichte*.

[36] Information regarding the professional activities of the younger Faviers in Dresden may be found in the annual publication *Königlich Sächsischer Hof- und Staats-Kalender* (Leipzig, 1732ff.; other titles: *Churfürstlicher Sächsischer Hof- und Staats-Calender*; *Staatshandbuch für den Freistaat Sachsen*), of the Italian Faviers in Hansell, "Opera and ballet" and Wiel, *Teatri veneziani*. For a brief discussion of several generations of Faviers, see Winter, *Ballet*, pp. 33–4. Winter, however, conflated the two Jean Faviers into a single person, as have other music and dance historians. We have not attempted to verify her accounts of Favier's descendents.

Six scenes, text only, music lost. Libretto bears the annotation: "La Scene des Medecins avec Lycas est une imitation de la scene de deux avocats consultés par Pourceaugnac." Undated, but must postdate 1669, when Lully's comedy-ballet *Monsieur de Pourceaugnac* was composed. Yet another scene imitates the Barbacola scene from Lully's ballet *Les Nopces de Village* (1663). Favier's mascarade thus probably postdates 1675, when Lully recycled both scenes at the Opéra in his pastiche *Le Carnaval Mascarade*.

3. *Ballet et musique pour le divertissement du roy de la Grande-Bretagne*. Imprimé aux depens de l'Autheur. Dans la Savoye par Thomas Nieucombe MDCLXXIV [1674]. Libretto in GB-Lad.

Libretto commissioned by Charles II to honor the wedding of the Duke of York (the future James II) and Mary of Modena. The text is by S[ebastian] Bre[mond]; the music is lost. The libretto includes a note to the reader by Bremond explaining that he had expanded this pastorale from the "petite demy heure de Divertissement meslé de Musique et de Dance" that Cambert and Favier had originally planned (see Grobe, "S. Bre.," Danchin, "The foundation," and Flood, "Quelques précisions").

B. Individual pieces found in musical sources

1. La Dauphine courante figurée de Mr Favier (La Dauphine de Mr Favier)
F-Pn Vm^{7}3555, p. 11; F-Po Mus. 2359, p. 95

2. Pavane de Monsieur favier
F-Pn Rés. F. 845, p. 159

3. La Pavane de Mad^e la Dauphine faite par Mr Favier (La Pavanne de Mr Favier)
F-Pn Vm^{7}3555, p. 16; F-Po Mus. 2359, pp. 94–5

4. La deuxieme Pavanne, de M. Favier
F-Pn Vm^{7}3555, p. 18 (Listed in table of contents, but page missing in manuscript. May be same as B-2.)

5. Passepied de M^r favier (Passepied de Favier laisné)
F-Pn Rés. F. 845, p. 158; F-Pn Vm^{7}3555, p. 115; F-Po Mus. 2359, p. 138

6. Rigodon de M^e la Dauphine fait par Mr Favier (Rigodon de Mr Favier pour Mme la Dauphine; Rigaudon de M^r favier l'ainé)
F-Pn Rés. F. 845, p. 173; F-Pn Vm^{7}3555, p. 28; F-Po Mus. 2359, p. 52; F-Pn Vm^{6}5, fol. 342^r

7. Rigaudon de Mr Favier L'aisné (Rigaudon de Mr Favier)
F-Pn Rés. F. 845; F-Pn Vm^{7}3555, p. 27; F-Po Mus. 2359, p. 50

8. Rigaudon de Mr Favier
F-Po Mus. 2359, p. 48

9. Autre [rigaudon] de Mr Favier
F-Pn Vm^{6}5, fol. 343

10. Le Trianon de Mr Favier
F-Pn Vm^{7}3555, p. 37
F-Po Mus. 2359 (Listed in table of contents as "la gigue de trianon par M. Favier," but page missing in manuscript.)

C. Choreographies in Feuillet notation

1. Sarabande de M^r favier [LMC 7720]
In F-Pn Ms. fr. 14.884, pp. 29–36. For a solo man, set to the "Premier Air des Espagnols" from Lully's *Bourgeois Gentilhomme* [LWV 43/27].

2. Le nouveaux Rigaudon de M^r favier [LMC 6240]

In F-Pn Ms. fr. 14.884, pp. 465–72; and F-Po Rés. 934, pp. 399–405. In Feuillet notation, for a man and a woman. Source of tune unidentified. In three musical anthologies, this piece is called the "Rigaudon de Pécourt."

3. Rigaudon de Mre Favie

In D-W Codex Guelf. 244 Blankenburg, No. 43. Contredanse in modified Feuillet notation, set to the rigaudon from Lully's *Acis et Galatée* [LWV 73/6].

Musical and choreographic sources for Favier's works

F-Pn (Musique) Vm^{7}3555. Suite des dances pour les violons, et hautbois. Qui se joüent ordinairement à tous les Bals chez le Roy. Recueillies, mises en ordre, & composées la plus grande partie, par M. Philidor l'aîné, Ordinaire de la Musique du Roy, & Garde de tous les Livres de sa Bibliotheque de Musique, l'An 1701 [inked over to read 1712].

A large manuscript collection (although the title page and table of contents are printed), partially in the hand of Philidor *l'aîné*, of tunes for ballroom dances, arranged by dance type. Includes the treble parts only.

F-Po Mus. 2359. Livre du bal / dessus de violon

A collection very similar to Vm^{7}3555, also partially copied by Philidor, with many of the same pieces.

F-Pn (Musique) Rés. F. 845. Airs propres pour le Timpanon

An anthology of instrumental and untexted vocal pieces, treble part only, from the early eighteenth century.

F-Pn (Musique) Vm^{6}5 [untitled]

A large collection of dance music, treble part only, arranged in chronological order from a *Ballet Royal* of 1654 through a *Serenade de Mr de Lalande* of 1691. Contains mostly stage music, but includes some ball dances.

D-W Codex Guelf. 244 Blankenburg, No. 43.

A manuscript dated 1717 compiled by a dancing master named Jayme containing English-style contredanses in modified Feuillet notation.

F-Pn (Manuscrits) Ms. fr. 14.884

A manuscript collection containing seventy-five choreographies in Feuillet notation. Some of the dances also appear in prints published by Feuillet between 1700 and 1709.

F-Po Rés. 934

A manuscript collection containing fifty-seven ball dances in Feuillet notation. Some of the dances also appear in prints published by Feuillet and Dezais between 1700 and 1714.

THE SINGERS

All of the seven singers and five dancers whose names appear in the manuscript had associations with the royal musical establishment. The singers had regular appointments either in the chapel or the chamber, and were also called upon to perform in productions of Lully's stage works at court.[37] Several of them were also involved in Philidor's two other theatrical works from 1687 and 1688, *Le Canal de Versailles* and *La Princesse de Crète*.

The role of Monsieur Dupont was performed by Jean Borel, called Miracle (d. 1728), a singer in the chapel. Although he only entered the chapel in 1687, he had already been singing at court for many years, having appeared in Lully's tragedy-ballet *Psyché* in 1671 and in a number of Lully operas during the following decade. During the 1688 carnival season he also sang in Philidor's other theatrical work, *La Princesse de Crète*. Pougin claims that Miracle had been brought to Paris from Languedoc by Perrin and Cambert to sing in

---

[37] Much of the biographical data regarding the singers in *Le Mariage de la Grosse Cathos* has been derived from the documents cited in Benoit, *Musiques de cour*. Information about stage appearances comes from the published librettos.

the short-lived opera company they founded in 1669, and that he was reputed to have a beautiful tenor voice (Pougin, "La troupe de Lully," p. 324).

The Monsieur Le Roy who sang the role of Madame Dupont could be one of two people by that name. Fursy Le Roy (d. 1726) was a singer in the royal chapel who is first mentioned in documents from the court in 1685. He was listed as a *haute-contre* (high tenor) in 1717, the voice range of Madame Dupont. The other Le Roy, Philippe Le Roy de Beaumont had been a singer in the king's chamber since at least 1664 and remained there until his death in 1704. The name Le Roy appears in fifteen Lully operatic librettos between 1677 and 1699; which of the two singers is intended is not clear.

Antoine Morel (Maurel), who sang the role of the Abbé du Plessis, had been a singer in the royal chapel since 1673. Around the time of *Le Mariage de la Grosse Cathos* he also received a post in the chamber, but he had already performed in a large number of productions of Lully comedy-ballets and operas starting in 1670 in addition to Philidor's two theatrical works from 1687–88. Morel died in 1711. Gripetout, the character in the mascarade with whom Morel fought in his stage persona as the Abbé, was one of his colleagues in the chapel, Louis Gingant. Gingant had been in the chapel since 1664, and had also performed in comedy-ballets such as *Georges Dandin* (1668) and *Le Bourgeois Gentilhomme* (1670). His name appears much less frequently in both court documents and Lully librettos than does Morel's, perhaps indicating that he was less active professionally. The date of his death is unknown.

As with Madame Dupont, the role of the Dame Ragonde could have been performed by one of two singers. According to Benoit, there were two brothers at court by the name of Jonquet, Jean and Pierre. Jean is mentioned as a singer in the king's chamber between 1680 and 1732, a remarkably long career if, in fact, he kept performing during the entire period. Pierre only appears in documents from the chapel in 1717 and 1721, but Jonquet, without indication of first name, is listed as performing in a number of Lully's works from *Le Triomphe de l'Amour* in 1681 to a revival of *Le Bourgeois Gentilhomme* in 1698. For this last performance, documents record the expenses incurred for his shoes, silk stockings, and Spanish wig. The name of Jonquet also appears among the cast for both of Philidor's other two stage works from 1687–88.

André Guillegau, or Guillegault (d. 1702) who played Grosse Cathos, had been a singer in the king's chapel since 1680. He sang at least occasionally in theatrical productions at court; records show that he performed in *Le Triomphe de l'Amour* in 1681, *Atys* in 1682, and *Le Bourgeois Gentilhomme* in 1698. He seems to have been something of a regular in Philidor's productions, having sung in *Le Canal de Versailles* during the summer of 1687, in *La Princesse de Crète* and *Le Mariage de la Grosse Cathos* during the 1688 carnival season, and in *Le Roy de la Chine* in 1700. He has at least one little composition – a menuet tune – to his credit, but evidently was not well enough versed in harmony to be able to supply the bass: this job went to Philidor.[38] Perhaps in addition to his low voice Guillegault was endowed with a physique of generous proportions, which might account for his selection for the role of Grosse Cathos.

The most colorful member of the cast was Philbert, also known as Philibert Rebillé, who played the role of La Couture. Unlike the other singers, Philbert was primarily an instrumentalist, but his multiple talents brought him into the limelight at court in many different capacities.

Philbert had joined one of the ensembles of the *grande écurie*, the *hautbois et musettes de Poitou*, by 1667 (Benoit, *Musiques de cour*, p. 18), if not before. At the time he occupied the place in the ensemble reserved for the young son of one of the other members, Jean Brunet. Philbert was evidently a very talented performer on both flute and oboe; already

---

[38] "Menuet de Monsieur Guillegaut. La Basse par Monsieur Philidor l'aîné," in *Suite de danses pour les violons et haut-bois qui se joüent ordinairement aux bals chez le Roy* (Paris: Christophe Ballard, 1699), p. 35. In distinction to many other anthologies of the period (see the Favier work list above), in this collection the preposition "de" is almost always used to indicate the name of the composer; when it means "performed by," Philidor is careful to distinguish between performer and composer, as in the following example on p. 42: "Menuet de Madame la Duchesse de Bourgogne, fait par Monsieur Philidor l'aîné."

in the same year he also held a place in the king's chamber as a flutist, in which capacity he is singled out for mention in the payment records (Benoit, *Musiques de cour*, p. 19). For many Lully productions, starting in 1666 with the *Ballet des Muses*, he appears to have been an indispensable member of the cast.

In his early years at court, so the story later went, Philbert's colleague Jean Brunet developed strong feelings of friendship toward the young flutist; so, apparently, did his wife, Catherine Bonnières. Jean Brunet, blind to the affair going on between his friend and his wife, arranged the marriage of his daughter, Marie-Catherine, to Philbert. In 1672, the day before the wedding, Brunet died of "apoplexy." Marie-Catherine was packed off to a convent and after a decent interval of two years, the widow Brunet married Philbert. All was peaceful for a few years, and Philbert was appointed guardian of his stepson Jean-Louis, the boy whose position in the *écurie* he had originally occupied.[39] Then in 1679 the "affair of the poisons" broke at court. Madame Voisin and her fellow poisoners began naming names. Madame Brunet-Philbert was accused of having poisoned her husband; she was condemned and publicly executed. Louis XIV, assuming that Philbert had been involved in the crime but not wanting to see one of his favorite musicians condemned, advised him to flee France. Instead, Philbert turned himself in to the prison at Vincennes, maintaining his innocence and demanding to be exculpated. When in due course he was declared innocent he returned to his musical duties at court, his reputation infinitely enhanced by appearing as the kind of man for whom a woman had committed murder.[40]

As an instrumentalist Philbert was best known as a flutist; along with his colleague Descouteaux he is reputed to have been one of the earliest players on the new transverse flute in France.[41] According to a biographical sketch of Philbert published in the *Mercure de France* in 1725, "Louis XIV greatly appreciated listening to these two people perform melodious tunes on their flutes and often called them for that purpose into his apartments or into the gardens at Versailles."

But Philbert was also evidently a born mimic, with a fine singing voice. The *Mercure* report continues:

> Philibert [sic] sang very well; and to give more expression to his singing, he knew how to sweeten his voice, and he would inflate it all of a sudden in order to go from a graceful sound to a noisy one and to a martial one. He had the talent of mimicking all kinds of jabberings or corrupt accents – Gascon, German, and frenchified Swiss; he could imitate the speech and manner of young girls or mimic old ladies. He was, so to speak, the monkey of the human race. He was often included in the king's ballets in order to represent comic characters, at which he succeeded perfectly.[42]

---

[39] As guardian, Philbert was entrusted with the wages of his stepson and Mme Brunet was granted half of the amount until the time of her son's majority (see Benoit, *Musiques de cour*, pp. 42, 64, et passim). Jean-Louis Brunet eventually took over his father's positions among the *hautbois et musettes de Poitou* and, more importantly, as *huissier des ballets du roi*, the person in charge of administering the ballet performances at court. He died in 1709.

[40] The story of Philbert and Madame Brunet has been considerably embellished in the many retellings it has had since the seventeenth century (for citations and excerpts from some of the more colorful versions, see Ecorcheville, "Quelques documents," pp. 634–7). The account presented here is based on that in Benoit, *Versailles*, p. 140, who relies on contemporary documents to support the outline of the case.

[41] The dating of the transformation of the Renaissance transverse flute into the French three-piece Baroque model has been the subject of some dispute. (The same is true regarding the evolution of the shawm into the oboe; see chapter 4.) Philbert's presence in the ensembles of the *écurie* starting in the 1660s has sometimes been interpreted as evidence that the new transverse flute was in existence by that time. Jane Bowers points out, however, that the early documents mentioning Philbert only refer to his instrument as a *flûte*, a term that could (and still can) mean either the transverse flute or the recorder. The first unambiguous scoring for transverse flute in the works of Lully is in 1681 in *Le Triomphe de l'Amour*. (See Bowers, "New light," pp. 11–12.)

[42] "Philbert chantoit fort bien; & pour donner plus d'expression à ses chants, il sçavoit adoucir sa voix, & la grossissoit tout-à-coup, pour passer du gracieux, au bruyant & au martial. Il avoit le talent de contrefaire toutes sortes de baragoüins, ou langage corrompu, le Gascon, l'Allemand, & le Suisse francisé; il imitoit les manieres, & le parler des jeunes filles, & contrefaisoit les vieilles; il étoit, pour ainsi dire, le singe du genre humain. On l'admettoit souvent des les ballets du Roi pour y representer tous les personnages comiques où il réüssissoit parfaitement bien." *Mercure de France*, June 1725, pp. 1081–2.

One of the roles that must have made the most of Philbert's comic talents was as the Mufti in *Le Bourgeois Gentilhomme*, a role that Lully himself had originally created, and which Philbert performed in 1691 and 1698, if not on other occasions. According to the *Mercure*, Philbert was also known for a parlor trick of making an old frying pan sound so much like a carillon that people in neighboring rooms thought they were hearing church bells. He was sometimes called upon by the king to serve essentially as a clown in order to amuse the king's grandchildren (Dangeau, *Journal* VII, p. 12 [21 January 1699] and *Mercure de France*, June 1725, pp. 1082–3). In his more formal performances, he appeared both as an instrumentalist and as a singer; sometimes he even exhibited his two talents in the same performance, as, for example, when he appeared in *Orontée*, "singing and playing the flute."[43] His singing roles in Lully operas at court performances during the 1680s, such as nymphs, children, and pages, suggest that he could sing high parts as well as the bass role for which he is scored in *Le Mariage de la Grosse Cathos*.[44]

Philbert's versatility and his comic abilities made him a natural choice for the role of La Couture, in which role he was required to sing, dance, and act in the manner of the *comédie italienne*. Given both the nature of the part and his own natural inclinations, it is safe to assume that he exploited the burlesque possibilities of the mascarade well beyond what appears on the written page.

THE DANCERS

Of the five identified dancers who performed in *Le Mariage de la Grosse Cathos* – Favier, Germain, Dumirail, Barazé, and Richer – Favier seems to have been the most senior; he is the only one who appears to have begun his career during the 1660s. On the whole the dancers in the mascarade were quite an elite group; four of the five were or were to become members of the Académie Royale de Danse, the select group of thirteen dancing masters that had been established by Louis XIV in 1661 to promote the art of dance.

There were two dancers by the name of Germain – Antoine and Louis. Both achieved the honor of being elected to the Académie Royale de Danse; their names appear on membership lists from 1695 and 1719.[45] The name Germain first appears in librettos for court performances of Lully's works in 1671 (*Psyché*) and can be seen in many librettos thereafter. Antoine Germain was a dancer at the Paris Opéra, as a list of personnel from 1704 shows (La Gorce, "L'Académie Royale de Musique," p. 175); thus he is probably the Germain mentioned in eighteenth-century librettos from Parisian operatic performances.[46] Which Germain is meant for the earlier period, and which danced in *Le Mariage de la Grosse Cathos*, is unclear. Germain, like Favier *l'aîné*, was named by Pierre Rameau in his 1725 book, *Le maître à danser*, as one of the outstanding dancers that Beauchamps had available while he was choreographer at court and at the Opéra. Both Germains lived in Paris and gave dancing lessons (Du Pradel, *Livre commode*). One of them was still alive in 1732 when his name appears on a membership roll of the Académie Royale de Danse (*Mercure de France*, September 1732).

Romain Dumirail was another member of the Académie Royale de Danse (his name appears on the list for 1719) and like Germain was considered to be one of Beauchamps's leading dancers. His earliest documented appearance at court was in a revival of the

---

[43] [Lorenzoni], *Orontée*, tragédie en musique ornée d'entrées de ballet, Act IV, Scene 8. This work was performed at Chantilly in honor of the Dauphin in 1688. Philbert's name is listed in many ballet and opera librettos as an instrumentalist, in fewer as a singer.

[44] This hypothesis is based on a comparison of the librettos and scores of the works in which Philbert sang. In Act IV, Scene 1 of Lully's *Proserpine*, for example, Philbert sang as one of the blessed spirits (*ombres heureuses*) whose chorus is scored for three high voices, notated in treble, soprano, and mezzo-soprano clefs.

[45] The first names of the dancers are given in the list from 1719 (Benoit, *Musiques de cour*, p. 306); the list from 1695 refers to them only as Germain *l'aîné* and Germain *le jeune* (for which list see n. 29 above).

[46] Germain appears in librettos of revivals of Lully's *tragédies lyriques* until 1716. If these entries refer to the same dancer as the one who debuted in 1671, then he had a remarkably long performing career of forty-five years.

comedy-ballet *Monsieur de Pourceaugnac* in 1671, and he was one of the French dancers who went to England with Cambert two years later (see above, p. 23). His name may be found in librettos for such works as *Le Triomphe de l'Amour* and a 1691 revival of *Le Bourgeois Gentilhomme*. Although Dumirail was not named as a dancer at the Paris Opéra in the 1704 list, he seems to have danced with the troupe, judging from the appearance of his name in librettos from the first decade of the eighteenth century. He probably died before 1732, since he is no longer named among the members of the Académie Royale de Danse at that time.

Barazé was the fourth member of the Académie Royale de Danse to perform in *Le Mariage de la Grosse Cathos*. His name appears on the list from 1695 but not that of 1719, suggesting that he had died by that time. He had already danced at court at least as early as a production of Lully's *Thésée* in 1675, but he did not perform there nearly so often as the dancers already mentioned; perhaps his principal place of employment lay outside the court. If he was a member of the dance troupe at the Paris Opéra, his activities there ceased before the turn of the century when the librettos begin to print the dancers' names in the Parisian performances.

Even less is known about Richer than about Barazé. He danced two roles in a court performance of *Atys* in 1682 and appeared as a *fille de la noce* in *Le Mariage de la Grosse Cathos* in 1688.

THE ITALIAN COMEDIANS

The cast list for *Le Mariage de la Grosse Cathos* does not reveal the names of the performers who filled the spoken roles of Harlequin and Mezzetin, but this omission is not surprising, given that individual Italian comedians tended to adopt only one character and thus were identified by their roles, whether in or out of costume. The Italian performers in this mascarade undoubtedly came from the troupe of *comédiens italiens* established in Paris in the theatre of the Hôtel de Bourgogne, which enjoyed royal patronage and was frequently summoned to perform at court.

At the time the role of Harlequin was filled by the leader of the troupe, Domenico Giuseppe Biancolelli, known in Paris simply as "Dominique." Born into a family of actors in Bologna in 1636, Dominique came to France in 1661 or 1662 to join the Italian troupe in Paris, where he remained for the rest of his life.[47] As Harlequin he shaped the central character of the Comédie Italienne, one which had an immense success with the public over several decades. He is described as using a voice that sounded like a parrot, a mannerism that was imitated by subsequent Harlequins. Dominique could sing, dance, and perform acrobatics as well as act. If the self-deprecatory remarks in some of his routines are to be believed, he was short and somewhat fat. In what surely must be seen as a tribute to his abilities, the king himself stood godfather to Dominique's son Louis, born in 1666. It was reportedly Dominique who in the early 1680s requested permission from Louis XIV for the troupe to perform in French as well as Italian. Toward the end of his career he drew up a series of notes about scenes from seventy-nine plays in which he had played Harlequin, of which a free translation into French has been preserved.[48]

Despite his ribaldry on stage, Dominique was reputed to be a great family man who led an upright life. He and his wife, an actress in the troupe, had eleven children, of whom eight grew to adulthood and three of whom also went on the stage. Dominique's premature death was brought about by an excess of zeal in the service of the comic muse. Pierre Beauchamps had recently performed a remarkable dance before the king. In a divertissement that the Italian comedians added to one of their plays, Dominique did a

---

[47] Biographical information regarding Biancolelli and Constantini has been taken primarily from Scott, *Commedia dell'Arte*, chapters 5, 6, and 11.
[48] "Traduction du scenario de Joseph Dominique Biancolelli, dit Arlequin," discussed in Scott, *Commedia dell'Arte*, pp. 125ff.

comic imitation of Beauchamps's dance. The king was so amused by his performance that Dominique could not resist prolonging it for as long as he could still dance. Lacking the time to change his clothes before having to leave, Dominique went outside in his overheated state. He caught a cold which quickly became a serious illness and he died eight days later on 2 August 1688, that is, only a few months after his probable performance in *Le Mariage de la Grosse Cathos*. The stunned Italian troupe closed its doors for a month.[49]

Dominique's colleague Angelo Constantini was born in Verona around 1655. He came to Paris and joined the Italian troupe in the early 1680s. According to the Parfaict brothers (*Histoire*, pp. 83-94), he was hired at first to serve as a second Harlequin, but Dominique decided that he did not need a backup. Constantini thus developed a new role for himself, that of Mezzetin, whom he played unmasked to great success. The fact that many of the plays in the Gherardi collection have stage directions calling for Mezzetin to sing suggests that he must have been a good musician. When Dominique died, Constantini filled in as Harlequin until Gherardi took over the role in 1689, at which time he returned to playing Mezzetin. He is reputed to be the author of *La vie de Scaramouche* (1695), a fanciful biography of the eminent Tiberio Fiorilli, the troupe's Scaramouche for many years. When the Italian comedians were expelled from France in 1697, he was hired by Augustus I, King of Poland and Elector of Saxony (at the same court in which Jean Favier the son was to find employment twenty years later). Constantini made the mistake of behaving in too free a fashion towards the king's mistress and spent the next twenty years in prison.[50] Upon his release he returned to Paris where the Italian troupe had now been reestablished. In February of 1729 the aged actor attracted large crowds when he once again appeared in his old role of Mezzetin, but the novelty of his return wore out after only seven performances. Constantini died later the same year.

[49] Dominique's death was recounted in the middle of the eighteenth century by Thomas Gueullette in a manuscript history of the Italian troupe. His account was included by the Parfaict brothers in their *Histoire*, pp. 58–62 and is also cited in Scott, *Commedia dell'Arte*, p. 271.

[50] The story of Constantini's amorous adventures and subsequent imprisonment, which also originated with Gueullette, has been qualified by Scott as "a little too good to be true and very similar to some of the adventures in *La vie de Scaramouche*" (*Commedia dell'Arte*, p. 347).

3

Le Mariage de la Grosse Cathos in performance

THE PERFORMANCE CIRCUMSTANCES

Le Mariage de la Grosse Cathos was probably performed at Versailles during February of 1688. The year is confirmed by the dates on the scores from both the Bibliothèque Nationale and the Bibliothèque de l'Arsenal, and by a document listing payment made to Philidor for the copying of this work as one of the entertainments of that season (see chapter 7, pp. 185 and 186). The month and place are suggested by entries in the diary of the Marquis de Dangeau describing the events of that particular year.

At the French court, the carnival season that preceded Lent was the high point of the year for entertainments that involved dancing; balls alternated with ballets, and the festivities always culminated in a masked ball hosted by the king on Mardi Gras.[1] In its write-up of the 1688 carnival season, the *Mercure galant* reported that court practice had changed somewhat in recent years. Formerly, said the *Mercure*, the carnival had always featured an elaborately staged work – in early years a ballet, later a comedy-ballet, and more recently an opera – that was performed several times over a period of a few weeks. But in the past few years, operas had been replaced by "diverse little mascarades," not in order to save money, but to provide more varied pleasures.[2]

The *Mercure*'s observation of a general trend toward small-scale entertainments is confirmed by the records of performances at court,[3] and for 1688 in particular by the diary of the Marquis de Dangeau, who conscientiously noted the daily activities of the court and the events of the season as they occurred (Dangeau, *Journal* II, pp. 81-114). That year, in addition to a number of plays and several masked balls, there were three entertainments of a balletic nature. One was a divertissement consisting of six little scenes drawn from various Lully operas, each incorporating a small number of vocal pieces and dances, for example the "Jeux Junoniens" from the first act of Lully's opera *Persée*. The singers in this divertissement came from the Paris Opéra, but the dancers were primarily royal or aristocratic ladies, supported by several professional male dancers including Beauchamps,

---

[1] For information about balls at the court, see Harris-Warrick, "Ballroom dancing." In 1688 Mardi Gras fell on 2 March.

[2] "L'usage estoit autrefois à la Cour, de faire un grand divertissement qui duroit tout le Carnaval. C'estoit ordinairement un grand Balet en Machines meslé de recits, dont le tout ensemble formoit un sujet, comme par exemple, le Balet des Arts [1663], & le Balet de la Nuit [1653] . . . Ensuite le fameux Moliere introduit les Comedies meslées d'entrées, & de recits. Ces divertissemens plurent encore davantage que n'avoient fait les Balets. Les Opera succederent à ces sortes de Comedies . . . Cependant depuis quelques années, la Cour n'en fait plus faire pour ses divertissemens du Carnaval, ce n'est pas pour épargner la dépense, mais parce qu'elle a trouvé que le mesme divertissement pendant un mois estoit un plaisir trop uniforme. Ainsi au lieu de ces Opera, elle fait diverses petites Mascarades, qui ne coustent guere moins, mais dont la diversité empeschant que les mesmes plaisirs ne soient continus, les rend plus touchans & plus agreables. C'est ce qu'on a fait depuis trois ou quatre années, & ce qu'on a fait encore dans le dernier Carnaval." *Mercure galant*, March 1688, pp. 25–33.

[3] The most recent operatic productions at court had occurred in 1685, when Lully's operas *Roland* and *Amadis* were performed during carnival. For a list of the operas and major ballets performed at court between 1671 and 1715, see La Gorce, "L'opéra français à la cour."

Pécour, Létang, and Favier *l'aîné*.[4] The scenes were performed between the acts of five different five-act plays put on by the French comedians on 28 and 30 January, and 6, 14, and 27 February.

On another evening, Philidor's ballet *La Princesse de Crète* was performed by an all-professional cast. This "petit spectacle qui divertit fort" was interpreted, according to Dangeau, as a satire on the princes then vying for the hand of the widowed Princesse de Conti, daughter of the king.[5]

The remaining danced divertissement mentioned by Dangeau probably refers to *Le Mariage de la Grosse Cathos*. On 17 February he reported that, "After supper there were some *entrées de ballet* and a few scenes of Italian comedy in the apartment of the Princesse de Conti, where Monseigneur was and where very few people entered."[6] The scanty information provided here concords with what can be derived regarding the performance circumstances from the scores and contemporary references to the work. The title page of the Bibliothèque de l'Arsenal score indicates that the mascarade was "représentée devant Monseigneur," and the catalogue entry for the no longer extant libretto (see chapter 7, p. 186) says that it was "représentée devant Monseigneur et Madame la princesse de Conti." It was common practice for an apartment within the château of Versailles, usually that of the person hosting the entertainment, to serve as the venue for little works of this nature,[7] and the choreographic notation for the mascarade, which suggests a relatively restricted performance space with a single point of entry, is consistent with performance in a large room rather than on a stage.

The two for whom this entertainment was arranged were members of the royal family. *Monseigneur* was the title by which Louis XIV's eldest son Louis (1661–1711), the Dauphin, was commonly known at court; Marie Anne de Bourbon (1666–1739), the Princesse de Conti, was Monseigneur's legitimized half-sister, daughter of the king and of

---

[4] *Divertissement, Meslé de Musique & d'Entrées de Ballet, Dans des Entr'Actes de Comedies. Representé devant Sa Majesté en son Chasteau de Marly le 28. Janvier 1688*. The libretto of this divertissement was printed by Ballard by order of the king (copy in F-Pn [Imprimés] Yf Rés. 2006). Some of the noble dancers were the Princesse de Conti, Madame la Duchesse, the Marquise de Seignelay, and the Comte de Brionne.

[5] Dangeau's diary does not mention this work by name, but his account of the entertainment for 9 February appears to refer to it. "Avant souper, il y eut comédie. Après souper, M. de Luxembourg mena chez madame la princesse de Conty, où étaient Monseigneur et madame la Duchesse, trois comédiens italiens, quelques-uns des meilleurs danseurs [de l'Opéra] et mademoiselle de la Lande, et donna un petit spectacle qui divertit fort. Il avoit fait déguiser quatre gardes de compagnie de Noailles, qui avoient des tailles de géant et qui étoient habillés en filles; il y a eu des courtisans qui ont voulu fronder ce divertissement-là, qui attaquoit un peu les princes qui veulent épouser présentement la princesse de Conty." ("Before supper there was a play. After supper, Mr de Luxembourg led people to the apartment of the Princesse de Conti where there were Monseigneur [the Dauphin], Madame la Duchesse, three Italian comedians, a few of the best dancers [from the Opéra] and Mademoiselle de la Lande [a professional singer], and gave a little entertainment that was very amusing. He had disguised four guards from the Noailles company, who were the size of giants and who were dressed as girls. There were some courtiers who objected to this divertissement, which attacked a little the princes who currently want to marry the Princesse de Conti.") (Dangeau, *Journal* II, p. 106). There are a few discrepancies between Dangeau's account and the libretto for this work. Mlle de la Lande did sing in the *Princesse de Crète*, and the plot does call for four giants; they were not, however, dressed as girls. Nor do Italian comedians appear in this work. It seems likely that Dangeau conflated this performance with the other work by Philidor performed that season, *Le Mariage de la Grosse Cathos*, which did involve both Italian comedians and men disguised as women. In his desire for completeness Dangeau sometimes reported events which he himself had not attended, and his diary, although generally very reliable, is not without errors of detail, as Saint-Simon, who made extensive use of it in writing his own memoirs, was fond of pointing out.

[6] "Après souper, il y eut des entrées de ballet et quelques scènes de comédie italienne chez madame la princesse de Conty, où étoit Monseigneur et où fort peu de gens entrèrent." (Dangeau, *Journal* II, p. 109). "Chez madame la princesse de Conty" refers to her apartment in the château of Versailles, not in the king's smaller château, Marly, where the royal family spent part of every carnival season and where the plays with danced entr'actes had been performed. At Marly, the only available performing space was the salon of the main pavilion; individual suites were very small. Moreover, Dangeau indicated the place that he wrote this particular diary entry as Versailles, not Marly.

[7] A series of mascarades during the 1683 carnival, for example, were all performed in various apartments in the château, including those of Monsieur le Grand, the Dauphin, Monsieur le Duc, and Madame de Thiange (*Mercure galant*, March 1683, pp. 316–42).

his first mistress, Louise de La Vallière. Both were balletomanes: the Princesse de Conti was by all accounts a beautiful and skilled dancer, and the Dauphin organized a number of ballets in which he and his sister performed. He loved masked balls, in which his greatest pleasure was to disguise himself so well that no one could recognize him, an understandable desire on the part of one who led so public a life. Both had danced in court entertainments with Favier, and Favier was also the dancing master to the Dauphin's wife.

The Princesse de Conti's apartment was on the ground floor of the château in the south wing, the *aile du midi* (see a plan of its layout in plate 1).[8] The largest of her rooms, the *grand cabinet*, measured 3.63 by 4.55 *toises*, or 23.6 by 29.5 feet, excluding the deep indentations for the two windows across one width of the room. There were two doors, opposite each other on the upper end of the two lengths closest to the windows. If this was indeed the room in which *Le Mariage de la Grosse Cathos* was performed, then the audience must have been seated at the foot of the room, facing the windows, while the performers made their entrance and exit from the door to the audience's left, as shown in the choreographic notation. The full width of the room would probably have been available to the performers, but the length would have been reduced in proportion to the number of people watching; an area of 23 feet across by 15 feet deep is probably a reasonable approximation. If the space seems very restrictive for a production involving twenty-eight people, it must be remembered that most of the performance spaces at Versailles were surprisingly small. By way of comparison, the stage of the only theatre in the château at the time, the Salle de Comédie, had a very similar area, that is, approximately 26 feet wide by 16 feet deep (Coeyman, "Theaters," pp. 29–30). The largest room in the king's apartment, the Salle de Mars, measured 55 by 30 feet. Although it was often used for balls, much of the floor space had to be devoted to the spectators, who were much more numerous than the dancers. At the wedding ball for the Duc de Chartres in 1692, the space in the room defined as the dance floor measured about 27 feet long by 12 feet wide (Harris-Warrick, "Ballroom dancing," p. 44).

According to Dangeau, very few people were in the audience for the ballet and comedy on 17 February. At the château of Versailles, where hundreds of people routinely tried to crowd their way into balls and other diversions, "very few" undoubtedly meant something greater than it does to us; nonetheless, this seems to have been a private event, probably restricted to a relatively small number of people in the circle of the Dauphin and the Princesse de Conti. When balls and mascarades were performed in the apartments at Versailles, it was not uncommon for the court carpenters to erect tiered benches for the spectators. Such an arrangement was made for a mascarade performed in the apartment of Monsieur le Duc in 1683. The illustration published in the *Mercure galant* (plate 2) shows the performers on the far left, including the Princesse de Conti on the throne in her role as Queen of Egypt, the *petits violons* on risers in the window openings, and the audience around the sides. The people on the dance floor are servants bringing refreshments during a break in the dancing.[9] Perhaps the Princesse de Conti's apartment was set up in a similar way for the performance of *Le Mariage de la Grosse Cathos*, although for an event on a much less sumptuous scale, the erection of benches may have been unnecessary.

Le Mariage de la Grosse Cathos was probably performed only once, or at best, in a short run of a few performances. Little works of this nature were seasonal events at the court and were rarely revived.

---

[8] Information about the Princesse de Conti's apartment in the château of Versailles comes from Marie, *Mansart à Versailles* I, pp. 273–4. The apartment is no longer in existence, this wing of the château having been completely remodeled in the nineteenth century.

[9] A description of this event was published in the March issue of the *Mercure galant*, pp. 320–33. The engraving, designed by Jean Berain and engraved by Le Pautre, appears between pp. 322 and 323.

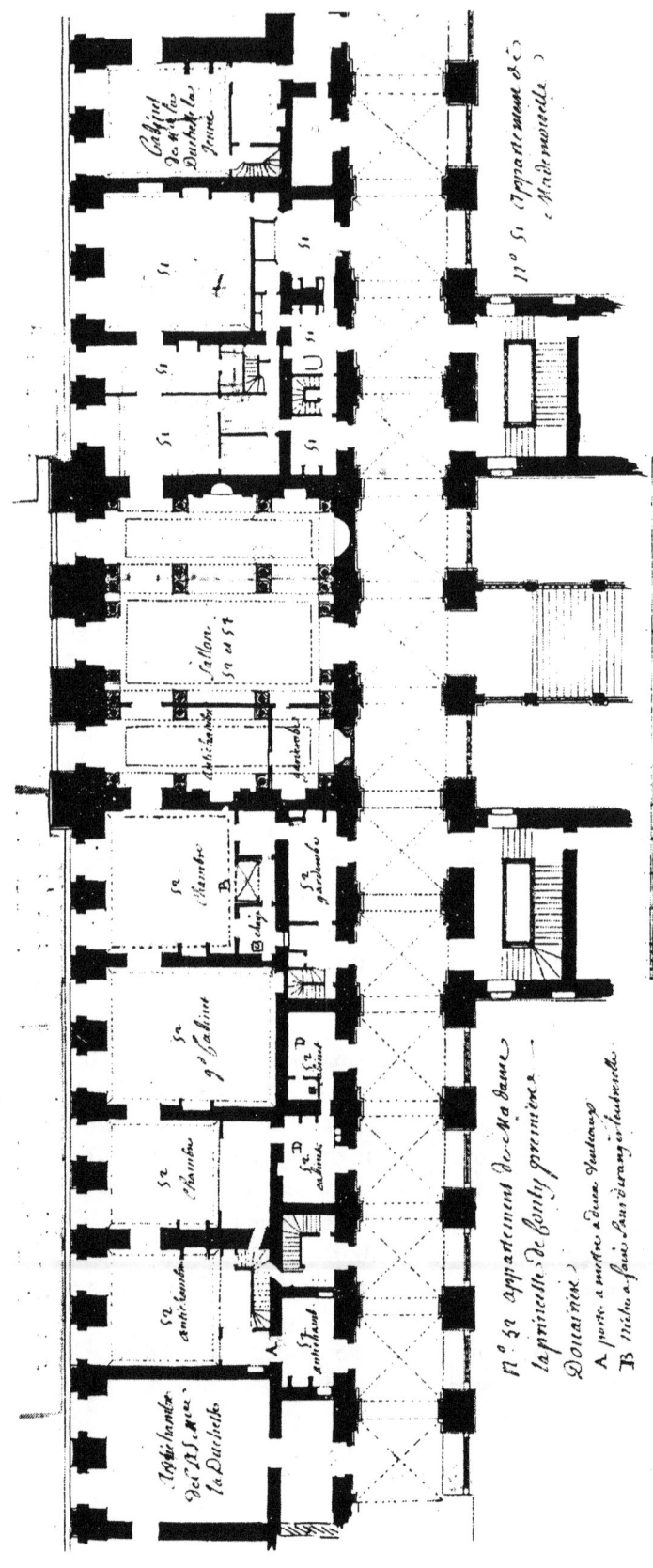

PLATE 1 Floor plan of the apartment of the Princesse de Conti at Versailles. The rooms belonging to the Princesse de Conti, numbered 52 on this plan, were located on the ground floor of the south wing of the château. The largest room, the *grand cabinet*, was probably the site of the performance of *Le Mariage de la Grosse Cathos*. (F-Pan O¹ 1781)

PLATE 2 Mascarade in the apartment of Monsieur le Duc, March 1683. The musicians are seated on stands in the window openings on the left, surrounding the Princesse de Conti, playing the Queen of Egypt, on her throne. Servants are shown bringing in refreshments to members of the audience seated on stands on the right. The engraving by Le Pautre after a design by Jean Berain was published in the March 1683 issue of the *Mercure galant*.

THE WORK

The mascarade itself is a small-scale entertainment, to be performed without a break and lasting approximately forty minutes. It requires little or nothing in the way of scenery – none, at least, is either mentioned or implied in the manuscript. The costuming, on the other hand, may well have been quite sumptuous, judging from performances of a similar nature.[10] The twenty-eight performers called for by the dance notation appear to represent the entire cast: nine singers, each of whom has a solo role and who collectively make up the chorus; a nine-member oboe band that provides the instrumental accompaniment; eight dancers who fill subsidiary roles as guests at the wedding; and two actors from the Italian theatre, Harlequin and Mezzetin, who have speaking roles and appear in one scene. Although it is not beyond the realm of possibility that the numbers of both singers and instrumentalists could have been augmented by performers other than those identified in the manuscript, the likelihood of additional performers is small.

The cast list given below combines information from both parts of the manuscript. The singing roles come from the list of characters that follows the title page in the musical score; the vocal ranges given in brackets are derived from the score itself. The dancing roles are listed as they appear in the choreographic portion of the manuscript. No separate list of dancers is provided there, but roles and names are indicated at the beginning of two of the dances (see the facsimile, pp. 43 and 61).[11] In both portions of the manuscript some of the performers' names are inexplicably lacking. The musical score does not provide any explicit information regarding the number of instrumentalists, but the dance notation calls for nine "oboes," that is, an ensemble of double-reed instruments. With the possible exception of the two Italian comedians, whose comings and goings are discussed below, all of the performers remained on stage for the duration of the mascarade.

Singing cast

La Couture, époux de la Grosse Cathos (the bridegroom)	Mr Philbert	[bass]
Grosse Cathos, épouse de La Couture (the bride)	Mr Guillegau	[baritone]
Monsieur Dupont, bourgeois de Paris	Mr Miracle	[tenor]
Madame Dupont, sa femme, maîtresse de la Grosse Cathos (his wife, Grosse Cathos's mistress)	M^r Le Roy	[haute-contre]
Abbé du Plessis, oncle de La Couture (La Couture's uncle)	Mr Morel	[bass]
Gripetout, écornifleur (scrounger)	Mr Gingant	[tenor]
Maître Simon, Suisse ami de la Grosse Cathos (Swiss friend of Grosse Cathos)	M^r [blank]	[haute-contre]
Dame Ragonde, parente de la Grosse Cathos (relative of Grosse Cathos)	Mr Jonquet	[haute-contre]
Un garçon de la noce, chantant à la sérénade de la mariée (a male wedding guest who sings in the serenade for the bride)	M^r [blank]	[bass]

Speaking cast

Harlequin, fourbe se disant mère nourrice de La Couture
 (scoundrel pretending to be La Couture's wet nurse)

---

[10] Records from carnival seasons at court show that large sums of money were often spent for mascarades, much of it on costumes. Elaborate costume designs by Jean Berain survive for several of the mascarades Philidor composed for the carnival season of 1700 (see chapter 2, p. 18).

[11] The cast list in the musical score purports to include the dancing as well as the singing roles; there are, however, certain discrepancies between this list and the dancing roles as they appear in the dance notation (see chapter 7, p. 187).

Mezzetin, fourbe se disant père nourricier de La Couture
   (scoundrel pretending to be La Couture's foster father)
La Couture

Dancing cast

Deux garçons de la noce	Messrs Dumirail & Favier *l'aîné*
(two male wedding guests)	
Deux filles de la noce	Messrs Germain & Richer
(two female wedding guests)	
Deux paysans	Messrs Barazé & [blank]
(two peasants)	
Deux Dames Gigognes	Messrs [blank]
(two Dames Gigognes)	
La Couture	

Instrumentalists
Nine unnamed "oboes"

As this list suggests, the mascarade drew its characters from the pool of stock comic types that appeared over and over in the theatrical entertainments of the seventeenth century. The topic of the village wedding was a frequent one, although it could be treated in a variety of ways.[12] In Lully's opera *Roland* (1685), the rustic bride and groom of the fourth-act divertissement who are presented as idealized representatives of the joys of love, serve to emphasize the sufferings of Roland whose own failure in love has driven him mad. Most village weddings, however, have a comic or even burlesque slant in which at least some of the characters become objects of ridicule. In them, as in *Le Mariage de la Grosse Cathos*, a parade of familiar types appears: the bumbling country bumpkins, the self-important bourgeois, the scoundrels trying to turn the occasion to their own advantage, the obligatory drunk. In this particular case the sense of the ridiculous was heightened by using men in all of the women's roles. Although seventeenth-century male dancers and singers had to be capable of performing female roles in a serious way, casting the bride as an enormous baritone suggests that all of the cross-dressing in this work had a burlesque intent. In fact, the mascarade explicitly addresses the issue of cross-dressing: in the spoken scene Harlequin tries to pass himself off as a woman but is discovered. Even the costuming may well have contributed to the humor of the work: by theatrical convention village characters were generally clothed in decidedly old-fashioned styles, as an engraving of the 1683 village wedding performed at Versailles shows (plate 3).

The Dame Ragonde and Dame Gigogne mentioned in the cast list were stock comic figures associated more with the musical than the spoken theatre.[13] A Dame or Mère Gigogne often wore enormous skirts that hid a crowd of children (it is this character who was to appear much later in Tchaikovsky's *Nutcracker Ballet*), although the characters by that name in this particular mascarade do not have any discernible progeny. The records of the Comédie Française show that a "danse de Gigogne" was performed on at least two occasions in 1684 in addition to the regularly scheduled play,[14] and the following year, the eleven-year-old daughter of Louis XIV performed a dance for a Dame Gigogne at a ball at Versailles.[15] Dame Ragonde appears as a dancing role in works such as Philidor's later mascarade, *Les Savoyards* (1700), and in an opéra comique by the Italian comedians entitled *La Désolation des Deux Comédies* (1718), in both of which the Dame Ragonde dances with Harlequine, Scaramouche, and Polichinelle. In a lyric comedy by Mouret called *Le Mariage de Ragonde* (1714), the title character, sung by a man, is an elderly

---

[12] For a discussion of the village wedding as a theme in seventeenth-century danced entertainments, see Harris-Warrick, "La Mariée."

[13] Neither Dame Gigogne nor Dame Ragonde appears in seventeenth- or early eighteenth-century French dictionaries, and only the former is listed in modern etymological dictionaries. All of the references we have found to the two comic characters are in a musical or dance context.

[14] See the *Registre de la Grange* (facsimile Paris: Droz, 1947), entries for 23 November and 19 December 1684.

[15] "Mlle de Nantes finit le bal par y danser une dame gigonne, le plus joliment du monde." Dangeau, *Journal* I, p. 173, entry for 16 May 1685.

PLATE 3 Mascarade of a village wedding performed at Versailles, March 1683. The performers in this *Noce de Village*, members of the royal family and of the highest aristocratic echelons at court, included the Dauphin as the bailiff of the village, the Dauphine as a sister of the bride, the Princesse de Conti as the bride, and the Comte de Brionne as the groom. The engraving by Le Pautre after a design by Jean Berain was published in the April 1683 issue of the *Mercure galant*.

widow competing with her daughter for the affections of a young peasant.[16] A late seventeenth-century engraving of a Dame Ragonde depicts her as a long-in-the-tooth coquette extravagantly got up in fashions a good half-century out of date (see plate 4). In *Le Mariage de la Grosse Cathos* Dame Ragonde and Dame Gigogne appear to be synonymous: Philidor's cast list calls for two Dames Ragondes, one who sings and another who dances, whereas in the dance notation the corresponding dancing roles are for Dames Gigognes.

If the Dames Ragondes/Gigognes are supposed to be ridiculous old ladies, then the two "peasants" appearing among the dancers may well represent their male counterparts. Certainly the middle-aged peasant portrayed at the Opéra by one of the Dumoulin brothers (plate 5) would have made a fitting partner for Dame Ragonde. Perhaps a generational distinction among the eight dancers in the mascarade was intended: two each of young *filles* and *garçons* on the one hand, and of old men and women on the other. Although the choreography does not disprove such a hypothesis, it does little to support it. There is a menuet for the two young couples, but nothing identifiably for the oldsters; in the group dances the steps are the same for everyone. Moreover, the dancers are sometimes identified in ways that gloss over any potential distinctions: in the rigaudon, four *filles de la noce* perform, while an annotation in dance IX identifies all four men collectively as *paysans*. Perhaps the differentiation by age, if such existed, was communicated via the costumes and through gestures not susceptible to choreographic notation.

By the musical symbolism of the day the rustic subject of the mascarade meant that the use of woodwind instruments was virtually obligatory. Although in theatrical scenes of a similar character wind instruments were often used to color the basic string sound, in this case the on-stage oboe band seems to have constituted the entire instrumental body (see chapter 4). In fact, the woodwind frame of reference extends beyond the instrumentation into the text of the work. The bridegroom's name, for example, appears to make reference to the Norman village of La Couture-Boussey which had sent many woodwind players and makers to Paris, most notably the extended Hotteterre family, and which at the time still supported a number of instrument makers. (When Philidor retired from the court, he settled in the nearby village of Dreux.) The name chosen for another of the characters, the Abbé du Plessis, may possibly have to do with an oboe and bassoon player called du Plessis who is known to have performed in other works by Philidor dating from 1700.[17] The text, whose authorship is unknown, gives the impression of containing many other topical references to familiar people, places, or events; their full implications escape us today, but would not have been lost on the original audience.

Another important element of the text, one that must have been exploited in performance, is parody, particularly of the conventions of opera in the Lullian manner. Operatic parody was part of the stock-in-trade of the Italian comedians,[18] but in this work the parody resides in the sung portions of the mascarade, not in the Italians' scene. The opening of the mascarade, for example, recalls the beginning of the first act of Lully's *Atys* (1676). In this opera the words, "Allons, allons, accourez tous / Cybèle va descendre," announce the descent of the goddess from the heavens to earth; they are sung first as a solo, later in the scene repeated as a duet, and finally set as a four-part ensemble, each reiteration of the text being separated by recitative. The mascarade opens with a similar exhortation to people to gather; however, the announcement that follows, "La Grosse Cathos se marie" ("Fat Kate is getting married"), thrusts not a goddess but a gargantuan serving girl with a baritone voice into the limelight. As in the opera, the announcement is made first by a soloist ("Allons mes enfants, venez tous / La Grosse Cathos se marie"),

---

[16] This work, first performed privately at Sceaux, the château of the Duchesse du Maine, was revived at the Opéra in 1742 under the title *Les Amours de Ragonde*.

[17] *Le Roy de la Chine, Les Amazones, Les Savoyards, La Noce de Village, Le Lendemain de la Noce de Village, Le Vaisseau Marchand* (for fuller references to these mascarades, see Philidor's work list in chapter 2, p. 19). Since the manuscript of *Le Mariage de la Grosse Cathos* does not provide the names of the instrumentalists, it is not possible to know whether du Plessis was also involved in this performance.

[18] See Grout, "Seventeenth-century parodies."

PLATE 4 Dame Ragonde. A late seventeenth-century French engraving of a Dame Ragonde. (From the private collection of Jérôme de La Gorce)

Le Mariage de la Grosse Cathos in performance 45

PLATE 5 Dumoulin costumed as a peasant. One of the Dumoulin brothers dancing at the Opéra in the role of a peasant. Engraving after a design by Jean Berain

expanded to a duet following a passage in recitative, and then sung by a chorus in four parts ("Allons, accourons tous / La Grosse Cathos se marie"). The text of another chorus in the mascarade, "Chantons le choix charmant / De cet heureux amant," recalls any number of operatic choruses, as, for example, one from the end of Lully's *Psyché* (1678): "Chantons les plaisirs charmants / Des heureux amants." Much of the humor of the work derives from the discongruity between elevated language borrowed from operatic conventions and the burlesque reality to which it is applied. The element of parody even extends into the dances; one particularly noteworthy example is discussed below.

The mascarade cannot be said to have a plot, but merely a sequence of events, beginning with the announcement of the wedding and proceeding through the festivities. It opens with a procession of the performers, led by the oboe band, into the room. Following a group dance, Monsieur and Madame Dupont, a bourgeois couple from Paris, announce the news that their servant girl, known as Grosse Cathos (Fat Kate), is marrying La Couture. The wedding guests, who include a scrounger named Gripetout, a priest who is the bridegroom's uncle, and a Swiss whose drunkenness compounds his thick accent, comment in flowery language on the appropriateness of the match. Although there are no physical descriptions of the characters, numerous references in the text make it clear that Grosse Cathos lives up to her nickname. When the happy pair appear, Grosse

Cathos's first words, sung in recitative, are to tell the wedding guests that they are breaking her eardrums with all this racket of singing. She is not interested in an opera, she says; it is better to get down to important matters – food.

After the bridal couple and the guests withdraw, Harlequin and Mezzetin arrive, the former disguised as a woman. In a spoken scene they reveal that they are going to have a good laugh at La Couture's expense. When La Couture returns, they compliment him on his new wife who, they insist, is worth her weight in gold. With many false tears and caresses they tell him that Harlequin had been his wet nurse, that Mezzetin is her husband, and that the two of them had taken care of him as a baby. After his first transports of joy, La Couture begs them to tell him about his father who had died when he was four. When it becomes clear that Harlequin is inventing his answers, La Couture gets angry and chases them away. Throughout this scene there are abundant opportunities for slapstick and sight gags.[19]

In the sung scene that follows, the abbé and Gripetout, whom La Couture has called for help, now get into a fight with each other. They are calmed by the Dame Ragonde, who announces that the guests want to dance. This statement sets up what amounts to a divertissement in the operatic manner; the action, such as it is, is suspended while a series of dances, interspersed with a few related vocal numbers, celebrates the wedding. Seven of the ten dances in the mascarade occur here. Following three dances involving the four young wedding guests (the *filles* and *garçons de la noce*), Maître Simon, a Swiss friend of the bride, sings a song in pidgin French about the consolations of drink which leads naturally into a comic entrée for two drunks. The bridegroom then participates in two group dances – one with the village women, the other with all the guests – and the divertissement culminates in a choreographed chorus in praise of the pursuit of pleasure. The "action" resumes when La Couture asks for his nightclothes and retires with his bride. The peace is broken by the traditional raucous wedding serenade or *charivari*, following which all the performers process off stage to end the mascarade.

The following outline shows the relationship of sung to danced sections of the work in greater detail. It incorporates information from both parts of the manuscript and thus also serves as a table of contents to both sections of the facsimile. The column on the left lists the pieces and their page numbers as they appear in the musical score; the column on the right lists the corresponding titles and location in the dance notation. The seventeenth-century spelling has been modernized. The center column identifies the performers both of the sung and danced pieces, and establishes a numbering system for the choreographies that is used in the discussions below. The mascarade contains ten dance pieces – or fourteen, if one counts as separate the sections within pieces where the number of dancers changes. In addition there are two places where the dance notation indicates that a solo dance was performed, but does not supply the choreography, plus another movement, the *charivari*, for which some kind of movement by the dancers was undoubtedly required.

Outline of the Mascarade

Music score			*Dance score*	
Page	*Title*	*Description, performers*	*Page*	*Title*
1	La Pavane	IA. Processional for all the performers	41–2	Marche pour 9 hautbois, 8 danseurs, et 9 musiciens
1	[repeat]	IB. Dance for 4 couples	43–51	Marche dansante pour les 8 danseurs
2	"Allons, mes enfants"	[Air] Mme Dupont	—	

---

[19] This scene is very much of a piece with other French plays performed by the Italian comedians (see *Le théâtre italien*, a collection of plays made at the end of the seventeenth century by Evaristo Gherardi, a member of the Italian troupe).

Music score			Dance score	
Page	Title	Description, performers	Page	Title
2		[Recitative] Mr Dupont, Abbé du Plessis, Gripetout	—	
2–3	"J'y trouve moi"	[Air] Maître Simon	—	
3	"Allons, mes enfants"	[Duo] Mr and Mme Dupont	—	
4	Chœur: "Allons, accourons tous"	II. Choreographed pantomimically for the 8 dancers	53–9	Chœur d'Allons, allons accourons tous
5		[Recitative] Gripetout	—	
5	"La Couture souffrait"	[Bass Air] Abbé du Plessis	—	
6	Chœur: "Chantons le choix charmant"		—	
7	"Je n'ai que faire d'opéra"	[Recitative and Air] Grosse Cathos	—	
8	"Il est vrai"	[Bass Air] La Couture	—	
9–12	*Scène Seconde*	Spoken scene: Harlequin, Mezzetin, La Couture	—	
13–14		[Recitative] Abbé du Plessis, Gripetout	—	
14–15	"Si tu n'apaises mon courroux"	[Duo] Abbé du Plessis, Gripetout	—	
15–16		[Recitative] Maître Simon, Abbé du Plessis, Gripetout	—	
16–17	"Si tu n'apaises mon courroux"	[Duo] Abbé du Plessis, Gripetout	—	
17		[Recitative] Maître Simon	—	
17	"Sortez, allez dans la rue"	[Recitative and Air] Dame Ragonde	—	
18	1ᵉ Entrée 2 Filles de la Noce[20]	III. Dance for 2 male guests	61–4	Entrée de 2 garçons de la noce
18–19	Gigue	IV. Dance for 2 female guests	65–7	Entrée de 2 filles de la noce
19	Menuet	V. For the 4 dancers of the 2 previous entrées	69–76	Entrée des 2 garçons et des 2 filles de la noce
20–1	Chœur: "Dans ce grand jour"		—	
21–2	"J'aime la pance, j'aime la dance"	[Duo] La Couture, Grosse Cathos	—	
22–3	"Pour moi qui n'aure point d'amour"	[Air] Maître Simon	—	
23–7	Chœur: "Passons toujours la vie"[21]		[99–105]	

[20] The title in the F-Pn score incorrectly assigns this dance to two women. Both the dance notation and the F-Pa score identify this dance as intended for two men.

[21] The score and the dance notation disagree about the location of the chorus "Passons toujours la vie" relative to the group of three dances that opens with the "Air des Ivrognes"; for a discussion of this point, see below, p. 54.

Music score			Dance score	
Page	Title	Description, performers	Page	Title
28	Air des Ivrognes	VI. Dance for 2 drunks	77–81	[untitled]
29	Rigaudon pour les filles de la noce	VIIA. For 5, the 4 women and La Couture	83–8	[untitled]
	[repeat]	VIIB. Unnotated solo for La Couture	88	La Couture danse seul une fois l'air
29–30	Passepied	VIIIA. Line dance for the 8 dancers and La Couture	89–91	[untitled]
	[repeat]	VIIIB. Figure dance first for the 4 women, then the 4 men, then all 8	91–8	[untitled]
[23–7]	Chœur: "Passons toujours la vie"	IX. For the 8 dancers, first in groups of 4, then together, plus one unnotated solo for a *paysan*	99–105	[untitled]
30–1	"Que chacun se retire"	[Recitative and Bass Air] La Couture	—	
31–9	Chœur: "Charivari"	[No choreography notated but dance or pantomime probably done during this chorus]		[3 unnumbered blank pages between pp. 105 and 106]
39–40	La Pavane	XA. March for the entire cast	106	[untitled]
	[repeat]	XB. Dance for 8	107–15	[untitled]
	[repeat]	XC. Procession of everyone off stage	116	[untitled]

THE WORK ON STAGE

The plot synopsis given above suggests entrances and exits on the part of the performers that were, in fact, more symbolic than real. All of the performers, with the exception of the two actors, entered to the sounds of the pavane and remained on stage until they processed out to the same music at the conclusion of the work. In the interim they either stood around the periphery of the stage area when not performing or moved into a position where attention would be focused on them when their turns came to sing, dance, or play. Thus they remained at all times within the visual field of the audience.

The dance notation provides the full choreography for the dances, but only shows movement by the singers and instrumentalists that occurred during the dance numbers. Thus the changes of position made by the soloists during the extended sung sections are not preserved, nor are staging indications for the spoken scene. Within these parameters, the movements of the performers have been worked out with remarkable precision. Such attention to detail by Favier was necessitated in part by the small size of the performing area. However, it also is indicative of the care he lavished on the preparation of this manuscript, and his compulsive rendering of so many small facets strengthens its value as a document that reflects an actual performance. The following discussion provides a general perspective on the staging over the course of the mascarade along with brief descriptions of the dances; more detailed information about each dance and about the movements of individual performers appears in chapter 6.

Favier used two forms of his notation system to show the movements of the performers. In both forms the floor pattern traveled by the performers must be deduced by comparing successive "frames" of the notation. (A frame is defined as any segment of the five- to seven-line music staff between two vertical lines; although a frame looks as though it would be equivalent to a bar of music, it usually represents only one or two beats of a bar.) Favier's "score" notation is used for the fully choreographed dances, with their varied step sequences and individual floor patterns; each frame shows the position of a single dancer at a given moment. The positions of the other dancers at that moment as well as the shape of the floor patterns are not immediately apparent (see, for example, p. 43 of the facsimile). In the abbreviated or "freeze-frame" notation, on the other hand, the symbols for a number of performers are included in the same frame (e.g., p. 42). This notation is sufficient when the performers are moving as a group, that is, when they are using the same step and traveling in uncomplicated floor patterns in which the positions of the performers relative to their neighbors remains more or less constant. The abbreviated notation is always used to indicate the movements of the singers and oboes, and is also used for the dancers in parts of the processional, recessional, and passepied.

From the movement notations several general staging principles may be inferred. First, the space on stage is divided into two areas, each with its own purpose. The three sides of the perimeter away from the audience serve as home locations for the performers, each group having its own position; the central area framed by the members of the cast serves as the active part of the stage into which individual performers emerge when the dramatic focus falls upon them and from which they retreat when the focus shifts. Second, the focal point of the dramatic or choreographic action is in the center, usually downstage, and the orientation of the performers is forward, directly toward the audience. The action is normally oriented around an invisible axis drawn back to front through the middle of the stage. Third, the staging of the mascarade promotes a flow of movement between numbers that minimizes pauses in the action or the music. Individual vocal or dance pieces are not set off into separate units, but are connected into a continuous progression that begins with the first sounds from the oboes and ends only when the last performer has left the stage. Fourth, the dancers often function as surrogates for the singers, setting into motion the words of singers who remain stationary. This is apparent not only in the choreographed choruses, but also in the links between adjacent vocal and instrumental numbers. The dances do not interrupt the dramatic progression, but participate in it.

The opening pavane (dance IA), called a "march" in the choreographic portion of the manuscript, functions as a processional to bring all the performers into the space. Taking the Princesse de Conti's *grand cabinet* as the probable venue for this performance (see plate 1), the performers would have entered from the room to the left as one looks at the plan, i.e., from upstage right. Although the notation does not differentiate among the three groups of performers, it is clear from their positions in the subsequent section that their entries follow the order given in the title of the piece, that is, with the oboes leading in three rows of three abreast, followed by the dancers and then the singers, both groups processing two abreast with one singer at the end of the procession (see p. 41 of the facsimile). Taking a single walked step per bar of music the performers process counterclockwise around the perimeter of the performing space, then take up positions facing the audience. The pavane is played twice to accommodate all of their entrances. It is enlightening in this context to read Arbeau's description of the pavane from one hundred years earlier: "On solemn feast days the pavan is employed by kings, princes and great noblemen . . . accompanied by queens, princesses and great ladies, the long trains of their dresses loosened and sweeping behind them . . . And it is the said pavans, played by hautboys and sackbuts, that announce the grand ball and are arranged to last until the dancers have circled the hall two or three times . . . Pavans are also used in masquerades to herald the entrance of the gods and goddesses in their triumphal chariots or emperors and kings in full majesty."[22] Whereas the formal elements of Arbeau's pavane still apply to its use in *Le Mariage de la Grosse Cathos*, the affective content is completely different. A processional intended for rustic, burlesque characters turns the noble, solemn pavane on its head.

During the last few bars of the processional the front two rows of oboes merge to form

[22] Arbeau, *Orchesographie* (trans. Evans), reprint p. 59.

a line of six; likewise the last five singers form a line at the back of the performing area. In the last frame of p. 42 the three groups are positioned as shown in ill. 3.1:[23]

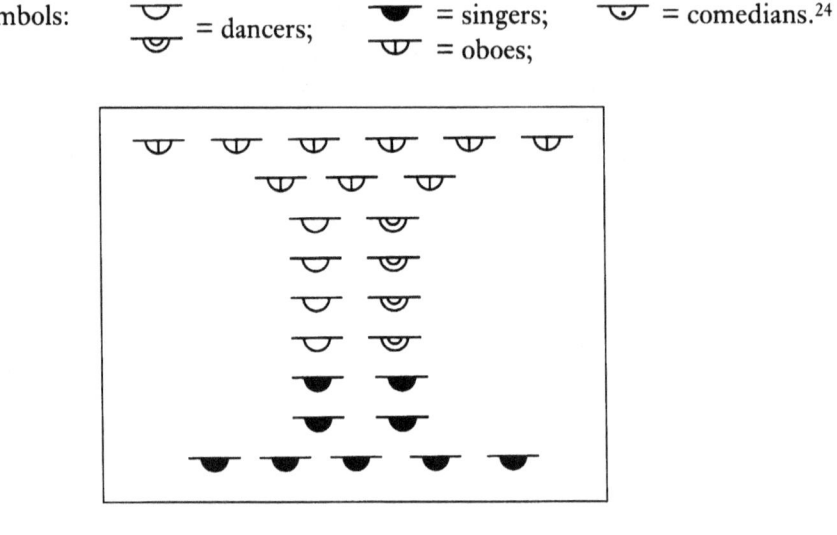

Ill. 3.1

As the eight dancers begin to dance to a third repetition of the pavane (IB), the oboes shift slightly from a 6-3 formation to a 5-3-1 formation, backing up a bit to occupy the space vacated by the dancers; likewise, the singers shift from a 2-2-5 formation to a 2-7 formation. For much of the rest of IB the oboes and dancers share the performing area, the oboes remaining upstage in their triangular formation while the dancers first move downstage to the left of the oboes and then occupy the rectangular space defined by the front of the oboe formation and the audience. By thus positioning the instrumentalists Favier establishes the centrality of the oboe band to the entire mascarade. They are clearly not a "pit band" that has been placed on stage for lack of a pit; in addition to their role of accompanying the singers they also function as the dance band for the wedding, a role made explicit not only in this dance but in the other dances that emphasize the village community of which the musicians are a part.

While the purpose of the processional is to bring the characters on stage and to introduce the entire cast to the audience, the second part of the dance serves as a reminder that the mascarade is set at a wedding celebration. Although dance IB begins with the dancers moving downstage in a formation which seems to grow out of the processional, the couple-oriented character of this dance soon emerges. The courtship motif, introduced here for the first time, is one that recurs in other dances throughout the mascarade.

The step vocabulary of the danced pavane, while not technically demanding, is lively and varied. The relatively large number of sprung steps – hops and leaps – contrasts markedly with the staid quality of the preceding march. However, the real interest of this choreography lies in its floor patterns, which utilize asymmetrical shapes both for the group as a whole and for the couples within the group of eight. For example, during part of the first twelve bars the dancers are arranged with one couple on stage right while the other three couples remain on stage left. Such asymmetry is in marked contrast to dances in Feuillet notation, almost all of which adhere to strict principles of symmetry.

By bar 17 the performers have reached the positions shown in ill. 3.2. During the final

---

[23] In practice, certain adjustments to this formation are necessary to facilitate a smooth connection between IA and IB; these are discussed in more detail in chapter 6.

[24] Favier was not consistent in his choice of symbols from dance to dance; for example, in some dances (IB, III, and V) he uses a filled-in symbol to represent the male roles and distinguish them from the females. Yet elsewhere this same symbol represents the singers. Our symbols follow the usage in the final section of the recessional (XC), the only dance in which Favier unambiguously differentiates all four performing groups. In addition, we have adopted Feuillet's double half circle to represent female roles.

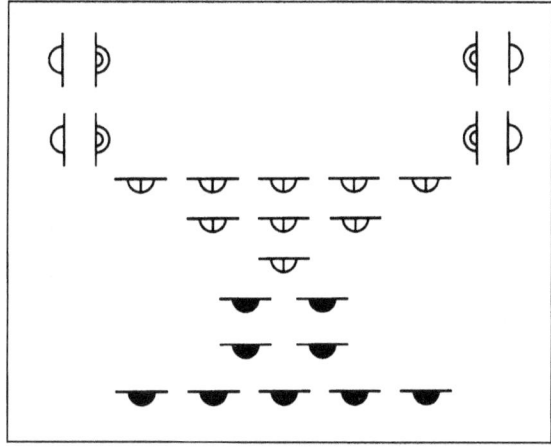

Ill. 3.2

third of the dance the oboes split into two groups, gradually moving to a new formation at the sides of the stage. They begin by walking towards the sides, turning to face each other when they have reached their new positions. By the last bar of music the dancers have retreated upstage, forming a kind of funnel shape through which two singers move forward. These are presumably Monsieur and Madame Dupont, who are the first to sing in the scene that follows. The other seven singers remain in a flattened semi-circle at the back of the stage. Ill. 3.3 shows the position of the performers at the end of IB. The closing bars of dance IB thus serve simultaneously as a conclusion to the processional and as a preparation for the first scene of the mascarade. The musicians and dancers who had occupied the center of the stage yield to the singers, two of whom advance even as the dancers retreat. By the time the pavane ends, most of the cast has set up a frame around the stage that shifts the focus from themselves onto Monsieur and Madame Dupont. Since the transition has been built into the dance, no more time need elapse between the end of the pavane and Madame Dupont's first words than a breath for the bassoonist; the movement is continuous. The kind of choreographed retreat apparent at the end of the pavane is a consistent feature of Favier's dances: each of them concludes with the dancers clearing the space in such a way as to allow for an easy transition to the next event in the mascarade.

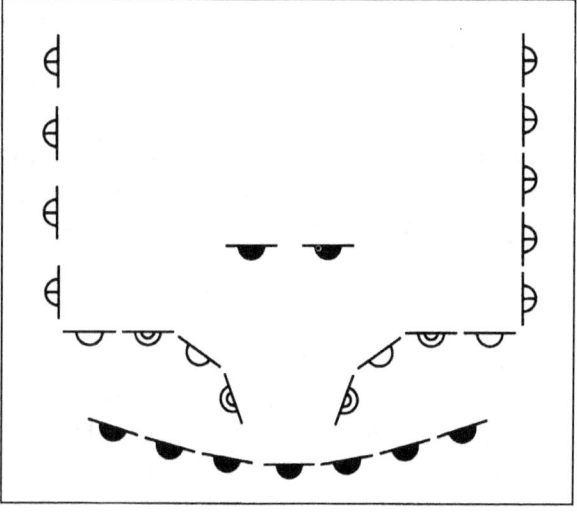

Ill. 3.3

The positions that the singers and oboes take up at the end of the pavane – the oboes along the sides of the performing area, four of them stage left and five stage right, the singers in a semi-circle across the back – represent their home positions for the rest of the mascarade. The oboes play from this position until they once again participate in the choreography during the passepied, following which they return to the sidelines. When the singers perform as a chorus, they remain in their home positions at the back of the stage; when they have solos or duets to sing, they emerge from the group into the center area. The freeze-frame notation never shows the home positions for the dancers, but their places when they are inactive are probably in the upstage corners of the performing area; these are the spots to which they retreat following dance II (see ill. 3.4 below) and in this position they are out of the way of both the oboes and the singers during the purely musical numbers.

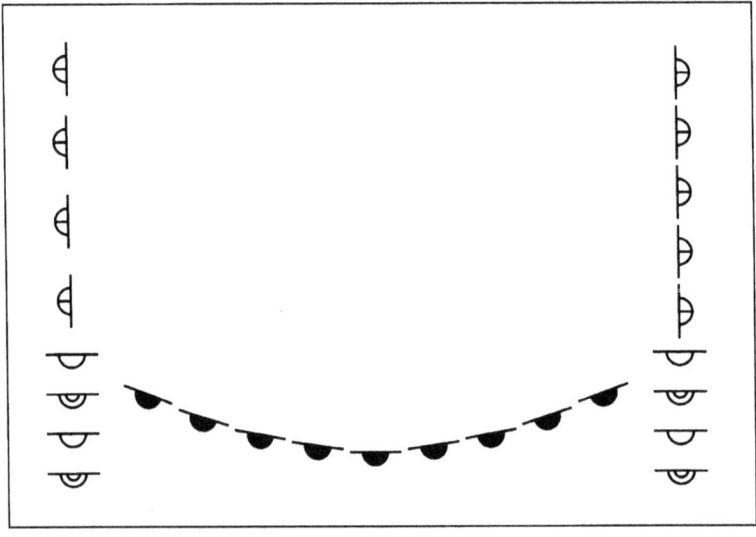

Ill. 3.4

It is likely, however, that during the brief sung scene that follows the pavane, the dancers do not go all the way to their home positions but remain, at least initially, where they ended the pavane. Since the dancers do not participate in the first part of this section, there is no notation showing their movements or those of the singers. The three soloists who add their comments on the approaching nuptials to Monsieur and Madame Dupont's announcement presumably step forward at the appropriate moments; meanwhile, the dancers need to move into two columns parallel to the oboes in readiness for their participation in the following chorus. By the end of this sung section the singers must have returned to their home positions, since the dancers' subsequent movements require the use of the center of the performing area.

In the brief chorus that now follows (II), the dancers, representing a stylized crowd scene, act out the words of the singers. The text of the chorus consists exclusively of three repetitions of the words, "Allons, accourons tous, la Grosse Cathos se marie" ("Come on, let's all hasten, Grosse Cathos is getting married!"). On the words "Allons, accourons tous" the two columns of dancers rush forward on either side of the stage, then stop abruptly in place on the syllable "Gros-[se]" while they listen to the surprising news. When the chorus again exhorts everyone to hurry over, the dancers spring into action; this time their running steps carry them across the stage in two groups that change places, freezing as before to hear the announcement of the wedding. During the final repetition of the text, the dancers retreat upstage more slowly, finishing in two columns in their home positions. Their movement effectively clears the stage so that a maximum of space is available for the subsequent scenes. Illustration 3.4 illustrates the position of the performers at the end of the chorus.

Following this chorus comes a long section that contains the dramatic core, so to speak, of the mascarade. Two relatively extensive sung sections frame the spoken scene, in which there are no notated dances and thus no movement indications for any of the performers. During this long sequence the oboes and dancers presumably remain in their home positions, while the vocal soloists move forward from their chorus positions when appropriate.

Harlequin and Mezzetin, who did not take part in the opening procession, must have made an entrance just in time for their scene with La Couture. With four of the dancers in the upstage right corner, it would certainly have been possible for them to have entered the performing area unseen during the singing. Or perhaps they had been concealed in the window bays at the back of the room. In either case, their absence from the processional suggests that their arrival was reserved as a surprise for the audience. The two comedians are chased away at the end of the spoken scene, presumably disappearing from sight. However, they reappear in time for the recessional in which they are notated as participants.

The dances numbered from III to IX on the outline enclose the part of the mascarade that functions as the divertissement: these are the wedding festivities proper. The short sung section between dances V and VI involving Cathos, La Couture, Maître Simon, and the chorus also functions as part of the general celebration, not as a contribution to the plot. The divertissement is even introduced by a straightforward announcement from the Dame Ragonde that "we intend to dance here." Four of the guests, identified in the dance score as *garçons* and *filles de la noce*, oblige, performing three dances (III, IV, and V) in quick succession. This sequence of dances can easily be read as a stylized courtship ritual, with the two men and two women dancing first in single-sex pairs and then together. The divertissement begins with the two men positioned about half-way downstage, they and their partners having apparently emerged from their home positions during Dame Ragonde's exhortation. While the women watch, the men perform a difficult entrée (III), showing off their technique in the execution of the varied and demanding steps.[25] The men end facing each other rather than the audience, the width of the stage between them, in effect inviting the women to dance. The *filles de la noce* respond to this invitation with a gigue (IV). Even though the "women" are male dancers, Favier observes the convention seen in the dances of Pécour and others of keeping the step vocabulary of the women's dances somewhat simpler than the men's. In the women's duet the steps are not only easier to perform, but they are part of the noble-style step vocabulary found in dances in Feuillet notation; in contrast, the male duet includes features associated with character dances, such as false positions of the feet and wider than normal steps, as well as a number of steps not found in theatrical dances by Feuillet or Pécour.[26] Both duets utilize symmetrical floor patterns of the type found in Feuillet-notated dances of the period.

The two women finish the gigue on the opposite sides of the stage from which they started, so that their partners for the following menuet (V) are not the same men with whom they danced in IB. Like the ballroom menuets of the early eighteenth century, this two-couple dance relies almost entirely on a single step, the *pas de menuet*, that is repeated throughout the dance.[27] This step, however, differs from any previously known version of the menuet step both in its rhythmic profile and in its execution (see chapter 5 for a more detailed discussion).

Another interesting feature of this dance, found also in the other dances in the mascarade that involve male–female couples, is that considerations of symmetry override

---

[25] A reading of this dance as a comic attempt at the noble style is proposed in chapter 6.

[26] Fifteen theatrical choreographies by Feuillet are included in his *Recueil de dances* (1700), a companion volume to *Chorégraphie*, and a number of other theatrical male solos survive in manuscript. Pécour's two large collections of theatrical dances, *Recueil de dances* (1704) and *Novueau* [sic] *recueil de dance* [1713], contain a total of sixty-five theatrical choreographies. For more detailed information see Little and Marsh, *Inventory*.

[27] Early eighteenth-century ballroom menuets fall into two categories. "Generic" menuets were danced by one couple at a time; the partners moved through a series of prescribed figures (although with some latitude regarding the number of times each figure could be repeated), using the menuet step and occasionally inserting other steps. Any menuet music could be used. The figured menuet, on the other hand, was a choreography in which the floor patterns and steps were notated, and were specific to a given piece of music. While most of these dances are also for one couple, a few notated menuet choreographies for two couples also survive.

the convention in which the woman starts and ends the dance to the right of her partner. Favier's menuet begins and ends with the woman in the right-hand couple standing to her partner's left, in mirror-image symmetry with the left-hand couple.[28]

The choreographic interest of the menuet is centered in the floor patterns, through which the courtship theme hinted at in the two duets is made explicit. The women circle their partners while the men feign indifference; after a back-to-back circling figure the men take charge, moving forward and forcing their partners to retreat to the sides of the stage. The floor patterns assume a variety of shapes: lines, squares, and diamonds; and the dancers move not only in straight and circular paths but in spirals. At the end of the dance the two couples move to the sides and then downstage, in a reversal of the upstage choreographic retreat seen in the other group dances in the mascarade. Perhaps the dancers were kept in the foreground to emphasize the connection between the menuet and the following chorus, the text of which echoes the sentiments implied by the menuet: "Dans ce grand jour unissons-nous / Pour partager des jeux si doux" ("On this great day let us join together / To share such sweet pastimes"). Although the dancers do not participate in this chorus, the triple meter and key of G major that continue from the menuet into the chorus increase the impression that the two pieces offer complementary expressions – one through dance, the other through song – of a single idea. The following duet by La Couture and Cathos switches the focus from the tender passions to more earthly pleasures, and Maître Simon, Cathos's Swiss friend, rounds off this solo section with a song in praise of the pleasures of drink.

At this point the two portions of the manuscript disagree as to the next event. In the musical score the celebratory chorus "Passons toujours la vie" occurs here, followed by the three remaining dances of the divertissement: the drunk dance (VI), the rigaudon (VII), and the passepied (VIII). In the dance notation the relative positions of the chorus and the three dances are reversed, which means that Maître Simon's drinking song leads directly into the dance for two drunks, while the choreographed chorus (IX) rounds off the three dances. The dance score further supports this order by notating the advance of a single singer downstage at the end of the chorus. If a dance is to follow the "Passons" chorus, as it does in the musical score, the emergence of a singer toward the front of the stage makes no sense. If, on the other hand, the next piece is a solo air, as is the case when the order of the dance notation is observed, such movement notation is to be expected. However, it is just possible that both portions of the manuscript are correct: perhaps the chorus was intended both to precede and to follow this series of dances. Certainly rounded structures involving repetition of a chorus may be found in Lully's divertissements. If the chorus was danced only upon its second appearance, then its first hearing would have left no trace in the dance notation, and Philidor's error in the musical score would not have been in misplacing the chorus, but merely in neglecting to call for its repetition.[29]

Arguing against this compromise hypothesis, however, is the close relationship between Maître Simon's drinking song and the drunk dance. Just as the consecutive menuet and the chorus "Dans ce grand jour" express via different media the same idea, so the two dancers of the "Air des Ivrognes" act out the drunkenness which Maître Simon has just expressed in song. A chorus praising the pursuit of pleasure fits into the spirit of general celebration, but if interpolated between Maître Simon's song and the drunk dance undermines the unity of expression created when the two numbers are performed consecutively. Nonetheless, either of the two possible orders for this sequence – the "Passons" chorus performed only once at the end of the section (as indicated in the dance notation) or this same chorus used as a frame for the three dances but choreographed only the second time (thus respecting the readings of both the music and dance portions of the manuscript) – implies the same staging for the dancers; that is, none of them would have

---

[28] Since there are no dances for a single mixed couple in Favier notation, and no theatrical dances for two couples in Feuillet notation, we cannot say for sure whether Favier's practice is unique. However, in all but one of the ballroom dances for two couples in Feuillet notation the men begin and end on their partners' left. The exception is Dezais's "L'Italiene," a *contredanse* for four published in his 1719 *Recueil de dances*.

[29] The F-Pa score follows the same order as the F-Pn musical score.

danced during the sung scene that intervenes between the end of the menuet (V) and the beginning of the drunk dance (VI). The notation does not specify which of the men now appear inebriated, and certainly any two of the four could have stepped forward in time to perform this dance.

To a late seventeenth-century audience familiar with the conventions of the noble style, the "Air des Ivrognes" (VI) would have been immediately recognized as a burlesque of the *entrée grave*, the noblest and most difficult of the theatrical dances of the time, usually performed by one or two men. The minor key, the slow duple meter with two step-units per bar of music, and the difficult step vocabulary are all characteristic features of this dance type.[30] The two peasants begin in a promising fashion but their inebriated condition soon threatens to destroy the dance. The sudden stops and starts and abrupt changes of direction suggest that their spatial orientation is rapidly deteriorating, and this impression is confirmed by an eight-bar passage in which the dancers simply walk around each other, nearly colliding at one point. Although no body gestures are indicated it seems clear that a certain amount of pantomime would have been used – staggering, reeling, and similar gestures associated with drunks. Certainly movements of this type are implied in one of Lully's ballets, *La Revente des Habits*, whose libretto describes the six drunks as "tottering often without falling or losing the beat of the music, so well are they attuned to the sound of the violins even in their cups."[31]

In both the music and dance parts of the manuscript the drunk dance is followed immediately by the rigaudon, but in performance a break of some sort must have occurred between the two choreographies. In the first place, the drunk dance is a real show-stopper, and regardless of the manner in which audiences of the period expressed their appreciation it seems likely that some time would have been taken here. There is also a practical reason why a short pause is needed between the drunk dance and the rigaudon: the two drunks end their dance in the same space where the rigaudon begins. It seems reasonable to assume that after the drunks had finished they would stagger to the upstage corners to sober up for their next appearance, while the four women and La Couture would take their places for the rigaudon (VII). If this hypothesis is correct, this is the one place in the mascarade where a small break may occur between numbers.

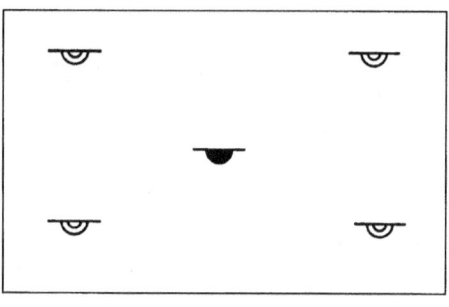

Ill. 3.5

The rigaudon is performed by the four women plus the bridegroom, La Couture. This unusual choreography begins with the women in a rectangular formation and La Couture in the middle (see ill. 3.5). Initially the women seem oblivious to the presence of the bridegroom: they interact with each other in their rectangular formation, and their curved floor patterns contrast with La Couture's movements forward and back along a straight line. The women all perform the same steps, while La Couture has his own more vigorous step sequence. These differences in both figures and steps not only underline the

---

[30] A number of examples of the *entrée grave* can be found in the collections listed in n. 26. See, for example, LMC nos. 1320a, 2720, 2740, 4000, 4180, and 4260, all choreographed to music by Lully.

[31] "V. ENTREE. Trois Sobres, Six Yvrognes. Six Crocheteurs . . . s'estans enyvrez sortent & dansent ensemble, chancellans souvent sans tomber ny sortir hors de cadance, tant ils ont parmy le vin l'oreille faite au son des Violons." *Ballet de la Revente des Habits*; the printed libretto (F-Pn [Imprimés] Yf 1038) lacks title page and imprint.

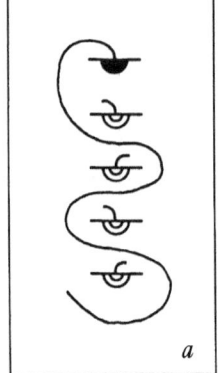 

Ill. 3.6

gender distinctions but also provide the only known example of a Baroque choreography in which two contrasting step sequences occur simultaneously for more than a few bars.[32] By bar 24 of the dance the village women have succumbed to the bridegroom's charms, and they rush to fall in line behind him. He proceeds to weave between them, each woman in turn joining the line after it passes her, and the column quickly dissolves into a semicircle (see ill. 3.6a and 3.6b). This figure, reminiscent of the weaving pattern or hey found in many contemporary English country dances, appears again in the second part of the following dance. As is true elsewhere in the mascarade, the complexity of the figure is offset by the use of a simple repetitive step vocabulary.

The end of the group dance is followed by a solo dance for La Couture, which, like the solo dance in the chorus "Passons" (IX), is not notated. Both solos may well have been left up to the individual performers rather than choreographed by Favier; in this case, the known talents of Philbert, the man who played La Couture, suggest that choreographic improvisation was easily within his capabilities.

If the theme of the rigaudon is seduction, that of the following passepied (VIII) is communal celebration, a point that is underscored by the reappearance of the oboes as participants in the choreography. The passepied begins with a serpentine line dance in freeze-frame notation (VIIIA) for the eight dancers led by La Couture. All nine performers hold hands in a curved line, the men presumably having moved into position while La Couture was performing his solo at the end of the rigaudon. The oboes, who have been in their home positions along the sides of the performing area since IB, now return to center stage, forming an outward-facing circle. The dancers travel once around the oboe circle, moving clockwise to their left while facing the instrumentalists, after which they turn and circle the oboes again, this time with their backs to the instrumentalists. A late seventeenth-century audience would have recognized the similarities between this dance and the branle, a traditional line or circle dance dating back at least to the Renaissance but also danced during this period at the opening of formal balls.[33] Favier's choreographic image thus simultaneously evokes folk tradition and parodies aristocratic ceremonies.

Midway through the second circling figure La Couture breaks away from the line and rejoins the singers at the back of the stage. The eight dancers split into two groups of four, while the oboes, still in their circle formation, move upstage (see p. 90 of the facsimile, last system). The passepied continues with a more elaborate choreography in score notation (VIIIB) for the eight dancers. It begins with two short sections, in which the women, and then the men, rotate as a group 90° clockwise; during these figures the oboe circle breaks into two lines parallel to the sides of the performing area. As in IB, the presence of the oboes upstage center restricts the floor space available to the dancers to a narrow

---

[32] Some duets in Feuillet notation include a short "courtship figure" in which, for example, the man dances around the woman, who pirouettes in place, but these passages are never more than three or four bars long.

[33] For a contemporary illustration of this dance see Israel Silvestre's engraving "Le Branle au Louvre," reproduced as plate I in Guilcher, *La contredanse*, following p. 112.

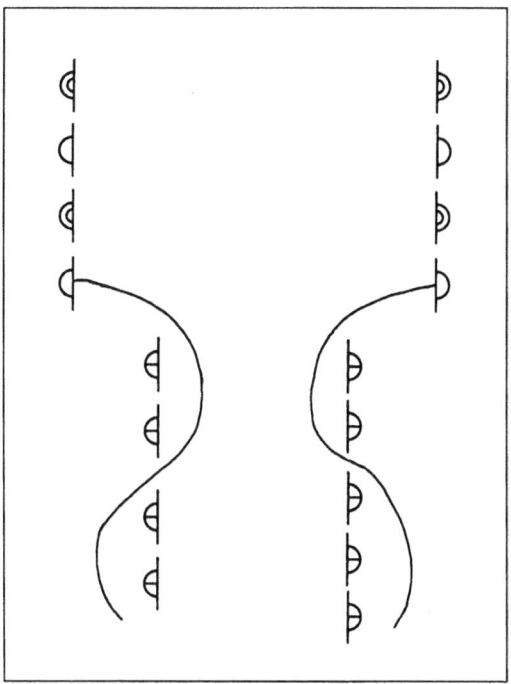

Ill. 3.7

rectangular area downstage. The final figure of the dance makes even more explicit the role of the oboes as members of the wedding party. The eight dancers form two lines and weave through the two lines of instrumentalists, in a figure which combines elements of the line dance and the hey (see ill. 3.7). By the end of the choreography the oboes have returned to their home positions along the sides of the performing space while the dancers end as they started, in a flattened semi-circle upstage.

As in the menuet (V) the step vocabulary of the passepied is limited. In VIIIA only the menuet step is used, always performed traveling sideways, usually to the left. In VIIIB other variants of the menuet/passepied vocabulary are used. As in the rigaudon Favier assigns somewhat more vigorous steps to the men's section of the dance than to the women's.

Although our analysis of this dance divides it into two parts based on the use of two different kinds of dance notation, a careful study of the choreography reveals that the dance has an organic unity: VIIIB flows seamlessly out of VIIIA, and the intermingling of dancers and oboes in the final figure of VIIIB is a logical extension of the opening circling figure of VIIIA. On another level the entire dance can be read as a stylized ritual ceremony: the "magic circle" around which the participants dance, the spinning circular figures of the women and then the men, and the final hey figure all have ritual resonance. This ceremonial quality is reinforced by the fact that the passepied is a "couple-less" dance; although men and women alternate in the line dance, and stand next to each other in VIIIB, there is no interaction between the men and the women, and none of the courtship figures found in the other group dances is present.[34]

The following chorus, "Passons" (IX), begins with the dancers in a straight line upstage, a position reached by flattening out the semi-circle at the end of the passepied. This number, the text of which celebrates living for pleasure, is the culmination of the divertissement within the mascarade and involves the whole cast, with movement notation for the oboes and singers as well as the dancers. Musically it alternates eight-bar phrases sung by the full chorus to the accompaniment of the oboe band with repetitions of another

---

[34] Carl Wittman has argued convincingly that such seventeenth-century English country dances as "Sellinger's Round" and "Jenny Plucked Pears" are stylized versions of pagan ritual dances ("An Analysis of John Playford's *English Dancing Master* [1651]," master's thesis, Goddard College, 1981, pp. 130–2). See also Guilcher, *La contredanse*, pp. 187–91, for a discussion of the ritual meanings of the branle in French folkdance.

eight-bar phrase played only by the instruments. The dancers remain motionless during each of the first three vocal statements, but dance to the interspersed instrumental phrases, reinforcing the phrase structure of the music. The first dance phrase is performed by the four women who come forward in a leisurely fashion, turning to the right and left as they move downstage. The singers repeat their text to new music, after which the men move forward, but much more quickly as if anxious to regain their partners, around whom they circle, holding inside hands. The third repetition of the instrumental phrase calls for a solo dance by one of the men ("un paysan"), which, like La Couture's solo at the end of the rigaudon, is not notated in the manuscript. The dancers join the singers and instrumentalists for the concluding phrase, a precisely notated retreat by the entire cast. This not only reaffirms the communal spirit of IX but serves a practical purpose as well, clearing the stage for whatever antics may take place during the subsequent *charivari*. The oboes, still in their two rows along the side, move upstage. The chorus, already upstage, retreats even further back to make room for the dancers who are also moving backwards in a "V" formation that gradually flattens out as it moves upstage. During the last four bars, a singer, undoubtedly La Couture, comes forward to sing the short air that introduces the *charivari*.

An enigmatic symbol,[35] appearing for the first time in the dance notation on p. 103 of the facsimile, suggests that the last eight bars of "Passons" are more than just a carefully choreographed retreat for the dancers, along with the singers and oboes. This symbol may indicate that some of the dancers, still in their "V" formation, form arches with their arms. Such a gesture, unique in notated dances of this period, is also curious in that it is not performed symmetrically. In other words, if this were an abstract choreographic gesture one would expect couples on both sides of the V to raise and lower their arms at the same time, which does not happen. Perhaps Favier was merely trying to notate the sort of gesture one sees in illustrations of peasant dancers from the period.[36] An attractive but considerably more speculative hypothesis is that the purpose of the arches is to allow someone to pass under them, in which case a sequential pattern of raising and lowering arms makes perfect sense. Since all of the singers, oboes, and dancers are accounted for in the movement notation, the only characters who could be passing under the arches are the Italian comedians; they have presumably been in hiding since their spoken scene but now emerge to participate in various outrageous antics during the *charivari*. This hypothesis is further supported by the fact that the comedians are shown exiting with the other performers in the recessional that follows, indicating that they did not exit the performing area after their spoken scene. Ill. 3.8 shows the positions of the dancers at bars 49–51 and a possible path traveled by the two Italians.

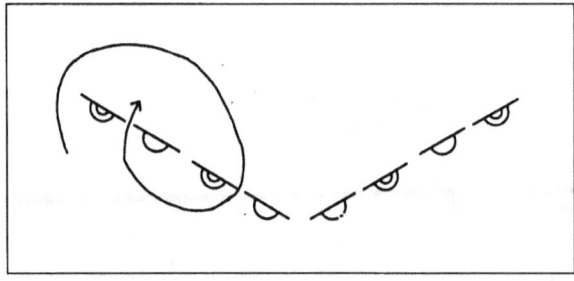

Ill. 3.8

---

[35] This symbol, a letter "b," may stand for "bras" (arm), just as "m" stands for "main" (hand). See chapter 5 for a more detailed discussion.

[36] A contemporary illustration by Berain of a peasant couple dancing appears as item 9 of the Drouot auction catalogue. The couple's inside hands are joined with the arms lowered, and the man's free arm is raised above his head. The dancers appear to be hopping on one leg, the free leg in the air with the knee bent, a posture that is not inconsistent with the first step of the *contretemps balonné*. For a similar pose, see the illustration of Dumoulin in the role of a peasant, plate 5.

No sooner has La Couture called for his nightcap than we are plunged into the *charivari*, the traditional wedding serenade intended to disrupt the nuptial bliss of the couple. Musically this is a loose rondeau structure, in which an oboe/chorus refrain alternates with a bass solo, sung by a "garçon de la noce." The refrains display bizarre instrumentation – the normal four-part texture of the oboes has been supplemented by two additional bass parts and a drum – and ostinato-like outbursts of the single word "charivari" by the chorus. Although no movement notation for this piece was entered in the manuscript, it seems certain that pantomime by the Italian comedians as well as dancing, at least during the instrumental and choral sections, took place. The clearing of the stage during the previous number, the blank pages in the dance portion of the manuscript at this point, and the nature of the celebration all strongly suggest that movement of some sort occurred. It is possible to imagine a dance so improvisatory in character that Favier despaired of trying to notate it. Such an "unchoreographed" finale would have been the ultimate burlesque of the noble-style *grand ballet*.

In any case, movement by all of the performers would have been necessary at some point during the *charivari* to get into position for the recessional (X). This dance, to the same music as the opening processional, has the three groups exiting in the same order in which they entered: oboes first, followed by the dancers and the singers. The recessional reverses the path of the opening dance, beginning upstage left and moving around the perimeter of the performing area, this time in a clockwise direction, and out the door or opening used for the entrance. As in the opening march, the music is repeated three times – perhaps more if necessary to get everyone off stage. The position of the performers at the end of the first time through the music can be seen in the last frame on p. 106 of the facsimile; the oboes are at stage right and the dancers are in front of the singers in the column at stage left.

At this point the recessional is interrupted by a notated choreography for the eight dancers, performed to the second time through the music. For the first seventeen bars this dance (XB) is nearly identical to dance IB, with the notable exception that the oboes are not positioned upstage center; instead, during the first six bars of XB they continue to travel upstage right in their column formation, turning to face the audience in bar 7. Likewise, the position of the singers is different from that in IB; here they remain in their column formation at stage left. In spite of these differences, the floor pattern of the dance is not altered; that is, the dancers move downstage during the opening segment of the dance and remain there performing within a narrow rectangular space. If anything, this rectangle is positioned slightly farther downstage than in IB, perhaps to avoid contact between the dancers and the two groups of performers on the sides of the stage. During the last eight bars of XB the dancers reform into a column two abreast across the front of the stage; one couple at a time they peel off in military fashion, falling in behind the column of oboes at stage right. The formal recessional resumes, with one walked step to each bar of music, until all the performers are off stage.

The positions of Harlequin and Mezzetin, who bring up the rear of the procession, are notated for the first time at the beginning of XB, where they are shown standing side-by-side behind the oboes. While the two Italians probably did not interfere with the notated choreography, it seems likely that once the march resumed and they came into full view of the audience they would have returned to character, carrying on outrageously until everyone had left the room.

THE PERFORMANCE PRACTICES

Le Mariage de la Grosse Cathos is but one of the many carnival mascarades performed at the French court over the years and the performing practices it reveals must have owed a good deal to longstanding traditions. But even though this work is a burlesque mascarade, the staging practices that may be abstracted from the rich documentation in the manuscript seem to be based on general principles that are not grounded in any single genre. This may be seen by comparing seventeenth-century documents having to do with the *ballet de cour* and the opera such as librettos, scores, choreographies, and descriptive and theoretical writings with the information derived from this mascarade. The performance indications provided by *Le Mariage de la Grosse Cathos* do not resolve all of the questions that an attempt at a faithful reconstruction of the mascarade itself raises, let alone a Lully opera; nonetheless they do offer important guidelines for interpreting the primary material that survives for such works.

The choreographic notation for the mascarade provides at least some information on a number of overlapping topics: the definition of the space on stage; the placement of the performers in the space; the relationships of different groups of performers to each other; the relationship of the individual to the group; how and when movement on stage is effected; how and where the focus of the audience is directed; the way in which the work as a whole progresses from beginning to end; the extent to which different modes of expression may serve the same dramatic ends; the function of dance within the work; the mimetic possibilities of choreography; and the ways in which dances are constructed.

In *Le Mariage de la Grosse Cathos* all of the performers, with the exception of the two Italian comedians, are on stage all of the time. This fact is fundamental to the staging because it means that twenty-six people must share a relatively small space – probably around 23 feet wide by 15 feet deep (see above, p. 37) – in a way that permits the necessary movement and directs the attention of the audience to the appropriate characters. This situation was handled by defining certain areas of the stage as the territory for each group of performers who thus framed the stage in a flattened U: the singers in a line across the back, the dancers divided between the two upstage corners, and the oboes along the two sides. This is a visually symmetrical arrangement, the only imbalance being the presence of five oboes on one side, four on the other. It establishes a difference between the perimeter of the stage, where the characters are perceived by the audience as a group of villagers, and the center, which they enter as individuals. The perimeter and the center are also differentiated on the basis of activity: when the performers are on the edge of the stage, they stand in place; if they are to move, they advance into the center. The performers' positions relative to the space thus define the ways they are viewed by the audience: when individuals emerge from the group into the center area, they call the attention of the audience to themselves; when the entire cast is in its home positions, it becomes a unit that the audience perceives collectively.

The inference of this treatment of the space on stage is that at any one time there is but a single focus for the audience and a single idea being expressed. The notion of a single focus does not mean that only one person or one group moves at a time, but it does imply that all of the people participating in the action act in concert. Thus if four dancers perform a menuet, that menuet represents the action of the moment, and none of the remaining characters would do anything that could draw the attention of the audience to themselves. Two singers would not, for example, choose that moment to pretend to engage in a game of cards. Similarly during the time when Cathos and La Couture exchange endearments, the dancers would not stroll around the stage. It is true that some of the numbers in this work, the passepied (dance VIII) for example, involve simultaneous movement by two or more groups, but such passages express celebration by the whole community, and even if the oboes walk while the dancers do menuet steps, all are participants in a single group choreography and all are moving in time to the same music. The principle of a single focus may be observed in Favier's choreography for the chorus "Passons toujours la vie" (dance IX). This chorus alternates four eight-bar sung phrases with three purely instrumental ones of the same length. The dancers remain motionless during the first three vocal phrases, but move during the instrumental sections; thus the audience shifts its attention from words to dance and back again. Only in the last vocal phrase, when the text has become familiar through four-fold repetition, do the dancers join forces with the singers to draw the number to a close.

The other choreographed chorus in the mascarade, "Allons, accourons tous" (dance II) might seem to provide a counter example to the idea of a single focus in that the dancers participate from the start, while the text is being sung for the first time. However, the text of this chorus has already been heard virtually verbatim in the mouths of Monsieur and Madame Dupont; moreover, the dancers act out the singers' words, serving as active bodies for the choir, who remain motionless. This chorus, in fact, demonstrates a phenomenon observable elsewhere in the mascarade: the use of dancers as surrogates for the singers. The full casting of the chorus requires singing villagers and dancing villagers, singing bodies and dancing bodies, who represent essentially the same people. It is not the singers who act out their own words, but rather the dancers who are, in a sense, their doubles.

In this chorus the dancers' expression of the idea is concurrent with the singers' words, but other parts of the mascarade show that the visual and textual manifestations of a single idea may be consecutive rather than simultaneous. During the mascarade's divertissement, for example, Cathos and La Couture allude in their bouncy duet to the pleasures that wine brings. After Maître Simon reveals the consolation he finds in drinking all day long, two dancers vividly portray the results of such behavior. It does not seem to be necessary that there be a one-to-one correspondence between singing bodies and dancing bodies: the dance represents the idea of drunkenness, not the person of the drunk Maître Simon. Slightly earlier in the mascarade, the relative position of dance and vocal number is reversed. Following a series of three dances (III–V) in which two young couples first perform for each other and then finally come together, the chorus rounds off the sequence by exhorting the assembly towards amorous unity. Although the music of this chorus is not choreographed, the text sums up ideas already made visible through dance.

In this mascarade the chorus is made up of the solo singers, but this is not the case in larger stage works such as Lully's court ballets or operas, where there is a clear distinction between the soloists, all of whom play specific roles, and the members of the chorus, who are collectively identified as, say, "villagers" or "inhabitants of Phrygia." In Lully operas the dancers are identified in the same general way as the singers, and his librettos often list the singing and dancing characters in parallel, as for example a "troupe de Phrygiens chantants" and a "troupe de Phrygiens dansants." The implication of such listings – that, as in *Le Mariage de la Grosse Cathos*, the dancers and singers fulfill two different functions for essentially the same roles – is supported by evidence that the chorus at the Paris Opéra "was no more mobile than the scenery." In fact, all the available evidence suggests that the chorus stood in a single row around the perimeter of the stage, leaving the center to the vocal soloists and the dancers.[37] In a Lully opera the principal singers presumably made entrances and exits as the plot demanded, rather than emerging from and retreating into the chorus as they do in this mascarade, but the fundamental principles regarding the definition of the space on stage and the relationship between chorus members and dancers would appear to function for both genres.

Although the division of labor between singers and dancers seems to apply most particularly to the choruses, the drunk dance in the mascarade shows that even a solo vocal number may be embodied in dance. But if dancers sometimes represent the moving bodies even of solo singers, to what extent would solo singers have been expected to move around when they are the center of the audience's attention? Would La Couture, for example, have walked about while singing that he is transported by love and wishing someone would bring him his nightcap? Or would he have stood still once he reached his position in the middle of the stage? His air here is not analogous to Maître Simon's drinking song in that it does not have a corresponding dance number (although it sets up the *charivari*), so perhaps in the absence of a dancer/surrogate, the singer was expected to provide his own movement. Regrettably, the manuscript does not answer the question of how much – or little – the singers may have moved during their solos; since the notated portion of the manuscript includes only the dance pieces, it is not possible to reconstruct the singers' movements during the purely vocal numbers. However, the manuscript does

[37] See Rosow, "Performing a choral dialogue," especially pp. 329–31.

provide one suggestive detail. In the two places where the movements of solo singers are notated – at the ends of dances IB and IX (facsimile, pp. 51 and 104–5) – the singers are shown advancing into the center during the closing bars of the dance. This means that by the time the dance is over, they are downstage and ready to sing. Although it is impossible to know whether they moved away from that spot once they were singing, at the very least this dovetailing of dance and vocal number suggests that the singers were not expected to open their mouths until they were in place.[38]

In these two notated passages, the route the singers are shown to follow as they advance is straight down the middle of the stage. La Couture comes forward by himself, whereas Monsieur and Madame Dupont walk in tandem, side by side – all three in rhythm with the music. Their trajectory – and perhaps their subsequent position – maintains the visual symmetry already established by the positions of the performers who frame the stage. Given the paucity of the evidence, it would be dangerous to propose that the singers in this mascarade must therefore always have arranged themselves symmetrically when in center stage. Nonetheless, what is merely hinted at for the singers is fundamental for the dancers. With few exceptions (discussed above and in chapter 6), Favier's choreographies arrange the dancers in symmetrical patterns, such that a couple on one side of the stage is mirrored by another couple opposite. In this respect his choreographies are very much of a piece with those preserved in Feuillet notation, where symmetry of both floor patterns and steps is a basic principle of construction. The same concern for visual symmetry is also apparent in contemporary theatrical designs, as sets for such Lully operas as *Thésée*, *Atys*, and *Isis* show (see Lesure, *L'opéra classique français*, plates 28–31).

The advance of the singers during the end of a dance in preparation for their own participation seems to represent a paradigm for the way in which numbers in the mascarade should connect. Because the singers have moved into position during the preceding number, no break is necessary between the end of the dance and the start of the vocal piece. In a similar manner, each choreography ends with a retreat by the dancers that clears the stage in readiness for the next event. The score supports the paradigm of continuous movement that is inherent in the dance notation: musical continuity is provided not only by the Lullian practice of welding recitative and air into a seamless flow, but by joining pieces to each other such that the end of one becomes the beginning of the next. See on p. 3 of the facsimile, for example, the join between Maître Simon's air and Monsieur and Madame Dupont's duet. When a change of key occurs between numbers, Philidor provides a modulatory tag in the bass, as may be seen on p. 30 at the end of the passepied. These indications, taken together, demonstrate that the mascarade was intended to proceed in a continuous flow of music and movement from beginning to end, with little or no pause between numbers. There are very few places in the work which might permit interruption by applause, the only obvious spot being the end of the drunk dance (VI), where a bit of time is needed for the two dancers to retire while the next five take their places. The mascarade is very clearly not constructed around a series of individual numbers intended to show off the talents of a particular singer or dancer; rather, what matters, even in a work as frivolous as this one, is dramatic continuity. Philidor's aesthetic stance on this point is identical to Lully's: Lully's opera scores are replete with compositional and notational continuities that undoubtedly served as a model for Philidor.

Another area in which Philidor clearly followed in the Lullian tradition was in having instrumentalists appear on stage with the other characters (see chapter 1). The librettos for Lully's works, however, rarely convey much information beyond the names of the performers and an occasional vague remark about roles or staging. The precise movement

---

[38] The art of acting in the eighteenth century, particularly as it was practiced in tragedy and serious opera, has been the subject of several studies by Dene Barnett, most notably "The performance practice of acting" and *The Art of Gesture*. Barnett's findings suggest that eighteenth-century tragic acting was quite static and for expression relied primarily on gestures with the hands, arms, and eyes. The applicability of his sources, most of which come from the late eighteenth or even early nineteenth century, to a comic seventeenth-century mascarade is unclear.

indications in *Le Mariage de la Grosse Cathos* are thus particularly welcome. Although the manuscript does not explicitly assign a role to the musicians, they obviously had one – that of the village dance band, whose job it is to provide music for festivities such as weddings. In a similar mascarade, *Le Lendemain de la Noce de Village*, composed in 1700 by Philidor's son (see chapter 2), the members of the oboe band are identified as "garçons de la noce"; the musicians in *Le Mariage de la Grosse Cathos* were undoubtedly conceived of in the same way and costumed appropriately.

The oboes fulfill a double function in this work. When they stand in their home positions on the two sides of the stage, they are viewed as part of the village community and recede into the background, both visual and aural, while individual actions take place center stage. Within the artificial world of musical theatre, where speech is replaced by song, the instrumentalists support the artifice by providing the necessary musical accompaniment to the singers' words. From this position they also accompany the small group dances. When, on the other hand, the oboes share the center stage with the dancers, they call attention both to their reality as musicians and to their participation in the life of the community. The places where the oboes become visually prominent (dances I, VIII, IX, and X) are ones which in real wedding festivities require music: processionals, recessionals, and dances of communal celebration; the musicians' contribution to the community thus becomes part of the subject of the dance. This idea, apparent in all four choreographies, comes particularly to the fore in the passepied (dance VIII), where the dancing villagers make visible their connectedness with the village musicians by first encircling and then weaving among them.

Like the singers, the oboes always move in time to the music; Favier even specifies which foot they all step out on. Clearly he saw the singers and oboes as participants in the overall choreography of the work. And even more clearly, as all of the above discussion has shown, Favier designed his choreographies not as diversions within a fundamentally vocal framework, but as an essential part of a dramatic structure that integrated music, dance, and poetry. In this entertainment dance is central, not peripheral. It was conceived not as an interruption of the drama for the sake of pure spectacle, but as an integral part of the fabric of the work, one that participates in the expression of the work's meaning. The expressive goals of this particular work are admittedly modest, but the integrative stance that supports them was fundamental to French aesthetics, not peculiar to Favier. Because this mascarade presents an unprecedented opportunity to grasp a late seventeenth-century work whole, it becomes important to abstract Favier's general choreographic practices in order to find out which ones might be applicable to other theatrical genres. The following observations do not offer detailed analyses of the movements in the dances (for which see chapter 6), but rather Favier's general approaches to the setting of dance to music.

1. In *Le Mariage de la Grosse Cathos* purely instrumental pieces are choreographed, as are some of the choruses, but solo vocal numbers and duets are not. This is true despite the fact that several of the airs in the mascarade have eminently danceable rhythms. However, as was shown above, a vocal air may nonetheless be related dramatically to an adjacent dance piece, thus juxtaposing poetic and choreographic modes of expression. A similar phenomenon seems to happen in the divertissements of Lully's operas, which often contain rounded structures in which an instrumental dance is surrounded by two verses of a vocal air or duet set to the same or very similar dance music. The libretto may contain incomplete staging indications on the order of "Arbas et la Nourrice . . . viennent mesler leurs chants avec les Dançes" (*Cadmus et Hermione*, V, 3) that make it clear that dancers are to participate in such a tripartite unit, but that fail to specify how or when. The example of *Le Mariage de la Grosse Cathos* suggests that the dancers would have performed during the instrumental statement of the air but have remained motionless during the vocal section.

2. The criteria for whether a chorus is choreographed seem to depend on the dramatic situation and the text, and a variety of choreographic approaches is possible. The first

chorus ("Allons, accourons tous") invites – and receives – pantomimic treatment. The second chorus ("Chantons le choix charmant"), despite its very danceable rhythm, is not choreographed, probably because it occurs in the middle of a solo vocal section and because its key word, "Chantons" ("Let's sing") suggests a non-choreographic mode of expression. The third chorus ("Dans ce grand jour") is not choreographed either, but as already has been seen, it serves to round off the three dances that precede it. The fourth chorus ("Passons toujours la vie") sums up the divertissement in both song and dance. The last chorus, the *charivari*, has no notated choreography, but was probably danced in a very free way.

3. There are at least two kinds of dance within the mascarade, one mimetic, the other abstract. In the first chorus and the "Air des ivrognes" the dancers imitate movements observable in ordinary life – running in the first case, drunken staggering in the second – although they do so through recognizable dance steps. The other dances do not imitate non-choreographic gestures and are constructed largely of familiar dance steps and abstract figures such as squares and circles. This does not, however, mean that their content is neutral. On the contrary, through a complex web involving number and identity of the dancers, steps, figures, and the relationships between a dance and its neighboring pieces, these choreographies may express ideas such as community or courtship – or even a man's last bachelor fling.

The *charivari* hints at a third kind of dance, a stepless, pantomimic style to which a number of contemporary texts allude. In a discussion of Lully's operas that dates from 1719, the Abbé Dubos singled out for praise those dance scenes "which had scarce any dancing movements, but were only composed of gestures, external signs, and in a word, of a dumb show," citing among other examples the funeral scenes in *Psyché* and *Alceste* and the depiction of the shivering people who live in frozen climes from *Isis*. "The latter was composed entirely of gestures and external signs of people shivering with cold; and had not so much as a single step of our ordinary dance."[39]

4. In instrumental pieces the dance is continuous for as long as the music sounds, but in choral pieces it may be disjunct. Here the choreography appears to depend upon the structure of the piece and the meaning of the text. In "Passons toujours la vie" (dance IX) the dancers alternate phrases with the singers and move only during the instrumental passages up until the last phrase when everyone participates. In "Allons, accourons tous" (dance II) which is sung throughout, the dancers react to the text, running or freezing in place depending on the words being sung.

5. The number of dancers within a given choreography may vary from phrase to phrase or from section to section. In "Passons toujours la vie" (dance IX) each of the four choreographed phrases uses a different group of dancers: first the four women; second the four men, who rejoin the women after two bars; third a solo man; and last all eight dancers. In this case sung phrases intervene between the danced passages, but in the second part of the passepied (dance VIIIB), the women and men alternate consecutive phrases.

6. A single piece of music, when performed more than once in succession, may encompass more than one choreography. This phenomenon occurs four times in the mascarade: in the opening and closing pavanes (dances I and X), the rigaudon (VII), and the passepied (VIII). The pavane is played three times at each occurrence; in both instances, two repetitions of the music serve as a march for all the performers, while one repetition features only the eight dancers. The passepied begins as a line dance for nine, but one phrase into the second playing of the music becomes a figure dance for eight and remains such until the end. The rigaudon music is played twice, once for five dancers, the second time as a solo for one of them. Continuity is provided not only by the music but by maintaining at least some of the same performers between sections. The passepied is further unified by the reuse of similar figures in the two parts of the dance. Nonetheless, the stringing together of different yet related choreographies to repetitions of the same music has many potential ramifications for the works of Lully. It certainly provides a

---

[39] Dubos, *Réflexions critiques* (trans. Nugent), pp. 186–8.

useful model for entrées in the court ballets, where the dance pieces may be as short as eleven bars, but for which the descriptions in the librettos suggest so much action that multiple repetitions of the music must have been necessary.

7. The choreographies in the mascarade vary the number of dancers required from one to nine, but tend to favor an even number. Leaving aside the processionals for the entire cast and without counting the oboes, there are four and a half dances a8, three dances a2, and one a4. For an odd number of dancers, however, there are only half of a dance a9, one dance a5, and two unnotated solos, one of them only a phrase long. This distribution suggests that Favier favored groupings that lent themselves to symmetrical treatment. In fact, his dances for eight often use figures that subdivide the dancers into two groups of four, which are further subdivided into couples. By way of comparison, Feuillet's "Ballet de neuf danseurs" (from the collection of Feuillet's own dances published with *Chorégraphie*), the only theatrical choreography in Feuillet notation for more than two dancers, exhibits similar tendencies. The nine men never dance all together: the dance alternates phrases performed by one, four, or eight.

8. The two notated choreographies requiring an odd number of dancers are quite different, both from the other dances in the mascarade and from each other. The rigaudon (dance VII) sets one dancer apart from the other four through differences both of figures and steps. The first part of the passepied (VIIIA) arranges the nine dancers in an open chain that winds through the performing space. These two choreographies suggest that the use of an odd number of dancers solicited special choreographic treatment.

9. Neither of the two solo choreographies called for in the manuscript (in dances VII and IX) is notated. The first was performed by Philbert in the role of La Couture, the second by "un paysan." Perhaps the two improvised their solos. Or perhaps, as has been suggested, solo dances were choreographed by the performers themselves, not by the choreographer of the rest of the work. These two dances may well have been quite virtuosic: there are a number of solo theatrical dances in Feuillet notation that showcase the technical prowess that professional male dancers possessed.

10. The greater the number of dancers, the more complex the figures and the simpler the steps. Conversely, the smaller the number of dancers, the simpler the figures and the more technically demanding the steps. The duets are thus the most virtuosic of the dances in the mascarade, while in the large group dances, choreographic interest is concentrated in the patterns the dancers trace through the space.

Many of these observations about Favier's choreography, as well as the observations about staging made above, are discernible only because they are based upon a complete theatrical work for which movement has been notated in very great detail. Regrettably, nothing comparable has been preserved in Feuillet notation. So whereas comparisons between individual Favier dances and dances by other choreographers are possible, thanks to the preservation of over 335 dances in Feuillet notation, there exists no other fully choreographed work that may be compared with *Le Mariage de la Grosse Cathos*. In the absence of the kind of mutual reflection that two such works might have provided, it will be necessary to make use of other kinds of sources – ballet and opera librettos, scores, archival documents, write-ups of performances, iconography, not to mention the practical experiences of people working in the field of reconstruction – in order to see the extent to which Favier's practices were part of a larger performing tradition, and to what extent individual. It is already clear, however, that there are numerous points of contact between this mascarade and the works of the man who dominated French musical theatre, Jean-Baptiste Lully. Surely Favier and Philidor, both of whom had spent virtually all of their professional lives working under Lully's direction, could not but have been shaped by him. In fact in Philidor's case, Lully's influence is easily demonstrable (see chapter 4). In terms of the visual side of the performance, none of the information provided by this manuscript contradicts anything that is known about the staging and the choreography of Lully's theatrical works; on the contrary, the information about Favier's practices helps make greater sense of the fragmentary evidence from other contemporary sources.

Even though *Le Mariage de la Grosse Cathos* is a comic mascarade, a lighthearted work with no pretensions to grandeur, it takes seriously certain fundamental aesthetic principles. One is the emphasis on dramatic continuity, a continuity that is expressed not only in the work's construction but in its choreography. Another is the integral role of dance, not as decoration or diversion, but as one of the fundamental modes of the work's expression. Surely Philidor's and Favier's artistic precepts could profitably be scrutinized for their relevance to performances in the royal châteaux and on the stage of the Académie Royale de Musique.

4

The music

The dual origins of *Le Mariage de la Grosse Cathos* in the *ballet de cour* and opera are readily apparent in its music. The burlesque subject and its concomitant musical elements – vocal scoring for humorous effect, the use of wind instruments, comic dances – come from a long tradition of carnival mascarades and ballet scenes built around rustic characters; the vocal forms, however, derive from French operatic practices. In both cases, the overwhelming influence on Philidor's compositional style was the music of the recently departed Jean-Baptiste Lully. Like his model's operas and late ballets, Philidor's mascarade strings together a supple progression of recitatives, airs, duets, choruses, and dance numbers that flow easily from one into the other. Philidor's pieces, however, are all on a miniature scale. The vocal writing is restrained – primarily syllabic and moving largely by step – and the choral textures are homophonic. The harmonic vocabulary is conservative and relies heavily on root-position chords. The work is almost entirely in two keys, G major and C major, but the rapid pacing and frequent changes of musical textures keep the work lively.

VOCAL SCORING

All nine of the singers in the mascarade, including those who sang the three female roles, were men. The clef usage and range of the parts shows the following distribution of voice types: three *hautes-contre* (Madame Dupont, Maître Simon, Dame Ragonde); two *tailles* (Monsieur Dupont, Gripetout); one *basse-taille* (Cathos); and three *basses* (La Couture, Abbé du Plessis, the *garçon de la noce*). The *haute-contre*, a peculiarly French phenomenon, was a high natural tenor voice with a range close to that of an alto.[1] It was always sung by men (French female singers did not sing in this low a range at the time) and was used both for many male roles in operas and as the second highest voice part in a four-part choral texture. The other three voice types correspond to tenor, baritone, and bass respectively. The ranges demanded by the parts in the mascarade are as follows:[2]

haute-contre (notated in alto clef)	g–b'
taille (tenor clef)	$f\sharp$–$f\sharp'$
basse-taille (baritone clef)	d–$f\sharp'$
basse (bass clef)	G–d'

The voice type conspicuous by its absence is the *dessus* or soprano. In French operatic practice, the *dessus* part was identified with female roles; solo *dessus* parts, Lully's

---

[1] See Zaslaw, "The enigma of the haute-contre." Zaslaw concluded that "the haute-contre was a high tenor who normally sang in a natural voice but occasionally was heard using falsetto at the top of the range." In recent years a number of tenors have begun to specialize in *haute-contre* roles.

[2] The actual sounding pitch may have been as much as a whole tone lower than these pitches suggest: French chamber and operatic pitch at the end of the seventeenth century was quite low, with a' equal to approximately 392–400 Hz (by way of comparison, when $a' = 440$ Hz, $g' = 392$ Hz). See Haynes, "Bach's pitch standards," especially pp. 85–7 and 95.

heroines, for example, were performed by women. In choruses, however, men singing falsetto sometimes reinforced the predominantly female *dessus* section, and in the French royal chapel it was primarily male singers – falsettists, boys, and castrati – who sang the soprano parts.[3] In the ballets and comedy-ballets he composed before devoting himself to opera, Lully occasionally assigned a comic role to a man singing soprano; one such is the nattering lawyer in *Monsieur de Pourceaugnac* (1669). Thus it certainly would have been feasible for Philidor to find men among the king's musical establishment capable of singing soprano for the female roles in *Le Mariage de la Grosse Cathos*, had he so desired. However, the humor in the vocal scoring of the mascarade derives not from men dressed as women singing in high voices, but from just the opposite: men in women's clothes singing with unambiguously male sonorities.

In this mascarade all of the singers served in a double capacity, that is, both as soloists and as chorus members; their combined voices made up the chorus without further vocal reinforcements. There are a number of points that make this dual function clear. First, the dance notation shows the presence of only nine singers, the same as the number of soloists. Second, the clefs used for the rather unorthodox chorus are the same as those representing the solo singers. Third, none of the solo roles is very large, sometimes being limited to only a few bars in a single "scene" – Monsieur and Madame Dupont, for example, sing solo only at the very beginning of the mascarade – yet all the soloists remain on stage throughout. In a work on the scale of *Le Mariage de la Grosse Cathos*, this kind of economy of personnel makes sense, and the vocal forces provided are certainly adequate to fill out the choruses. If in the ensemble numbers the soloists sang the same parts that they did in their solo sections, then the distribution of parts in the choruses must have been three *hautes-contre*, two tenors, one baritone, and three basses.[4]

INSTRUMENTAL SCORING

As can be seen from the facsimile, no instrumentation is specified in the musical score, but four different instrumental groupings are apparent: (1) an unfigured bass line, used to accompany most of the vocal solos and duets; (2) a trio texture, notated for two treble parts and bass, used in airs in which the bass voice and instrumental bass double each other; (3) a four-part texture used both for the purely instrumental dance pieces and as accompaniment to most of the choruses; and (4) a seven-part instrumental scoring used only once, in the *charivari*. The dance notation provides a point of departure for interpreting the score: it indicates the presence on stage of nine *hautbois*; no other instrumentalists are mentioned in either part of the manuscript. The intersection of the information from the two parts of the manuscript raises questions as to the makeup of a group of nine *hautbois*, the distribution of the instruments into the textures mentioned above, and whether any other instruments – strings or continuo instruments, for example – might have been involved in the musical realization of the score.

In the French musical establishment, the term "hautbois" was used generically to indicate all members of the double-reed family from oboe to bassoon, just as the term "violon" included all string instruments of the violin family. Thus the ensemble known as the *douze grands hautbois du roi* did not consist merely of high instruments, but incorporated a full texture from treble to bass. This group, like other French wind ensembles, played as a four-part consort, in distinction to string ensembles which generally played in five parts. In documents of the period the four parts were labeled, from top to bottom, *dessus de hautbois*, *haute-contre de hautbois*, *taille de hautbois*, and *basse de hautbois*. Similarly the members of the five-part string ensemble were called *dessus de violon*, *haute-contre de violon*, *taille de violon*, *quinte de violon*, and *basse de violon*, the fifth

---
[3] Regarding Lully's theatrical practice, see Rosow, "Performing a choral dialogue," pp. 326–7; regarding the royal chapel, see Sawkins, "Who sang the soprano?"
[4] In practice these choruses have a five-part texture, the *dessus* line lacking in the vocal parts being supplied by the highest oboe. For further discussion of this point, see below, p. 76.

part being the one just above the bass. In addition to their participation in the full consort of double-reed instruments, oboes and bassoons were scored for in two other ways: to double the outer voices of the five-part string ensemble; and in a trio texture, with two oboes and a bassoon. These last two textures were used frequently in Lully's operas, and the prominence given to oboes was an important characteristic of the French orchestral sound.

The use of oboe consorts in outdoor performances where loud instruments were required or in important ceremonial events such as coronations is well documented. A portion of the repertoire used by the wind ensembles of the *grande écurie* at such events is even preserved in a volume copied by Philidor *l'aîné*;[5] this contains primarily marches and other military airs, many of them identified as "pour les hautbois" and set in the standard four-part scoring, often with the addition of a drum part. Oboe ensembles also performed in theatrical works, particularly when the subject was pastoral. So strong was the association between rustic settings and woodwind instruments, that terms such as *concert champêtre* or *harmonie rustique* served as a kind of shorthand to indicate scoring for woodwinds such as oboes, recorders, flutes, and musettes. Such ensembles were virtually obligatory when the subject involved a village wedding, as, for example, in the ballet *L'Amour Malade* (1657), the mascarade *Les Nopces de Village* (1663), or the fourth act of the opera *Roland* (1685), all works by Lully whose librettos call for rustic instruments in the appropriate scenes.

Beyond the general indication for woodwinds, however, the precise instrumentation of a given piece is often difficult to determine in light of the paucity of instrumental indications in scores.[6] Nonetheless, it is clear that Lully made at least occasional use of the four-part oboe band as well as of the more frequent trio of two oboes and bassoon. *Les Festes de l'Amour et de Bacchus*, Lully's first work for the Académie Royale de Musique, contains a "Symphonie pour les hautbois et les musettes qui se répondent" in the prologue. The score here is in four parts instead of the five of the surrounding pieces. In the "Entrée des Zéphirs" in the second act of the opera *Atys* (1676), the five-part string orchestra alternates phrases with a four-part consort of oboes. Similarly, in Philidor's own *Canal de Versailles* (1687) a reduction in texture from five instrumental parts to four occurs for a "Simphonie de flustes pour Apollon" and again within a chorus for an instrumental interlude played by oboes. In all of these cases the reduction in texture is indicative of a change in scoring from strings to winds. Thus the four-part scoring in *Le Mariage de la Grosse Cathos*, particularly when taken together with the village wedding subject, would strongly suggest the use of an oboe band even if the word "hautbois" were not mentioned in the dance notation.

The question of exactly what kind of double-reed instrument was meant by the word "oboe" in the seventeenth century has caused much ink to flow. It was in France during this period that the Renaissance shawm was remodeled into what is now known as the Baroque oboe. The difficulty in charting the change lies in the fact that the French used the same term, "hautbois," throughout the century for the instruments of this family, regardless of their position in the evolutionary line of development; thus French terminology is useless for establishing when the shawm became the oboe. According to a highly speculative, yet nonetheless extremely influential article by Joseph Marx, the Baroque oboe was "invented" before 1660. More recently, Bruce Haynes has convincingly argued that there was not an abrupt transition from shawm to oboe but rather a gradual evolution, and that the "prototypical baroque oboe" can only unambiguously be documented starting in 1688, although it must have been in existence somewhat earlier,

---

[5] F-Pn (Musique) Rés. F. 671: *Partition de plusieurs marches et batteries de tambour tant françoises qu'etrangères, avec les airs de fifre et de hautbois à 3 et 4 parties et pl[usieu]rs marches de timballes et de trompettes à cheval avec les airs du carousel en 1686, et les appels et fanfares de trompe pour la chasse. Recueilly par Philidor lainé . . . l'an 1705.* Sandman, "Wind band music," a dissertation on the subject of this manuscript, includes transcriptions of all the pieces.

[6] The most extensive study of the subject is J. Eppelsheim's book, *Das Orchester in den Werken Jean-Baptiste Lullys* (regarding Lully's scoring for oboes, see pp. 103–13); see also La Gorce, "Some notes."

perhaps by 1680.[7] Given the 1688 date of *Le Mariage de la Grosse Cathos*, oboes or some kind of transitional instrument seem likelier than shawms to have been used in the mascarade, although the use of shawms cannot be ruled out and perhaps would not have seemed out of place in a burlesque work of this nature.[8]

A related question concerns the choice of instrument for each of the four parts. In this mascarade, as in the four-part scores of the *écurie* repertoire and of Lully's stage works, the parts are notated in four different clefs: from top to bottom, G^1 (French violin clef), C^1, C^2, and F^4 (bass clef) which are, respectively, a fifth, a third, and a fifth apart. Each corresponds to one of the four parts listed in documents describing oboe bands, that is, *dessus*, *haute-contre*, *taille*, and *basse* and each has a progressively lower range in this work: the *dessus* from d' to a'', the *haute-contre* from b to d'', the *taille* from $f\#$ to c'' and the *basse* from C to d'. The differentiation in names, clefs, and range suggests that four different sizes of instruments played the parts. Whereas there is no doubt that there were at least three members of the oboe family in use in France at this time – a treble instrument in C, a *taille* or tenor in F, and the bassoon – the possibility that there existed an intermediate instrument – a *haute-contre de hautbois*, probably pitched in A – has only recently been proposed. Researchers who posit the existence of only three instruments hypothesize that the French oboe band made use of either two treble instruments, one tenor, and one bass, or one treble, two tenors, and one bass over its four parts. A 2-1-1 distribution, however, is contradicted for both *Le Mariage de la Grosse Cathos* and the repertoire of music for oboe band from the *grande écurie* by the range of the *haute-contre* part, which descends below the range of a treble oboe.[9] A 1-2-1 distribution, on the other hand, can accommodate these pieces, but raises question as to why there should be distinctions of nomenclature, range, and clef if the instruments playing the two inner parts were identical. (In contexts when two identical instruments were desired, such as a trio texture when the two upper parts are to be played on treble oboe, both lines use the same clef.) It seems likelier that in France, at least, the oboe band made use of four different sizes of instrument, not three.[10]

The above discussion shows that the four-part ensemble scored for in *Le Mariage de la Grosse Cathos* was a well-established one, even if uncertainties remain regarding some aspects of its instrumentation. The fact that there are no pieces in the mascarade in a five-part instrumental texture strongly supports the implications of the dance notation that the instrumental music was supplied entirely by the nine-member oboe band, with no string instruments involved. Although it is not impossible that a string ensemble could have played from somewhere in the room besides the stage area, there is no evidence in

---

[7] See Haynes, "Lully and the rise of the oboe." Marx's article, "The tone of the Baroque oboe" (see especially pp. 10–15) was published in 1951 and has been widely cited ever since; its premises regarding the supposed "invention" of the oboe do not, however, stand up to scrutiny (see Harris-Warrick, "A few thoughts").

[8] Shawms and oboes coexisted for several decades. In her above-mentioned dissertation, Sandman demonstrates that considerations of range permit performance of this repertoire on either shawms and their relatives such as the dulcian, or on oboes and bassoons ("Wind band music," pp. 215–28 and 238–45). Haynes in "Lully and the rise of the oboe" makes the same observation about the treble parts scored for oboe in Lully's stage works. We have chosen to use the words "oboe" and "bassoon" throughout this book for convenience and do not intend the terms to be construed as eliminating shawms or transitional instruments from consideration.

[9] In the repertoire of pieces for *hautbois* found in Philidor's manuscript for the *écurie* (see n. 5 above), the ranges of the four parts are as follows (Sandman, "Wind band music," p. 226): *dessus*, c'-c'''; *haute-contre*, b-f''; *taille*, f-d''; *basse*, C-f'; as for the music in *Le Mariage de la Grosse Cathos*, both the bottom and top range get progressively lower for each part.

[10] The possible existence of an *haute-contre de hautbois* was raised by Haynes in n. 24 of his article "Lully and the rise of the oboe," on the basis of conversations with oboist and maker Marc Ecochard; the issue is discussed at greater length in Harris-Warrick, "A few thoughts." A thorough investigation of the organological questions is underway by Marc Ecochard, who has also developed a prototype for such an instrument.

It has been suggested that the *haute-contre de hautbois* might have been pitched in G rather than in A; this would solve the problem of the one piece in the mascarade (the "Air des ivrognes") that is in G minor, which on an instrument in A necessitates fingerings equivalent to playing in $B\flat$ minor, an uncomfortable key on a Baroque instrument. Bruce Haynes, however, finds the *haute-contre* part in the "Air des ivrognes" playable on an instrument pitched in A (personal communication).

either portion of the manuscript to suggest such an eventuality. Certainly an oboe band was not only adequate to the musical demands of the score, the use of oboes for at least some of the music was virtually obligatory given the rustic subject of this work.[11]

One of the pieces in the mascarade provides important clues as to how the nine "oboes" may have been divided on the parts. The final chorus of the mascarade, the *charivari*, is scored for an ensemble consisting of four vocal and seven instrumental parts performed in alternation with a vocal solo supported by three instrumental parts (see the facsimile, pp. 31–9).[12] The clefs of the seven-part instrumental texture read, from top to bottom, G^1, C^1, C^2, F^4, F^4, F^4, C^3. The last of these eternally repeats the same pitch; it is, clearly, a part for the *tambour*, the side or snare drum that frequently appears as a fifth part in the oboe pieces from the *écurie*.[13] The top four parts represent the grouping of clefs familiar from the other pieces for oboe band. The remaining two parts, both in bass clef, play simplified versions of the bass of the four-part ensemble, one at the octave below, the other at yet another octave below wherever possible. In the trio sections which alternate with the full texture, the two G^1 clefs indicate that at least two treble instruments are required. (The notation of the *second dessus* part on the same staff as the *haute-contre* part with an intervening change of clef [see, for example, p. 32 of the facsimile] was a space-saving measure common to both manuscript and printed scores of the period. It should not be taken as an indication that the *haute-contre* and *second dessus* parts were played by the same instrument.) Thus in the *charivari* eight of the nine instrumentalists can be accounted for: one drummer, two treble oboes, three bassoons, and a player on each of the remaining two inner parts. The ninth player must have doubled one of the parts, although certainly not either the drum, which was used in the *charivari* only, or the bass, which was already heavily reinforced. It seems unlikely that he would have doubled the *taille* part which is the least important of the four, although he might have doubled the *haute-contre* which is more melodic and often moves in parallel thirds with the *dessus*. The most likely possibility is that he added a third instrument to the treble line, thus providing parity in number, as well as more balance in volume, between the highest and lowest instruments. Such reinforcement of the outer parts was typical of French string ensembles: the distribution of players among the five parts of the king's *grands violons* for the years 1692–94, for example, was 7-4-4-2-8; similar proportions may be found among the *petits violons* and in the string section of the Paris Opéra orchestra.[14]

Given that the instrumentalists were on stage during the entire mascarade and probably operating in a very small area, it seems unlikely that the players could have changed instruments during the course of the performance. It is difficult to imagine that one of the bassoonists could have tucked his instrument under his arm and taken something else out of his pocket to play in one of the other pieces. Thus the distribution of the wind instruments in the *charivari* is likely to have been the same as for the four-part pieces in the work, that is, probably 3-1-1-3. The drummer presumably marched with the

---

[11] Modern performances of this work have shown how rich a sonority Philidor's writing for oboe band produces, one certainly in no need of fuller instrumental support.

[12] The *eight* instrumental parts indicated on the first page of the *charivari* (facsimile, p. 31) result from a copying error on Philidor's part. On the sixth line down from the top of the chorus (notated in C^1), instead of copying in the *haute-contre* part Philidor began entering the *taille* part, a mistake undoubtedly due to the fact that the upbeat and first measure of both parts sit on the middle line of the staff (they are, in fact, a third apart given the different clefs). He recognized his error by the fourth full measure where he decided not to erase what he had written, but to turn this part into one that fit in with the surrounding harmony (the repeated g' is consonant with the only two chords, tonic and dominant in C major, used in this passage) and to add the *haute-contre* part at the bottom of the page beneath the bracketed system. In the last measure of the page he brought the accidentally added part into conformity with the true *haute-contre* part in order to prepare for the page turn; starting on p. 32 the seven instrumental parts are correctly notated. This chorus is notated for only four instrumental parts in the F-Pa score, but the *haute-contre* part, as seen here on the bottom of the page, appears there in its proper place.

This passage is not the only one that gave Philidor trouble on this page; see, for example, the erasures in the *taille* in bar 4 and in the uppermost bass part in bars 4–6.

[13] For a discussion of the *tambour* in this repertoire, see Sandman, "Indications of snare-drum technique."

[14] La Gorce, "Some notes," p. 111 and the same author's "L'Académie Royale de Musique."

others but remained silent until the plot demanded his participation in the noisy wedding serenade. It is tempting to imagine that Philidor himself might have served as drummer; the *tambour* was one of the instruments he played, and in this capacity he would have been free to direct the other performers, drumstick, instead of the traditional rolled piece of paper, in hand.[15]

In the mascarade the full oboe band played for the dance movements and provided the accompaniment for the choruses. Fewer instrumentalists were required to accompany the vocal solos and duets. One standard texture, used in four places in the mascarade and also common in Lully's operas, involves a solo bass voice accompanied by an instrumental trio. In it the instrumental bass doubles the voice while two treble parts, both notated in the same clef, weave their melodic lines above. (It is this texture which is labeled "bass air" in the outline of the mascarade in chapter 3.) In Lully's works a trio of strings generally played for the bass airs, although an ensemble consisting of two oboes and bassoon, as in this mascarade, was not uncommon. Given that there were at most three treble oboes among the nine members of the oboe band for the mascarade, the trio textures were probably performed one on a part. A light scoring also seems indicated in order to avoid overbalancing the single singer. Purely instrumental trios, which Lully called "ritournelles" in his theatrical works where they are used in association with vocal airs, do not appear in *Le Mariage de la Grosse Cathos*.

The vocal duets and those solos for voices other than bass have still less accompaniment: here the vocal parts are supported only by an unfigured instrumental bass line. Under the operatic conventions of the period, one would expect the melodic bass to be supplemented by chordal continuo instruments such as theorbo or harpsichord. It has already been pointed out, however, that the only references to instruments in the manuscript are to "hautbois." This means that the solo singers would have been accompanied by bassoon alone, since no chordal instrument seems to have been available to provide additional support. In order to determine whether this was indeed the case, it is necessary to consider certain practical matters, to examine the internal evidence of the mascarade, and to compare Philidor's practices here with those in his other theatrical compositions.

The absence of figures from the bass line would not in itself prevent a competent theorbo player or harpsichordist from realizing the part. In practical terms, there are two ways in which a chordal instrument might have been accommodated in this work. Of the nine instrumentalists on stage, the scoring of the *charivari* accounts for eight; perhaps the ninth person played not the oboe, but theorbo, lute, or guitar. Alternatively, perhaps there was a group of continuo instruments to the side of the stage that played only for the solo singers, leaving the dances and choruses to the oboes.[16] Neither of these alternatives can be entirely discounted, but a number of factors make them seem unlikely.

Given the small space on stage allotted to the instrumentalists (see chapter 3), a marching continuo player would have had certain practical difficulties to confront, depending on the size of his instrument. These would not necessarily have constituted an insurmountable obstacle, as eye-witness accounts of a similar event attest: in a mascarade performed for a ball during the 1700 carnival season representing a great lord in his menagerie, the theorbo player not only had to march around the room while playing, but did so in a tiger costume, in which he accompanied a duet sung by two parrots.[17] However, this theorbo player appears to have been the only instrumentalist who

---

[15] The libretto and the score show that Philidor played the *tambourin* in *Le Vaisseau Marchand*, one of his mascarades from the 1700 carnival season. In three other mascarades from the same season Philidor was also assigned instruments that may not have played all the time and thus might have allowed him more freedom to conduct: musette in *La Noce de Village* and *Le Lendemain de la Noce*; *basse de cromorne* in *Le Roi de la Chine*.

[16] Sadler in "The role of the keyboard continuo" has argued persuasively that continuo instruments did not generally play in dance pieces in French theatrical music.

[17] See Sourches, *Mémoires* VI, pp. 231–3 and the *Mercure galant* (February 1700), pp. 222–6.

participated in the parade; the other, unspecified instrumentalists were those who also played for the rest of the ball, presumably from the side of the room. The theorbist thus functioned as a single continuo player in relation only to the singers, not as part of a larger instrumental ensemble. This separation between continuo instruments on the one hand and string or wind ensembles on the other shows up in the groupings of instrumentalists listed in some of the librettos for Lully's ballets; it appears to have been a functional, not merely an administrative, distinction. In terms of *Le Mariage de la Grosse Cathos*, it thus does not seem likely that a single continuo player would have been considered part of an ensemble of *hautbois*. The integrity of the performing groups of the period suggests, particularly in cases such as this modest mascarade, that they functioned as a unit, not as a mixed ensemble. Thus if any continuo instrument or instruments were used by Philidor in this mascarade, it seems more probable that they functioned as a separate group from the oboes. This manuscript, however, presents the mascarade very much as a self-contained unit. There is no suggestion in either the score or the dance notation that any performers beyond the twenty-eight already identified were involved.

In further support of this view, it is instructive to examine Philidor's own practices, both as a copyist and as a composer. Philidor's theatrical works (listed in chapter 2) fall into two groups: the first represents multi-act works with large numbers of singers and dancers and a full string ensemble supplemented by winds and percussion; the other is of brief mascarades such as *Le Mariage de la Grosse Cathos* that involve reduced instrumental forces. The one fully surviving example of the first group is *Le Canal de Versailles*, a ballet performed during the summer of 1687. In this score the vocal airs and recitative have figures in the bass line, although the dance pieces do not. This pattern of figuring also prevails in the Lully ballet scores that Philidor copied in his role as royal music librarian. In large works of this type, continuo accompaniment of the vocal music appears to be expected.

The situation is quite different in Philidor's mascarades, of which a group composed for the carnival season of 1700 is preserved. Like *Le Mariage de la Grosse Cathos*, at least some of these works require only a few musicians who are on stage with the other performers. Both the librettos and the scores list the names and functions of the instrumentalists involved, and the instrumental scoring accords with this information, even when it is quite unusual. The libretto for *Le Roy de la Chine*, for example, calls for four *tailles de hautbois*, two *tailles de violon*, one *basse de cromorne*, one *basse de violon*, two bassoons, and one *tambour*. The score uses only those clefs appropriate to such an assortment of instruments, that is, C^2 for the *tailles*, F^4 for the *basses* and bassoons, and C^3 for the drum; for some of the pieces it specifies which groups are to play which lines. In the *Mascarade des Amazones* this low sonority is replaced by a high one: four *dessus de hautbois*, three *dessus de violon*, two each of *tailles de hautbois* and *tailles de violon*, and one drummer, notated in the appropriate clefs of G^1 (*dessus*), C^2 (*tailles*), and C^3 (*timballes*). As in *Le Mariage de la Grosse Cathos*, nothing in the scores of these mascarades suggests that any instruments beyond the ones listed were involved.[18] And, once again, none of the bass lines in any of these mascarades is figured. The relative simplicity of the works seems to allow for a lean instrumental accompaniment, one that excluded a realized continuo part. Thus, unfamiliar as such a sound may be to our ears, the appropriate instrumental accompaniment for the vocal solos and duos in *Le Mariage de la Grosse Cathos* would appear to be bassoon alone.[19]

---

[18] The only musical source for these two and five other mascarades by Philidor and his relatives from the 1700 carnival is US-BE Ms. 455, a manuscript in the hand of Philidor himself. Although the instrumental indications – noted both in the scores and in the printed librettos – appear to be complete, the scores themselves are reduced, that is, only the outer parts are notated for the dance pieces.

[19] In performance the bassoon accompaniment works well, particularly when a Baroque bassoon with its full sound is used. Because only male voices sing in the mascarade, the gap in pitch between voice and instrumental bass is relatively narrow, and the absence of chordal accompaniment is less noticeable than it might be were a soprano singing.

VOCAL FORMS

Seventeenth-century French vocal music adhered closely to the rhythms and structures of the poetry on which it was based; for this reason it is important to begin any examination of the music with an understanding of the way the text is constructed. Although it is not known who wrote the libretto for the mascarade, the author adopted the norms for music theatre in evidence in the librettos Quinault wrote for Lully's operas.

A line in French poetry is defined not by a pattern of stresses that form metrical feet, as in English verse, but by the number of syllables it contains. French classical tragedies, most notably those of Corneille and Racine, adhered consistently to a single structure for each line, the twelve-syllable alexandrine, arranged in a sequence of rhymed couplets; Molière's comedies used either the alexandrine or, in some cases, prose. Verses written to be set to music, however, had considerably more rhythmic freedom in that they were composed as *vers libres* or free verse; this means that the number of syllables is allowed to vary from line to line. Although freer metrically, *vers libres* nonetheless conform to seventeenth-century conventions in their alternation of masculine and feminine rhymes. (The latter refers to rhyming words, such as "cruelle" in the example below, in which the last syllable contains a mute "e"; this syllable is not counted for purposes of defining the meter, but it was pronounced in spoken drama and set as a separate syllable by seventeenth-century composers. In the diagram below it is indicated by a little cross.)[20] The following example from the mascarade, a quatrain with a rhyme scheme of *abba* that is set as an air for the Abbé du Plessis, gives a sense of the metrical variety which *vers libres* allowed. The variability – in this example between six and twelve syllables per line with no two lines having the same meter – is not a function of the comic subject; similar structures abound in the verses Quinault wrote for Lully's *tragédies en musique*. However, in this case the disjunction between a vocabulary borrowed from high theatre that is applied to low characters is definitely exploited for comic effect.

```
1  2  3  4  5   6  7  8  9  10 11 12 +
La Cou-tu-re souf-frait u-ne pei-ne cru-el-le

1  2  3  4  5  6  7  8 9 10
Pour la beau-té dont son cœur est é-pris.

 1  2  3   4 5  6 7 8 9
Mais la Gros-se Ca-thos est le prix

1  2  3   4  5   6 +
De son a-mour fi-del-le.
```

("La Couture was suffering a cruel pain / For the beauty of whom he is enamored. / But Grosse Cathos is the reward / For his faithful love.")

Because the text setting is almost exclusively syllabic in all of the vocal pieces, the variability in the number of syllables per line frequently results in phrases of unequal lengths. This particular quatrain is set as a very simple bass air in triple meter (facsimile, p. 5) moving mostly in quarter notes whose phrasing is nonetheless quite irregular: the first line of text is set to a five-bar phrase, the second to a four-bar phrase, while the third and fourth lines together make up a phrase of seven bars. In recitatives the flexibility of the poetic line is often reflected in changes of meter designed to insure that the important syllables, particularly rhymes, fall on downbeats. In the first recitative of the mascarade, for example (facsimile, p. 2), the time signature changes eight times in fifteen bars.[21] This

---

[20] For a fuller discussion of the principles of French versification as they apply to the theatrical music of this period, see Rosow, "French Baroque recitative."

[21] The best overview of the complex question of the relationships between meters in French music, one that brings seventeenth-century theory and recent scholarship to bear on a number of specific passages from Lully's works, is Lois Rosow's article "The metrical notation of Lully's recitative."

flexible treatment of both air and recitative represents another point that Philidor's style has in common with Lully's.

The division between recitative and air does not necessarily respect poetic structures. La Couture's text just before the *charivari*, for example, consists of six lines rhymed *aab ccb*. The first three lines each contain six syllables, the next three five.

> Ma foi, c'est assez rire.
> Que chacun se retire
> Sans tumulte et sans bruit.
> L'amour me transporte,
> Je veux qu'on m'apporte
> Mon bonnet de nuit.

("Well, that's enough laughing. / Let everyone retire / Without commotion or noise. / Love carries me away, / I want someone to bring me / My nightcap.")

This text is not, however, treated musically as a single unit: the first line is set in recitative, the remaining five as an air. Nor does the treatment of texts as either air or recitative depend on a distinction between static moments and those that propel the action. The commentary on La Couture's success in love by the Abbé du Plessis cited above follows a similar comment regarding Cathos from Gripetout: "Elle obtient l'objet de ses feux / Que son sort est heureux" ("She has obtained the object of her desire / How happy is her lot"). Yet despite their similarity in content, Gripetout's text is set as recitative, the Abbé du Plessis's as an air. As in Lully's operas, it is not always apparent from the libretto alone what musical structures the composer will choose to use in setting the text.

The minimizing of textual distinctions between recitative and air is supported by the musical similarities between them. With the exception of the bass air, the texture is the same for both: solo voice supported by the bass line. There are no ritournelles or other instrumental interventions to set off the airs, and a syllabic declamation, closely wedded to the rhythms of the text, pertains in both. The melodic lines are similar in their general adherence to step-wise motion interspersed with a few larger intervals. The differences primarily concern metrical regularity and text repetition. Passages in recitative tend to change meter frequently and to use little or no text repetition. Airs and duets, on the other hand, have a regular meter and repeat portions of the text. The metrical regularity of airs and duets does not, however, preclude all changes of meter. Dame Ragonde's air ("Sortez, allez dans la rue," facsimile, p. 17) changes from duple to triple meter at the midpoint and the duet between Grosse Cathos and La Couture ("J'aime la panse," facsimile, p. 21) moves between triple and duple meter at regular intervals. As a concomitant of their more regular meter, the airs and duets have a more regular and somewhat more rapid harmonic rhythm than does the recitative, whose bass varies from long, sustained notes to running eighth notes. The vocal lines in airs also tend to have a more uniform rhythm, often moving in quarter and half notes, whereas recitative introduces somewhat more rhythmic variety by using shorter note values and more dotted patterns.

The patterns of textual and musical repetition define various formal structures in the airs and duets. Dame Ragonde's air ("Sortez," facsimile, p. 17) is unique in the context of the mascarade in that it has a standard binary form with both sections repeated, thus giving it an AABB structure. Much more frequent are pieces in which repetition of the text is exact while that of the music is not: the music maintains the rhythms of the original phrase but uses different pitches which may or may not maintain the initial melodic shape. The most common formal structure in which this kind of repetition appears is an extended binary form in which the second part of the text is repeated to the original rhythmic pattern (ABB');[22] examples include both of La Couture's airs ("Il est

---

[22] The term "extended binary air" is borrowed from James Anthony's studies of Lully's vocal airs; see in particular his two articles, "Lully's airs – French or Italian?" and "The musical structure of Lully's operatic airs."

vrai," and "Que chacun se retire," facsimile, pp. 8 and 30) and the air by the Abbé du Plessis cited above ("La Couture souffrait," facsimile, p. 5). Philidor undoubtedly adopted the extended binary air from Lully's works where it is very common; Lully in turn appears to have acquired it from mid-seventeenth-century Italian models. A variant on this structure may be seen in Grosse Cathos's air ("Je n'ai que faire d'opéra," facsimile, p. 7). Here both parts of the text are repeated to the same rhythms, yielding an AA'BB' form. In places where the text being set consists only of a couplet rather than four or more lines, the same principle obtains but the form may be even simpler: Madame Dupont's opening air ("Allons, mes enfants," facsimile, p. 2) has an AA' form, the duet between the Abbé du Plessis and Gripetout ("Si tu n'apaises mon courroux," facsimile, pp. 14–15) an AA'A" form.

The single exception to Philidor's practice of accompanying one or two voices with a bass line only, is the bass air. Since the singer doubles the instrumental bass line, melodic interest is provided by two treble parts, both notated in French violin clef, that play primarily in parallel thirds. The character of the vocal line is quite different from those in the other airs, particularly in its wider range – typically an octave and a fifth – and in the more extensive use of leaps that results from the tendency of Philidor's bass lines to provide the roots of chords. In *Le Mariage de la Grosse Cathos* Philidor used this texture for three bass airs and for two interpolations by a *garçon de la noce* within the choral *charivari* (facsimile, pp. 32–7). Like so many other aspects of Philidor's style, this texture is also found frequently in the works of Lully. In the latter's early operas, in fact, the bass air represents the only instance in which a solo voice is accompanied by anything other than a single bass line; it was not until 1679 in *Bellérophon* that Lully introduced orchestral accompaniment for some other solo vocal pieces.

In the two duets involving a bass singer ("Si tu n'apaises mon courroux" and "J'aime la panse," facsimile, pp. 14–15 and 21–2), the lower voice doubles the instrumental bass, while the upper line, sung by a tenor or baritone, carries the melody. Both contain phrases that begin either imitatively or in alternation; homophony, however, quickly returns. The duet between Monsieur and Madame Dupont ("Allons, mes enfants," facsimile, p.3, for *haute-contre* and tenor) is actually a trio in that it has an independent instrumental bass. Philidor constructed it by simply taking Madame Dupont's preceding air complete with melody and bass and adding a middle voice for Monsieur Dupont.

The chorus in the mascarade always sings in four parts (*haute-contre*, tenor, baritone, bass), although its sonority is dark given the absence of a soprano part. It is accompanied by the oboe band, which also plays in four parts, but which does not merely double the vocal parts. In fact, the addition of the oboe band expands the texture to five, or even six parts. For most of the choruses the following pattern of doubling, moving from bottom up, prevails: the bass lines are virtually identical for voice and bassoon; the baritone voice, for which there is no corresponding oboe, is not doubled; the *taille de hautbois* doubles the *taille*, or tenor voice (notated on the second stave from the top) at pitch; the *haute-contre de hautbois* doubles the highest voice in the choral texture, the *haute-contre*. The treble oboe does not double a voice, but plays above the highest choral part, in some ways providing the melodic *dessus* part that the male chorus lacks. This part is not, however, perceived as the "tune" of the chorus. It is slightly more decorative than a vocal line would be, in that it sometimes breaks up a note into an ornamental turning or scalar figure, and it jumps around more than Philidor's vocal melodies do. Still, it provides a fifth part at the upper end of the texture and helps brighten the choral sound. In "Chantons le choix charmant" there are six sounding parts, owing to the fact that the *haute-contre de hautbois* functions like a second treble oboe and plays above the *haute-contre* voice, which is thus left undoubled. Thus despite the absence of a treble vocal part, Philidor's voicing provides for a full, very rich sonority. The homophonic texture is slightly ornamented by the oboes, particularly at resting points in the vocal line where the oboes carry on with the motion.

The formal structures of the five choruses follow the same principles found in the airs: textual and rhythmic repetitions that provide a framework for the through-composed melody and harmony. The first three choruses ("Allons, accourons tous," "Chantons le choix charmant," and "Dans ce grand jour," facsimile, pp. 4, 6, and 20–1) are sung throughout with no independent instrumental passages. Like those airs that also only have two lines of text, the structure of these choruses consists of a three-fold repetition of the text set to the same rhythm, but with different pitches that allow for cadences on different scale degrees; the structure may be outlined as AA'A". In "Chantons" and "Dans ce grand jour" there is even less variety than this simple scheme suggests: each of the two lines of text that constitutes each section has the same rhythm, thus leading to a six-fold repetition of a single rhythmic pattern. However, these choruses are far too short – on the order of fifteen or twenty seconds each – to become monotonous.

The remaining two choruses ("Passons toujours la vie," and the *charivari*, facsimile, pp. 23–7 and 31–9) are constructed on a larger scale that interleaves the repeated rhythmic framework with instrumental or solo vocal passages into a rondeau structure. In "Passons toujours la vie" the four lines of text are set to an eight-bar rhythmic phrase whose pitches vary somewhat upon repetition due to fleeting tonicizations of closely related keys. This choral phrase is heard four times in alternation with a rhythmically similar eight-bar instrumental phrase that is played first in the tonic, then in the dominant, and finally in the tonic again. Thus the overall form of the piece may be represented as follows, where B stands for the instrumental phrases and A for the choral phrase and its variants:

A B A' B' A" B A

Greater musical variety is found in the *charivari*, although the text for the choral sections is confined to a single word. The three-fold repetition of "charivari" constitutes a two-bar refrain that is used as the conclusion to each of the five sections of the piece. The beginning of each section consists alternatively of an instrumental phrase played by the full oboe band and of solos for a bass *garçon de la noce*, doubled by bassoon and accompanied by two treble oboes. In the following diagram of the form of the *charivari*, "i" and "s" represent the instrumental and bass solo sections respectively, "R" the choral refrain. The number of bars per phrase includes the two-bar refrain. The letters A through C show how the structure combines elements of rondeau and arch form:

i R s R i R s R i R
A   B   A'   C   A
9   12   7   16   9

The only movement away from the tonic of C major occurs in the middle of the piece: A' cadences in the dominant as does the first phrase of the following vocal solo, which nonetheless returns to the tonic in time for the refrain. The irregular phrasing is indicative of the greater variety built into this chorus: only the refrain adheres to the usual pattern based on identical text and rhythm; the instrumental and solo sections are allowed more rhythmic and melodic freedom. There is even a meter change from duple to triple for the *garçon*'s second solo. The departure from Philidor's formal norms, combined with the unique sonority provided by the three instrumental bass parts and the drum, set this piece apart from the others in the mascarade.

Philidor made a copying error at the end of the *charivari* that makes performance of its final bar problematic. Because the *charivari* is in C major and is followed by the pavane in G major, Philidor composed a modulatory tag in the bass to join the two pieces. However, in the F-Pn score (facsimile, p. 39) the join does not work either melodically or rhythmically because the bass appears to jump up a minor seventh to the pickup into the pavane. The F-Pa score resolves the problem. It contains an extra bar that Philidor omitted here: a dotted half-note *G* for the bass instruments that finishes the melodic descent and supplies the right number of beats to make a smooth join with the pavane.

The last page of the *charivari* also shows another phenomenon that raises questions for performance. This chorus, like all of the others and also like some of the vocal airs, ends with a double bar that has dots inside. This is the same double-bar notation Philidor uses to indicate repeats in the binary dance pieces. However, if this notation were intended to call for a repeat here, then the entire *charivari* would have to be repeated. A look through the manuscript reveals that Philidor uses no other double bar notation – that is, there are no instances of a double bar *without* dots – even in places where no repetition could have been intended (see, for example, the top of p. 17 of the facsimile). In fact, a comparison between Philidor's copies of Lully's ballets and ones by other copyists shows that Philidor had the habit of putting dots in virtually all his double bars, regardless of the musical context. Performers should not assume that a double bar with dots at the end of a number automatically calls for its repetition.

INSTRUMENTAL FORMS

All of the purely instrumental pieces in the mascarade are dances. Of the seven, five belong to familiar dance types, whereas the other two are simply labeled "entrée" or "air," terms that by themselves do not define the meter, tempo, or affect. The identification as to type comes from the music part of the manuscript; Favier, as choreographer, was more concerned with clarifying who was dancing than with identifying the dance type. Even his title for the first dance ("Marche"), by way of contrast with Philidor's ("La Pavane"), places the emphasis on what the dancers do with their feet. In the following list, the first title given is the one found in the music section, the second provides the first word of the title in the dance section; for the first four dances, the title in the dance notation continues with a list of the dancing characters.

1 La Pavane/Marche (music the same for dances I and X)
2 Entrée/Entrée (III)
3 Gigue/Entrée (IV)
4 Menuet/Entrée (V)
5 Air des Ivrognes/[untitled] (VI)
6 Rigaudon/[untitled] (VII)
7 Passepied/[untitled] (VIII)

Philidor's choice of dances provides a variety of meters and tempos; however, he avoids the slower, more serious dances such as the sarabande and the loure as well as the lengthy passacaille, none of which would have been appropriate to the comic subject or the rapid pacing of the mascarade. The variety extends to the relative age of the dances, from the old-fashioned pavane to the new rigaudon. The dances are all very short, the longest of them having only twenty-four bars, without counting repeats. Except for the through-composed pavane, all of the dances are in binary form with both sections repeated. Although the music notation does not so indicate, the choreography for some of the dances requires that the dance be played more than once. The pavane must be played three times at the beginning of the mascarade, and at least three times at the end. The menuet, rigaudon, and passepied are all played twice; full repeats are taken both times through the dance, yielding an AABB AABB structure.[23]

While several of the dances – the "Entrée de deux garçons de la noce" (III), menuet (V), rigaudon (VII), and the first strain of the passepied (VIII) – exhibit very regular phrase structures based on four-bar repeated or antecedent and consequent phrases, the others incorporate the kinds of irregularities that are typical of much French dance music of this period. Such irregularities are often the result of stretching phrases by avoiding melodic or harmonic articulation. The second strain of the passepied, for example, consists of a twelve-bar unit that overrides potential divisions into four-bar phrases and whose harmonic rhythm accelerates at the end via the hemiola. Although the gigue (IV) consists of three phrases that are identical in length – one in the first strain, two in the second –

---

[23] The repeat structure of the passepied is ambiguous in the dance section of the manuscript; the problem is discussed in chapter 6, p. 170.

each is six bars long. The "Air des ivrognes" (VI) has eight bars in the first strain and ten in the second, but both resist breaking down into shorter units. The somewhat long-winded quality thus created can be seen at its most extreme in the pavane, which has repeated rhythmic groups but no clear-cut phrases in its entire twenty-four-bar length. The phrase structure of Lully's dance music is similarly elastic – or even more so. Contrary to oft-repeated assumptions about the relationships between the structure of dance music and the nature of choreography it accompanies, there is no simple equation to be seen in this mascarade between regularity or irregularity of phrase structure in the dance pieces and the affective qualities of the corresponding choreographies.

Several of the dances open with a triadic motive, the most apparent example being the pavane, where the first three bars are elaborations of the first, third, and fifth scale degrees respectively. This opening is similar to other marches by Philidor, for example to the processional from his 1700 mascarade *La Noce de Village*, and even more strikingly, to the "Marche Liegeoise" from the repertoire of the *grande écurie*,[24] both of which are also through-composed. The "Entrée de deux garçons de la noce" and the rigaudon both open with an almost identical melodic line which outlines a rising triad; the opening bars of both the menuet and the drunk dance also show triadic derivations, but rearrange the order of the chord tones. Other dances in the mascarade are also related through their melodic construction. The second section of the rigaudon and the opening of the passepied are both built on the same six-note motive (b' c'' d'' e'' d'' b'; facsimile, p. 29); since the second dance follows the first without a pause, the transformation of the duple-meter phrase into a triple-meter one was surely intentional, and is reminiscent of procedures found in Renaissance dance pairs such as the pavane and gaillarde. Another interesting aspect of Philidor's melodic construction is his use of small rhythmic cells that are repeated either on the same pitch or in sequential fashion on different pitches (see, for example, bar 5 of the pavane, which is repeated exactly in bar 15 and also appears in bars 8, 10, and 17 starting on different notes). This spinning-out technique, while most obvious in the through-composed pavane, is also used in some of the other dances, where it contributes to the irregular phrase structure.

The harmonic language of Philidor's dances is similar to that of the choruses: simple progressions based on closely related chords that never go farther afield than to briefly tonicize a closely related key such as the dominant or the relative major. Other factors that contribute to the overall conservative effect of Philidor's harmonic language include the relatively slow harmonic rhythm and the tendency to alternate two chords – usually I and V or I and IV. At times, particularly in the pavane, the harmony seems to get stuck on one chord, remaining there for up to three or four bars.

The texture of the dances is homophonic, the melody being supported harmonically by the three lower parts. As in the vocal music, a treble–bass polarity dominates, but in many of the dance pieces the second oboe part (the *haute-contre*) moves in parallel thirds with the top part, thus creating the impression of a trio texture. The third part (the *taille*), on the other hand, never deviates from its role as a harmonic filler. The bass line, as in the vocal music, functions as a harmonic bass, and since the majority of the chords are in root position this line tends to have rather more leaps than do the other parts. Sometimes these leaps are filled in by eighth-note passages in step-wise motion (see, for example, bars 2 and 11 of the pavane).

On the whole, Philidor's dance pieces conform to the models provided by Lully and his successors. For example, the gigue exhibits the characteristic 6/4 meter, dotted rhythms, and two-note upbeat associated with this dance type. Although Philidor's gigue is homophonic in texture – unlike many Lully gigues which begin contrapuntally – it displays the irregular phrase structure typical of gigues from this period. Similarly Philidor's rigaudon adheres to the pattern of other late seventeenth-century examples in its use of regular four-bar phrases; the eighth-note turning figure found in bar 4 is almost an identifying characteristic of this dance type. The passepied also conforms to established

---

[24] In F-Pn Rés. F. 671; see Sandman, "Wind band music," Appendix II, p. 85.

norms in its melodic simplicity, its phrase structure, its use of an upbeat, and the presence of hemiola. It is only slightly unusual in that it is notated in 3 rather than 3/8 or 6/8.

Philidor's menuet (facsimile, p. 19) is noteworthy not for its phrase structure or its melodic profile, both of which are perfectly conventional, but for its rhythm. The two-bar rhythmic pattern that recurs in the melody at the beginning of every four-bar phrase consists of an iamb followed by a trochee, that is, of a 1, 2, 2, 1 pattern over six beats, that is reinforced by the homophonic texture. This rhythm is identical to that of Favier's menuet step, a fact that would not be surprising were it not that Favier's step rhythm differs from any of the other known menuet step rhythms from this period (see chapter 5, p. 115). However, this rhythmic pattern is not unique to the mascarade; Philidor himself wrote other menuets in this rhythm, as did Lully, Lalande, Campra, and even Jean-Philippe Rameau. The pattern is also found on the other side of the channel in the works of Henry Purcell, sometimes in pieces that are not identified as menuets in the score: the best-known example is his chorus "Fear no danger" from *Dido and Aeneas*.[25] The relative frequency with which this pattern appears in menuets, particularly those from the late seventeenth century, suggests both that the composers may have been influenced by the rhythm of the menuet step itself, and that use of this particular step may have been quite widespread.

The words "entrée" and "air" are general terms found in theatrical scores, usually followed by the names of characters dancing, as is the case in this mascarade (e.g., the "Air des ivrognes," and the "Entrée de deux garçons de la noce"). The term "air" may be applied to either vocal or instrumental music, whereas "entrée" is reserved for dance pieces. While such designations may sometimes mask other dance types – either an air or an entrée may turn out to be a gavotte, for example – often pieces do not fall into any particular category. This is true of Philidor's "Entrée de deux garçons de la noce." There was, however, one reproducible type of entrée, generally referred to in choreographic sources as an "entrée grave," of which the "Air des ivrognes" is an example. Such pieces are in duple meter, often in the minor mode, and have dotted rhythms that provide a forceful, or even aggressive character. The choreographies use a virtuoso step vocabulary with two step-units per bar, thus requiring a slow tempo. A notable example is Lully's "Entrée d'Apollon" from *Le Triomphe de l'Amour* (LWV 59/58), for which there are two choreographies in Feuillet notation (LMC 2720 and 2740). Philidor's dance adopts most of these musical characteristics – although it has fewer dotted figures, especially in the first strain – but the serious affect of the music is completely undermined by the choreographed staggering of the two drunks.

Like many of his contemporaries, including Lully, Philidor was not averse to recycling his music, and several of the dances in *Le Mariage de la Grosse Cathos* can be found in his later mascarades. He may also not have been averse to borrowing from other composers – namely, from Lully himself. The first three bars of Philidor's pavane are almost identical to the beginning of the B section of the "Marche des sacrificateurs" from the opera *Cadmus et Hermione* (III, 5; LWV 49/42); thereafter, however, the two pieces diverge markedly, particularly with respect to harmonic language, which is much more sophisticated in the Lully dance. Perhaps Philidor did not borrow from Lully so much as internalize his style; certainly in his double role as performer and copyist he had more than ample opportunity to get to know Lully's compositions.[26] It is also possible that Philidor himself was borrowed from, and that one of the dances in this mascarade may have served as a model for a dance further removed both chronologically and geographically. The first strain of Philidor's passepied melody is virtually identical to the first strain of a menuet

---

[25] Daniel Heartz in his article "Branle" in *The New Grove Dictionary of Music and Musicians*, III, p. 201, associates this chorus and its characteristic rhythm to the Renaissance *branle gay*, but does not mention the prevalence of this rhythm in the seventeenth-century menuet.

[26] Philidor's relationship to Lully's compositions is a complex one that has posed a number of problems for the editors of the new Lully edition and that remains to be completely sorted out. In his role as copyist of Lully's ballets Philidor may even have composed some of the pieces that he attributed to Lully; see Schmidt, "Berkeley Ms. 454."

choreographed by the English dancing master Thomas Caverley that first appeared in an early eighteenth-century manuscript.[27]

In setting the libretto of *Le Mariage de la Grosse Cathos*, Philidor used many of the same vocal forms as are found in Lully's operas – solo airs, recitative, small ensembles, and choruses – but with everything in miniature. Madame Dupont's opening air, for example, is only ten bars long, the first chorus only eleven. The dance pieces are also relatively brief, although comparable in length to the dances in Lully's *ballets de cour*; certainly there are none of the longer dances sometimes found in Lully's operas. The only two extended pieces in the mascarade – the "Passons" chorus (fifty-six bars) and the *charivari* (fifty-three bars) – are also the only two pieces that include separate vocal and dance sections; both achieve their length by use of a rondeau structure.

A visual inspection of the score, with its almost unbroken succession of diminutive vocal pieces and short dances, might give the impression of a rather fragmentary and disjointed work. Yet just the opposite is true. The key relationships, the repetition of melodic material in the vocal pieces, and the similarities in thematic ideas in the dances all combine to provide musical coherence. In many of the vocal pieces meter changes are indicated in the final bar of the previous piece, thus deemphasizing any metrical contrast and ensuring a smooth link between the two numbers. Furthermore, when there is a change of key between numbers Philidor adds a short connecting passage to the final bar of the bass line, thereby ensuring that the next piece will follow *attacca*. On p. 4 of the facsimile, for example, the last bar of the chorus "Allons" adopts the duple meter of the following recitative and the instrumental bass plays a descending line that modulates from G major to the new key of C major (although Philidor, presumably thinking already in the new key, neglected to cancel the $f\sharp$). Even the dances, which might be thought of as set pieces, are choreographed to contribute to the continuity of the work. The mascarade functions as a single unit, which flows without break from beginning to end.

---

[27] See Tomlinson, *Workbook*, and Petre, "Six new dances." The second strains of the two menuets do not resemble each other.

5

The dance notation

Because the notational system used to preserve the ten dances of *Le Mariage de la Grosse Cathos* is completely different from Feuillet notation, this chapter aims to explain its workings in some detail. A study of the notation first serves the purely mechanical purpose of enabling people to reconstruct the dances of the mascarade, and is clearly important for this reason alone. But in a broader sense the discovery of another notational system widens the perspective on Baroque dance in general. Not only does an understanding of this notation provide access to Favier's own dances, it provides a different angle of vision from which to examine the entire repertoire and the dance technique on which it rests. A notator who attempts to map a complex art based on movement through time and space onto a two-dimensional sheet of paper has to select which aspects of the dance to communicate; the choices made say a good deal about what the notator considers fundamental. By seeing where Favier's and Feuillet's choices overlap it is possible to gain a deeper understanding of the bases of Baroque dance; the places where they differ, on the other hand, provide pieces of information – sometimes complementary, sometimes contradictory – that broaden our view of the art. This chapter focuses on Favier notation, but our study of its workings has obliged us to take a close look at Feuillet notation and to examine carefully what both systems do and do not communicate.

The fact that the dances in *Le Mariage de la Grosse Cathos* antedate the earliest publication of dances in Feuillet notation by twelve years raises the possibility of examining the repertoires for changes in style over time. It is certainly unlikely that French dance style and technique remained static over the twenty-five-year period (1700–25) for which there is the most documentation, and it is to be hoped that an understanding of Favier's notational system will prompt researchers to ask the kinds of developmental questions that to date have remained unexamined. Having issued an invitation, it is, however, also necessary to sound a warning: although Favier's dances can be precisely dated because they were performed in a particular work, dating Feuillet's dances is a complicated task, despite the publication dates on many of the collections. A number of the dances appear to have been choreographed well before they were published, and there are several undated manuscripts of choreographies that provide even less information about their origins.[1] However, the discovery of Favier notation raises other historical questions more amenable to examination; these concern the evolution of dance notation itself, a process which Favier notation casts into a whole new light. The desire for accurate preservation of dances evident starting in the 1680s demonstrates a certain historical awareness on the part of the notators, or at the very least a recognition that dances have more than ephemeral value. It is perhaps no coincidence that at the same time that dancing masters

---

[1] A *terminus ante quem* for many of the choreographies can be provided by identifying the source of the music; there are, however, a large number of dances for which the music has not yet been identified. Although many of the dances in the manuscript collections were copied from Feuillet's prints, others are unique, and some of these exhibit stylistic features suggesting that they may be older than the others. Evidence suggesting that at least one of the dances in Feuillet's 1700 collection of Pécour's dances may have been choreographed as early as 1690 may be found in Harris-Warrick, "La Mariée"; regarding the dating of some of Pécour's theatrical choreographies, see Harris-Warrick, "Contexts."

were seeking to preserve the choreographic repertoire of the court and the Opéra, Philidor *l'aîné*, the king's music librarian, was engaged in a massive project to preserve the compositions of the man who supplied much of the music for this repertoire, Jean-Baptiste Lully.

This chapter thus examines Favier notation from both historical and practical perspectives. It is designed to accommodate readers looking for an overview of the system as well as those interested in learning about it in depth.

THE INVENTION OF DANCE NOTATION

On 28 April 1704 the eminent choreographer Pierre Beauchamps (1636–1705), then at the end of his long career, lodged a complaint in the king's council against two younger dancing masters, Raoul Auger Feuillet and André Lorin. At issue was credit for the invention of dance notation, credit which Beauchamps claimed belonged to him. Four years earlier Feuillet had published a 106-page book entitled *Chorégraphie, ou l'art de décrire la danse* in which he claimed as his own invention an elaborate system of symbols by which the dances of the day could be transmitted on paper, initiating at the same time a series of collections of notated dances which continued annually until at least 1725. On 14 February, two months before Beauchamps filed his suit, Lorin had also been accorded a privilege to publish notated choreographies, and it was apparently this threat of further publications that pushed the seemingly passive Beauchamps, who had remained silent during the four years following the publication of *Chorégraphie*, finally to protest.[2] The depositions made by both sides in the ensuing dispute make it clear, however, that attempts to develop a system of choreographic notation antedated Feuillet's publications by many years, and that a number of people had been engaged in work toward that end. Favier's notational system, although not mentioned in the documents presented in the Beauchamps case, must thus be seen in light of the several competing systems that were developed in France during the late seventeenth century.

Prior to the burst of notational activity that occurred in the 1680s, instructions for dances relied primarily on verbal description. Italian dance manuals such as Caroso's *Il ballarino* (1581) and *Nobiltà di dame* (1600) or Negri's *Le gratie d'amore* (1602) first describe, not always without ambiguity, how to perform the basic dance steps of their respective styles, then provide narrative accounts of the step sequences and figures for a sizable number of dances. ("In the second figure, do two *semibreve steps* and one *breve sequence*, beginning with the left foot; repeat to the other side."[3]) Although the description of each dance includes its music, notated in lute tablature, matching choreography to music is frequently problematic. A French dance manual, Thoinot Arbeau's *Orchesographie* (1588), which Feuillet credits as having given him the idea to develop dance notation (*Chorégraphie*, Preface), is also based on verbal description of the dances, but clarifies the temporal relationship between steps and music by writing the step names next to the relevant notes in each tune. A few dance sources make use of rudimentary symbols for some aspects of the dance: fifteenth-century *basse danse* descriptions, for example, set letters underneath the music to indicate the step patterns (d = *double*, r = *reprise*, etc.), while some seventeenth-century sources for the *ballet de cour* use symbols that show the spatial relationships of the dancers at one fixed moment.[4] None of

---

[2] The scales may also have been tipped by a favorable review of *Chorégraphie* that appeared in the May 1704 issue of the *Journal de Trévoux*, pp. 692–703, assuming it was actually in print before May: the October issue of the same journal (pp. 1786–7) reported that Beauchamps had protested to the editors that they had attributed the glory of his invention to another, and that when they had justified themselves on the grounds of Feuillet's 1699 privilege from the king, Beauchamps had taken his case to the king's council.

[3] Example taken from the balletto "Conto dell Orco Nuovo" in Caroso, *Nobiltà* (trans. Sutton), p. 253.

[4] The main source for *basse danse* choreographies is the Brussels manuscript, B-Br ms. 9085. For two sample pages of dance figures – one showing primarily geometric shapes, the other letters – from the notebook of a seventeenth-century French dancing master working in Brussels, see Ward, "Newly devis'd

these, however, attempts to communicate both the steps and the figures of a dance through symbols alone.

Beauchamps's deposition to the king's council states that the impetus for developing a choreographic notational system had come from Louis XIV himself. Beauchamps claimed that about thirty years earlier – that is, in the 1670s – the king had ordered him to "discover the means of making the art of dance comprehensible on paper" and that he had "applied himself to shaping and disposing characters and notes in the form of tablature in order to represent the steps of the dances and ballets performed before the king and at the Opéra" in such a way that the dances could be learned "without need for personal instruction."[5] In support of his claim that Feuillet and Lorin had stolen and profited from the system that he had invented, Beauchamps entered as evidence a number of items, among them five volumes containing the notational symbols he had invented; a notated choreography dating from 1684 of the chaconne from Lully's opera *Phaéton*; letters from the chancellery granting Beauchamps a privilege for printing dances, dating from 1687 but unsigned and unsealed; and an attestation from twenty-five Parisian dancing masters stating that Beauchamps had shown them his dance notation more than twenty-five years previously. In its decision the king's council supported Beauchamps's contention that he was, in fact, the inventor of what today is generally called Feuillet notation, but denied him any legal redress for theft of his ideas on the grounds that he had failed to obtain the necessary privilege that would have allowed him to commercially exploit his invention.[6] Thus Feuillet, who had followed the proper administrative channels and had been granted a privilege on 22 August 1699, was permitted to continue his highly successful series of dance publications.

Feuillet never acknowledged his indebtedness to Beauchamps, having claimed the invention of dance notation as his own in *Chorégraphie*, with only perfunctory reference to his predecessors.[7] Nonetheless, it appears to have been widely known at the time that Beauchamps was the true inventor of the system. Not only did the *Journal de Trévoux* publish the text of the decision by the king's council in the issue of October 1704, a number of dancers and musicians commented upon the dispute. Siris, a French dancing master working in England, wrote in *The Art of Dancing* (London, 1706) that Beauchamps himself had taught him the notation "above Eighteen Years ago," but "through an unaccountable Negligence he delay'd the publishing of it." After Feuillet's death in 1710, another dancer and notator, Michel Gaudrau, wrote in the preface to his published collection of dances by Pécour (Paris [1713]) that "it is to M. Beauchamps . . . that we owe

---

measures," pp. 115 and 116. The printed libretto for the *Ballet de M. de Vendosme* (1610), performed at the court of Louis XIII, shows twelve figures, each reportedly representing one of the letters of "the alphabet of the ancient druids," formed by twelve dancers as part of the concluding grand ballet (reprint in McGowan, *L'art*, plates VI and VII).

[5] "Sur la requeste presentée au Roy en son conseil par Pierre Beauchamps Compositeur des ballets de sa Majesté et Directeur de l'academie Royale de danse, Contenant que pour obeir a l'ordre que luy donna sa Majesté estant a Chambort il y a trente années ou environ de trouver moyen de faire comprendre l'art de la danse sur le papier, il s'est appliqué a former et disposer des caracteres et des nottes en forme de tablature pour figurer les pas des danses et des ballets representez devant Sa Majesté et a l'academie de musique et qu'il a encore inventez depuis, et pour exprimer de maniere l'ordre des mesures et les mouvements qu'a l'inspection de ces caracteres les danses et les entrées de ballet puissent estre executées sans avoir besoin d'instruction personnelle . . . " F-Pan V^{6}796, document n° 10 (Arrêt du Conseil Privé du Roi du 28 avril 1704).

[6] For a list of some of the documents and books entered by all three parties to the suit, see Richardson, "Beauchamp"; additional discussion of the dispute, although also incomplete, may be found in Guilcher, "Lorin" and Derra de Moroda, "Chorégraphie." The documents themselves have not been found, but the complete list of them, as well as the decision of the king's council, is preserved in F-Pan V^{6}797, document n° 22 (Arrêt du Conseil Privé du Roi du 28 juillet 1704).

[7] "Plusieurs personnes avant moy ont travaillé en differens temps à mettre les Dances sur le papier, par le moyen de quelques Signes; mais comme leur travail est resté infructueux, j'ay tâché de conduire le mien assez loin pour le rendre utile au public . . ." [Here follows a mention of Arbeau's *Orchesographie*, which Feuillet knew only from the dictionary of Furetière.] "De tous les Signes, Caracteres & Figures *que j'ay pû inventer*, je n'ay employé dans cet Ouvrage que ceux qui m'ont paru les plus propres & les plus démonstratifs . . ." (Preface to *Chorégraphie*; emphasis added).

the invention of this new art [i.e., dance notation] and the late M. Feuillet, profiting from his [Beauchamps's] knowledge, brought forth *Chorégraphie* . . . " Sébastien de Brossard, making an entry for *Chorégraphie* in his 1724 catalogue of the books in his library (F-Pn [Imprimés] Rés. Vm⁸ 21), added the following note: "To my way of thinking M. Feuillet has claimed himself a little too freely as the author or first inventor of the art of writing dances on paper . . . everyone knows that the late M. Beauchamps, who was dancing master to king Louis XIV and choreographer of his ballets, is the true and first inventor and it was even the great king himself who gave him the idea; M. Feuillet can at best attribute to himself the glory of having perfected this art and of having communicated it to the public. But *facile est inventis addere*."⁸

Although there appears to be no reason to doubt that Beauchamps deserves priority for the development of dance notation, it is clear that he was not alone in his work in this area. Feuillet's codefendant in Beauchamps's suit, André Lorin, had also been working on dance notation during the 1680s, although unlike Feuillet, he never published any dances.⁹ The surviving record of Lorin's labor in this field consists of two manuscripts of *contredanses*, one almost certainly from 1685, the other dated 1688 (F-Pn [Manuscrits] Mss. fr. 1697 and 1698). The first contains thirteen dances which Lorin says he brought back from England (the English country dance had been introduced at the French court just one year earlier);¹⁰ the second, beautifully decorated for presentation to the king, has but a single dance, "Le carillon d'Oxfort," known in England as "Christ Church bells." This spectacular manuscript includes laudatory poems in honor of members of the royal family and beautiful color drawings in which the four dancing couples, fashionably dressed in bright colors that distinguish each one from the others, are shown moving through the figures of the nine repetitions of the dance. The care lavished on preparation of this manuscript demonstrates just how high the stakes in the contest to produce dance notation were perceived to be: if the impetus for developing dance notation had indeed come from the king, then glory and wealth – so Lorin clearly hoped – would devolve upon its "inventor," a title Lorin claimed as his due.¹¹ Yet Lorin's self-glorification notwithstanding, the notation itself is restricted in scope, probably because it was designed to accommodate the relatively simple *contredanse* with its stereotypical figures and limited step vocabulary. It separates the floor patterns of the dance, which appear as line diagrams, from the steps, which are notated below the music using letter abbreviations (e.g., "J"

---

⁸ "Au reste M. Feuillet se donne à mon sens, un peu trop hardiment, pour l'autheur ou le premier inventeur de l'Art de Décrire les dances sur le papier . . . tout le monde sçait que feu M. de Beauchampt qui avoit été le Maistre à Dancer du Roy Louis XIV et compositeur des Ballets en est le veritable et le premier Inventeur, ce fut même ce grand Roy qui luy en fit naitre la pensée; Le Sr Feuillet ne peut donc au plus s'atribuer la gloire d'avoir peut estre perfectionné cet art et de l'avoir communiqué au public. Mais *facile est inventis addere*." Other contemporary testimonials from England and Germany supporting Beauchamps's claim are cited in Derra de Moroda, "Chorégraphie."

⁹ As far as we have been able to determine, Lorin appears never to have followed through on the privilege for printing dance notations he acquired on 14 February 1704 (his privilege is recorded in F-Pn [Manuscrits] Ms. fr. 21.948: *Registre des privileges accordés aux auteurs et libraires* [1703–05], pp. 39–41). No records of any publications by Lorin have been found, either in the form of surviving copies or by mention in catalogues and other secondary sources. For further discussion of Lorin's notational system, see Guilcher, "Lorin," pp. 261ff.

¹⁰ 27 October 1684: "Le soir il y eut appartement; on y dansa pour la première fois les contredanses qu'un maître anglois, nommé Isaac, avoit apprises à toutes les dames." ("That evening there was *appartement*; *contredanses* that an English [dancing] master named Isaac had taught to all the ladies were danced for the first time.") Dangeau, *Journal* I, p. 63.

¹¹ A dedicatory poem to the king (quoted in Guilcher, "Lorin," p. 258) claims the notation as "a new invention which no one before me had thought of." ("Dans ce concours heureux je fais tout mon employ / De te marquer icy mon zèle / Par une invention nouvelle / Dont on ne s'estoit point avisé devant moy . . .") Further indications of the importance Lorin attached to priority in the development of dance notation come from the fact that as late as 1716, when his son was married, Lorin described himself as "seul inventeur de l'art d'écrire la danse" (document cited in Brossard, *Musiciens*, p. 201). In 1721 Lorin, who had reacquired his beautiful manuscript following the death of the Duchess of Burgundy, wrote a new dedication for it and presented it to her son, the eleven-year-old Louis XV, who had ascended the throne six years earlier. A reproduction of one page of this manuscript may be seen in Hilton, *Dance of Court and Theater*, p. 14.

means *jeté*) and whose direction is shown by their position relative to a vertical line. Lorin does not describe how to do the steps he names; he seems to have taken for granted the existence of a shared dance vocabulary between himself and his readers.[12] Although his notation aims to communicate both steps and figures in relation to the music, it does not represent the same level of conceptual sophistication as does Beauchamps/Feuillet notation. The king's council correctly deemed that as Lorin's system was different from the one Beauchamps had developed, the latter had no grounds for lodging a complaint against Lorin.

The Beauchamps documents provide a hint of yet a third notational system that was under development during this same period. One of the items entered as evidence in the case was an intriguing "placard de 1689 d'une danse décrite par le Sr Delahaise." A search through the records of the printers' guild reveals that in 1686 a certain Sieur De La Haise, dancing master, was granted a privilege to publish a book entitled *L'art de danser*, which was described as "a new method of learning dance invented by him," and also granted the right to publish plates of dances for fifteen years.[13] No trace of such a book has as yet turned up, so it would appear that De La Haise, like Lorin, failed to get his book into print. Although it is currently impossible to know how this system may have related to any of the others, it may be that this is the system based on assigning each letter of the alphabet to a particular dance step to which an allusion is made in the *Encyclopédie* (see below).

Favier's dance notation represents yet a fourth system from the same period and milieu. *Le Mariage de la Grosse Cathos* shows that this notation was well developed by 1688; Favier must have been working on it for some time before then. It seems very unlikely that Beauchamps could not have known about the work of a man who had been one of his own dancers for many years. Presumably the reason Beauchamps did not mention Favier in his suit was that Favier never attempted to exploit his system commercially. The other three dancing masters whose names appear in the Beauchamps documents – Feuillet, Lorin, and De La Haise – all applied for and were granted privileges to publish books of dance notation. Favier's work, which remained in manuscript, must not have represented a threat to Beauchamps.

Thus within the relatively small circle of professional dancers that worked at court and in Paris at the end of the seventeenth century, there were at least four systems of dance notation under development.[14] However active Beauchamps or the others may have been still earlier, the 1680s evidently represent a period of intense work in this direction, as the following recapitulation of the datable documentary evidence shows: Beauchamps's notation of the chaconne from *Phaéton* (1684); Lorin's first *contredanse* manuscript (1685);

---

[12] In F-Pn (Manuscrits) Ms. fr. 1697 Lorin included symbols for the following steps: *pas simple, pas jeté, pas assemblé, pas sauté, pas sauté et le demeuré en l'air, pas sauté et assemblé, pas sauté et assemblé en présence, pas reculé, pas dégagé en avant, pas dégagé à côté, pas tourné au quart de tour (à demi tour, à un tour), pas balancé, pas de menuet, pas de bourée à deux mouvements, fleuret, pas de sissonne, chassé, coupé ordinaire, coupé en l'air, coupé en arrière*, and *cabriole de côté*.

[13] F-Pn (Manuscrits) Ms. fr. 21.946, Enregistrements des Privilèges [23 October 1673–31 December 1687], 10 December 1686: "Le Sr de la haise maistre a danser nous a presenté un privilege à lui accordé par sa maiesté pour l'impression du livre intitulé *l'art de danser* nouvelle methode d'aprandre la danse inventée par lui comme aussy de faire graver les planches ou cartes de dances pour quinze année."

[14] In early eighteenth-century German dance books, there are indications of two other notational systems designed to transmit French-style dances. The one put forth in 1705 by Johannes Pasch, who says that he had studied with Beauchamps, is like a hybrid between Arbeau and Feuillet: each dance figure requires two pages of notation, one that includes the music with the steps of the dance either named or explained in words below each measure, and a second that shows the track of the dance, drawn the same way as in Feuillet notation ([Pasch], *Maître de Danse, oder Tantz-Meister*). Meredith Little has suggested that Pasch may have derived his notation from Beauchamps rather than Feuillet (see Little, "French dance in Germany"), but in view of the fact that two of Pasch's four notated dances come from Feuillet's first published collection (the other two, both bearing French titles, are unique to Pasch's book) and that these two notations are strikingly similar to Feuillet's in layout and steps, it seems likelier that Pasch's notation represents his own modification of Feuillet notation. Another system, one that uses symbols along a track to indicate the steps (these symbols being different from those of any other known system), was published by Behr in his book *Anderer Theil der Tantz-Kunst*; Behr did not, however, include any dances notated using this system.

the granting of a privilege to publish notated dances to De La Haise (1686); Beauchamps's own privilege for publishing dances, which remained unsigned and therefore invalid (1687); Lorin's second *contredanse* manuscript (1688); Favier's notations for *Le Mariage de la Grosse Cathos* (1688); and De La Haise's unnamed notated dance (1689). It is inconceivable that any of the four notators could have thought that he was the only one trying to develop a workable system of dance notation. Beauchamps and Favier had known each other all their lives, and Lorin was likewise attached both to the court and to the Académie Royale de Danse.[15] Nothing is known about De La Haise, but he probably also belonged to Parisian dance circles.[16] It is perhaps a reflection on the demanding life of the professional dancer that none of the four succeeded in publishing his work. Feuillet's act of plagiarism, however deplorable, had the fortunate result of preserving over 335 choreographies for posterity.

THE KEY TO FAVIER'S NOTATIONAL SYSTEM: THE *ENCYCLOPÉDIE*

Although Favier did not obtain a privilege for printing dances using his notational system, a mid-eighteenth-century source reveals that he wrote a book about it. The source in question is the *Encyclopédie ou dictionnaire raisonné des sciences, des arts et des métiers*, the enormous and invaluable compendium of French Enlightenment thought, conceived and edited by Denis Diderot and Jean le Rond d'Alembert. Published in stages over a period of almost thirty years (1751–80), with volumes both of text and of very detailed plates, the *Encyclopédie* contains numerous articles regarding dance and dance music. The largest number of dance articles was written by Louis de Cahusac (1706–59), author of the three-volume treatise *La danse ancienne et moderne* (The Hague, 1754); others were contributed by Jean-Jacques Rousseau and by the two editors, Diderot and d'Alembert, *inter alios*. The substantial article entitled "Chorégraphie," however, was contributed by a mathematician and painter by the name of Louis-Jacques Goussier (1722–99) and appeared in volume 3 (published in 1753; the two accompanying plates were published in 1762 in volume 3 of the plates).[17] In it two notational systems are described at length: Feuillet notation and another by the "sieur Favier," whose undated manuscript book had "fallen into" Goussier's hands. Although no trace of the book itself has been found, Goussier's article about it provides the key to unlocking the notation of *Le Mariage de la Grosse Cathos*.

Goussier was originally engaged by d'Alembert to work on the plates for the

---

[15] In his 1685 manuscript Lorin identifies himself as "académicien de Sa Majesté pour la Dance"; in the privilege of 1704 he is referred to as "André Lorin Conducteur de notre Academie Royale de Danse & Syndic des Maistres à Danser suivant nostre Cour." "Conducteur," however, does not seem to mean that he was a member of the Academy, as his name does not appear on any of the known membership lists (1661, 1695, 1719); perhaps the position was an administrative one. Nonetheless, that he was well connected at court can be seen in the fact that Philippe d'Orléans, the king's nephew and regent of France following the king's death in 1715, served as godfather to Lorin's son (document relative to the mariage of Philippe Lorin in 1716, cited in Brossard, *Musiciens*, p. 201). Lorin also rented an apartment from Beauchamps for at least eight months in 1692–93, in the same street (rue Bailleul), and perhaps even the same building, where Beauchamps lived. This business connection emerges from the two rent receipts, dated 17 July 1692 and 10 February 1693, that Beauchamps entered as evidence in his suit against Feuillet and Lorin, and from a document giving Lorin's street address in February 1693 (Brossard, *Musiciens*, p. 201). Reading between the lines, it would appear that Beauchamps might have suggested to the king's council that Lorin had taken advantage of his access to Beauchamps's home to steal his ideas from him.

[16] The possible variant spellings of this name have complicated the search for information about him. In the Beauchamps documents his name is written "Delahaise," in his own privilege as "de la haise" (possibly "de la haize"). Searches in various sources under D, L, and H have as yet failed to turn him up.

[17] The article and the plates also appeared in subsequent editions of the *Encyclopédie*; in addition, they were reproduced without attribution in Charles Compan, *Dictionnaire de danse* (Paris, 1787). Several dance historians, familiar with this article but unaware that Favier notation had ever been put to use, have assumed that the system was contemporaneous with the *Encyclopédie* or with Compan's dictionary, that is, from the middle or end of the eighteenth century.

Encyclopédie and more than 900 are signed by him.[18] Perhaps it was his experience in preparing the two detailed plates of dance notation that qualified him to write the article itself; he also contributed other articles such as "coupe de pierres" and "facture d'orgue." Whatever the case may be, he approached his task systematically, using as his sources Feuillet's book *Chorégraphie*, Favier's now missing manuscript book, and information, including part of a notated choreography, supplied to him by the dancer Dupré.[19] He does not go beyond these sources in his discussion (he does not, for example, mention Beauchamps's contribution to dance notation or either of Pierre Rameau's two books), nor does he give the impression that he himself had experience as a dancer beyond what might be expected from a well-bred man of his day; he examines dance notation as a system of symbolic representation, viewed rather from the perspective of someone sitting at a desk than from that of someone accustomed to holding a book of notations in his hand as he moves around the room.

The long article – twelve columns over seven double-column pages (the article and the corresponding plates are reproduced in Appendix B) – may be divided into four parts: the elements of Feuillet notation; a description of part of a notated dance; the elements of Favier notation; and a brief comparison of the two systems. In the first section, occupying five of the columns, Goussier provides a summary of *Chorégraphie*, without, however, citing its author by name. In fact, it is only in the third and fourth sections that he refers briefly to Feuillet as the author of this system. Nonetheless, it is abundantly clear that he had a copy of Feuillet's book at his elbow while writing his own article. Goussier adheres to Feuillet's ordering of the material as it had appeared in *Chorégraphie*, although he concentrates on Feuillet's statements of general principles and confines himself to the basic notational symbols (e.g. *plié*, *sauté*, *en l'air*, *tourner*), omitting the ways in which these symbols are combined to form steps.[20] (It is presumably because his focus is on the system itself and not on its practical applications that Goussier reproduces virtually all of Feuillet's extensive section about the notation of arm and hand gestures [illustrated in Goussier's plate I, figs. 45–76], even though such notations are not used in actual choreographies.) Goussier paraphrases the text of *Chorégraphie*, sometimes remaining very faithful to the original, but often reshaping or even expanding Feuillet's telegraphic prose into fuller and clearer explanations. (Feuillet, p. 2: "Plié, est quand on plie les genoux. Elevé, est quand on les étend." Goussier, p. 367, column 2: "Le plié est l'inflexion des genoux. L'élevé est l'extension des genoux pliés; ces deux mouvements doivent toujours être précédés l'un de l'autre.") Goussier keys his discussion to the numerous notational examples from *Chorégraphie* contained in his own two plates. At two places in this section he explains how the notation of the foot sign can be modified to communicate the rhythm of the step in relation to the music. Although it is embedded in Goussier's summary of Feuillet's book, this idea is not one that originated with Feuillet; in fact, Goussier reveals elsewhere in the article that this improvement had been communicated to him by Dupré.

In the second section of the article Goussier explains at considerable length (over two columns on pp. 370–1) the notational symbols as they function in the first five bars of a ten-bar excerpt, shown in his plate II, from the "Pas de deux lutteurs" (Dance for two

---

[18] See Dulas, "J. Goussier."

[19] The Dupré family included many dancers, but the one mentioned by Goussier is probably Louis Dupré (1690 or 1695–1774), known as "le grand Dupré," who had a long career at the Paris Opéra (see Winter, *Ballet*, pp. 56–7). Like Favier's son (see chapter 2), Louis Dupré spent part of his professional life at the Polish court; perhaps Dupré was the conduit through which the elder Favier's manuscript reached Goussier.

[20] Goussier's article includes information from the following portions of *Chorégraphie*: the preface, pp. 2–15, 87, 90, 92–3, and 96–9. It omits, among other topics, all of Feuillet's tables of steps.

Goussier was but one of a large number of eighteenth-century authors who recirculated material from *Chorégraphie* in the form of translations, paraphrases, excerpts, abridgments, or even wholesale borrowings. The most egregious example of the latter is the *Principes de chorégraphie* (Paris, 1765) by Magny, who admits in his introduction – although not on the title page – that the book consists of Feuillet's *Chorégraphie* virtually intact. For a bibliographic study of many such works, see Rebman, "*Chorégraphie*."

wrestlers) from the ballet héroïque *Les Fêtes Grecques et Romaines* by Collin de Blamont (first performed at the Paris Opéra in 1723, revived in 1733 and 1741), as danced by Dupré and Javiliers. This choreography, as the date of composition of the music reveals, postdates Feuillet's *Chorégraphie*, nor is the dance known from any later choreographic source. Although Goussier does not say so, he presumably received this choreography from Dupré himself. The excerpt incorporates the notational precisions regarding rhythm mentioned in the first part of the article and much of Goussier's explanation is devoted to pointing out how the notation shows the rhythmic value of each gesture.[21] It is indicative of Goussier's general focus that he explains the movements of the dance in terms of each successive notational symbol, not by reference to any step-units of which the movement represented by the symbol might be a part. In fact, the notation of the steps lacks the lines of liaison that for Feuillet serve to join the component parts of a step-unit.

The third section of the article, as long as the first, is devoted to Favier's notational system. Goussier's introduction to the subject reveals next to nothing about the origin of the book he had come across, nor when the book might have been written: "A manuscript by the sieur Favier having fallen into my hands, I thought to oblige the public by explaining this author's system, all the more since his book will probably never be printed" (p. 371, column 1). As he had done for Feuillet, Goussier summarizes the elements of the system, concentrating on the notational symbols and omitting any discussion of steps per se. If he adopted the same procedure as he had for *Chorégraphie*, then he probably followed the order of Favier's original, paraphrasing and clarifying the text, but possibly omitting certain parts of it. Cueing his discussion to forty-six figures on his plate II, Goussier begins with the way the dancing space is represented, the symbol for the body of the dancer, the way his spatial orientation is indicated, and modifications made to the body sign used to indicate bending of the upper body on the one hand, or the rhythm of the steps on the other (figs. 3–16). He next proceeds to outline the symbols used to show the movements or positions of the feet and the ways in which the basic symbols may be modified or used relative to the body sign (figs. 17–40). This part of the article gives the impression of staying close to Favier's original material; the explanations are brief and to the point (e.g., "La ligne horizontale [fig. 19] marque qu'il faut marcher"). When Goussier arrives at the section where he begins to discuss ways in which the basic symbols can be modified or recombined to produce different meanings, his text gets wordier and the reader receives the impression that he is abstracting general principles from what probably were lengthy lists of combinations of symbols with minimal commentary. He introduces this section by a direct quote from Favier's manuscript (p. 372, column 1).

"These are all the different signs with which one may notate the movements, actions, and positions that may be done in dance; it only remains to assemble them. But this is done in so many different ways that if I can succeed, as I hope to, I will have reason to be satisfied with my reflections," says the author.

We will see to what extent the author succeeds.

---

[21] It is not clear whether or not Goussier was aware of Pierre Rameau's attempts to improve the rhythmic accuracy of Feuillet notation, put forth in his *Abrégé* [1725], or whether Rameau's and Dupré's ideas had a common origin. Both indicate the timing of the step by modifying the foot sign, although somewhat differently. Goussier never mentions Rameau, but in his plate of Feuillet symbols gives as the second of two for "poser la pointe" (plate I, fig. 35) a symbol found in Rameau's *Abrégé* (p. 18) but not in Feuillet's *Chorégraphie*.

Four years after the publication of the *Encyclopédie* volume containing Goussier's article on dance notation – although still twelve years before the publication of the plates – a book entitled *Méthode pour apprendre de soi-mesme la chorégraphie* was published in Le Mans. Despite its title it contains no actual notation but describes in words the notation of a number of dances, most of them previously published in Feuillet's system. For one of the dances, "tirée de la chorégraphie nouvelle d'un maître de Paris," the author describes the use of white and black "heads" to indicate step rhythm. In the absence of the notation, it is hard to establish what connection, if any, there may have been between this modification of Feuillet notation and the ones proposed by Rameau and Goussier. But it is nonetheless intriguing that the author of this *Méthode* was named Dupré – even though the fact that he describes himself as a dancing master in Le Mans almost certainly eliminates the possibility that he could have been the *premier danseur* by the same name at the Paris Opéra.

Despite the tantalizing come-on, the section of Goussier's discussion covering figures 41–8 appears to have significantly telescoped Favier's original. That Goussier made cuts is suggested by language such as "And so on for all the possible combinations... which it would take too long to enumerate" or "and vice versa for all the combinations to which these arrangements are susceptible" (p. 372, column 2). In some cases Goussier may only have omitted permutations of a type that readers could easily figure out for themselves, by recombining the basic elements; Favier may have shared the encyclopedic impulses that led Feuillet to include the notation for the same motion done on the right foot, on the left foot, forwards, backwards, to the right, to the left, etc., while Goussier felt that an example could stand in for the whole. On the other hand, Goussier alludes to the fact that certain aspects of the notation may be combined with other symbols without, however, either discussing or illustrating more than a few examples. Although it is impossible to reconstruct exactly what Favier's original contained, one suspects that Goussier's deliberate concentration on notational symbols at the expense of their larger implications for sequences of movement may have led him to eliminate whatever Favier might have written about the notation of step-units. If any such information was, in fact, contained in Favier's manuscript, its loss is regrettable.

Goussier concludes his summary of Favier notation by briefly describing the layout of a typical page of a dance. "In this new system the melody is written above the dance, and the whole thing is written on ordinary music paper, such that, at first glance, a dance notated in this way looks like a duet or a trio, etc. if two or more dancers dance together" (p. 373, column 1). This brief paragraph sounds not like a paraphrase of Favier's text but like Goussier's own voice and strongly suggests that Goussier must have seen at least one page from an actual choreography, even though he does not reproduce a dance in Favier notation in either of his plates. The impression of his having been able to look at dances notated in both systems side by side is strengthened in the fourth and final section of the article, where Goussier makes good a promise to judge the relative merits of the two systems. Even though Goussier admits that Favier's system is ingenious, he finds in favor of Feuillet, because dances notated using the latter system make the floor plan readily visible, whereas Favier's do not.[22]

Goussier's article provides a literal guide to the basic principles of both Feuillet and Favier notation. For neither system, however, does Goussier's discussion cover all of the symbols used in actual choreographies. In the case of Feuillet notation, the numerous other extant sources render Goussier's omissions unimportant, whereas for Favier notation the only means of filling in the lacunae is by deducing the meaning of the undescribed notational symbols from the ways they function in the dances. Thus this article serves as a fundamental point of entry into Favier notation, but is not by itself sufficient for reconstructing the dances of the mascarade.

Goussier's point of view is strikingly ahistorical; he treats all of his topics – Feuillet notation, Dupré's modification to it, Favier notation – as if they were contemporaneous, even though he must have known, by looking at the title page, that Feuillet's book had been published around fifty years before he himself was writing. Thus Goussier's comments do not contain the slightest hint as to when Favier's manuscript might have been written, much less help resolve the narrower question of whether Favier's notation manual was prepared before or after 1688, when Favier notated the dances for *Le Mariage de la Grosse Cathos*. Although this latter question must be addressed primarily by comparing the descriptions of the notation with its actual workings, a direct quotation Goussier provides from Favier's manuscript has a bearing upon it. Before proceeding to

---

[22] "We promised to compare these two ways and we keep our word. We believe, even though this author's invention is ingenious, that one should prefer Feuillet's system in which the track is represented, especially given that we have made the change communicated by M.Dupré, by means of which the rhythm of the steps is communicated via the color of their heads, as was explained in the first part of this article. The drawback of not marking the tracks is much more serious than the drawback of not notating music on the lines and spaces, as several authors have proposed. See the article MUSIQUE, where these things are discussed." (p. 373, columns 1–2; this last remark refers to reforms in music notation proposed by Rousseau.)

his exposition of the principles of Favier notation, Goussier had explained that he first wished to report Favier's own assessment of the different systems for notating dance. Because of its relevance to the competition for the development of dance notation, this passage (p. 371, column 1) is translated here in full. The remark enclosed in parentheses is an explanatory note added by Goussier.

> "Some people," says [Favier], "try to notate dance by using the letters of the alphabet, having reduced, by their own estimation, all the steps that can be done to the number of twenty-four, which is the same as the number of letters. Others have added ciphers [initials] to this letter-based invention, and give as a mark to each step the first letter of its name, for example a *B* for the *pas de bourrée*, an *M* for the menuet step, a *G* for the *pas de gaillarde*, etc. These two methods are, in truth, very frivolous, but there is a third" (that of the sieur Feuillet which we have followed above, while making a few improvements in it)[23] "which seems to have more weight. This one uses lines showing the figure or path that the dancer follows, to which lines are added everything that the two feet do, etc.
>
> But whatever success this [system] may have, I will nonetheless put forth the one I invented on the same subject, and perhaps my work will be as favorably received as his, without, however, diminishing in any way the glory this famous genius has acquired through the beautiful things he has given us."

Favier's discussion of his competitors is regrettably vague as to their identity, but it does confirm the existence of at least four competing notational systems. Moreover, a number of things can be inferred from what he does say. The third system to which Favier refers is undoubtedly Feuillet notation, as Goussier points out. The second system he mentions, the one using the first letter of the step name as a shorthand reference, is probably Lorin's notation. Although there is no way of proving the connection, it is tempting to identify the first system as the one developed by De La Haise, whose notation was entered in evidence in Beauchamps's suit. At the very least, Favier's comments suggest that his own manuscript was written during the period when the ferment over the invention of dance notation was at its height, that is, between approximately 1685 and 1705. The dating could be narrowed, however, if it could be determined whether in his last two sentences Favier is referring to Feuillet, as Goussier seems to think, or to Beauchamps; the remarks could conceivably apply to either. If Favier meant Feuillet, whose dance publications were without doubt "favorably received," then the comment was probably penned after 1700 when Feuillet began his series of publications. If, on the other hand, Favier meant Beauchamps, the inventor of the system and choreographer of countless "beautiful things," then the comments probably date from before the time when Feuillet claimed Beauchamps's invention as his own. The answer lies, perhaps, in Favier's choice of words: surely he was more likely to apply the term "famous genius" to his own teacher, the leading choreographer at court and in Paris, than to the otherwise obscure man who had stolen his teacher's work.

Thus it would appear that Favier's missing manuscript and the dances in *Le Mariage de la Grosse Cathos* were probably prepared relatively close in time to each other, but the question of which one came first is harder to answer. Each contains some notational symbols not found in the other and one could make the argument in both cases that these modifications appear to be later refinements of the system.[24] One difference, however, a

---

[23] In this parenthetical remark Goussier – not Favier – is referring to the refinement brought to his attention by Dupré, which incorporates rhythmic indications into the step notation.

[24] An analogous situation exists in regard to Feuillet notation: *Chorégraphie* includes three pages (97–9) describing the notation of arm motions and three more devoted to notation for castanets played by the dancer (100–2); there are virtually no examples of either notation in the known choreographies. If *Chorégraphie* were not dated, one might conclude that these constitute later notational refinements and that Feuillet's book must therefore postdate the choreographies, when, in fact, it was published concurrently with the earliest published notations. By the same token, the choreographies contain a few symbols not found in *Chorégraphie*. Clearly the presence or absence of symbols does not provide a sufficient basis for establishing relative dates.

All of the symbols associated with Favier notation – including those Goussier mentions that are not found in the mascarade and the ones used in the mascarade but not mentioned by Goussier – are discussed below in the detailed study of Favier notation.

case involving a single notational problem with two possible solutions, seems to argue in favor of the lost manuscript having been written earlier than the dances in the mascarade. Goussier's biggest concern, one that he returns to several times in the article, was that dance notation should specify the precise rhythm of each notated gesture. He felt that he had improved Feuillet notation by incorporating Dupré's system of drawing the foot sign in such a way that it could indicate the note value to which it corresponded, and he implies that the idea may originally have come from Favier.

> The idea of marking the beats of the steps by the shape or color of their head [by this Goussier means the little circle showing the heel of the foot] had occurred to this author [i.e., Favier]; but it was communicated to us by M. Dupré, and we have introduced it into the *Chorégraphie* of Feuillet where it is lacking. The main difference between these two ways is that in this one [Favier's] the value of the steps is marked on the body sign. See fig. 16, which shows the different shapes of the body sign with the corresponding note values marked above.
> These marks in truth would be very useful; but the author advises not to make use of them unless one is very skilled in dance notation and music. (p. 371, column 2)

In *Le Mariage de la Grosse Cathos* Favier did indicate precisely the rhythm of the steps, but not by using the system proposed here. Given the tiny size of the notational symbols used in the manuscript of the mascarade, such subtle modifications to the body signs would have been very painstaking to notate and difficult to read. For notating rhythm Favier used a much clearer and more accessible system, one that breaks down the melody of the dance, written above the choreography, into note values that correspond to each physical gesture (see discussion below). This system is such an improvement over the one described by Goussier, that it must have represented a later stage of Favier's thinking. It seems improbable that Favier could have thought of this system first, then rejected it in favor of modifying the body signs. It also seems unlikely that the Favier dances Goussier presumably saw could also have used the same rhythmic notation as the dances in *Le Mariage de la Grosse Cathos*; not only would this have been redundant, but given Goussier's obsession with rhythmic accuracy, he surely would have mentioned it. Thus it appears probable that Favier's lost manuscript was drawn up before the performance of the mascarade in February 1688; if so, it provides further confirmation that the 1680s were the crucial decade in the development of dance notation.

THE ISSUE OF TERMINOLOGY

The question of the dating of Favier's manuscript relative to the dances in *Le Mariage de la Grosse Cathos* is not academic, but is tied up with the development of Baroque dance style and its terminology. Even prior to the discovery of this mascarade it was clear that French dance was technically and aesthetically sophisticated well before 1700: Feuillet's book *Chorégraphie* represents not the invention of a new dance style, but a notational intabulation of a style that had been developing for a long time and was by then highly codified, a codification that is most apparent in its terminology. Feuillet's numerous tables of steps show that dance was conceived as based upon a limited number of fundamental movements, each of which could be varied in a large number of ways. A *demi-coupé*, for example, may be done *en avant, en arrière, ouvert en arrière, ouvert en arrière avec un rond de jambe par devant*, and so on for fifty-four more ways. More important than the variety, however, is the concept of the individual unit of motion: the movements of the dance are conceptually broken down into a series of fundamental building blocks that can then be assembled at will.

The basic idea was not new: at least as far back as the fifteenth century dancing masters had been conceiving of certain stereotyped sequences of motions as units or steps. The treatises left by late sixteenth-century Italian dancing masters such as Caroso and Negri make use of a dance vocabulary that, like Feuillet's, draws upon the concept of fundamental step-units that are subject to modification. But terminology is not fixed;

Caroso and Negri may apply different terms to the same movement or may ascribe different movements to the same term. Since the dances in *Le Mariage de la Grosse Cathos* are communicated exclusively through symbols, not words, and since Goussier does not discuss steps per se in his article, very little can be established about Favier's own dance terminology. Yet in order to discuss both Favier's notation and his dances, it was necessary for us to find a usable vocabulary. The problem was twofold: first, to determine whether Favier's choreographies fit into the same conceptual framework as the other known Baroque dances; and second, to identify which existing terms might represent the movements Favier notated. The situation was delicate because we wished to avoid imposing preconceived ideas of what Baroque dance was like upon this newly discovered repertoire; we considered it important to remain open to the possibility that the dances and the notation might change some of the ways we think about Baroque dance. Thus it became necessary to examine what was already known about Baroque dance terminology in general.

The terminology used by today's practitioners of Baroque dance derives primarily from two sources: Feuillet's *Chorégraphie* (1700), which gives the names and notations of the steps but does not describe how to execute them, and Pierre Rameau's book, *Le maître à danser* (1725), which lacks notation but provides step names and descriptions. Other French dance sources that contain at least some terminology are Lorin's 1685 manuscript, the four-page supplement included in the second edition of *Chorégraphie* (1701), the introduction to Feuillet's *Recueil de contredanses* (1706), and Rameau's second book, *Abrégé de la nouvelle méthode* (also 1725). Information can also be gleaned from contemporary dictionaries, music treatises, and the like.[25]

All of these sources, while differing in content and manner of presentation, nonetheless clearly operate within the boundaries a single style of dance; moreover they all assume the existence of the *pas composé* or step unit as the concept fundamental to the construction of dances.[26] Favier's dances as seen in *Le Mariage de la Grosse Cathos* fit squarely into this conceptual and stylistic framework. The fundamental motions, as filtered through Goussier's presentation of them, presuppose a technique in common with Feuillet's dances, and the dances themselves are built around recognizable and recurrent step-units. Moreover, their choreographic syntax – the way in which the elements of the dances are combined – follows the same tradition found in the social and theatrical dances of Feuillet and Pécour. Goussier even indirectly reveals that Favier made use of the same kind of terminology as his contemporaries: in one of the passages taken directly from Favier's manuscript (quoted above), Favier mentions the *pas de bourrée*, the *pas de menuet*, and the *pas de gaillarde*, all three of them step-units in common use. In addition, Goussier uses a number of familiar terms in his descriptions of Favier notation that were probably taken directly from Favier's own text: *plié, élevé, marcher, tour de jambe en-dehors, tour de jambe en-dedans, à plat, à terre, en l'air, de côté, sauté, cabriolé*, etc.

It thus appears clear that Favier shared at least some terminology with Lorin, Feuillet, and Rameau; this is certainly to be expected, given that all of them belonged to the same relatively small dance world. However, because Favier's dances date from twelve years before the publication of *Chorégraphie* and thirty-seven years before the publication of Rameau's two books, there is a danger of anachronistically applying to Favier's step-units terms that had not yet come into use. Certainly there are a number of differences in usage

---

[25] The development of French dance terminology has recently been the subject of a momumental study drawing upon many such sources: Kougioumtzoglou-Roucher, "Aux origines."

In addition to the French sources, there are treatises from outside of France that deal with the French style of dancing; the two that contain the greatest amount of information regarding dance terminology are Taubert, *Rechtschaffener Tantzmeister* (1717) and Tomlinson, *The Art of Dancing* (1735). Because of their foreign origin and late dates, these were not included in the present study.

[26] These remarks are not intended to deny the differences in function and complexity between, say, a *contredanse*, a ballroom *danse à deux*, and a theatrical entrée, nor the changes in execution and style that may have occurred over time. Nonetheless, these dances share a basic technique, step vocabulary, and choreographic syntax.

between Feuillet and Rameau, at least some of which may be attributable to the twenty-five-year gap between them, and there may also have been similar differences between Favier and Feuillet. There is the further danger that naming a step-unit will call up preconceived ideas about the nature of a step bearing that name, leading one to ignore the specific characteristics of the step as it is notated. Nonetheless, we have chosen to apply to Favier's step-units those names from other French dance sources that appear to represent the same sequences of movements, favoring, whenever possible, those terms that are closest in time to Favier and omitting entirely terms found only in Rameau. It seems reasonable, for example, to identify a bend and rise symbol placed on a step sign as a *demi-coupé*, and the sequence of a *demi-coupé* followed by a single step as a *coupé*. The latter is a term already used by Lorin in 1685 and one whose movement content seems to have remained stable for a long time.

Readers are warned, however, that our use of a term also found in *Chorégraphie* does not necessarily mean that the execution of the step-unit is identical for Favier and for Feuillet. The menuet step serves as a case in point. In this instance the appropriateness of the term cannot be questioned: Favier himself, as quoted by Goussier, mentions it, and two dances in the mascarade – the menuet and the passepied – are based on a repeating step-unit that could be nothing other than a menuet step. However, its execution, both in rhythm and in technique, is somewhat different than the step-unit by the same name as notated by Feuillet and described by Rameau. The difference may be due to a change in style over time, or may simply represent yet another variation on the basic step. It does not negate the applicability of a single term to a step that exists in different versions, but it does serve as a useful reminder that identity of terminology does not necessarily require immutability of content.

Even though we cannot be certain that the terminology we have applied to Favier's steps is the same as his, we know at least that we have chosen terms that were current in his milieu during his lifetime. Our decisions regarding the appropriate terms to use for Favier's step-units had to rest upon close analyses of his notational symbols as they function in the dances of the mascarade. In order to classify sequences of motions, it was necessary to identify their significant taxonomic characteristics; this process served to illuminate both similarities and differences between Favier's and Feuillet's steps. The application of terminology thus is not restrictive, but on the contrary, serves as a useful point of entry to this new repertoire of dances. It ultimately will serve to help place Favier's dances in a larger context, to make it possible to pursue comparisons between Favier's choreographies and the Feuillet repertoire, and to study the works of Favier in relation to those by other choreographers such as Pécour. Our goal in finding a usable vocabulary for Favier's dances has not been to narrow the view of this new repertoire, but to open it out.

Since Feuillet notation is already familiar to many people and serves of necessity as a point of reference for investigations into Favier notation, we have followed Goussier's organizational plan and introduce our discussion of Favier's notational system with a brief review of Feuillet notation.

FEUILLET NOTATION IN BRIEF[27]

The Feuillet system of notation (see plate 6) utilizes a track or floor pattern, showing the path followed by the dancer or dancers. At the top of each page of dance notation is the melody line of the music corresponding to that segment of choreography. Individual dances in Feuillet notation are normally about four to ten pages in length, and the number of measures of music and dance on each page varies from four to twenty or more, depending on the complexity of both the steps and the floor pattern. Short perpendicular

---

[27] For a detailed investigation of Feuillet notation see Hilton, *Dance of Court and Theater*, particularly chapters 5 and 6.

The dance notation

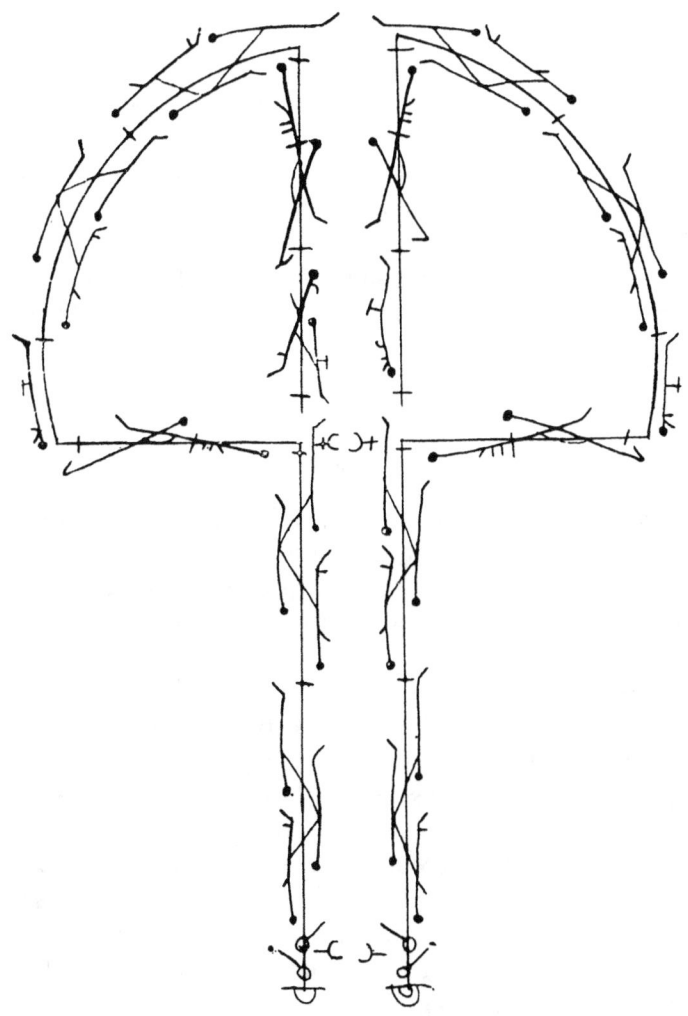

PLATE 6 Example of Feuillet notation. The first page of the "Bourrée d'Achille," a social dance for one couple choreographed by Pécour and notated by Feuillet. Published in Feuillet's *Recueil de danses, composées par M. Pecour* (Paris, 1700)

lines on the track correspond to the barlines of the music, marking off the measures of dance. Symbols representing the motions of the feet, body, and – occasionally – hands are placed along the track. Stationary foot positions are represented by pinlike schematic drawings of the feet in one of the five positions:

     ᑐᑐ first position
     ᑐ ᑐ second position
     ᑐ third position
     ᑐ fourth position
     ᑐ fifth position.

A traveling step is notated by a line, with a dot showing where the step begins and a flag showing where it ends. A step forward on the right foot would be notated as follows:

This basic step may be modified by the addition of one or more symbols. Feuillet includes seven such symbols in *Chorégraphie*: *plié* (bend), *élevé* (rise), *sauté* (hop or leap), *cabriolé* (beaten hop or leap), *tombé* (fall), *glissé* (slide), and *pied en l'air* (foot in the air). In addition, the placement of a dot by the flag indicates that the toe or heel rests on the ground, but the weight of the body remains on the other foot. The *demi-contretemps* shown here illustrates how several of these symbols can be combined. The dancer bends on the left foot, hops on the same foot, and finishes by stepping into *plié* on the right foot. Although the left leg initiates the action, all of the modifying signs are placed on the symbol for the right foot, because it is the foot that travels.

Individual step symbols are usually combined into *pas composés* or step-units, each of which normally corresponds to a measure of music. Certain slow dances, such as the *entrée grave* and the loure or slow gigue, require two step-units for each bar of music; conversely, in menuets and passepieds notated in a meter of 3/4 or 3/8, one step-unit requires two bars of music. A liaison line connects the various steps that make up the step-unit. This line may be modified to indicate the relative speed of any individual step: two steps connected by parallel lines are to be performed twice as fast as the other steps in the step-unit. A liaison line stopping short of the step symbol indicates that the step in question is to be performed twice as slowly as the other steps in the step-unit. However, there are inherent ambiguities in this system, particularly for dances with a meter of 3/4 or 6/4 – the *pas de menuet*, in which four steps are distributed among six beats of music, is a good example. Theatrical choreographies, most of which contain complex step-units, also pose a problem in this regard. Furthermore, many notators of the time did not observe these conventions and used a single, connected liaison line regardless of the rhythm of the steps.

The step symbols are placed along the track or floor pattern followed by the dancer. Although these floor patterns are not always drawn to scale, the overall shape of the dance figure is clearly visible. A change in direction of the dancer relative to the track or floor pattern is shown by a small curve placed on the step sign, the degree of turning being indicated by the shape of the curve. Symbols for taking and dropping of hands are placed to the side of the step symbols. In *Chorégraphie* Feuillet includes symbols for the motions of the wrists and arms, along with a sample dance excerpt for which the arm movements have been notated; however, almost none of the surviving notated dances include symbols of this type.

The strengths of Feuillet notation – the clear floor patterns and the easily understandable step symbols – were as obvious to eighteenth-century dancers and choreographers as they are to us. In fact, Goussier singled out the clarity of the floor patterns as the chief advantage of Feuillet notation over that of Favier. The elaborate foot and leg gestures associated with theatrical dance can also be illustrated with little difficulty. However, the system has a certain number of weaknesses; in particular it is not well suited for notating choreographies involving more than a few dancers. Even in certain *danses à deux* the overlapping floor patterns, with their accompanying step symbols, can be difficult to decipher; when four or more dancers are involved the difficulty is compounded (unless, of course, all the dancers are moving downstage in straight lines). Thus, of the more than 335 dances preserved in Feuillet notation, fewer than 20 are for more than two dancers, most of them relatively simple non-theatrical dances. Only one French theatrical choreography for more than two dancers survives, Feuillet's "Ballet de neuf danseurs" to music by Lully (LMC 1320).[28] A second weakness is that the apparent clarity of the Feuillet floor patterns can be misleading. Stationary steps such as the *pas de rigaudon* appear to travel, since they take up space in the floor pattern, when in fact they are done in place; in addition, the floor patterns must often be displaced on the page to show the patterns of two dancers who are following the same track.[29] Finally, the precise rhythm or timing of step-units within the measure is not always indicated.

FAVIER NOTATION: AN OVERVIEW

Our understanding of Favier notation draws on three types of information: Goussier's article "Chorégraphie" in the *Encyclopédie*; the dances preserved in *Le Mariage de la Grosse Cathos*; and the information regarding Baroque dance derived from both theoretical sources and surviving choreographies. This synthesis is necessary for several reasons. Although Goussier's article was invaluable in the initial stages of decoding Favier notation, it soon became apparent that it was not sufficient for a complete understanding of the system. A number of the symbols included in Goussier are not used in Favier's mascarade; conversely, several symbols found in the mascarade choreographies either do not appear in Goussier or are used in ways not explained in the *Encyclopédie* article. Furthermore, the important issue of how these symbols combine to form steps and step-units is almost completely ignored by Goussier.

Although Favier notation bears certain similarities to that of Feuillet, the differences between them, both conceptual and symbolic, are much more numerous. For those familiar with the attractive floor patterns of Feuillet notation, the most striking feature of Favier notation is that neither the floor patterns nor the step-units are readily apparent. Both must be synthesized from several disparate elements. These elements are presented in a "grid" comprised of three or more horizontal layers and a number of columns (see, for example, p. 43 of the facsimile, a dance for eight performers). The horizontal layers, reading from the bottom to the top of the grid, include (1) the symbols for the steps – *demi-coupé*, *jeté*, etc.; (2) the spatial orientation of the dancer as well as the choice and position of the feet, shown on what looks like a music staff, a separate one for each of the eight dancers; and (3) the music for the dance, as in the Feuillet system, but with the melody broken up into short rhythmic units, usually of a quarter note or half note in duration.

The bottom layer: the step symbol

The simplest movement, a plain step or *pas marché*, is indicated by a short horizontal line (−). To this line are added various modifying symbols to indicate such movements as a

---

[28] The eight dances in Pemberton, *Essay*, are for three to twelve women, but were probably performed as graduation exercises at London finishing schools for young ladies (see Marsh, "French dance," p. 197).

[29] For example, in Feuillet's 1710 "Passepied à quatre" (LMC 6660), a rather simple dance for two couples, Feuillet includes small inserts on a number of pages labeled "Comme il faut être après la figure" to show the true positions of the dancers at the end of the figure on that page.

bend and rise or *demi-coupé* (symbol) and a leap or *saut* (symbol). The presence of two horizontal lines rather than one indicates that two feet are involved in the step. For example, an *assemblé* or spring from one foot onto both feet would be written as follows: (symbol).

The middle layer: position and feet

The five- to seven-line "music staves," one per dancer, are divided into segments or frames by vertical lines. Each frame represents the performing space, downstage at the top of the staff, upstage at the bottom. The dancer is indicated by a half-circle, closed by a straight line that represents the front of the body (this symbol is also used by Feuillet). The position of the body symbol within the frame indicates the dancer's position on stage at the beginning of the step element. Only by comparing the placement of the symbol in two or more consecutive frames can the path of the dancer be determined.

Several other symbols are used in conjunction with the half circle. The addition of a small curved line to either side of the body sign indicates a turn to that side: (symbol). Unlike Feuillet notation, where the degree of turning is indicated by the shape of the turn sign – ¼ circle for a 90° turn, ½ circle for a 180° turn, etc. – the turn sign in the Favier system indicates the direction of the turn only. Again, a comparison of the orientation of the body signs in two consecutive frames is necessary to determine the degree of turning required. The letters "*d*" (*droit*, or right) and "*g*" (*gauche*, or left) refer to the feet; the placement of the letter relative to the half circle signifies the positioning of the foot relative to the body, i.e., in front, to the side, or to the back. Both letters have two forms: the relatively straight ascender or descender (∂ or ɡ) shows a weight-bearing foot, while the curved form of the letters (∂ or ɡ) means that the foot in question is in the air.

Ill. 5.1 shows the same step-unit, a *fleuret*, as notated in both systems. The dancer begins facing the audience, and in the course of the step-unit (a *demi-coupé* followed by two plain steps) travels forward, gradually turning 90° to his own left. This example also illustrates a somewhat disorienting aspect of Favier notation, namely that the notation is always read from left to right, regardless of the direction in which the dancer is moving.

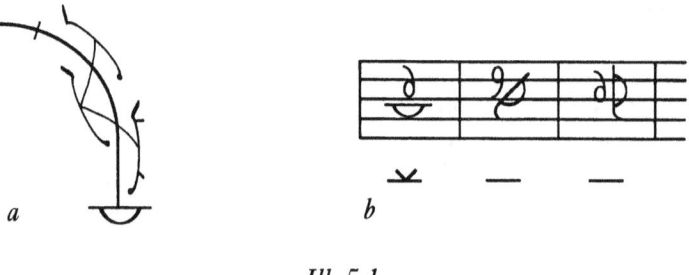

Ill. 5.1

The top layer: the music

Both notation systems place the music accompanying each frame of dance at the top of that segment. In Feuillet notation a measure of music is usually equal to a measure of dance, but the relationship of the beats within the measure of music to the various elements of the step-unit is not always clear. As a result, performers today will often arrive at different rhythmic interpretations of the same notation. The Favier system, in contrast, permits each note of the melody to be subdivided without limit, so that a quarter note can be notated as four tied-together sixteenth notes. Example 5.1 illustrates the same melodic fragment as it appears in the music score (p. 18 of the facsimile) and in the dance score (p. 61 of the facsimile). Since each melodic segment corresponds to the element of the step-unit in the column beneath it, rhythmic values for these elements are thus established with a precision that is unimaginable in the Feuillet system. The superiority of Favier notation in this respect is unquestionable.

Ex. 5.1 a, b

As example 5.1b illustrates, there are almost no bar lines in the music itself in the dance section of the manuscript, except in dances with upbeats, when a bar line is used to separate the pickup from the first beat of the following measure. However, in the first five dances as well as the final recessional, short vertical lines appear below the music staff to mark off the measures of music. The spacing of the individual notes of the melody bears no relationship to their rhythmic durations. On the contrary, the first note within each frame is aligned with the step symbol below – usually in the center of the frame – and the remaining notes (if there are any) are bunched together at the right of the frame, sometimes even overlapping into the next frame (see, for example, the ends of the first two lines of music on p. 41 of the facsimile). In the two danced choruses the dance notation has been cued to the text and the bass line of the music.

FAVIER NOTATION: A DETAILED STUDY

The detailed investigation of Favier notation that follows draws upon information both from Goussier's *Encyclopédie* article and from *Le Mariage de la Grosse Cathos*. Since the crucial point is to understand the way the notation actually functions in the dances, the material presented in this chapter does not limit itself to the individual symbols, as did Goussier, but goes beyond into the ways in which the symbols are combined. Because of this broader focus, the discussion does not adopt Goussier's organization; rather, we expand upon the framework established in the preceding section, by first listing all symbols from the bottom and middle layers that are used in the mascarade (symbols mentioned by Goussier but not used in *Le Mariage de la Grosse Cathos* are treated separately) and then by showing how the symbols combine to form step-units. This is followed by a section devoted to the information about step rhythms contained in the top layer. Although Favier's notational intentions are for the most part clear, even as to symbols not covered by Goussier, a certain number of ambiguities remain. The implications for performance that these ambiguities suggest are also discussed.

In the following lists, Goussier's own explanations are provided for those notational symbols included in his article. The original French (spellings modernized) is followed by a translation or paraphrase, and by comments when necessary. The symbols are cued to the figures from plate II of the *Encyclopédie* article (see appendix B), although our order does not adhere to Goussier's. Square brackets enclose terms that are not taken from Goussier.

Notational symbols used in the mascarade

The bottom layer

The bottom layer includes the step symbols, which usually consist of a horizontal line upon which various modifying symbols have been placed. Each symbol is allocated a separate frame, regardless of its rhythmic duration, and is centered below it.

— "La ligne horizontale marque qu'il faut marcher" (fig. 19). (A horizontal line indicates a plain step.) This corresponds to Feuillet's step or *pas droit*.

100   Musical Theatre at the Court of Louis XIV

\ "[U]ne ligne inclinée de gauche à droite, marque qu'il faut plier les genoux" (fig. 17). (A line slanting [downwards] from left to right indicates a bending of the knees.) Feuillet also uses a short slanting line to indicate a *plié*.

/ "[Une ligne inclinée de droite à gauche,] marque au contraire qu'il faut les élever" (fig. 18). (A line slanting in the opposite direction indicates a rise.) Figs. 17 and 18 correspond to Feuillet's *plié* and *élevé* respectively.

⌒ "[L]e mouvement qu'on appelle *tour de jambe en-dehors*" (fig. 22). (A turning of the leg outward.)

⌣ "[L]e mouvement qu'on appelle *tour de jambe en-dedans*" (fig. 23). (A turning of the leg inward.) Feuillet uses the term *pas rond* or *rond de jambe* for both of these motions.

o ⁀o "[U]n *o*, indique qu'il faut pirouetter." (An "o" indicates a *pirouette*.) In *Le Mariage de la Grosse Cathos* this symbol is used either in combination with a short curved line (see figs. 20 and 21 below) to indicate a *pirouette* on one foot, or with another "o" to indicate a *pirouette* on both feet. The latter symbol does not appear in Goussier. According to Goussier's commentary (p. 372, col. 1) the *pirouette* is illustrated in figure 40 of plate II, but this statement is in error; figure 40 shows the feet in fourth position, as Goussier correctly points out in the next column on the same page.[30]

⌒ "[I]l faut marcher en avançant d'abord le pied dans le commencement du pas, et continuer en ligne courbe jusqu'à la fin de son action" (fig. 20). (A step, the free foot traveling forward in the curved path as shown.)

⌣ "[I]l faut marcher en reculant d'abord le pied dans le commencement du pas, et continuer en ligne courbe jusqu'à la fin de son action" (fig. 21). (As in the previous example, but the free foot follows its curved path backward rather than forward.) In *Le Mariage de la Grosse Cathos* these two symbols appear only in conjunction with the *pirouette* symbol; in this context they seem to indicate that the free foot moves in a circular path as the body turns.

= "Ces deux lignes indiquent que le pied droit commence et achève son mouvement, et que le pied gauche commence et finit le sien après." (The two lines indicate that the right foot starts and finishes its movement after which the left foot starts and finishes its movement.) When both feet are involved in a single step – for example, in a spring from one foot to two feet – two horizontal lines appear in the same frame. The upper of the two lines always represents the right foot, while the lower always represents the left foot. The vertical alignment of the two symbols indicates their timing relative to each other: for example, if the two lines overlap, the second foot begins moving before the first foot completes its action. Goussier discusses this principle at great length and includes six examples in his commentary as well as the two examples in plate II (see figs. 47 and 48).[31]

∧ [*Tombé*]. The inverted "V" – a rise followed by a bend – may indicate a *tombé* or fall. Goussier neither mentions this term nor provides a symbol in his plates, although it is an important element in the Feuillet dance vocabulary. In *Le Mariage de la Grosse Cathos* the *tombé* appears only in conjuction with a jump from two feet to two feet, and we have identified the resulting step as a *pas échappé*.

[30] Goussier's error may be explained by the fact that figure 40 of plate I (the plate illustrating Feuillet notation) *does* illustrate a *pirouette* or 360° turn.

[31] Perhaps one reason why Goussier devoted so much space to a discussion of this issue is that it is inherently confusing. Since the notation proceeds from left to right across the page, it would be more logical for the upper line to represent the left foot and the lower line the right. Favier himself apparently had trouble remembering this principle: in a number of instances in *Le Mariage de la Grosse Cathos* it is clear that the feet have been reversed. These errors are detailed in chapter 6.

The middle layer

The middle layer includes the position and orientation of each dancer in the performing space, the choice of foot or feet for each step, the positions of the feet, and the use of hands and arms.

"[L]a salle où l'on danse [est représentée] par des divisions faites sur les cinq lignes d'une portée de musique" (fig. 3). (The room where one dances is represented by the divisions [vertical lines] made on the five lines of the music staff.) The frames of dance notation created by these divisions should not be confused with measures of music, each of which will usually contain several frames of dance notation. The orientation of these frames is the same as in Feuillet notation: downstage at the top of the staff and upstage at the bottom. Although Goussier does not mention this possibility, in most of those choreographies in *Le Mariage de la Grosse Cathos* involving all eight dancers, one or two additional lines are added to the original five- or six-line staff to allow for greater detail in the floor patterns.

"Le caractère de présence du corps" (fig. 4). (The symbol for the dancer.) The straight line represents the front of the body, the semi-circle the back. This symbol is also used by Feuillet for male dancers.

[Other symbols used to represent performers.] The three symbols shown here are used in the final recessional (XC) to differentiate the various performing groups: the singers are represented by a filled-in half circle, the oboes by a half circle bisected by a vertical line, and the Italian comedians by a half circle with a dot. Elsewhere in the manuscript (dances IB, III, and V) the filled-in half circle is used to identify the male dance roles.

The filled-in half circle and the half circle with a vertical line also appear as the third and fifth symbols in Goussier's figure 16; however, these symbols were used to indicate step rhythms, a system of rhythmic notation that had apparently been discarded by Favier before he notated the mascarade. (See below, "Notational symbols found only in the *Encyclopédie*," for further discussion.)

"[L]e corps doit tourner du côté droit, [ou] du côté gauche" (figs. 5 and 6). (The body must turn to the right side [or] to the left.) A small curved arc added to the body sign signals a turn towards the side on which the sign is placed. The extent of the turn can only be determined by comparing the positions of the body signs in two consecutive frames (see ill. 5.1b). Goussier goes on to explain that the turn sign appears on the first of the two consecutive body signs, i.e., on the body symbol representing the orientation of the dancer *before* the turn has taken place. However, this explanation does not conform to the usage in *Le Mariage de la Grosse Cathos*, where the turn sign appears on the body symbol showing the dancer's orientation *after* the turn is made.[32]

"[U]n *d*, indique le pied droit" (fig. 25).

"[U]n *g*, indique le pied gauche" (fig. 26). The letters "d" – *droit*, or right – and "g" – *gauche*, or left – refer to the feet. The shape of the letter determines the performance of the step. Here, the relatively straight ascender or descender signifies a weight-bearing foot.

"[L]es pieds sont en l'air, ce que l'on connaît par leur queue qui est recourbée du côté de la tête" (fig. 32). (The feet are in the air, which one recognizes by the curved tail of the letter.) Almost all of the steps in *Le Mariage de la Grosse Cathos* use either these letter shapes or the ones shown in figs. 25 and 26.

---

[32] Although it is possible that Favier changed his notation system between the time that he wrote his treatise and when he notated *Le Mariage de la Grosse Cathos*, it seems equally plausible that Goussier confused Favier's use of the turn sign with Feuillet's.

"[Les pieds] sont tournés en-dedans, comme dans les cinq fausses positions" (figs. 35 and 36). (The feet are turned inward, as in the five false positions.) As Goussier explains in his article, false positions of the feet are represented by upside-down letters. Although Goussier's text distinguishes between figs. 35 and 36 – the former is *à terre*, the latter *en l'air* – the two examples in plate II are very similar. Two examples of false positions occur in *Le Mariage de la Grosse Cathos*, both of them in the first entrée (III). In both instances Favier reverses the foot letters as well as placing them upside down; thus an inverted "d" represents a false position with the *left* rather than the right foot.

[The placing of the feet.] The positioning of the letter or letters relative to the body symbol signifies the placement of the foot or feet relative to the body: as shown here, in front, to the side, or in back. The letters representing the feet always appear in an upright position (with the exception of the false positions described above), even if the orientation of the body symbol changes. When both letters appear with the body sign, the resulting foot placement normally corresponds to one of the five positions codified in Feuillet's *Chorégraphie*. Favier apparently did not use this terminology, preferring instead to classify the foot positions into three categories: *naturelle* (natural), *ensemble* (closed), and *écartée* (wide).

Naturelle (figs. 37 and 40). "[Les pieds sont] éloignés l'un de l'autre de la distance d'un des pieds. Il [i.e., Favier] marque [cette position] par les lettres *d g* jointes au caractère de présence, sans y rien ajouter." (In the natural positions the feet are separated by the distance of the dancer's foot. They are indicated by placing the letters for the feet adjacent to the body sign, without adding other symbols.) Favier's natural positions correspond to Feuillet's second and fourth positions. In second position the letters are on either side of the body sign, as shown in the first example. In fourth position the letters are above and below the body sign. Either foot can be in front; in the example shown here it is the right foot. We have modified Goussier's drawing of figure 40, making the tail of the "g" less curved to correspond to his description of this position.

Ensemble (fig. 38). "[Les pieds] se touchent. Il met un point, en sorte que la lettre du pied soit entre le caractère de présence et le point." (In the closed positions the feet touch. These positions are indicated by dots placed next to the letters for the feet.) Favier's closed positions correspond to Feuillet's first and fifth positions. Goussier's example of first position (fig. 38) is shown here, but he does not provide an example of fifth position. The latter, however, occurs frequently in *Le Mariage de la Grosse Cathos*; in the example shown here the right foot is in front of the left, but as in fourth position, either foot can be in front.

Favier's choice of the terms *naturelle* and *ensemble* – rather than Beauchamps's terminology (the five positions) – suggests that the latter terminology may not have been in general use at the time Favier's treatise was written. Furthermore, it leaves open to question whether Favier even envisioned a third position. Although it is possible that the placement of the dot on the opposite side of the body symbol from the foot letter indicates a step into third position, as in the example shown here, it seems more likely that the dot in this context represents a beaten step. (Evidence for this assertion will be presented later in the chapter.) It is even more difficult to imagine how Favier notation might represent both feet in third position, and there are no symbols in the mascarade that are susceptible of this interpretation.

 *Écartée* (fig. 39). "[L]a distance d'un pied à l'autre est plus grande que celle d'un pied. Il [Favier] marque [cette position] par une petite ligne verticale placée entre le caractère du pied et celui de présence." (In the wide positions the feet are farther apart than in the natural positions [i.e., second and fourth positions]; they are notated by placing small vertical [or horizontal or diagonal] lines between the body and foot symbols.) Favier's wide positions have no equivalent in Feuillet notation.

 Although Goussier only mentions the use of a vertical line to indicate a wide position, and only illustrates a wide second position (fig. 39),[33] it stands to reason that a wide fourth position is also possible, and that it would be indicated by short horizontal lines, as shown here. Indeed, a number of examples of wide fourth position are found in *Le Mariage de la Grosse Cathos* in both male duets (III and VI). The horizontal line is often slanted, perhaps to allow it to be more easily distinguished from the horizontal stave lines.

 "[L]e pied gauche à terre devant, et le pied droit en l'air derrière. On connaîtra la position en ce qu'elle sera toujours la première de chaque danse" (fig. 43). (The left foot in front and the right foot behind in the air. This position is familiar since it is used to begin every dance.) Goussier discusses this symbol at some length, stating that it is to choreography what the clef is to music – i.e., it shows the dancer where and on which foot he begins the dance. The symbol appears at the beginning of almost all of the dances in the mascarade. Most dances in Feuillet notation begin in a similar fashion.

The following four examples, all drawn from *Le Mariage de la Grosse Cathos*, show how these symbols are used when stepping into the various positions.

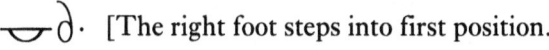 [The right foot steps into first position.]

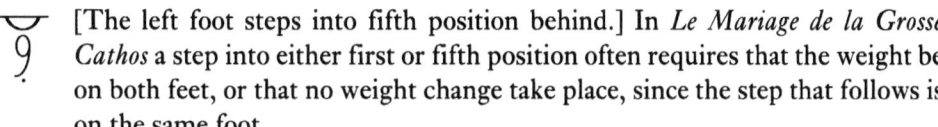 [The left foot steps into fifth position behind.] In *Le Mariage de la Grosse Cathos* a step into either first or fifth position often requires that the weight be on both feet, or that no weight change take place, since the step that follows is on the same foot.

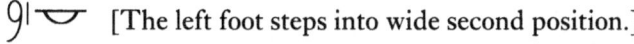 [The left foot steps into wide second position.]

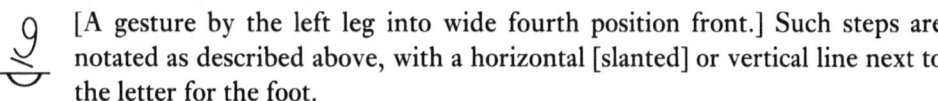 [A gesture by the left leg into wide fourth position front.] Such steps are notated as described above, with a horizontal [slanted] or vertical line next to the letter for the foot.

• [The dot]. The dot has two, or possibly three, meanings, only one of which – the closed or *ensemble* position – is mentioned by Goussier. When a dot appears in the middle layer on the opposite side of the body symbol from the foot letter, it may signify a beat with the free foot (see discussion below, p. 00). The dot is also used in the bottom layer as part of a modified *demi-coupé* symbol (see *pas de gaillarde* in the inventory of steps.)

m [*Main* or hand]. This letter appears in three of the mascarade dances – nos. IV, V, and IX – to indicate that partners should take hands. The placement of the "m" – below the lower left or right corner of the frame – indicates that the left or right hand respectively is intended. Unlike Feuillet notation there is no symbol to indicate the dropping of hands, and verbal instructions are given instead: for example, "l'on quitte les mains." Verbal instructions are sometimes used in place of or along with the "m": for example, "la m[ain] d[roite] à la 3me personne" (dance V, frame 1). Neither this nor the following symbol is mentioned by Goussier.

---

[33] In Goussier's figure 39 the vertical line between the left foot and the body symbol is missing.

b [*Bras* or arm]. The letter "b" is only used in one dance, the chorus "Passons" (IX), and there are no verbal instructions to help decipher its meaning. By analogy with Favier's use of the letter "m" it would seem that the "b" stands for *bras* or arm. Precisely what the arms in question are supposed to do is less clear. However, the appearance of a "b" first above and then below consecutive frames (or vice versa) suggests that the arms are being raised and then lowered.

[*Cabriolé*]. The short horizontal line extending from the middle of a foot letter to either side may indicate a *cabriolé* or beaten *saut*. Goussier lists the term *cabriolé* along with the terms *plié*, *élevé*, and *sauté* – all of them modifying signs that are placed on the line for the step in the bottom level. However, no symbol for the *cabriolé* appears in Goussier's plates, and there are no unidentified symbols in the bottom layer of the mascarade notation that could be interpreted as a *cabriolé*.

Our identification must remain tentative, since the symbol appears in the middle layer rather than the bottom layer of notation. Nevertheless, in the mascarade it always occurs in conjunction with a *saut*, apparently calling for some sort of leg gesture in the air.

Notational symbols found only in the *Encyclopédie*

"[L]e corps penché" (figs. 12–15). (The bending of the body.) Modifications of the body symbol that show the body bending in various directions – forward, to the right, backwards, and to the left; they do not appear in Favier's mascarade. These symbols have no counterpart in Feuillet notation. However, their inclusion in Favier's treatise suggests that they represent one aspect of the movement repertoire of late seventeenth-century theatrical dance. Contemporary illustrations, notably of Harlequin and some of the other *commedia* characters, support this notion.

"[L]a valeur des pas [marquée] sur les caractères des présences" (fig. 16). (The rhythmic value of the step shown on the body symbol.) These modifications of the body symbol indicate the rhythm of the step, ranging from a sixteenth note, the first symbol, to a dotted whole note. This system is not used in *Le Mariage de la Grosse Cathos*; instead Favier indicates step rhythm by subdividing the note values in the top layer (see p. 98). The similarity of the third and fifth symbols in this figure to Favier's symbols for the singers (or male dancers) and oboes respectively has already been mentioned.

.... "[L]e pied fait quelque mouvement, sans sortir cependant du lieu qu'il occupe" (fig. 24). (A movement by one foot while the body remains stationary.) This symbol does not appear in *Le Mariage de la Grosse Cathos*; perhaps it is similar to Feuillet's *pas tortillé* or waving step, a term not mentioned by Goussier.

Goussier's plate II includes seven additional shapes of the letters "d" and "g" (see figs. 27–31 and 33–4) in which the ascender or descender has been modified in some way. None of them is used in the dances in *Le Mariage de la Grosse Cathos*, although given the small size of the letters in the manuscript of the mascarade, the subtle distinctions shown in Goussier's plate would have been almost impossible to distinguish. Figures 27–31 represent various ways of placing the foot on the floor – toe followed by heel, toes only, flat, and so on. Feuillet notation also includes symbols for such gestures, and they are occasionally found in theatrical choreographies in Feuillet notation. Figures 33 and 34 represent, respectively, the foot in the air, toe pointed up; and the foot in the air, level with the ground. No equivalents for these gestures exist in Feuillet notation. Favier's inclusion of such symbols in his lost manuscript treatise provides another hint of the broad range of movement vocabulary in use at the time.

Goussier's plate II also illustrates two other positions involving both feet; neither has an equivalent in Feuillet notation.

"[L]e pied droit devant et de côté, et par conséquent le pied gauche derrière et de côté" (fig. 41). (The right foot in front and to the side and as a result the left foot behind and to the [other] side.) This position appears to be a combination of second and fourth positions.

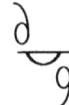
"[L]a situation qu'on appelle *croisée*, le pied droit devant la partie gauche du corps, et le pied gauche derrière la partie droite" (fig. 42). (A crossed position, the right foot in front of the left part of the body, and the left foot behind the right part of the body). Although Feuillet also uses the term *croisée*, he does not intend the feet to cross further than fifth position.

"Missing" symbols

Goussier neither mentions nor illustrates several other symbols that are important elements in the Feuillet dance vocabulary, in particular a beat or *battu* and a slide or *glissé*. Nor do there appear to be dedicated symbols for these elements where one would expect to find them – in the bottom layer of the mascarade dance notation. The absence of these elements may indicate either that the actions they represent were not part of Favier's dance style, or that the actions were implicit in the particular step notation. The *battu*, however, may be indicated by the dot, as will be discussed in detail below.

Inventory of steps and step-units

Step symbols in Favier notation, as in Feuillet notation, are formed by placing modifying signs on the basic step sign. Goussier alludes to this process by saying that one places on the step sign "les signes des agréments, comme *plié, élevé, sauté, cabriolé*, etc." (p. 373, col. 1; the signs for the "ornaments" such as bend, rise, hop or leap, cabriole, etc.) Although the resulting movements are neither discussed nor illustrated by Goussier, it is clear from the dances in *Le Mariage de la Grosse Cathos* how this system works in practice. A single step or movement in Favier notation normally corresponds to a single frame. The basic action of the step is notated in the bottom layer of the frame, but it is necessary to consult the middle layer to determine which foot performs the action. The middle layer must also be consulted for steps involving jumps or leaps, since it is the shape of the foot letter in that layer that distinguishes between the two actions. The rhythmic duration of the step is shown in the top layer.

The formation of *pas composés* or step-units, each of which is made up of two or more individual steps or movements, is a somewhat more complicated procedure in Favier notation than in Feuillet notation. Since Favier's step-units almost always comprise two or more successive frames, it is necessary not only to synthesize vertically the elements of each frame, but also to synthesize horizontally, comparing adjacent middle-layer frames in order to determine the amount of turning, the direction of travel, and the interpretation of hops or leaps. Feuillet's liaison line visually defines the step-unit by joining its elements; it has no equivalent in Favier notation. However, as in Feuillet notation, Favier's step-units usually begin with a *mouvement* (bend/rise or bend/*saut*) and this *mouvement* usually corresponds to the beginning of a bar of music (or half-bar in the case of dance VI).

All ten dances in *Le Mariage de la Grosse Cathos* are constructed entirely or in part of step-units that have recognizable counterparts in Feuillet notation; these step-units are listed in the inventory. However, four of the dances also use step-units that are composed of recognizable elements but that have no name in Feuillet notation.[34] For example, within

---

[34] It should be noted that unnamed step-units are also found in theatrical dances in Feuillet notation. No systematic study of this dance vocabulary has been undertaken.

a single measure a *demi-contretemps* might be followed by a *coupé*. Most such step-units appear only once in the mascarade, but one is sufficiently intriguing and appears with enough frequency that we have dubbed it the Favier step and included it in the inventory. The remaining unnamed step-units are described in the narrative accounts of each dance found in chapter 6.

The step names used in the inventory have been taken from several sources: most of them are found in the 1700 edition of Feuillet's *Chorégraphie* or in the four-page supplement included in the 1701 edition; one comes from the same author's 1706 treatise on contredanse, *Recueil de contredanses*. Concordances with Lorin's list of steps in his contredanse treatise (c. 1685) are also cited, as evidence that the nomenclature existed prior to 1688.[35] In a number of instances more than one version of a particular step-unit is found in the mascarade. In such cases the version that occurs most frequently is reported first, with the other versions reported as variants.

The inventory begins with a discussion of the *demi-coupé* and the *saut*; not only do these steps exist independently but almost every step-unit includes either one or the other (or both) of these steps. The remainder of the steps and step-units are presented in alphabetical order. The illustrations show the simplest form of each step as it appears in *Le Mariage de la Grosse Cathos*; turns are omitted for ease of comparison, and no attempt has been made to indicate traveling. Although only one form of each step is shown, almost all of them occur beginning on the opposite foot as well. In *Le Mariage de la Grosse Cathos* turns are frequent, and step-units often do not progress in one direction throughout. For example, a *fleuret* may move forward on the first step, to the side on the second, and backwards on the third, all while turning 90° to one side. In step-units beginning with a hop or leap it is sometimes necessary to show the position of the feet at the end of the previous step; in such cases the symbol preceding the step-unit in question is enclosed in square brackets. Since most of the step-units can be performed in more than one meter, with a subsequent change in timing, step rhythms are discussed in a separate section following the inventory. The descriptions in the inventory assume a basic knowledge on the part of the reader of Baroque dance terminology and at least a rudimentary understanding of the technique. It should be emphasized again that we have used Feuillet terminology for the sake of convenience, and that the execution of steps in Favier notation may not be the same as in Feuillet notation, even if the names are the same.

 [*Demi-coupé*]. Bend and rise while transferring the weight of the body from one foot to the other (here from the left foot to the right). This step, the building block of Baroque dance technique, initiates the majority of step-units in *Le Mariage de la Grosse Cathos*.

 In this variant of the *demi-coupé* the bend and rise signs are placed at the beginning of the step sign, usually in conjunction with a step into fifth position behind as shown here. This variant occurs only in the context of a step-unit, for example as the first element of the *coupé* or the third element of the *contretemps de menuet*.

 Saut. "Le saut se connaît lorsque la ligne *élevé* placée sur la ligne *marché*, est plus grande que la ligne *plié* placée sur la même ligne *marché*" (p. 372, col. 1). (A leap or hop is indicated when the rise symbol placed on the step line is longer than the bend symbol placed on the same line.) This is the only step symbol that Goussier describes, but he does not provide an illustration in plate II. The symbol shown here is a "generic" *saut*. The French word can mean either hop or leap, and in Favier notation the differentiation can only be made by the shape of the letter that accompanies the body sign: the curved form of the letter, a foot-in-air sign, signals

---

[35] See also n. 12 above. According to Kougioumtzoglou-Roucher, "Aux origines," many of Feuillet's step names appeared in print for the first time in Antoine Furetière's *Dictionnaire* (1690), gathered by Furetière during his visits to dance academies.

a hop, while a letter with a straight tail denotes a leap. See the entries below for the *contretemps* family and the *jeté*.

This variant of the *saut* is analogous to the *demi-coupé* variant shown above. The bend and hop or bend and leap signs appear at the beginning of the step sign; if a leap or *jeté*, it is usually taken into fifth position behind. Like the *demi-coupé* variant it is found only as part of a larger step-unit. The hop variant is found as the first element of the *contretemps* family and as the second element of the *pas de sissonne*; the leap variant is used as the third element in the *contretemps de menuet* and in some unnamed step-units. The implications of this notational variant – and its *demi-coupé* analogue – for the performance of the step will be discussed later in this chapter in the section on notational ambiguities.

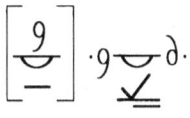
[*Assemblé*]. A springing step from one foot to two feet, ending in first position. In this example the previous step ends with the weight on the left foot; thus the right foot, represented by the upper horizontal line, begins the step and is joined by the left foot, represented by the lower horizontal line.

In the late seventeenth century the term *assemblé* (or *pas assemblé*) more often referred to the *à terre* or *sans sauter* version of the step, shown at left.[36] Both versions of the step are used frequently in *Le Mariage de la Grosse Cathos*, the springing version appearing often as a punctuation step at the ends of phrases. The *assemblé* is also combined with other steps to create step-units, and in the mascarade such combinations often coincide with musical cadences.

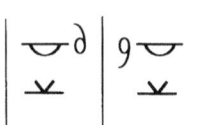
[*Balancé, pas*]. Two *demi-coupés*, performed from side to side, here beginning to the right; each *demi-coupé* takes a measure of music. In Feuillet notation the *pas balancé* is also shown as being performed forward and backward. Feuillet does not use the term "balancé" until his 1706 *Recueil de contredanses*, but the step-unit is found in dances from 1700 on, and Lorin lists the term in his c. 1685 manuscript. Favier's *pas balancé* occurs in the "Passons" chorus (IX).

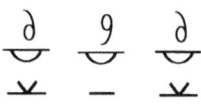
[*Bourrée, pas de*]. A *fleuret* of two movements: *demi-coupé*, step, *demi-coupé*. The step-unit is used in several of the dances in *Le Mariage de la Grosse Cathos*, but does not appear nearly as frequently as the *fleuret*.[37] As in the *fleuret* each of the component steps can be performed in a different direction: for example, a *demi-coupé* to the front, a step to the side, a *demi-coupé* behind. The *pas de bourrée* was one of the three step-units mentioned in the lost Favier treatise.

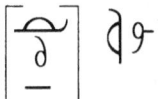
[*Cabriole*]. A leap, here onto the left foot, during which the legs beat together while in the air. This identification is somewhat more tentative than are the other entries; see the discussion of the *cabriolé* sign above.

In Feuillet's table of *cabrioles* the beat can occur during either a hop or a leap, but no examples of the former are found in the mascarade.

---

[36] See Kougioumtzoglou-Roucher, "Aux origines," vol. I, p. 356.
[37] Feuillet (1700) does not distinguish between the *fleuret* and the *pas de bourrée*, calling his table initially "Table des Pas de Bourée, ou Fleurets" and thereafter simply "Table des Pas de Bourée"; however, all of the examples in his tables are of a step-unit with one movement. Lorin (c. 1685) distinguishes between the *fleuret* and the *pas de bourrée à deux mouvements*, although he does not explain what the difference is. In *Le maître à danser* (1725) Rameau defines the *pas de bourrée* as having two movements, as opposed to the *fleuret*, which has only one (p. 122). He describes the second movement of the former step as a *demi-jeté*, a subtlety of performance which may not have existed in Favier's time. This question is addressed at the end of this chapter in the section discussing the placement of the modifying signs.

The *cabriole*, followed by a plain step, is found three times in the first entrée of the mascarade (III). This step-unit functions cadentially, always appearing as the last bar of an eight-bar music/dance phrase.

[*Chassé*]. The characteristic feature of the *chassé* in both Favier and Feuillet notation is that of a "chasing" of one foot into the air by the other foot. The foot that was chased then either remains in the air (one change of weight) or steps (two changes of weight). Feuillet does not distinguish in his terminology between these two types. This chasing action happens almost simultaneously, as is indicated by Favier's use of a single frame for the *chassé*, even though two feet and two step symbols are involved. In *Le Mariage de la Grosse Cathos* the *chassé* is usually combined with one or more other elements to create a step-unit; these elements vary widely, from another *chassé* to a combination that we have identified as a *pas de rigaudon* (see below).

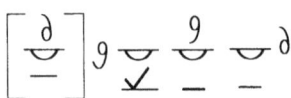

A *chassé* to the side: a leap onto the left foot, "chasing" the right foot into the air to the side. This version of the *chassé* occurs in the gigue (IV). The step can also be performed with the chasing action moving forward and backward, as in the following example from the drunk dance (VI).

In the example given here the left foot closes in from behind, chasing the right foot forward into the air. In some of the *chassés* in the drunk dance both letters are either in front or in back of the body sign, rather than on opposite sides as in our example. It is not clear whether this configuration represents a different manner of performance. The *chassé* is also performed *sans sauter* in several dances.

[*Contretemps*].³⁸ A hop on the supporting leg, in this example the right, followed by two steps, here forward on the left foot and to the side on the right. One of the most common of Baroque dance steps, it is used in six of the dances in *Le Mariage de la Grosse Cathos*. In one variant of this step-unit, found in the march (IB), the third element is replaced by a *jeté*, resulting in a *contretemps à deux mouvements*. The *contretemps* is performed *sans sauter* in the rigaudon (VII). (See also *demi-contretemps*.)

An interesting and very useful aspect of Favier's *contretemps* notation that applies to all members of the *contretemps* family is that the position of the free leg during or after the hop is always indicated. This position, as can be seen in many of our *contretemps* examples, is usually to the side rather than to the front, regardless of the direction of travel.

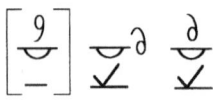

[*Contretemps balonné*]. A hop on the supporting leg, in this example the left, followed by a leap onto the free foot. As in the *contretemps* the position of the free leg, usually to the side during the hop, is clearly indicated. The step-unit is used in five of the dances in *Le Mariage de la Grosse Cathos*. It can also be performed *sans sauter*, in which case it is equivalent to a bend and rise without a transfer of weight, followed by a *demi-coupé* (see dance VII).

---

³⁸ We are following Feuillet's terminology in using the simpler term *contretemps*, rather than Rameau's *contretemps de gavotte*, which he used to differentiate the forward-moving version of the step from the *contretemps de chaconne* and *contretemps de côté* that travel to the side.

[*Contretemps de menuet*]. A hop on the supporting leg, in this example the left, a step onto the right foot, a *demi-coupé* on the left foot to fifth position behind, and a step on the right. Favier's *contretemps de menuet* does not correspond precisely to Feuillet's step-unit by this name. While both begin with a hop/step or *demi-contretemps*, the third and fourth elements of Favier's step-unit are replaced in the Feuillet version by a hop followed by a leap. Two of Favier's *contretemps de menuet* performed in succession will alternate starting feet, whereas Feuillet's version always starts with the same foot. This step-unit is found in both the menuet (V) and the passepied (VIIIB).

Another version of the *contretemps de menuet*, in which the third element is a *jeté* rather than a *demi-coupé*, is found only in the passepied (VIIIB). A more energetic step-unit than the previous version, it is closer in character to Feuillet's *contretemps de menuet*.

A step-unit with identical notation to the first *contretemps de menuet* shown above appears in both duple-meter entrées (III and VI), with, however, a different rhythm.

[*Coupé*]. A *demi-coupé*, in this example on the right foot, followed by a plain step on the left. The *coupé*, along with the *fleuret*, is one of the most common step-units in dances in both notation systems. It is frequently combined with other steps as well.

Although the *coupé* normally takes an entire bar of music, the gigue (IV) includes a step-unit comprising two *coupés* traveling quickly to the side, followed by a *demi-coupé* lasting a full bar. A similar *enchaînement* can be found in a number of dances in Feuillet notation, but with the addition of a *glissé* to the second step of each quick *coupé*. This step-unit was labeled a *glissade* by Rameau in 1725.

[*Coupé à deux mouvements*]. Two consecutive *demi-coupés*; it can be distinguished from the *pas balancé* both by its timing and by the fact that it travels rather than remains in place. It is used in the "Passons" chorus (IX).

In Feuillet's version of this step-unit the second *demi-coupé* is notated with the bend and rise signs in the middle of the step symbol. In both of Favier's examples the bend and rise signs of the second *demi-coupé* are placed somewhat further to the left than is the case in the first *demi-coupé*.

[*Courante, temps de*]. A bend and rise, here on the left foot, performed before the transfer of weight takes place, followed by a step forward. The *temps de courante* takes an entire bar of music. In Feuillet notation the step forward – it can also be to the side or behind – is always notated with a *glissé* or sliding of the foot along the floor. Since Favier notation apparently has no symbol for the *glissé*, this characteristic element of the *temps de courante* cannot be indicated. Perhaps the performance of the *glissé* was a convention that was taken for granted, and Favier did not consider a separate notation symbol necessary; alternatively, perhaps in 1688 the *temps de courante* was performed without a *glissé*.

The step is used once in the gigue (IV).

[*Demi-contretemps*]. A hop on the supporting leg, here the left, followed by a step on the right. This step-unit, in essence a *contretemps* minus the third element, is first mentioned by

Feuillet in his 1706 collection of *contredanses*, both as a *demi-contretemps* and as a "saut contretemps," but it is found in dances in Feuillet notation before this date. The step-unit can be performed quickly or slowly; in the gigue (IV) it is lively, with two *demi-contretemps* per bar of music, whereas in the drunk dance (VI), the rigaudon (VII) and the "Passons" chorus (IX) there is only one step-unit per bar (or half-bar, in the case of the drunk dance). In the rigaudon (VII) it is also performed *sans sauter*.

[*Échappé, pas*]. Starting from fourth position, a simultaneous collapse with both feet into wide second position. The identification of this step is based on our assumption that the inverted "V" represents a *tombé*. This step is used once in the drunk dance (VI), where it is preceded by a jump to fourth position and followed by an *assemblé*. This *pas composé* resembles the step sequence described by Rameau in 1725 as a *saillie* or *échappé*. Although Feuillet does not include the *pas échappé* in his tables in *Chorégraphie*, he does notate and describe earlier in his treatise the slipping and collapsing motions characteristic of the *échappé*. The step appears in a few solo male dances in the noble style, but it seems to be primarily associated with character dances, such as the three Harlequin dances in Feuillet notation.

[*Entrechat à quatre*]. A leap into the air with a rapid crossing and re-crossing of the legs in fifth position front and back, landing in a wide second position. Favier's single example of the *entrechat* begins from second position, but in Feuillet notation other options are possible as well. The *entrechat* is one of the more difficult and showy of Baroque dance steps; in dances in Feuillet notation it is found almost exclusively in male theatrical choreographies. In the drunk dance (VI), the only one in the mascarade where this step is used, ties are used to connect the three successive frames of notation, apparently to indicate that together they constitute a single step rather than form a step-unit. The same practice occurs in one of the *pirouette* steps (see below).

["Favier step"]. This step-unit has no equivalent in Feuillet notation; we have named it in honor of our choreographer. It begins with a *pas de gaillarde* (see below) ending on a flat foot – here the left – followed by a step into *élevé* with no *plié*. The second step is usually taken to fourth position behind as shown here, and one or both of the steps are performed with a turn. The Favier step is always embedded in a larger step-unit; in the mascarade it is preceded variously by a *demi-coupé*, a hop, or a *demi-contretemps*, and is usually followed by a *demi-coupé*. These larger step-units appear in dances III, IV, and VII. Since they usually take two bars of music, the two elements of the Favier step are often performed across the barline.

[*Fleuret*]. A *demi-coupé* followed by two plain steps. It can be done in any direction, often with turns. The most common step-unit in Baroque dances, the *fleuret* is used in all the dances in *Le Mariage de la Grosse Cathos* except the menuet and passepied. (See also the *pas de bourrée*.)

[*Gaillarde, pas de*]. This symbol is similar to that of the *demi-coupé*, but here the diagonal *plié* sign has been replaced by a dot and a shorter diagonal line; no explanation for this symbol is found in the Goussier article. We have tentatively identified this symbol as a *pas de gaillarde*, that is, the seventeenth-century *pas de gaillarde* shown in Feuillet's tables of steps (*Chorégraphie*, p. 48), not the later version described by Rameau,[39] both because Favier's step, like Feuillet's, invariably travels to second position, and because the *pas de gaillarde* was one of the three steps actually mentioned by Favier in his treatise. If this identification is correct, the step would be performed as follows: during the *plié* the free foot – here the left – closes to first position (hence the dot at the beginning of the *plié* symbol) and then steps to second position with an *elevé* or rise *only* to a flat foot. This latter qualification, while not implicit in the notation, is necessary because in *Le Mariage de la Grosse Cathos* the *pas de gaillarde* is always followed by a step into *elevé* with no preparatory *plié*. We have named this two-element combination the Favier step (see above).

[*Jeté*]. A leap from one foot to the other, here from the left foot to the right.

Occasionally Favier notates a *jeté* with a foot-in-air sign, as shown in the second example (dance III), presumably to indicate that the free leg moves in an unexpected direction. Here the *jeté* is onto the left leg, traveling forward, as is indicated by the relative positions of the two body signs (not apparent in the example but clear in the manuscript). During the *jeté* the right leg remains to the side of the body; the leap is followed by a step forward. This *jeté* notation can only be distinguished from a *contretemps* on the basis of the previous step. If no change of weight has taken place the step-unit is a *contretemps*, not a *jeté*.

A *jeté* followed by two steps, this step-unit might best be described as a high-energy *fleuret*; it is used in both male duets (III and VI). The step-unit is also found in dances in Feuillet notation, and in 1725 Rameau labels it a *pas de bourrée sauté*.

[*Menuet, pas de*]. A *demi-coupé* on the right foot, a step into *plié* on the left, a step with an *elevé* on the right, and a *demi-coupé* on the left. Favier's *pas de menuet* exists in only one version, and it differs from all of the versions of this step-unit preserved in Feuillet notation, both in execution and in timing. Early eighteenth-century treatises describe the most frequently encountered menuet steps as being of two movements (a movement consists of a bend and rise) – a *demi-coupé* plus a *fleuret* – or of three movements – a *demi-coupé* plus a *pas de bourrée*. Favier's step-unit bears a superficial resemblance to Feuillet's menuet step of three movements, since both step-units contain four changes of weight and three bends and rises. However, the timing of Favier's *pas de menuet* – its quick first and last *demi-coupés* contrasting with the deliberate quality of the central *mouvement* – lends a completely different character to the step-unit. (The rhythm of the *pas de menuet* is discussed in more detail below.)

---

[39] For an excellent discussion of the two versions of the *pas de gaillarde* and the confusion that these versions have caused twentieth-century writers on Baroque dance, see Kougioumtzoglou-Roucher, "Aux origines," vol. I, pp. 351–4.

The step-unit is used both in the menuet (V) and in the passepied (VIII). It always begins with the right foot, unlike Favier's *contretemps de menuet* that can begin with either foot.

[*Pirouette*]. Two types of *pirouettes* are used in *Le Mariage de la Grosse Cathos*. The first example is a *pirouette* on two feet, as indicated by the use of two circles instead of one. The amount and direction of the turn is indicated in the same way as all other turns in Favier notation; this example begins with a 45° turn to the right, a turn back to the starting position, and then a 180° turn to the right. The apparent change in the position of the feet from frame to frame is a result of the turning motion of the body; the feet make no independent movements.

A 360° *pirouette en dehors* on one foot, here turning to the left on the left foot, the right remaining in the air behind the body. The curved line above the circle in the step symbol indicates the path traveled by the free foot. As was the case in the *entrechat*, the two frames of dance notation are connected by a tie to indicate a continuous single step rather than a step-unit. Both *pirouettes* occur in the drunk dance (VI).

[*Rigaudon, pas de*]. Only one step-unit in *Le Mariage de la Grosse Cathos* seems close enough to Feuillet's *pas de rigaudon* to be so identified. It comprises a hop on the right foot, during which the left leg moves into the air in front of the body; a *chassé*, the left foot leaping into first position and sending the right foot into the air in front (rather than to the side as in Feuillet's step-unit); and an *assemblé*. This step-unit appears in dance IV; curiously, there are no *pas de rigaudon* in the rigaudon dance (VII).

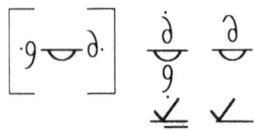

[*Sissonne, pas de*]. Starting from first position, a jump into fifth position, the right foot in front; a hop on the left foot, the right foot remaining in front in the air. The *pas de sissonne* occurs only in the gigue (IV) and is followed by two more repetitions of the same step-unit; thus the subsequent step-units start, not from both feet in first position, but from one foot. In the Feuillet version of the *pas de sissonne* the springs onto two feet land in *plié*, but this is apparently not the case in Favier's version of the step.

Favier's vocabulary of steps and step-units can be summarized as follows: the majority of the identifiable step-units seem to be similar in structure and performance to their counterparts in Feuillet notation; this group includes the *coupé, fleuret, contretemps*, and the other basic step-units found in almost all dances in Feuillet notation. In *Le Mariage de la Grosse Cathos* these basic step-units are also found in most of the dances, although they appear with greater frequency in the large group dances than in the duets and smaller group dances. A second group consists of Favier step-units that share certain characteristics with their Feuillet counterparts, but that also contain some significant differences. Step-units in this category include the various *chassées*, the *entrechat à quatre*, the *pas de rigaudon*, and the *pas de sissonne*; usually only one or two examples of each step-unit is found in the mascarade. The third group of step-units is large and diverse, comprising all of those step-units for which no equivalent terminology exists in contemporary sources, and which therefore do not appear in the inventory. Some of these step-units are made up of recognizable steps; in other cases, particularly in the two male entrées, the step-units often resist analysis.

Table 1. *Rhythms of step-units in* Le Mariage de la Grosse Cathos

	Step-units		
	Two elements: *contretemps balonné* *coupé* *demi-contretemps* Favier step *pas de sissonne* unnamed step-units	Three elements: *contretemps* *fleuret/pas de bourrée* *pas de rigaudon* unnamed step-units	Four elements: *pas de menuet* *contretemps de menuet* unnamed step-units
Meter of music			
Duple (IB, III, VI, VII, IX, XB)	a: 𝅗𝅥 𝅗𝅥	c: 𝅘𝅥 𝅘𝅥 𝅗𝅥 d: 𝅗𝅥 𝅘𝅥 𝅘𝅥	i: 𝅘𝅥 𝅘𝅥 𝅘𝅥 𝅘𝅥 j: 𝅘𝅥𝅮𝅘𝅥𝅮 𝅘𝅥 𝅗𝅥
Triple (II)	—	e: 𝅗𝅥 𝅘𝅥 𝅘𝅥	—
6/4 (IV)	b: 𝅗𝅥. 𝅗𝅥.	f: 𝅗𝅥 𝅘𝅥 𝅘𝅥.	k: 𝅗𝅥 𝅘𝅥 𝅘𝅥 𝅘𝅥 l: 𝅘𝅥𝅮𝅘𝅥𝅮 𝅘𝅥 𝅗𝅥.
Triple: one step-unit for two bars of music (V, VIII)	—	g: 𝅘𝅥 𝅘𝅥 ǀ 𝅗𝅥. h: 𝅘𝅥 𝅘𝅥 ǀ 𝅗𝅥.	m: 𝅘𝅥 𝅘𝅥 ǀ 𝅗𝅥 𝅘𝅥 n: 𝅘𝅥 𝅘𝅥 ǀ 𝅘𝅥 𝅘𝅥

Step rhythms

Favier's ingenious system – subdividing the notes in the line of music at the top of each page and aligning these subdivisions with the corresponding gesture in the dance – means that the duration of each element of a step-unit can be precisely indicated.[40] In the mascarade these durations vary from a whole note (i.e., a whole bar) at one extreme, to a sixteenth note at the other, although most elements correspond to note values somewhere in between. An examination of all the step rhythms in the mascarade shows that the frequently used step-units such as the *fleuret* or *contretemps* tend to have the same rhythm within the same meter. In fact, there is a strong correlation between the number of elements contained in each step-unit and the rhythm of the step; for example, in the duple-meter dances the overwhelming majority of three-element step-units are performed to a short–short–long (SSL) rhythm. The unnamed step-units not corresponding to a step-unit in the inventory show somewhat more rhythmic variety.

Table 1 summarizes the rhythmic values of the most frequently used steps in *Le Mariage de la Grosse Cathos*, by comparing the number of elements in the step-unit with the meter of the dance; exceptional cases are discussed below. A dash indicates that no steps of that particular type are found in a given meter. The lower-case letters inside the table are used as points of reference for the more detailed discussion that follows.

The dances in duple meter include the pavane (IB and XB), the first male duet (III), the drunk dance (VI), the rigaudon (VII), and the "Passons" chorus (IX). All but one of the duple-meter dances have one step-unit per bar; the exception is the drunk dance with its two step-units per bar. For ease of comparison, we have chosen in this table to show the step rhythms of the drunk dance in the same note values as the other duple-meter dances; a *fleuret*, for example, is shown here as two quarter notes plus a half note, i.e., rhythmically equivalent to Favier's two eighth notes plus a quarter note. There are two compound-meter dances: the chorus "Allons" (II) and the gigue (IV). However, in the

---

[40] In the following rhythmic analysis the term "element" refers to the movement contained in a single frame of Favier notation.

former, there are two step-units per 6/4 bar, so that in effect the meter of the step-units is triple, and they have been analyzed as such in the table. This choreography has only a very limited step vocabulary, which means, regrettably, that the mascarade, and hence this table, provide no information about the step rhythms for common triple-meter dances such as the sarabande, chaconne, or passacaille. The other two dances in triple meter, the menuet and passepied (V and VIII), use step-units that require two bars of music. While superficially analogous to dances in compound duple meter such as the gigue (IV), the menuet and passepied differ from them in that they are based on step-units – the menuet step and its derivatives – that are exclusive to these two dance types. The rhythmic characteristics of these particular step-units are discussed in more detail below.

This table includes most of the step-unit rhythms that appear in the mascarade, omitting only the one-element steps – *assemblé*, *demi-coupé*, etc. – that take a whole bar of music and those step-units requiring special discussion. It does not, however, exhaust all the step-rhythms possible in Baroque dances, particularly not for triple-meter dances. What the table does illustrate is that most step-units have a stereotypical rhythm; this is especially true of step-units that can be identified by name. The exceptions to these rhythmic patterns occur in composite step-units in the more technically demanding duets.

Two-element step-units occurring in the duple- and compound-duple-meter dances always have a rhythm of two equal beats (rhythms a or b). Such step-units are not used in the triple-meter dances of the mascarade. Two of these step-units, the *coupé* and the *demi-contretemps*, also occur as components of larger three- or four-element step-units, in which case they are performed more quickly and, in the gigue (IV), in a LS rhythm (first two notes of rhythm f).

Three-element step-units demonstrate more rhythmic variety. The extra element almost always occurs in the first half of the measure. In duple-meter dances this produces a short–short–long (SSL) pattern (rhythm c), the only exception to which is a LSS pattern (rhythm d) found in the first male duet (III) for a composite step consisting of a *contretemps balonné* followed by a step. In this instance, the normal rhythm for a *contretemps balonné* (rhythm a) is preserved, the extra step taking time from the end of the step-unit. In the only triple-meter dance (II) rhythm e is used throughout. In 6/4 or compound-duple meter (dance IV) rhythm f is the norm, with the step rhythm reflecting the duple division and triple subdivision of the music. In the menuet and passepied (V and VIII), where the step goes over six beats, three-element step-units occur only at cadences; in such cases, the same pattern of placing two elements in the first group, one in the second, prevails, although the rhythm of the first group may be either SL (rhythm g) or LS (rhythm h). The increase to four elements per step-unit is accompanied by even more rhythmic variety. With the exception of the menuet step and the *contretemps de menuet*, such step-units are nameless composites – made up, for example, of a *fleuret* plus a step – and are therefore not listed in the inventory. In duple-meter dances an even distribution of elements over the four beats of music (rhythm i) is the norm. Rhythm j is found only in the first male duet (III), where it is used for composite step-units consisting of a three-element step-unit (*fleuret* or *contretemps*) followed by a plain step. In the compound-duple gigue (IV), the four elements of the step-unit are distributed in a LSLS pattern (rhythm k). The only exception, rhythm l, is used for the same composite step-unit as rhythm j.

In the menuet and passepied (V and VIII) two four-element step-units predominate: the menuet step and the *contretemps de menuet*. Both step-units require that four changes of weight be distributed among six beats of music, thus allowing for a variety of rhythms. Two timings are found in the mascarade: a SLLS pattern (rhythm m) is used for the menuet step in both the menuet and the passepied; it is also used for the *contretemps de menuet* in the menuet. The second timing, LSLS (rhythm n) is used only for the *contretemps de menuet* in the passepied.

A five-element variant of the *contretemps de menuet* occurs in both dances; the extra step is added in the second half of the step-unit, changing the rhythm from LS to three quarter notes (SSS). In both dances the rhythm of the first half of the step-unit remains in agreement with the other step-units of the dance – SL for the menuet, LS for the passepied.

Table 1 does not include the few steps that fall outside the norms shown above. One of these, the *entrechat à quatre*, is of particular interest. This step-unit is usually executed today with the landing on the downbeat. However, Favier's notation of an *entrechat à quatre* (dance VI) clearly shows the dancer in the air on the downbeat, with the rapid crossings of the feet occurring on the first two sixteenth notes of the bar, followed by the landing on the third sixteenth note. The rhythmic accent is thus perceived as the upward thrust, not the landing.

The *pas balancé*, as was mentioned in the inventory, requires two bars of music, one bar per step.

It is interesting to reexamine previous conclusions about Baroque step rhythms in view of the information provided by Favier's unambiguous rhythmic notations. Reconstructors of dances in Feuillet notation have not had to invent rhythms out of whole cloth; both the notation and contemporary treatises provide some guidelines for the timings of step-units, although the precision of Favier's system is lacking. For example, in *Chorégraphie* Feuillet describes how to modify the liaison line to indicate that a given element is faster or slower than the other elements in the step-unit; but such modifications are relative, and in compound-duple meters it is often difficult to determine the precise rhythm of a step-unit containing more than two elements. Furthermore, many of Feuillet's contemporaries do not utilize these modifications of the liaison line in their notated dances. Perhaps realizing the limitations of his notation in this regard, Feuillet included in his 1704 collection of Pécour dances a short "Traité de la cadence" [treatise on timings] that gives precise timings for many different step-units in both duple and triple meters.[41] Feuillet's 1704 examples demonstrate that the relationship between meter and number of elements in a step-unit is not always the same: for example, the *contretemps* in triple meter can be performed either in three equal beats or in a SSL rhythm – two eighth notes and a half note; four-element step-units demonstrate a similar variety. Feuillet gives no examples of compound-duple meter and does not include the menuet step in his tables. Rameau, in his *Abrégé* [1725], also includes a short "Traité de la cadence" (pp. 103–11) in which a number of step-units are analyzed by labeling their elements corresponding to the notes of music. Unfortunately, in several of his illustrations numbers are missing or appear to be misplaced, rendering them less than satisfactory, and Rameau himself admits that he is making no attempt to be comprehensive.

On the whole, the timings used by reconstructors today are in agreement with Favier's timings; his information regarding the step rhythms of compound-duple-meter dances will be particularly welcome, since there is more ambiguity in these dances than in duple-meter dances. The one area where Favier's timings differ substantially from what was previously known is in the menuet step and the *contretemps de menuet*.

Although Feuillet inexplicably omits any information on the timing of these two important step-units, other eighteenth-century theorists have provided us with a variety of rhythms. Three of the most common timings for the menuet step are shown below:[42]

(a) 2,1,1,2 – Rameau, menuet step of two movements
(b) 2,1,2,1 – Rameau, menuet step of three movements
(c) 3,1,1,1 – Tomlinson[43]

---

[41] Feuillet's "Traité" appears in his 1704 *Receuil de dances . . . de Mr Pécour*, pp. [vi–xii]. An English translation by John Weaver was published in London in 1706 as a separate pamphlet, *A Small Treatise of Time and Cadence in Dancing*.

[42] The numbers correspond to the changes of weight; they represent the number of beats during which the dancer remains with the weight on a given leg, regardless of bending and rising.

[43] See Hilton, *Dance of Court and Theatre*, pp. 191 and 194, for a discussion of the two Rameau timings. She does not mention the Tomlinson timing given here, the first of several timings which he includes in *The Art of Dancing* (see pp. 105–6). For further information on the timings of menuet steps in the eighteenth century, see Cobau, "The preferred *pas de menuet*" and Sutton, "The minuet: an elegant phoenix."

However, no eighteenth-century source mentions Favier's timing, 1,2,2,1, or, for that matter, his unique execution of this step-unit. As was mentioned in chapter 4, Favier's menuet step rhythm is also found in Philidor's tune for this dance and in other seventeenth-century menuet music.

The timing of the Feuillet version of the *contretemps de menuet* is subject to some disagreement, due no doubt in part to the ambiguities in Rameau's example.[44] The two most widely accepted rhythms in use by today's Baroque dancers are the following: SLLS (1,2,2,1) and LSLS (2,1,2,1).[45] Favier's *contretemps de menuet* uses both of these rhythms (see rhythms i and j in table 1).

We are not suggesting that Favier's menuet step timings should replace those in use for Feuillet notation. However, given the evidence presented in chapter 4 regarding the rhythms of late seventeenth-century menuet music, it seems plausible that Favier's rhythm represents an earlier timing of the menuet step than that presented by the eighteenth-century theorists, and it might be particularly appropriate to use Favier's menuet step when dancing to menuets by Lully or other composers whose tunes share Favier's step rhythm.

Notational ambiguities: implications for performance

With the aid of the Goussier article and our knowledge of late seventeenth-century French dance style we are confident that we have successfully decoded most of the symbols in the mascarade. There are, however, certain ambiguities and inconsistencies in the mascarade notation that may have implications for performance. Two such instances occur frequently and will be discussed in more detail here. They are the ambiguous use of the dot, and the placement of the modifying symbols on the step symbol.

Ambiguous uses of the dot

There are a number of instances in *Le Mariage de la Grosse Cathos*, particularly in the two male duets, where a middle-layer dot appears on the *opposite* side of the body symbol from the foot letter. No mention of this phenomenon is made by Goussier, and one could argue that no special significance should be attached to this placement, it being simply an alternative way of notating a closed position. This is particularly true when the dot and foot letter are on opposite *sides* of the body symbol – as opposed to above and below it – since this notation might be intended to represent a step into third position. The unusual placement of the dot could also be a copyist's mistake, since errors having to do with dots occur in the dance notation more frequently than any other type. However, there are several reasons for looking beyond these arguments and concluding that many of the dots used in this way indicate a beat with the free leg against the weight-bearing leg. At several places in the mascarade this reading makes sense of an otherwise problematic step-unit. Perhaps the best example occurs in the first male duet (III):

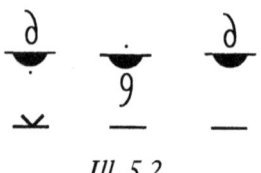

Ill. 5.2

---

[44] *Abrégé*, p. 104, fourth example. The numeral 5 is missing from the dance notation, and the numeral 8 is probably misplaced in the music notation.

[45] See, for example, Hilton, *Dance of Court and Theater*, p. 216, where both timings are presented as possibilities; and Witherell, *Pécour*, pp. 80–1, where only the timing 1,2,2,1 is considered. A third rhythm, consisting of four even dotted-quarter-note beats, is proposed by Mather, *Dance Rhythms*, p. 104. Her interpretation, based on Rameau's ambiguous diagram (see previous footnote), seems highly implausible.

If the dots in these two frames are read as fifth-position dots, the dancer will simply step in place, an action contradicted by the consecutive positions of the body signs, indicating that both men are to move forward on the *demi-coupé*, backward on the next step, and forward again on the third step. Reinterpreting the dots as beats, however, solves both of the these problems: the unconvincing stepping-in-place sequence has been replaced by a more vigorous forward and back motion with beats, and the required traveling takes place. There are other reasons why this beat hypothesis is attractive: since a beat is, in effect, a movement of the free leg into and out of a closed position, there is a certain logic in notating this action with the symbol used to notate a closed position. This interpretation also explains the lack of a dedicated sign for the beat in Favier notation, and brings Favier's step vocabulary more into line with the surviving male theatrical dances in Feuillet notation, where beats are commonplace.[46]

The beat hypothesis is not without its problems; in particular, it means that in any given situation the context must determine whether or not a beat is intended, and in certain cases the evidence is ambiguous. If our hypothesis is in fact correct, it appears that Favier had not fully worked out this particular detail of his system.

Placement of the modifying signs

In the following discussion we will examine the implications for performance of a literal reading of certain aspects of Favier notation. Comparison with Feuillet notation will be included as part of the discussion. It should be understood that this section is more speculative than the preceding material, and is intended more to stimulate thinking about the implications for performance of *both* Favier and Feuillet notation rather than to resolve performance issues definitively.

Two step symbols found in almost all of the step-units in Favier notation – the *demi-coupé* and the *saut* – have already been discussed in the introduction to the inventory. As was pointed out there, in the standard version of both steps the modifying signs indicating the bend and rise or bend and hop/leap are placed at (or slightly to the left of) the mid-point of the step sign.[47] Variant versions of both the *demi-coupé* and the *saut*, in which the modifying signs appear at the beginning of the step sign, also occur relatively frequently in the mascarade. These variant versions are always part of a larger step-unit such as the *fleuret* or the *contretemps*. The distinction between the standard and the variant notations is carefully preserved throughout the manuscript, suggesting that two different executions were intended.

A hint as to what this difference might be can be found in Goussier's explanation of how step symbols are formed in Favier notation, quoted earlier in this chapter. According to Goussier the position of the modifying signs – for example, bend and rise or bend and leap – on the step line indicates when these actions are to be performed relative to the step or movement of the foot. Although Goussier provides no examples of these principles in his plate of Favier notation, his commentary implies that distinctions in performance can be determined from the notation. One possible interpretation of these distinctions is presented in the following list that shows Favier's standard version of the *demi-coupé*, hop, and leap and the variant version of each step as found in the mascarade. For each symbol we provide a description of the execution of the step based on a literal reading of the notation. The variant *demi-coupé* and *jeté* are almost always taken into fifth position behind, and they are so notated here. (For clarity and ease of comparison all of the

---

[46] See, for example, Feuillet's 1700 "Sarabande pour homme" (LMC 7900) or the male dances in Pécour's 1704 collection.

[47] Given the small size of the notation and consequently the rather narrow margin for error, we have assumed that these slight variations in placement are not significant. However, as was noted in the inventory, in both examples of the *coupé à deux mouvements* the second *demi-coupé* symbol is positioned somewhat further to the left than is the first. Thus it is possible that Favier intended even more nuances of performance than we are proposing.

examples begin with the weight on the left foot; the steps may also be performed starting on the opposite foot.)

 standard demi-coupé: with the weight on the left foot, the free right foot begins to move to its new position;[48] halfway through this movement a quick bend and rise is made on the left foot. The right foot then completes the step making the transfer of weight as it arrives at its new position. (Since Favier notation does not indicate when the change of weight takes place we are assuming that it occurs as described here.)[49]

 variant demi-coupé: with the weight on the left foot a quick bend and rise is made at the *beginning* of the step, after which the right foot moves to its new position and the change of weight to this foot takes place.

 standard hop: with the weight on the left foot the right foot begins to move to its new position (in the air); the hop occurs in the middle of this movement.

 variant hop: the hop occurs *before* the movement of the right foot.

 standard leap: analogous to the *demi-coupé*, that is, the bend and leap into the air occur during the middle of the movement of the free foot; the transfer of weight occurs when the body lands on this foot.

variant leap: the bend (on the left foot) and leap into the air are made at the beginning of the step *before* the right foot moves to receive the weight of the body. Although the two symbols are clearly differentiated in appearance, the difference in execution is less obvious.

Favier's system could accommodate other possibilities than those that occur in *Le Mariage de la Grosse Cathos*: a *demi-coupé*, for example, could have a bend at the beginning of the step followed by a rise at the end of the step. It is interesting to note that both the actual and hypothetical configurations in Favier's system have certain parallels in Feuillet notation, and that both choreographers were concerned with the placements of the bend/rise signs relative to the step symbol. Since these distinctions have a significant impact on the performance style of all Baroque dances, a comparison of Favier and Feuillet notation with respect to this issue is of interest.

Feuillet, like Goussier, states clearly that the placement of the modifying symbols on the step symbol indicates when they are to be performed relative to the movement of the foot. For example, in discussing the execution of the bend or *plié* he declares:

> On pratique trois manières de plier dans le pas, savoir, plier avant de marcher, plier en marchant, et plier après avoir marché. Quand il y a un signe plié au commencement d'un pas, il signifie qu'il faut plier avant de marcher. Lorsqu'il y a un signe plié au milieu d'un pas, c'est marque qu'il ne faut plier qu'après avoir marché la moitié du pas. Quand il y a un signe plié à la fin d'un pas, il signifie qu'il ne faut plier qu'après avoir marché tout le pas entier. Il en est la même chose des signes élevés.[50]

---

[48] Favier notation, like Feuillet notation, usually does not indicate the position of the free foot at the beginning of a step-unit, unless the previous step-unit ended in a closed position with weight on both feet – e.g., an *assemblé*.

[49] Feuillet notation also fails to indicate when the change of weight takes place, and the way in which this question is answered accounts for some of the differences in style among present-day Baroque dancers. Verbal descriptions of step executions, in particular those by Rameau and Tomlinson, provide additional information about how the steps were performed. However, since the treatises by these men were written more than two decades after the publication of Feuillet's *Chorégraphie* it is possible that performance styles may have changed in the intervening decades.

[50] Feuillet, *Chorégraphie*, p. 14. Weaver's translation (*Orchesography*, p. 15) reads: "There are three ways of *Sinking*, viz. before the Foot moves, in moving, and after it has moved. When there is the Mark of a Sink at the beginning of a Step, the Sink must be made before the Foot moves. When the Sink is marked in the middle of the Step, the sink is not to be made 'till the Foot has made half the Step. When the Sink is marked at the end of the Step, the Sink must not be made 'till the Step is finished. It is the same thing in the Marks of a Rise."

However, the positioning of the modifying symbols in Feuillet notation differs from that of Favier notation. For example, Feuillet's standard *demi-coupé*, hop, and leap are usually notated with the bend sign in the first third of the step symbol and the rise or *saut* near the end of the step symbol. Conversely, Feuillet's variant *demi-coupé*, which he calls "jetté sans sauter ou demy coupé en l'Air," is notated with the bend and rise symbols in the middle of the step; thus from a visual standpoint this step appears analogous to Favier's standard *demi-coupé*. The following chart juxtaposes the six Favier symbols shown above with equivalent symbols in Feuillet notation. The comparison is of symbols, rather than step names; if no equivalent symbol appears in any of the known sources, a hypothetical example, enclosed in brackets, is supplied.

Favier   *Feuillet*[51]   *Comments*

Favier's standard *demi-coupé*, in the left column, is the notational equivalent of Feuillet's variant *demi-coupé* (or *jeté sans sauter ou demi-coupé en l'air*), shown in the right column. Both notations indicate a bend and rise after the right foot has started traveling, with the weight still on the left foot. The transfer of weight to the right foot probably occurs at the end of the step.

Favier's variant *demi-coupé*, at the left, would be notated in Feuillet notation as shown in the right column, a symbol that does not occur in *Chorégraphie* or in any dances in Feuillet notation. However, if a *glissé* sign (non-existent in Favier notation) were added to this symbol it would be equivalent to Feuillet's *temps de courante*.

Favier's standard hop, in the left column, appears to be the notational equivalent to Feuillet's *pas plié et sauté, le pied en l'air*, shown in the right column. Both notations indicate a bend and spring into the air in the middle of the movement by the free foot. Feuillet's symbol appears in the early section of *Chorégraphie* (p. 13), but not in the tables of steps; it is seldom used in actual choreographies, the hop normally being notated either as shown in the following example (equivalent to Favier's variant hop), or as a component of the *demi-contretemps*.

In Favier's variant hop the bend and spring occur at the beginning of the step before the free foot moves. The Feuillet equivalent, while not appearing in *Chorégraphie*, is quite common in choreographies. A slightly altered version appears as the second symbol in Feuillet's *contretemps de menuet* notation.

Favier's standard *jeté*, in the left column, is the notational equivalent of Feuillet's *pas plié et sauté*, shown in the right column. Feuillet's symbol appears in the early section of *Chorégraphie* (pp. 13 and 15) but it differs from the symbols in his table of *jetés* (see below) and is seldom, if ever, found in choreographies. A literal interpretation of the notation calls for a bend and rise into the air in the middle of the step.

---

[51] The Feuillet examples are taken from the 1700 and 1701 editions of *Chorégraphie*. Later notators do not always adhere precisely to Feuillet's illustrations. In English sources, for example, the bend sign normally appears near the beginning of the step.

Favier	Feuillet	Comments
⌄‾	∫	In Favier's variant *jeté* the bend and rise into the air occur at the beginning of the step, before the free leg moves. The Feuillet equivalent does not appear as an independent step in *Chorégraphie*, but a similar notation is used in the *chassé* and other composite step-units.

The following examples compare the standard versions of two steps in Feuillet notation with their hypothetical equivalents in Favier notation.

   ∫   The symbol in the left column is a hypothetical reconstruction in Favier notation of Feuillet's standard *demi-coupé*; no such symbol appears in *Le Mariage de la Grosse Cathos*. A literal reading of the symbol is as follows: bend on the left foot when the right foot has completed about one-third of the step, rise on the right foot at the end of step. The precise moment of transfer of weight is not indicated.

   ∫   The symbol in the left column is a hypothetical reconstruction in Favier notation of Feuillet's standard *jeté*; no such symbol appears in *Le Mariage de la Grosse Cathos*. A literal reading of Feuillet's notation suggests that the rise into the air does not occur until near the end of the step, that is, until the free leg has almost arrived at its new position.

The most significant differences that emerge from these comparisons occur in the notations of the *demi-coupé*. If we accept the idea that the placement of the bend/rise symbols in both Feuillet and Favier notation is meant to be interpreted literally – and the fact that both notation systems make such a distinction certainly suggests as much – we must conclude that more than one manner of performance of the *demi-coupé* was in use in the late seventeenth century. Since the *demi-coupé* is the initial step of almost all the non-sprung step-units in Baroque dance, this conclusion has important implications for today's reconstructors. Favier's standard *demi-coupé*, with its quick bend/rise in the middle of the step, results in a livelier and more animated style than that indicated by the more deliberate Feuillet *demi-coupé*. Feuillet does use a livelier version of the *demi-coupé* (his *jeté sans sauter*) but only as the second element in the *coupé à deux mouvements*, which begins with his more sedate *demi-coupé*.[52] If in fact Favier's *demi-coupé* represents the standard late seventeenth-century version of this step, it seems possible that a significant shift in performance style took place between 1688 and 1700. On the other hand, it is also possible that these notational variants reflect subtle differences in performance style among the Parisian dancers. Finally, it should be mentioned that these differences might tend to disappear at faster tempos; the performance of a *fleuret* at, for example, the lively tempo recommended for a rigaudon or a bourrée by several early eighteenth-century theorists (half note = MM120) does not allow much time for the articulation of the nuances described above.[53]

---

[52] Hilton's treatment of Feuillet's *jeté sans sauter* is problematic (*Dance of Court and Theater*, p. 174). On the one hand she equates it with Rameau's *demi-jeté* – presumably on the basis of Rameau's renotated versions of Pécour's 1700 dances – without considering the possibility that Rameau's step may have been executed differently. On the other hand, she claims that Feuillet does not provide a special sign for a *demi-jeté*, and that it can also be represented by the standard *demi-coupé* symbol if the latter appears at the end of a step-unit. Yet Feuillet is consistent in his notated choreographies: he reserves the *jeté sans sauter* symbol for the second step of the *coupé à deux mouvements*, and never uses it as the final step in the *pas de menuet à trois mouvements*.

[53] For a discussion of the tempo markings for French Baroque dances preserved in eighteenth-century theoretical sources see Harris-Warrick, "Interpreting pendulum markings."

AN ASSESSMENT OF THE TWO SYSTEMS

Both Feuillet and Favier notation have a number of ambiguities that the verbal explanations available regarding them do not fully resolve; the previous section, based on a literal reading of certain notational symbols, has demonstrated one of the ways in which the two systems can be used to shed light on each other. As more people become familiar with Favier notation, it will become possible to use the interface of the two systems to examine broader questions of technique, style, and evolution. Although our own investigations have of necessity focused primarily on Favier, we would like to follow Goussier's example by ending the discussion with an assessment of the two systems – not, however, of their relative value, but of their conceptual underpinnings.

The most striking point in common between the two notational systems is that both Favier and Feuillet focus their attention on the dancers' feet. The notated dances have virtually nothing to say about the rest of the body, the only exception being instructions to take or drop hands.[54] Although both systems developed symbols capable of notating other gestures – Feuillet movements of the hands and arms, Favier motions of the upper body – these symbols do not appear in the extant choreographies. The mere existence of such symbols, supplemented by descriptions, instructions, and iconographical evidence, proves that Baroque dance style depended on more than just correct placement of the feet, but both Favier and Feuillet clearly considered the steps more important to communicate than any other physical gestures.

The other concern that both systems strongly express is the centrality of the relationship between choreography and music. Both systems show precisely which measure of music goes with each measure of choreography such that there is never any doubt as to where in the music choreographic phrases occur. Favier notation further reveals the exact correspondence between each motion and its rhythmic placement within the measure. Feuillet, too, was concerned with this level of detail, as his 1704 "Traité de la cadence" shows. Both notators saw the relationship between music and dance as an intimate one that needed to be prescribed, not left to the vagaries of the performers. The notion of dance without music, or even of dance with an imprecise relationship to the music, would have been inconceivable to both Feuillet and Favier.

Although both Favier and Feuillet emphasized the movements of the feet, the ways they chose to communicate movement are quite different. Feuillet notated steps in relation to a line representing the floor plan of the dance. His notation emphasizes the continuous movement of the body and the relationship of the dancers to each other; it highlights both the figures of the dance and the sequences of steps, but it lacks the same degree of temporal precision possessed by Favier notation. The latter, on the other hand, does not make the sequences of either step-units or figures instantly apparent; these have to be synthesized from the different layers in the grid. However, Favier notation does indicate at any one time the exact location of each dancer in the space and the precise location of his feet relative to his body. It is possible to show, for example, that at a given point within a measure a dancer is standing on the left foot facing the top of the room with the right foot in the air out to the side. Favier notation shows a series of slices of time, of discrete moments within the dance; it is like a series of photos that stop time, and that when read in succession show the progression of the dancer's body. Moreover, the camera focuses on each dancer individually, not on the group as a whole. The view of each dancer at any given moment is quite exact, but the series of pictures must be reassembled in both time and space in order to see the whole dance with all of its participants. In this sense all of Favier notation is freeze-frame, not just the short-hand notation used in the march and passepied to show the movement of groups. These fundamental differences in

---

[54] A very small number of dances in Feuillet notation include drawings or symbols for other gestures: e.g., special hand holds in "l'Allemande" (LMC 1200), head gestures and the removal of the hat in the three Harlequin choreographies (LMC 1800, 1980, and 2760), and tambourine beats in the "Entrée de deux bacchante" (LMC 2880).

approach underlie the different visual impressions the two systems make. Feuillet notation encourages the eye to take in the whole page; Favier notation forces it to examine each piece of the page frame by frame. Feuillet notation abstracts movement into dynamic patterns; Favier notation insists on precision of gesture. Feuillet shows where a dance is going, Favier where it is. Feuillet emphasizes movement through space, Favier the passage of time.

Those who are already familiar with Feuillet notation may well feel that the accessibility it affords to the step-units and figures of the dance outweighs Favier's superiority in rhythmic precision. However, a drawback to Feuillet's beautifully represented figures is that group dances are difficult to notate. Patterns of any complexity in which the dancers' paths cross create serious problems for the notator, and these may represent one of the reasons that there are so few group dances in Feuillet notation. Favier notation, which gives every dancer his own stave, avoids such problems and makes notating choreographies for groups much easier. This capability is certainly of great practical value when the repertoire slated for preservation is theatrical, with its high proportion of group dances.

Favier, coming at the problem of dance notation from a well-established career as a professional dancer, wanted to be able to show the dancers how to move from one place to another in a very practical way; he did not seem to have been concerned about beauty of presentation, as a comparison between Favier's notations and Lorin's magnificent *contredanse* manuscript shows. As far as is known, Favier did not try to exploit his invention commercially; had his system been published in competition with Feuillet's, it undoubtedly would have fared less well. Feuillet not only chose his repertoire in order to appeal to upper-class amateurs interested in learning the latest dance from the court or the Opéra, he designed each page so that it looked beautiful and would appeal to the eye. The English dancing master Kellom Tomlinson, who adopted Feuillet's system, even went so far as to state that his plates of notation would make lovely pictures to hang on the wall.[55] Feuillet's emphasis on solo and couple dances probably reflects an understanding of his audience. For Favier, however, it is not at all clear what audience he had in mind for his dance notations. This mascarade is not the kind of work likely to have been revived, even at court. Nor does it seem likely that he would have substituted the use of dance notation for live instruction when teaching dances to professionals working under him. Given the fact that this volume ended up in the royal library, perhaps Favier intended it for the one audience that really mattered – the king.

Although Favier and Feuillet notation overlap in some of the choices made regarding what should be represented by the notation, each provides a somewhat different lens through which to look at Baroque dance. In addition, the repertoires they represent are different: Favier's dances are part of a complete comic work, and are for groups or for same-sex couples, whereas Feuillet's repertoire of set pieces includes primarily mixed-couple social dances and theatrical solos and duets. The discovery of Favier notation thus opens up three areas of opportunity for dancers and historians: it provides access to a new repertoire of dances; it makes possible a reexamination of the history of dance notation and of the development of ballet; and it invites new ways of looking at Baroque dance technique and movement.

---

[55] "The cuts [i.e. plates] were originally designed not only for the better explanation and understanding of my printed book ... but likewise to be proper furniture for a room or closet ... for if put in frames with glasses they will not only show the various positions or postures at one view but be very agreeable and instructive furniture." Tomlinson, *The Art of Dancing*, from the frontispiece to the plates.

6

The dances

INTRODUCTION

In this chapter we examine the ten dances in *Le Mariage de la Grosse Cathos* in greater detail, integrating information from chapters 4 and 5 and concentrating in particular on details of casting and staging as well as on the step vocabulary and floor patterns. Although the level of detail, at least in the step inventories, makes this chapter most appropriate to dancers and dance historians with an interest in reconstructing the work, the introductory and concluding sections for each dance will be of interest to a wider audience. Each of the ten dances is analyzed individually, the discussion being divided into seven parts: (1) introduction; (2) music; (3) casting and staging; (4) list of step-units; (5) step vocabulary; (6) floor patterns; (7) dance/music relationships.

The introduction contains an overview of the dance: the performers, the dance type, and any unusual features. Emphasis is on the dramatic function of the dance within the mascarade and on its character.

The section devoted to the music for each dance begins with a transcription of the melody – or bass line, for dances II and IX – as it appears in the dance notation. This transcription adds bar lines and meter signs where necessary and changes the French violin clef of the original to treble clef. Bar numbers have been added at regular intervals to provide a reference point for the analysis of the step-units. In the binary dances (nos. III–VIII) double – or even quadruple – numbers appear, one for each repeat of the strain: this double numbering reflects the fact that the choreography is through-composed even though the music repeats. Rhythmic values have been regularized and no attempt has been made to preserve the ties that are a characteristic feature of Favier's notation system – for example, four tied eighth notes are transcribed as a half note. Minor variants between the versions of the music preserved in the two sections of the manuscript are not recorded; more significant variants are mentioned in the comments to the list of step-units. The discussion that follows the transcription considers the musical form, the dance type, plus rhythmic, melodic, and harmonic characteristics that are of special interest.

The casting of the dances – which dancer performed which role in each of the choreographies – is given considerable attention in our discussion because the information about casting in the manuscript is incomplete. Annotations in the margin of dance IB (facsimile, p. 43) reveal that the eight dancers performed as two each of *garçons de la noce*, *filles de la noce*, *paysans*, and *Dames Gigognes*; these annotations further provide the names of five of the dancers. Dance III, the "Entrée de deux garçons de la noce," also gives the names of the performers, but none of the remaining dances does so. Nonetheless, a comparison of the titles of the dances with the choreographic notations generally makes it possible to establish which of the performers participated in each dance. The difficulty lies in determining which individual among the participating dancers corresponds to each staff of dance notation in the eight choreographies that lack verbal identification of the dancers. In dance V, for example, the title ("Entrée des deux garçons et des deux filles de la noce") makes it clear that the four participants are the two couples that had performed in the two previous dances. In addition, male and female roles are distinguished by differences in the body symbols. However, nothing in the choreographic notation indicates which of the two *filles* performs the third line of dance notation and which the fourth. The difficulty becomes even more acute in the group dances toward the end of the mascarade (VIII–X) for which the dance notation does not even distinguish between male and female roles.

In order to keep separate the issues of casting and staging in the subsequent analyses, two sets of labels are used to identify the dancers. Arabic numbers (1–8) identify the dancers in any given dance according to the order of their parts in the dance score. Thus, in dance IB the top stave is identified as dancer 1, the bottom stave as dancer 8. This system enables the reader to locate a particular stave in the manuscript without first having to determine who is dancing that part. It is important to remember that these numbers are used solely for analytical purposes, and are unrelated to questions of casting – the identity of dancer 1, for example, changes several times during the course of the mascarade.

A second set of labels – the upper- and lower-case letters A–D and a–d – are used to identify the performers. These letters have been assigned in accordance with the information provided in dance IB. Unlike the number identifications, which change from dance to dance, the letter identifications remain constant for the entire mascarade; thus, for example, dancer B is always Favier *l'aîné*.

A = Dumirail (*garçon de la noce*)   a = Germain (*fille de la noce*)
B = Favier *l'aîné* (*garçon de la noce*)   b = Richer (*fille de la noce*)
C = Barazé (*paysan*)   c = [unidentified] (Dame Gigogne)
D = [unidentified] (*paysan*)   d = [unidentified] (Dame Gigogne)
    X = La Couture (dances VII and VIIIA)

The use of matching upper- and lower-case letters (A–a, B–b, etc.) reflects the couple formation of dance IB; in addition, it also makes clear that these pairings do not remain constant throughout the mascarade. In dance V, for example, the two couples are comprised of dancers A–b and B–a.

The relationship between the number and letter identifications for each dance is provided in a key that shows how the order of the dance staves corresponds to the casting information for that particular choreography. For example, the key for dance V begins as follows:

Dancer 1 [i.e., first stave]   = B [i.e., Favier, *garçon de la noce*]
Dancer 2   = A [i.e., Dumirail, *garçon de la noce*]
Dancer 3   = a [i.e., Germain, etc.]

The issue of casting does not affect the reconstruction of any single dance, but becomes important when the entire mascarade is staged. In order to determine the path traced by Favier or any of the other dancers through the sequence of dances in the mascarade, it is necessary to compare the relative positions of the dancers from one dance to the next. To aid in this comparison, diagrams showing the beginning and ending formation of the dancers, using the letters we have assigned them, are provided for each dance. Our proposals as to the identity of each dancer rely in part on the principle of economy of movement, the premise being that as little movement as possible takes place between dances. For example, since dance IB ends, and dance II begins, with four dancers on each side of the performing area, it seems reasonable to assume that each group of four remains on its own side of the stage between the two dances. This principle not only makes sense from a practical standpoint – in view of the crowded performing area one would want to avoid any unnecessary movements such as crossing over to the opposite side of the stage – but it can also be observed in the staging of the singers and instrumentalists. Any other factors that influenced our ideas regarding the casting of each dance are discussed in this section. It should be pointed out that the solutions to casting and staging proposed in this chapter are based on principles which we have derived from the work itself, thus providing internal consistency to the staging; however, it is possible that more on-stage shifting of performers occurred, or that the dancers rearranged themselves in an order other than that presented here.

Implicit in the mascarade movement notation is the concept of "home positions" – the place or places on stage where each of the three performing groups is stationed when no notation is provided (see chapter 3, ill. 3.4). For the oboes, this is along the sides of the performing area, four oboes on stage left and five oboes on stage right. They move to these positions at the end of IB, remaining there until VIIIA when they again come to the center, returning to their home positions at the end of VIIIB. Home position for the singers is a single line along the back of the performing space. Individual singers advance downstage to perform solos or duets, retreating to their home positions when finished. When these solos or duets follow a notated dance the manuscript provides movement notation indicating that the singers move forward during the final bars of the previous piece, and it is clear that this seamlessness is a paradigm of the entire staging of the mascarade. Home position for the dancers, particularly the four who do not perform in dances III–VI, is not indicated in the manuscript. We are assuming that the dancers, when not performing, retreated to the two upstage corners, i.e., upstage from the oboes and to the right and left of the singers, since these are the only two unoccupied spaces available. Nothing in the notation indicates whether or not the commedia characters have a home position. They do not enter with the rest of the cast, but they bring up the rear in the recessional.

The heart of each dance analysis is the list of step-units, in which each step-unit is identified or described. The numbers in the left-hand column refer to the page numbers of the manuscript, those in the second column to the bar numbers of the music as they appear in the transcription. (It is important to remember that the vertical divisions in the dance notation mark off frames rather than bars, and that a bar of music can include as many as six frames of dance notation. Readers who wish to compare the analysis with the manuscript will need to add bar numbers to the facsimile.) The third column lists the step-unit or step-units for each bar of music, based on the definitions presented in the inventory in chapter 5. Unnamed step-units, which occur frequently in the two male duets (dances III and VI) and the rigaudon (VII), are analyzed according to their component parts. In some cases these elements are recognizable steps or step-units that are combined in unusual ways, e.g., a *demi-contretemps* followed by a *coupé*. In cases where even the component parts lack names (most notably in dance VI), a description of the step elements is provided. In this listing, elements within a single step-unit are separated by commas (e.g., *jeté, coupé*); where there are two step-units per bar of music, as is generally the case in dances II and VI, the step-units are separated by a semi-colon.

The final column of the list, labeled "Comments," includes a wide variety of information. Literal transcriptions of almost all of the textual material in the notation section of the manuscript are provided: dance titles, verbal instructions and cues, and other marginal comments, the only omissions being the texts of the two choruses, which may be found in the libretto (Appendix A), and the repeated running heads. When the original French seems particularly obscure it is transliterated into modern French and enclosed in square brackets. English translations of this material are provided when necessary and are also enclosed in square brackets. Other types of information mentioned in this column include movement notation for the singers and oboes; important choreographic structural points; and problematic passages in the notation – for example, symbols with ambiguous meanings or errors in the dance notation. These errors fall into several categories: copying mistakes, many of which have been corrected in the manuscript by the original copyist; omissions, either through copyist error or because the manuscript was trimmed; and situations in which the manuscript reading seems faulty, either because the notation symbols conflict with each other or because the paradigm of symmetry is violated. It is particularly important to identify these passages because of the possibility that they might *not* be errors, even though they violate principles of construction observed in dances in both Favier and Feuillet notation.

The list of step-units is followed by a discussion of the step vocabulary, which usually includes a table of the steps and step-units employed in the dance arranged by frequency of use. The character of the steps is considered – smooth vs.sprung, simple vs. complex, easy vs. difficult – and the relationship of the step vocabulary to other dances in the mascarade is mentioned.

Favier's floor patterns are not readily apparent from the notation, with the exception of the dance sections in freeze-frame notation, and we consider it important to make this information more accessible to readers. Our discussion utilizes both diagrams and verbal descriptions to consider issues of symmetry, types of shapes employed, and use of floor space. More attention is paid to the large group dances, particularly those in which interaction with the singers and instrumentalists takes place, since these pieces offer information about staging practices that is unavailable in any other contemporary source. The symbols we have used to represent the performers in the diagrams are the same as in chapter 3:

☋ = dancers;   ● = singers;   ☌ = oboes;   ☍ = comedians.

Previous knowledge of Baroque dance floor patterns has been derived from the surviving choreographies in Feuillet notation, which are almost exclusively for one or two dancers, and are always preserved as isolated set pieces.[1] These exhibit a very high degree of symmetry with respect to their floor patterns, that is, the dancers' movements in relationship to each other always adhere to one of three types of symmetry. In mirror-image symmetry the axis of symmetry is an imaginary line and the dancers move opposite each other and on opposite feet (ill. 6.1a); in rotational symmetry the dancers follow the same path around a point and move on the same feet (ill. 6.1b); in parallel symmetry, most often found in menuets and passepieds, the dancers perform the same figure in the same orientation and use the same feet (ill. 6.1c). The type of symmetry in effect generally changes several times in the course of a dance. Although Favier's dances make use of all three types of symmetry, they also exhibit uses of space not found in any other notated Baroque choreographies.

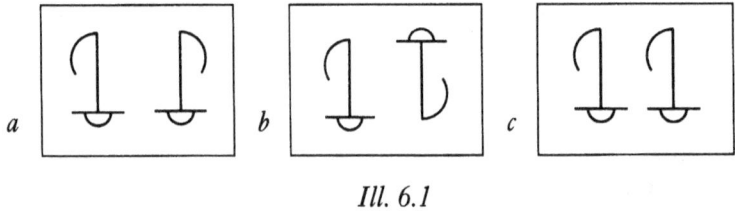

Ill. 6.1

The relationship of dance and music is addressed in the final section of each dance analysis. These sections consider some of the ways in which Favier's choreographies intersect with Philidor's music.

I. MARCHE POUR NEUF HAUTBOIS, HUIT DANSEURS, ET NEUF MUSICIENS

The opening march, the first piece of the mascarade, has two distinct choreographic sections, each with a separate function: in the first part (IA), the entire twenty-six-member cast is brought into the performing area; following this processional entry the second part of the dance (IB) introduces the eight dancers – the wedding guests – who celebrate in dance the impending union of La Couture and Grosse Cathos. Although in

---

[1] Dances in Feuillet notation for larger groups are mostly social dances a4; the one extant theatrical dance for a large group, Feuillet's 1700 "Ballet de neuf danseurs" (LMC 1320), is very different from Favier's large group choreographies.

the latter section a variety of steps and figures are used, in the processional (IA) only a plain walking step is prescribed, one such step per bar, while the performers circumnavigate the performing space. This simple entry is reminiscent of the Renaissance pavane, a processional dance that consisted of little more than stylized walking steps performed by a long column of dancers who promenaded around a performing space. This association is made explicit in the music section of the manuscript, where the piece is entitled "Pavane" rather than "Marche."

The second part of the dance also includes movement notation for the singers and oboes. In fact, the most striking feature of this dance is that the oboes share the performing space with the dancers for much of the choreography.

Ex. 6.1

Music

Philidor's march music is unlike the majority of Renaissance pavanes or Baroque marches in that it is through-composed rather than in binary or ternary form. In spite of the irregular internal phrase structure, a march *topos* is suggested by the triadic outlines of the melody, the regularity of the rhythmic patterns, and the primarily tonic and dominant harmonies. The music is repeated three times: twice for the processional and once for the figured choreography.

Casting and staging

None of the twenty-six performers in the opening processional (IA) is identified, nor is there any differentiation of body symbols to distinguish between oboes, dancers and singers. However, from the movement notation in the second part of the dance (IB) it is possible to work backwards and identify the order in which the groups enter the performing area. This order turns out to be the same as that listed in the title: the oboes come first, followed by the dancers and then the singers.[2] The oboes march three abreast, while the dancers and eight of the singers follow in a column two abreast, the last singer bringing up the rear. As can be seen in the last frame on p. 42 of the facsimile, by the end of the processional the oboes are in a two-line formation of six and three players respectively; behind them are the dancers, still in a double column, and bringing up the

---

[2] Favier follows common seventeenth-century practice in using the term "musiciens" to refer to the singers, as distinct from the oboes, who are always called "hautbois".

rear are the singers are in a 2-2-5 arrangement. Since the column formation of the dancers is the same at the end of IA and at the beginning of IB, it seems reasonable to assume that their order and relative positions remain unchanged. A similar logic suggests that the two Duponts lead the group of nine singers in the processional, since they are shown at the end of dance IB in front of the other singers. The order of the remaining singers in the procession cannot be determined from the notation and has no bearing on the staging of the work.

In contrast to the lack of information about the identity of the performers in the processional, at the beginning of dance IB all eight of the danced roles are labeled and five of the eight dancers are identified by name. Furthermore, Favier supplies gender identifications in this dance as well as in dances III and V – filled-in body shapes for the male roles, hollow body symbols for the female roles.[3] The key below lists only the dance roles (A, B, etc.); the actual names of the dancers are included in the master key in the introduction to this chapter, and in the "Comments" column of the "List of step-units."

Key for dance IB

Dancer 1 = A   Dancer 5 = C
Dancer 2 = a   Dancer 6 = c
Dancer 3 = B   Dancer 7 = D
Dancer 4 = b   Dancer 8 = d

Dance IB begins with the four couples in a column at stage left and ends with the funnel-shaped formation shown below, centered and upstage.

Beginning position   *Ending position*
A a   A   B
B b   a   b
C c   D   C
D d   d   c

Although it is clear that the dancers must shift from their center-stage position where they end dance IA to their stage-left position where they begin dance IB, no movement notation is provided to show how this shift takes place. The most likely possibility is that the dancers' arrival upstage center behind the oboes occurs slightly sooner than the freeze-frame notation indicates, after which they move to the left during the last few bars of IA. This solution allows dance IB to begin immediately after IA, thus preserving the continuity between numbers which is a paradigm of the mascarade.[4]

No movement notation for either the oboes or the singers is provided at the beginning of IB; however, later in the dance – bar 17 for the oboes, bar 24 (the final bar) for the singers – diagrams do appear, showing that both groups have rearranged themselves slightly from their positions at the end of IA. The oboes have shifted from their 6-3 formation to a 5-3-1 triangular formation, while seven of the singers have merged into a semi-circular formation at the back of the performing area, the other two singers remaining in the center and slightly in front of them. Although the manuscript does not

---

[3] As was pointed out in chapter 3, n. 24, Favier was not consistent in his choice of symbols. In dances IB, III, and V the filled-in half-circle represents male dancers, while elsewhere in the manuscript the same symbol represents singers. Similarly, in dances IV and V the hollow body symbol is used for the female roles, whereas in other dances it represents both male and female roles as well as oboes and singers. The symbols in our diagrams follow Favier's usage in dance XC; we have added the double half circle to represent female roles.

[4] The apparent imprecision of the freeze-frame notation at this point – relative to the very precise score notation – can also be observed in dance VIIIA. It would seem that Favier's freeze-frame notation was not always intended to be read literally; that is, while the floor pattern of the performers is clearly indicated, the correspondence between a given bar of music and the position of a particular performer is not necessarily exact. A good example occurs at the end of the processional: according to the notation the oboes and dancers require six bars, taking one step per bar, to travel from stage left to stage center, yet the last singer is shown covering the same distance in three bars, clearly a difficult if not impossible feat. What the freeze-frame notation *does* show clearly is the path followed by all the performers, and the relationship among the various individuals as they execute the floor pattern.

The dances

indicate when these shifts take place it seems likely that they occur at the beginning of dance IB. By the end of IB the oboes have moved to their home positions along the sides of the performing area.

List of step-units

Page	Bar no.	Step-unit or description[5]	Comments[6]
		[IA: Processional march for entire cast]	
41	0		"Marche pour 9. hautbois, 8. Dançeurs, et 9 Musiciens"
	1–24	The performers take one step per bar of music, beginning with the right foot.	In left margin: "marche de / 9 aubois de / 8 denceurs et / de 9 musiciens." The march begins with the right foot, as indicated by the small "d" in the first frame; foot signs continue throughout the dance.
42	1–24		The music is repeated a second time while the performers continue their processional. At the end of the dance: "Fin de la Marche."
		[IB: March for the eight dancers]	
43			"Marche dansante pour les 8. Danseurs." The eight dancers' parts are identified as follows: "1 / pas de mr / dumirail / garçon de la / nopce"; "2 / pas de mr / germain fille / de la nopce"; "3 / pas de mr / favier lesné / garçon de la / nopces"; "4 / pas de mr / richer fille / de la nopces"; "5 / pas de mr / berazé payison"; "6 / pas de mr / dame / gigogne"; "7 / pas de mr / / payisant"; "8 / pas de mr / dame / gigogne."
	1	*Contretemps balonné*	The sequence of step-units in bars 1–8 is repeated in bars 10–17, but with a different floor pattern. Dancers 1 and 3, first frame of this bar: the letters "d" and "g" respectively have been partially erased.
	2	*Contretemps balonné*	Dancer 6, second frame: a "d" is missing.
	3	*Pas de bourrée*	
44	4	*Pas de bourrée*	
	5	*Contretemps balonné*	
	6	*Contretemps balonné*	

---

[5] In the list of step-units the word "step" is used only in the narrow sense of a walking step or *pas marché*, rather than as a generic term for an element of a step-unit.

[6] The comments in this column are keyed to the bars of music and dance shown in the second column. Readers will need to annotate the facsimile with bar numbers if they wish to examine the dance notation to which a certain comment applies. A reference to a specific frame – for example, the second frame – is to the second frame of the bar under discussion.

Page	Bar no.	Step-unit or description	Comments
45	7	*Pas de bourrée*	
	8	*Assemblé*, step	Dancers 7 and 8, first frame: should have the same step symbol as dancers 3–6.
	9	*Assemblé*, step, step	Dancers 7 and 8, first frame: should have the same step symbol as dancers 3–6.
46	10	*Contretemps balonné*	Bars 10–17 repeat the step units of bars 1–8.
	11	*Contretemps balonné*	
	12	*Pas de bourrée*	
47	13	*Pas de bourrée*	Dancers 3 and 4, second frame: step should probably be to the side rather than to the front.
	14	*Contretemps balonné*	In bars 14 and 15 dancers 1, 3, 4 and 7 perform this step-unit with a hop to the side followed by a leap behind; the other four dancers perform both the hop and the leap to the side.
	15	*Contretemps balonné*	Left-hand margin, near bottom of p. 48: ["ha]ubois."
48	16	*Pas de bourrée*	Couples 1 and 2 must perform the first element of this step-unit without a weight change, since they ended the previous step-unit on the foot which begins this one.
	17	*Assemblé*, step	The oboes begin moving to their new positions along the sides of the performing space. On pp. 48 and 49 they take walking steps in the same rhythm as the dancers. On pp. 50 and 51 no step symbols are given, but presumably the walking steps continue since the oboes are still traveling.
49	18	*Contretemps*	
	19	*Pas de bourrée*	
	20	*Contretemps à deux mouvements*	
50	21	*Pas de bourrée*	
	22	*Contretemps à deux mouvements*	Dancer 3, last frame: the "d" has been crossed out.
51	23	*Fleuret*	Left margin: "9 / obois." Dancer 3, last frame: the "d" should be a "g."
	24	*Fleuret*	Above next to bottom stave: "2 musiciens entrent"; above bottom stave: "7 musiciens au fond de la sal" [*salle*]. Two singers, presumably M. and Mme. Dupont, take three steps downstage in preparation for the next scene; the other seven singers remain at the back of the stage in a semi-circular formation. Following bar 24: "fin dela marche / dencente" [*fin de la marche dansante*].
[52: blank]			

Step vocabulary

The step vocabulary of dance IA is limited to the *pas marché* or walking step, one per bar of music. The step vocabulary of dance IB, like most of the other group choreographies in the mascarade, is fairly restricted as the following summary illustrates:

pas de bourrée	8
contretemps balonné	8
other *contretemps* steps	3
assemblé, step, [step]	3
fleuret	2

During much of the dance the lively *contretemps balonné* alternates with the more flowing *pas de bourrée*, while the *assemblé* serves as a punctuating step for the dance phrase. In the last section of the dance (bars 18–23) this alternation occurs every bar, rather than every two bars.

Floor patterns

The floor patterns of the processional (IA) are relatively easy to discern from the freeze-frame manuscript notation. The performers enter from an opening upstage right, and traverse the performing area in a counter-clockwise pattern, processing downstage, across the front of the performing space, upstage, and into the position shown in the last frame on p. 42 of the facsimile.

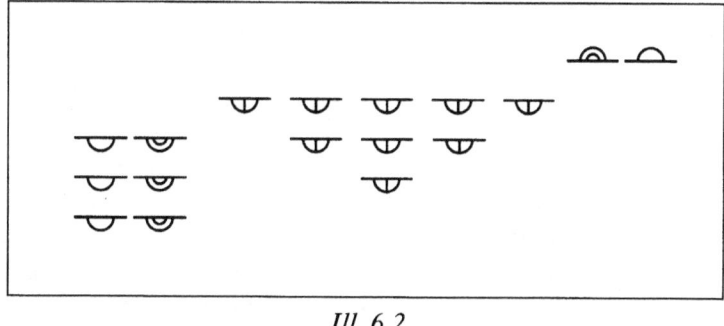

Ill. 6.2

Dance IB begins with the column of dancers, who have shifted to stage left, moving forward downstage, a floor pattern that suggests a continuation of the preceding processional. In bars 3–4 the first couple breaks off from the rest of the column, crossing to the opposite side while passing downstage from the oboes, who remain in a triangular formation in the center (ill. 6.2). The eight dancers remain in this asymmetrical formation for several bars, while the partners turn to face each other and then turn away from and back towards each other. In bar 10 the processional motif returns, with the couples moving into a rectangular formation, each couple traveling clockwise into place but following a somewhat different floor pattern. Here again the lack of symmetry in the individual floor patterns is striking: the overall effect recalls the organized chaos that occurs when a marching band changes from one formation to another. The asymmetry is compounded by the fact that each dancer executes the steps in a slightly different manner – for example, one stepping forward, another stepping to the side while turning – to accommodate the individual movements to the overall pattern. Symmetry is reestablished at the end of bar 15, and the dancers circle individually in place, turning 360°. The turning motion continues as they move to their new formation in bar 17, at which point the oboes begin traveling to their home positions along the sides of the performing space; ill. 6.3 shows the positions of the dancers and oboes at the beginning of bar 18. When the oboes have moved out of the center of the performing area the dancers begin their third and final pattern. The rectangular formation is broken into two diagonal lines, and the dancers move upstage to their home positions on either side of the singers,

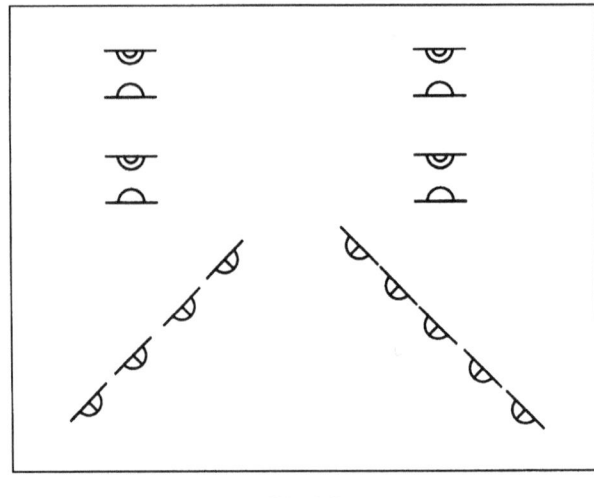

Ill. 6.3

embellishing this basic track with turns in bars 21–3. Each dancer turns a full 360° as he travels, those on stage left turning clockwise to their right while those on stage right turn in the opposite direction. This turning figure is imitated by the oboes in bars 21–2, with 180° turns in place.

The structure of the floor patterns parallels to some extent the repetition of step sequences discussed earlier. During bars 1–4 and again during bars 10–13 the dancers are moving to new positions; once these positions are established the partners circle each other, but do not change positions relative to the other couples (bars 5–8 and 14–17).

Dance/music relationships

The four-bar floor pattern segments just mentioned and the repetition of the opening eight-bar step sequence in bars 10–17 establish a choreographic regularity that has no counterpart in the irregular musical phrasing of this through-composed march. However, in at least one instance the choreography does reflect this very un-marchlike march: the unexpected addition of another *assemblé* in bar 9 – a repeat of the cadential *assemblé* in bar 8 – provides a choreographic analogue to the off-balanced music.

II. CHŒUR "ALLONS, ACCOURONS TOUS"

Two of the four choruses in *Le Mariage de la Grosse Cathos* are choreographed, although in both instances the dancing is not continuous throughout the chorus. In the very short (eleven bars) "Allons, accourons tous" the dancing might better be described as pantomime, in which the dancers, now functioning as individuals rather than as couples, as in the previous dance, represent in motion the words of the chorus: "Come on, let's all hasten. Grosse Cathos is getting married!" Both the floor pattern and the running steps suggest the use of pantomime. Although no hand or upper body gestures are notated, it seems likely that the dancers would have performed such actions as feigning surprise at the news and listening to make sure they had heard correctly.

Music

The music sets two lines of text, "Allons, accourons tous, / La Grosse Cathos se marie," that are repeated three times to the identical three-and-one-half-bar rhythmic pattern. During the first two statements of the text the dancers move only during the first part of the phrase, stopping on the syllable "Gros-"; the third and final pattern is danced throughout.

Ex. 6.2

Al - lons, ac - cou - rons tous, la Gros - se Ca - thos se ma - ri - e. Al - lons, ac - cou - rons tous, la Gros - se Ca - thos se ma - ri - e. Al - lons, ac - cou - rons tous, la Gros - se Ca - thos se ma - ri - e.

In the manuscript the music that appears at the top of the page of dance notation is taken from the bass line of the chorus. This unusual practice, found also in the other danced chorus (IX), is a departure from the normal procedure of relating the dance notation to the melody line, which in both choruses is played by the oboes but not sung. It would seem that Favier wanted to cue the choreography to the text; since the highest texted part was an inner voice, he chose the other structural part, the bass. Favier notated only those portions of the bass line that are actually danced; when the dancers have no movement notation the bass line has rests. Our transcription supplies, in square brackets, the notes that Favier omitted.

Casting and staging

The dancers are not identified by name or gender, but the casting information presented here is based on the assumption that the dancers remain on the same side of the stage and in the same relative positions in which they finished dance IB.

Key for dance II

Dancer 1 = A	Dancer 5 = D
Dancer 2 = B	Dancer 6 = C
Dancer 3 = a	Dancer 7 = d
Dancer 4 = b	Dancer 8 = c

The dancers begin in two single columns on either side of the stage, upstage of the oboes and presumably slightly more towards the center – the position of the oboes is not indicated in this dance – and end in a similar formation on the opposite sides of the performing area.

Beginning position		*Ending position*	
A	B	B	A
a	b	b	a
D	C	C	D
d	c	c	d

The transition from the funnel-shaped formation that ends the previous dance into the two columns is not notated in the manuscript, but could have taken place without any difficulty during the sung sections that separate dances I and II. Since the dancers now move into the space previously occupied by the Duponts – and presumably by L'Abbé du Plessis, Gripetout, and Maître Simon as well, although the lack of movement notation for the solo vocal sections makes it impossible to determine all the singers' movements – it seems certain that these five would have moved upstage to rejoin the other singers in their home positions by the start of the chorus.

List of step-units

Page	Bar no.	Step-unit or description	Comments
		NB: In this dance there are two step-units per bar; in the table below they are separated by a semi-colon.	
53	0	[Starting position]	Title of dance: "Chœur d'Allons, allons accourons tous." Dancer 2 is missing the letter "d" above the body symbol.
	1	*Fleuret; fleuret*	Dancers move forward downstage; the two columns are on opposite feet and remain so throughout the dance. Dancer 8, last frame on page: the letter "g" is missing.
54			
	2	*Fleuret; assemblé sans sauter*	On the *assemblé* the dancers turn towards each other, holding this position until half-way through bar 4.
	3	[Dancers remain in place]	
55	4	[Dancers remain in place]; *fleuret*	Dancers move across stage. The step sequence of bars 1–2 is repeated, but displaced by half a bar.
56	5	*Fleuret; fleuret*	
	6	*Assemblé sans sauter*; [dancers remain in place]	On the *assemblé* the dancers again turn to face across the stage, holding this position until bar 8. Dancer 2: a dot is missing.
	7	[Dancers remain in place]	
	8	*Contretemps; fleuret*	Dancers move backwards upstage until end of dance.
57			
58	9	*Contretemps; fleuret*	
59	10	*Demi-coupé; demi-coupé*	
	11	*Demi-coupé*	

Step vocabulary

The very limited step vocabulary of this dance—only three step-units are used—is not surprising given the purpose of the choreography. This is a miniature "crowd scene": the dancers, miming the action suggested by the chorus, rush forward at the words "allons, accourons tous," then stop to hear the news. The *fleuret*, a stylized running step, is a suitable choice for this action, while the *assemblé sans sauter* is used to halt the forward motion while the dancers wait for their next movement.

Floor patterns

From their starting positions—two columns on opposite sides of the stage—the dancers "run" forward downstage, then abruptly stop and turn towards each other, remaining in this position while the chorus finishes the phrase. In the second section they cross over to the opposite side of the stage, again stopping abruptly and turning to face each other during their rests. The cross-over pattern, in essence a straightforward choreographic device, has been very precisely notated with respect to the dancers' paths. Since the dancers in each column begin the cross-over figure standing close together, they must spread out somewhat in order for the two columns to pass through each other at the same time. However, this maneuver is not performed uniformly; instead the dancers furthest from the audience move in a "V"-shaped path, while the downstage dancers make only minor adjustments (ill. 6.4). In the third and last section the dancers remain facing each other while moving sideways upstage. This choreographed retreat, a feature of all of the group dances in the mascarade, is of particular significance here because the dancers do not perform again until the third scene of the mascarade; thus it is important that they clear the stage at this point.

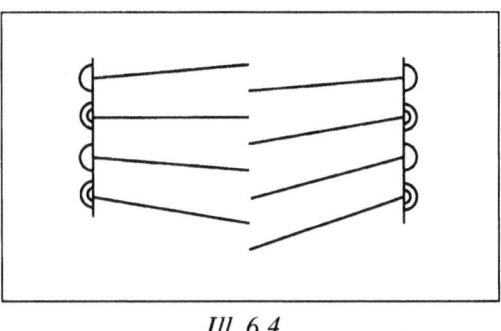

Ill. 6.4

Dance/music relationships

The three-fold musical repetition of this chorus is matched by repetitions in the step sequences – exact repeats in bars 1–3 and 4–6 (both the music and the steps being displaced by half a bar) and a slight variant in bars 8–10. The dancers "run" in a steady quarter-note rhythm, even though the rhythm of the text and music is more varied.

III. ENTRÉE DE DEUX GARÇONS DE LA NOCE

This duet is the first of three dances performed in sequence by the *garçons* and *filles de la noce* following a long section in which there has been no dancing. The opening male duet is the most difficult of the three, although not as demanding as the other male duet in the mascarade, the drunk dance (VI); it resembles many of the virtuoso male duet entrées by Feuillet and Pécour. The affective content, however, seems to differ from dances in the noble style. Several features of this choreography suggest that the dancers may be imitating clumsy rustics who can't quite get their steps right: the use of false positions, unusual gestures such as extra-wide steps and high kicks, awkward *enchaînements*, and rhythmic displacement of the steps which suggests that the dancers are unable to keep time to the music. This dance, along with some of the other dances in this mascarade, may thus add to the small stock of character dances in Feuillet notation in providing glimpses of how Baroque choreographers handled comic or low characters.[7]

The dance may well have operated on two levels: read literally it is a comic dance for two country bumpkins who are trying to perform their version of a noble entrée, without having quite mastered the necessary technique. An audience familiar with the demands of Baroque dance would also have admired the skill of the two performers who artfully imitate their rustic counterparts.[8]

---

[7] In addition to the three Harlequin choreographies mentioned in chapter 5 and Anthony L'Abbé's "Turkish Dance" (LMC 8220) there are several other dances in Feuillet notation with "character dance" elements. A few of these exist in unique versions in the manuscript F-Po Rés. 817: see, for example, "Entrée de paysant" (LMC 3060) and "Mama mouchy" (LMC 5340). Character dances are also the subject of Lambranzi's *Neue und Curieuse Theatralische Tantz-schul* (1716); unfortunately no choreographic notation is included in this work. The whole issue of character dance in the late seventeenth and early eighteenth centuries urgently needs study.

[8] It should be noted that the effects discussed here are more subtle than those in the drunk dance, and that the choreography works perfectly well when performed as a serious male duet. The other two dances in the sequence do not appear to have a humorous content.

Ex. 6.3

Music

The music is in binary form, with two repeated eight-bar strains, each of which is clearly articulated into shorter two- and four-bar phrases. The strong triadic outline in the first two bars of the melody is a characteristic shared by a number of the mascarade dances. The smooth melody and rhythm of the opening phrase belie the melodic character of the rest of the piece, in which there are not only frequent leaps but also a recurring two-bar dotted rhythmic pattern (bars 3–8 of both strains).

Casting and staging

As in dance IB, the performers are identified by name in the manuscript at the beginning of the dance.

Key for dance III: dancer 1 = A (Dumirail); dancer 2 = B (Favier)

The dance begins with the two men standing side by side (B A) about halfway downstage. Although there is no indication as to when or how they move to this starting position, it seems likely that they, along with the two *filles de la noce*, come forward at the end of Dame Ragonde's *récit* in response to her invitation to have some dancing. The dance finishes with the men further apart and also further upstage, facing each other on the same sides of the stage from which they began.

List of step-units

Page	Bar no.	Step-unit or description	Comments
61	0	[Starting position]	Heading: "Entree de deux Garçons de la Nopce." Both dancers are identified in the left margin: "Pas / de Mr Du / Mirail" (first dancer) and "Pas de / Mr Favier / laisné" (second dancer).
	1	*Contretemps* variant: hop, beaten step, free leg moves into the air in front of the body	
	2	As in bar 1, but with a hop in false position, the free foot in front of the body	The false position hops are indicated by the use of the "wrong" letter in an upside-down position. Dancer 1, frame 2: the notation has been corrected from a "d" to a "g."
	3	*Fleuret*	

Page	Bar no.	Step-unit or description	Comments
61	4	*Fleuret*, step	The quick *fleuret* – taking only one half of the bar – begins with a variant *demi-coupé* and ends with a wide step forward; the step-unit finishes with a step to fifth behind. Dancer 1, frame 3: the diagonal line found in the second dancer's part is missing, yet the position of this dancer's body symbol indicates that he has moved as far forward as dancer 2.
	5	*Jeté* to fifth position behind (or fourth position with a beat), free leg beats behind and in front	There are two separate but related problems in the notation of this bar. In the first frame of the top dancer's part there are dots both in front of and behind the body symbol, whereas the second dancer has a dot in front only. Even if we assume that the second dancer's part is correct, the meaning of the dot, particularly in conjunction with the step symbol, remains ambiguous, and solutions other than the one posed here are certainly possible.
	6	*Contretemps*, step	This composite step-unit is analogous to the step-unit in bar 4 in several respects; the identifiable step-unit (here the *contretemps*) is performed at twice normal speed, the third element of the *contretemps* is a wide step forward, and the final element is a step to fifth position behind.
	7	*Fleuret*	
	8	*Cabriole*, step	This step-unit is used to conclude three of the four strains of this dance. Corrections were made in both frames of the top dancer's part; the body symbol was originally placed incorrectly at the left side of the frame.
	9	*Contretemps*, step	This step-unit is similar to the step-unit in bar 6, but the wide step in the third frame of that bar is here replaced by a beaten step. In the last frame of this bar the dancers must keep their weight on both feet if the first frame of bar 10 is to be performed as notated.
	10	Bend and rise in fifth position on weight-supporting leg (no transfer of weight), step, leap to fifth position	In the last frame the step symbol is wrong for both dancers: the feet have been reversed.
62	11	*Contretemps*	In both bars 11 and 12 the dancers apparently remain more or less stationary while shifting their weight from one foot to the other.

Page	Bar no.	Step-unit or description	Comments
62	12	*Fleuret*	In the first two frames the dots on the opposite side of the body from the foot letters may indicate beats.
	13	*Assemblé*, step, step to first	Dancer 2, frame 3: missing dot. The step to first position in the third frame allows the weight to remain on both feet, so that bar 14 can begin with the same foot that ended bar 13.
	14	*Fleuret*, step	This step-unit has the same rhythm as the step-unit in bar 4, but with somewhat different components. The quick *fleuret* begins with a wide *demi-coupé* or lunge to the side, followed by a step to the opposite side, and a step to fifth behind; the step-unit finishes with a step forward.
	15	Hop (free foot to side), Favier step	Variants of this step-unit occur in bars 23 and 31; in all three instances the Favier step is preceded by another element, here a hop. At this point the dancers cross over to the opposite sides of the performing space.
	16	*Cabriole*, step	Same step-unit as bar 8.
	17	*Demi-contretemps, coupé*	This step-unit, which occurs three times in succession, is notated identically to Favier's version of the *contretemps de menuet* found in dance V, bars 25–7. However, here the timing of the step-unit is four even quarter notes.
	18	*Demi-contretemps, coupé*	
	19	*Demi-contretemps, coupé*	
	20	*Assemblé*, step	After the *assemblé* there is a change to rotational symmetry, coinciding with the circling pattern of the two dancers.
63	21	*Contretemps balonné*, step	The dot in the second frame may indicate that the second element of the *contretemps balonné* is executed with a beat. The rhythm of the *contretemps balonné* – a half note followed by a quarter note – is also unusual; the *contretemps balonné* in both Favier and Feuillet notation is normally performed to two notes of equal duration. There is a discrepancy between the two dancers in frame 1 regarding the placement of the free foot: to the front versus to the side.
	22	*Fleuret*, step	This step-unit is similar to the step-unit in bar 4, but without the wide step as the third element. The dancers are circling each other.
	23	*Demi-contretemps*, Favier step	This step-unit is similar to the step-unit in bar 15, but the opening hop has been replaced by a quick *demi-contretemps* which begins with a variant hop.

Page	Bar no.	Step-unit or description	Comments
63	24	*Jeté*, step, step	The discrepancies between the two dancers' parts in the second and third frames may be in part due to the change to mirror-image symmetry in the third frame.
	25	*Demi-coupé* while free foot moves to false position in the air, step, free foot gestures in front	The notation for the gesture in the third frame seems to call for a higher than normal movement. As in bar 2, the false positions of the feet are indicated by upside-down letters of the opposite foot. Dancer 1, frame 1: missing dot.
	26	Step, hop, gesture	The rather curious sequence of steps in the next three bars can be read as a series of three *contretemps*, displaced rhythmically by one half bar; if so, the sequence would start on the third quarter note of bar 26. In the first two of these *contretemps* the first step following the hop is replaced by the high leg gesture found in bar 25. Both dancers are facing the audience and do not travel except to turn in place on the third *contretemps*.
	27	Step, hop, gesture	
	28	Step, hop, step	Music, frame 3: this note should be a g', not an e'.
	29	Three steps [*fleuret?*]	The 180° degree turn in the first frame of this bar is difficult to perform without a *plié*, and the timing and direction (traveling sideways upstage) suggest that the step-unit might be a *fleuret*.
	30	*Pas de bourrée*	
64	31	*Demi-coupé*, Favier step	A third version of the step-unit found in bars 15 and 23.
	32	*Cabriole*, step	Same step-unit as in bars 8 and 16.

Step vocabulary

The wide variety of step-units and many unconventional variants found in this dance provide a dramatic contrast with the limited and highly conventional step vocabulary of the two previous dances. Most of the eight *contretemps* and six *fleurets* in the list of step-units are variants of the versions as they are described in the chapter 5 inventory and in contemporary treatises. The rather high percentage of sprung steps is also worth noting, in particular the *cabriole* which is used three times in this dance and nowhere else in the mascarade.

The possibility has already been mentioned that this dance was intended as a parody of a virtuoso male duet – two country bumpkins trying to impress their sweethearts with a dance in the noble style, a style that they can only attempt to imitate. Although the evidence for such an interpretation is not unambiguous, the following observations lend support to this reading. The dance opens with two *contretemps*, both of which go awry. In the first step-unit, instead of the normal hop, step, step the second step is omitted and the free leg moves to the front of the body, as if the men have forgotten what comes next. Their second try is even worse: the initial hop is made with the free foot in false position in front, and the ending is still not right. Another attempt at a contretemps (bar 6) involves unusual timing, a wide step or lunge forward, and an extra step at the end. Both of these motives – the false position and the wide step – return in the last strain of the dance. Bar 25 begins with a turn into a *demi-coupé*, the free foot moving into false position in front; the third element of this bar is a leg gesture, perhaps a high kick to the front, a step which returns twice more in the subsequent bars. This passage is further complicated by the cross-rhythms in bars 26–9: our poor peasants are *still* trying to get the *contretemps* right, and have managed to lose the beat. They finally succeed in bars 28–9.

Floor patterns

The floor patterns of this dance are quite straightforward, perhaps as befits two dancers whose energies are concentrated on the steps. Following the opening figure, in which the men move downstage, turning along the path, much of the rest of the dance involves travel upstage and downstage on each side of the performing area. The men stay on their own side of the stage for half of the dance, then cross over and circle each other back to their original sides. Everything happens rather deliberately – for example, the entire first strain is spent moving from mid-stage to down stage – and the only hint of a choreographic climax is the bumbling step sequence of the last strain. Mirror-image symmetry predominates, interrupted only once by a four-bar passage of rotational symmetry. Both the beginning and ending positions of the choreography are unusual compared to entrées in Feuillet notation: here the men start halfway down the performing space and end upstage, facing each other rather than the audience. Perhaps this posture was intended to suggest that the men are now directing their attention to the women, and to invite the audience to do likewise.

Dance/music relationships

The large-scale musical form of this dance is nicely articulated by both the steps and the floor patterns. Three of the four strains end with a *cabriole*, an emphatic cadential step; in addition, the penultimate bars of three of these strains (15, 23, and 31) contain the Favier step as a component of the step-unit. Changes in direction, shape and symmetry frequently correspond to structural divisions in the music; for example, at the beginning of the second strain the dancers turn towards each other for the first time, and begin to move upstage.

IV. ENTRÉE DE DEUX FILLES DE LA NOCE [GIGUE]

As soon as the men have finished their dance two women respond with another entrée, a dance which is both a complement to and a contrast with the previous piece. Musically more lighthearted, technically less difficult, these "women" have no pretensions to a level of proficiency above their social station.

Music

The music, a gigue in 6/4, is in binary form with strains of six and twelve bars respectively, the latter divided into two equal six-bar phrases. The repeated rhythmic motive of the opening bars persists throughout the dance, and lends a kind of breathless perpetual motion quality to the long-winded phrases. As is common in quick gigues in Feuillet notation, there is normally one step-unit per bar of music. The rhythm of the step-unit varies according to the number of elements it contains: for example, when there are two elements, each one lasts a dotted half note; when there are three elements, the rhythm is half note, quarter note, dotted half note.

Ex. 6.4

Casting and staging

Although the two performers are not identified by name in the manuscript, the use of hollow body symbols in the notation indicates that the dance is for two women, and the dance title tells us which: the two *filles de la noce*, performed by Germain and Richer in dance IB. The role assignment assumes that the dancers have remained in place on their own sides of the performing area since the end of dance II.

Key for dance IV: 1 = b (Richer); 2 = a (Germain)

The two women, who had probably moved in front of the singers at the start of the previous dance to watch the *garçons de la noce*, begin their dance about one-third of the way downstage and toward the center: b a. The ending position of the dance is almost identical to that of the opening, except that the women have changed places: a b.

List of step-units

Page	Bar no.	Step-unit or description	Comments
65	0	[preparatory position shown]	Heading: "Entrée de deux Filles de la Nopces."
	1	*Fleuret*	
	2	*Fleuret*	Dancer 2, frame 2: position of the body symbol should be the same as in the preceding frame.
	3	*Demi-contretemps, demi-contretemps*	
	4–5	*Demi-coupé*, Favier step, *demi-coupé*	The Favier step, here preceded and followed by *demi-coupés*, crosses the bar line and is performed to even dotted half note beats.
	6	*Pas de bourrée*	
	7	*Coupé, coupé*	The two quick *coupés* are performed traveling to the side, as the dancers cross to the opposite sides of the performing area.

Page	Bar no.	Step-unit or description	Comments
65	8	*Demi-coupé*	The presence of the dot may indicate a beat.
	9	*Coupé, coupé*	See comments to bar 7; here the dancers move quickly upstage.
	10	*Demi-coupé*	See comments to bar 8.
	11	*Demi-contretemps, demi-contretemps*	
66	12	*Pas de rigaudon*	This step-unit, while not identical to Feuillet's *pas de rigaudon*, contains similar gestures.
	13	*Contretemps*	The dancers change to rotational symmetry for the next six bars as they circle to their original sides. In the last frame of this bar the dancers must keep their weight on both feet if the first frame of bar 14 is to be performed as notated.
	14	*Fleuret*, step	The quick *fleuret*, which begins with a variant *demi-coupé*, takes only half the bar; the walking step completes the step-unit.
	15	*Assemblé*, step	There is an error in the step symbol: the short line (right foot) should be *above* the long line.
	16	*Contretemps*	This step-unit, along with the subsequent *contretemps* in this dance (bars 23, 28–31), begins with a variant hop.
	17	*Pas de bourrée*	
	18	*Assemblé*	
	19	*Pas de sissonne*	Change to mirror-image symmetry.
	20	*Pas de sissonne*	
	21	*Pas de sissonne*	
	22	*Pas de bourrée*	
	23	*Contretemps*	
	24	*Coupé*	
67	25	*Fleuret*	The *fleurets* in this bar and the next begin with a variant *demi-coupé*. The dancers change sides again for the third and final time.
	26	*Fleuret*	
	27	*Assemblé*, step	The small "m" (= *mains*) in the second frame indicates that the dancers take inside hands; the first woman takes a wide step to the left to bring her closer to her partner. This frame also marks a change to parallel symmetry, lasting for four bars.
	28	*Contretemps*	Both dancers move left for two bars, then right for two more bars.
	29	*Contretemps*	Dancer 2, frame 3: the dot is partially obscured by the barline.

Page	Bar no.	Step-unit or description	Comments
67	30	*Contretemps*	
	31	*Contretemps*, free leg moves into the air	"lon quite les m." [*l'on quitte les mains*]; dancers drop inside hands and change to mirror-image symmetry in the last frame of this bar.
	32	*Chassé, chassé sans sauter*, step	This unnamed step-unit bears some resemblance to the *pas de rigaudon* (bar 12), but lacks the initial hop. Dancer 1, frame 3: part of the notation extending into the right margin has been trimmed; presumably it mirrors that of the second dancer. Dancer 2, frame 1: missing dot. Music, frame 3: a quarter-note *g* has apparently been trimmed.
	33	*Temps de courante*	In the first frame dancer 1 has a dot while dancer 2 does not; the correct reading is not obvious from the notation.
	34	*Fleuret*	The *fleurets* in this bar and the next begin with a variant *demi-coupé*.
	35	*Fleuret*	
	36	*Demi-coupé*, [step to first position?]	Most of this bar has been trimmed, and there is probably at least one missing frame since the melody note appears to be tied to another note. A *coupé* to first position would be a plausible closing step-unit.

Step vocabulary

In keeping with the character of the music and perhaps the differentiation of genders, the step vocabulary is more conventional and less technically demanding than that of the previous dance. The following list summarizes the steps used:[9]

fleuret (and variants)	7
contretemps	7
assemblé, [step]	3
pas de bourrée	3
pas de sissonne	3
coupé: quick (two per bar)	2
slow (one per bar)	1 (or 2)
demi-coupé	2
demi-contretemps (two per bar)	2
Favier step	1
pas de rigaudon	1
temps de courante	1
unnamed step-units	1

All three duet choreographies contain a greater variety of step-units than do the group dances. However, in contrast to the men's duets, the women's duet consists almost entirely of recognizable step-units of the sort to be found in contemporary *danses à deux* in

---

[9] Here and in subsequent lists the total number of step-units does not always equal the number of bars of music, since a few of the step-units require two bars of music.

Feuillet notation, and even the single unnamed step-unit is made up of recognizable components. By comparison, both men's duets contain a significant number of unnamed step-units, and this distinction may be another way of signaling gender differences in the roles being danced. The step sequences of the gigue also exhibit more internal coherence than do either of the male duets. Although there are no lengthy repetitions of step-units such as are found in the group dances, there are a number of two-bar groupings of the same step-unit, as well as some repeated choreographic phrases which contribute to the sense of orderliness in this duet.

Floor patterns

The floor patterns in this dance are similar to those of the previous duet. During the first strain of music the women move slowly downstage, making 1/8th turns toward and away from each other in the first two bars, movements that might be seen as corresponding to the men's full turns at the beginning of their duet. The women turn and move sideways in bars 4 and 5. The repeat of the first strain of music is accompanied by a cross-over pattern and subsequent movement upstage, again corresponding to a similar floor pattern in the men's dance. The women, however, move in clearly defined two-bar segments, and their pattern unfolds more rapidly. The second strain of music (bar 13) is marked by a change to rotational symmetry, as the women circle each other, moving halfway around the room as they do so. From this point on the similarities between the two duets cease. An unusual figure occurs in bars 28–31: facing downstage, the women hold inside hands and move first to one side and then the other.

Dance/music relationships

The choreography at times subtly delineates the musical structure, at times works against it. As an example of the former, the repeat of the first strain is marked by new step-units with a faster rhythm, a change of direction, and the cross-over floor pattern; bar 18, the strong internal cadence of the B section, is marked by a cadential *assemblé* and a change of symmetry. On the other hand, in the repeat of this strain the choreography completely ignores the musical cadence.

Certain elements of this dance connect it to the previous male duet. In addition to the similarities in floor patterns discussed above both choreographies include a three-fold repetition of a step-unit: in bars 17–19 the men perform a *demi-contretemps/coupé* combination three times, while in bars 19–21 the women perform three *sissonnes* in succession. Both dances rely heavily on the *contretemps* and its variants, but with an important difference: the women perform the step correctly. It is certainly more than coincidence that in the sideways-moving passage mentioned above (bars 28–31) the women perform four *contretemps* in a row, two to each side, at a place in the choreography corresponding almost exactly to the spot where their hapless swains were two beats off the music.

V. ENTRÉE DES DEUX GARÇONS ET DES DEUX FILLES DE LA NOCE [MENUET]

As the manuscript title indicates, this choreography is for the four dancers who have performed the two previous duets. It rounds off the first sequence of three dances and makes explicit the courtship motive that may have been hinted at in the preceding duets.

In contrast to the two previous duets, in particular the male entrée with its challenging step vocabulary, this dance relies almost exclusively on one step; the choreographic interest lies in the floor patterns and the interaction within each couple.

Music

As is the case with almost all menuet choreographies in Feuillet notation, the music is in three [3/4] while the dance step is in 6/4; thus, one menuet step requires two bars of music. However, to simplify our discussion of the choreography we have barred the melody in 6/4; thus in the following discussion a bar of music equals a bar of dance.

The music is in binary form, with two repeated four-bar strains, resulting in a total length of sixteen bars; although there is no such indication in the music section of the manuscript, the entire piece with repeats must be played twice to accommodate the thirty-two bars of the choreography. Each of the strains is divided into two equal two-bar phrases, and in the A strain these are almost identical. The opening bars of both strains exhibit the triadic outlines common to several pieces in the mascarade. The rhythmic profile of the melody, reinforced by the homophonic texture, mirrors the SL LS rhythm of Favier's menuet step.

Casting and staging

The dancers are not identified in the manuscript, but the gender roles are distinguished by the use of hollow and filled-in body symbols for the women and men respectively, and the dance title tells us that it is performed by the four dancers of dances III and IV. As in the previous dances, we are assuming that no extraneous movement takes place between the choreographies, and that the dancers remain on the same sides of the stage where they finished the previous dance.

Key for dance V: 1 = B; 2 = A; 3 = a; 4 = b

The dance begins with all four dancers in a line near the back of the performance space, arranged in couples as follows: B a   b A. The men are already in place, having finished dance III in this position, and need only turn towards the audience, while the women must adjust their positions slightly, moving upstage and toward the center. The dance ends with the two couples again in a line, somewhat downstage from the starting position, and with the order of the dancers reversed: A b   a B.

List of step-units

Page	Bar no.	Step-unit or description	Comments
69	0	[Preparatory position]	Heading: "Entrée des 2. Garçons, et des 2. filles de la Nopce."
			Dancer 2: body symbol has been erased and moved to right.
	1	Pas de menuet	Above the first frame appear instructions for taking hands:
		Bars 1–24 use menuet steps exclusively. This column includes only those bars for which there is a comment.	Dancer 1: "la m.d a la 3e personne" [*la main droite à la troisième personne*; the right hand to the third dancer]
			Dancer 2: "la m.g. a la 4e personne" [*la main gauche à la quatrième personne*]

Page	Bar no.	Step-unit or description	Comments
69	1		Dancer 3: "la m.g. ala pr. personne" [*la main gauche à la première personne*]
			Dancer 4: "la m.d. a la 2e personne" [*la main droite à la deuxième personne*]
			These instructions result in the couples (dancers 1 and 3, 2 and 4) holding inside hands.
			The step symbols for the *pas de menuet* are given in bar 1 only. No further step symbols appear until page 75, where there is a change to a different step-unit.
70			
	6		A small letter "m" [*main* = hand] appears in the lower left or right corner of the fourth frame of this bar in each dancer's part, indicating that the partners must change hands due to the turning pattern. Thus the first dancer is now to the right of the third dancer, holding inside hands and the second dancer is to the left of the fourth dancer.
71			
	11		"quité les m." [*quitter les mains*]; at this point partners drop hands for the rest of the dance.
	12		Dancer 2, frame 4 (first frame of page 72): the third dancer's part was copied in error and then erased.
72			
	16		The last frame of this bar is missing: there should be a quarter-note *g'* in the melody (see bar 32) and a *demi-coupé* onto the left foot for all four dancers.
73			
74			
	24		This step-unit needs to end with the weight on both feet in second position, so that the following bar can begin with a hop on the right foot.
75	25	*Contretemps de menuet*	The rhythm of the *pas de menuet* (SL LS) is preserved in the *contretemps de menuet*. Dancer 2, frames 3 and 4: erasures have been made here and in the first frame of the next bar.
	26	*Contretemps de menuet*	
	27	Dancers 2 and 3: as bars 25–6; dancers 1 and 4: an extra step has been inserted as the fourth frame of this step-unit.	The extra step for dancers 1 and 4 allows them to draw somewhat closer to their partners. It is preceded by a standard *demi-coupé* to fifth position behind; the other two dancers perform the variant *demi-coupé*. Dancer 4, frame 4: missing dot.
	28	*Coupé, assemblé*	This step-unit is also used in the passepied (VIIIB). In both dances it functions as a cadence step, coinciding with the last bar of a musical strain.

Page	Bar no.	Step-unit or description	Comments
76	29–32	[*Pas de menuet*]	No step symbols are given for the last four bars, but a return to the *pas de menuet* is clearly intended. There are a number of minor differences among the four dancers – see, e.g., the second frame of bar 29 – necessitated by the floor pattern.

Step vocabulary

The limited step vocabulary of this dance – the *pas de menuet* for twenty-eight of the thirty-two bars and the *contretemps de menuet* for three of the remaining four bars – is characteristic of menuets in Feuillet notation, although in the latter there is usually a higher proportion of *contretemps de menuet*, and often other steps as well, such as the *pas balancé*.

Floor patterns

Since the women trade sides in their duet while the men do not, the couples have switched partners for the menuet. It is difficult to know whether this switch was of significance to the choreographer. It might not have been noticed by the audience unless the dancers had come forward in their original couple formation at the beginning of the divertissement, and in addition had indulged in some sort of flirtatious behavior during the duets.

Perhaps of more interest is the fact that the dance begins and ends with the positions of the couple at stage right reversed – the woman stands to her partner's left rather than his right. At the beginning of the dance couple A–b is reversed, at the end couple B–a. What makes this so unusual is the fact that at least since the Renaissance the man positioned himself at his partner's left, not only for dancing but in any social situation that involved movement as a couple. This convention is rigidly adhered to in one- and two-couple dances in Feuillet notation[10] as well as in the thousands of country dances and *contredanses* from the period. However, the two-couple dances in Feuillet notation are for the ballroom, not the stage; Favier's defiance here and elsewhere in the mascarade of the rules of etiquette suggests that in theatrical choreographies considerations of symmetry overruled those of social convention. However, the mirror-image symmetry of the floor patterns is not extended to the dance steps; as in ballroom menuets all four dancers begin the *pas de menuet* on the right foot throughout the choreography.

The courtship motive of this dance suggested by the opening figure is reinforced by the many circling patterns that the partners perform around each other. The choreography begins with the two men turning slightly towards their partners to take inside hands; forming diagonal lines, each couple moves downstage for the first strain of the music, the man leading his partner. The first circling figure is made by the women, who move downstage and then around their partners, still holding inside hands (ill. 6.5). As the women arrive on the outside of their partners (end of bar 6), the hand holds are changed

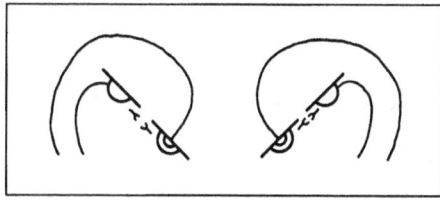

Ill. 6.5

---

[10] The one exception, Dezais's "L'Italiene", is mentioned in chapter 3, n. 28. Most of the two-couple dances in Feuillet notation are menuets and passepieds.

so that once again partners are holding inside hands. The strain finishes with all four dancers facing the audience and taking one menuet step backwards and one forwards.

The B strain (bar 9) begins with the two couples crossing to the opposite sides of the stage, moving sideways. Couple B–a passes downstage of couple A–b. The next circling figure begins in bar 11 with the couples dropping hands and then moving around each other in a figure reminiscent of a half *dos-à-dos* [do-si-do], a pattern found in many late seventeenth-century *contredanses*. However, in this figure all four dancers face the audience at all times, rather than each other. Again, mirror-image symmetry is in effect, the women moving downstage and away from each other, the men upstage and towards each other.

The repeat of the B strain (bar 13) begins with a figure similar to the opening of the dance: the couples form diagonal lines and move upstage for two bars. Another circling pattern follows, the women again taking the lead and moving inward and around their partners, who also turn in place. During bars 17–20 the couples separate, the women moving downstage; the turning figures continue, and at the end of this phrase all four dancers are in a line across the center of the performing space, the men inside facing downstage, the women outside facing upstage. The couple motive is reestablished in bars 21–2, as the partners spiral in towards each other, ending this figure in a slightly asymmetrical formation, the left couple further downstage than the right couple. As couples they move halfway across the stage, until the women have passed each other; then all four dancers travel backwards to stage left or right, the men to their original places and the women to the opposite side from which they started, ending in a rectangular formation. During the next four bars the figures change very quickly, helped in part by the use of the *contretemps de menuet*, a step-unit that allows more distance to be covered. In bar 25 the dancers move to a diamond figure, all facing in; during the following bar the diamond shape rotates 90° clockwise, ending with the dancers facing out; in bar 27 the diamond dissolves into a line across the center, the partners facing each other (ill. 6.6); the phrase closes with each dancer turning in towards his partner and ending facing downstage in the starting formation.

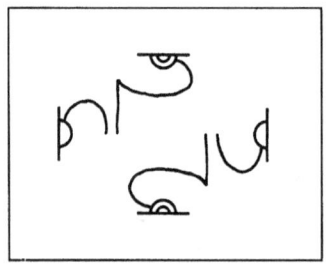

Ill. 6.6

The final four bars have the effect of a choreographic coda. The men make a half-circle around their partners, after which the couples change sides, couple B–a passing downstage of couple A–b. During the final two bars the expected choreographic retreat upstage is reversed as the couples move downstage and to the sides, clearing the performing area for the vocal soloists and chorus.

Dance/music relationships

As the previous discussion has illustrated, the floor patterns in this dance are not only very elaborate but they are also used to articulate the music strains more so than is the case in other dances in the mascarade. Perhaps this is not surprising, given the fact that until bar 25 only a single dance step is used.

VI. AIR DES IVROGNES

The title for this dance is found only in the music section of the manuscript, but the choreography makes it abundantly clear, even if the musical concordance had not done so already, that the title applies to this dance. The humor is created in part by the juxtaposition of incongruous elements – the elevated music is a foil to which are set steps requiring virtuoso technique, as well as steps totally inappropriate to the genre. Although it is not obvious from the choreography whether the dancers act drunk from the beginning, or get progressively drunker as the dance goes on, moments of attempted "sobriety" do occasionally occur – when, for example, the drunks summon all their energies to do one magnificent *entrechat à quatre*.

Ex. 6.6

Music

Another binary dance, the music is played once through (AABB) for a total of thirty-six bars. The music for this choreography stands in sharp contrast to the rest of the mascarade dances: in G minor, it is the only minor piece in the mascarade; both strains open in a quasi-imitative fashion, the melody beginning before the other voices, whereas the other dances are strictly homophonic; finally, the tempo is undoubtedly slower than the other dances, since there are two often complex step-units per bar of music. All of these are characteristics of the contemporary *entrée grave*, a technically demanding male solo or duet.

Casting and staging

From this point on in the manuscript annotations appear much less frequently; thus, casting decisions are correspondingly more tentative. The two drunks were undoubtedly men, not women, but otherwise there are no clues as to which man performed which role. Dumirail and Favier are the obvious choices, since they would have been in position after having performed the menuet. One might argue that it would make dramatic sense for the other two men, who had been standing in their corner home positions since the end of dance II, to have been seen tippling all this time and to now appear in a drunken state. However, such a staging would have created a distraction during the singing, in contravention of the principle of a single focus that seems to underlie the notation. The subject of this part of the mascarade is the state of drunkenness, not the process of getting drunk; moreover, the dancers are in a sense acting as surrogates for Maître Simon, who has just told the audience that he has to derive his pleasure from drink since he has no love life. It would thus have been dramatically acceptable for any of the four men suddenly to appear

150 Musical Theatre at the Court of Louis XIV

drunk, but as Dumirail and Favier are already in position, they are the likeliest candidates.

Key for dance VI: 1 = A; 2 = B

The dance begins with the two men about halfway downstage, each one near his own side of the performing area (A B). This starting position, is, in fact, very near to where the men were at the end of dance V; the intervening vocal music between V and VI would have allowed their partners a chance to retire to their home positions. The dance ends with the two men in the same relative positions, but further upstage.

List of step-units[11]

Page	Bar no.	Step-unit or description	Comments
77	0	The first frame shows the starting positions for the two dancers	
	1–2	Three springing step-units: a wide jump sideways, landing in fourth position followed by a jump to second position; a beaten *contretemps*; a *chassé*, the free foot subsequently swinging beind the body	These three step-units create a cross-rhythm of 3+3+2 with the duple meter of the music. The last two frames of bar 2 can also be read as a *jeté* forward, the free leg swinging in front and then behind.
	3	*Demi-contretemps*; *coupé*	Dots in the second and third frames may indicate beats.
	4	*Demi-coupé*; wide *demi-coupé* to side, *rond de jambe* with free leg	
	5	Two traveling jumps in first position, moving sideways downstage and then upstage	
	6	Three traveling jumps in first position, moving backwards and then forwards; step	
	7	*Coupé*; *assemblé*, step	
	8	*Assemblé*, step; two steps	Dancer 2, frame 1: missing dots.
	9	*Demi-contretemps*; *coupé*	
78	10	*Demi-contretemps*; *coupé*	
	11	*Assemblé*; jump in place, turning 360°	Dancer 2, frame 1: missing dots.
	12	*Demi-coupé* with *rond de jambe*; *fleuret*	The first step-unit is similar to the second step-unit of bar 4. The *fleuret* begins with a variant *demi-coupé*.
	13	*Demi-coupé*; *chassé*, step	In this and the next two bars the final step (to second position) must end with the weight on both feet if the following bar is to be performed as notated.

[11] Each bar of music comprises two step-units; they are separated by a semi-colon in the analysis.

The dances 151

Page	Bar no.	Step-unit or description	Comments
78	14	*Fleuret*, a beat on the last step; step	The *fleurets* in this bar and the next begin with a variant *demi-coupé*.
	15	*Fleuret*; *demi-coupé*	In the last frame of this bar and the first frame of the next dancer 1 has two consecutive *demi-coupés* on the same foot.
	16	*Fleuret*; *fleuret*	Change to rotational symmetry; dancers begin circling each other back to back.
79	17	*Assemblé*, [step]; two hops, during which the free foot moves to fifth behind, then fifth front	The step symbol in the second frame of this bar (first frame of page 79) is missing.
	18	*Fleuret*; *coupé*	The *fleuret* is performed moving from side to side, ending with a step backwards; the overall effect is of a stagger.
	19	Two hops; *fleuret*	The three step-units in bars 19 and the first half of 20 are a repeat on the opposite feet of the three step-units in bars 17½–18. The dot in the last frame of the second dancer's part indicates a step to fifth position behind, the weight on both feet, enabling the following bar to be performed as notated.
	20	*Coupé*; *coupé*	Change to mirror-image symmetry. Dots in the first and third frames may indicate beaten *coupés*. The second step-unit must end with the weight on both feet to begin bar 21 as notated.
	21	Jump to fourth position, turning 180°, *pas échappé* to wide second position, jump to first position; *fleuret*, closing to first position	
	22	*Coupé* backwards, *chassé sans sauter* to the side, the free foot opening to a wide position; two jumps to fifth position, the feet reversing after each jump	Dancer 1, frame 3: the "d" has been corrected to a "g" but without removing the stem of the former. In the next two frames there are horizontal lines above the body signs, indicating that the jumps travel upstage. These signs are missing from the second dancer's part.
80	23	*Assemblé* to fourth position, *pirouettes* on both feet, first turning 45° towards upstage center and back, and then 180°, turning in the same direction, step	The apparent change in foot positions relative to the body – e.g., for the first dancer the front foot in the first four frames alternates r, l, r, and l – is a result of the *pirouette* action; no additional foot movements are required.
	24	*Demi-contretemps*; *demi-contretemps*	In both step-units the free foot moves in front of the body.

Page	Bar no.	Step-unit or description	Comments
80	25	*Coupé*; *chassé* (the "chased" leg swinging wide in front), step	During this bar the dancers cross to the opposite sides of the stage, dancer 2 moving downstage of dancer 1; slight adjustments in frames 2 and 4 are necessary to accommodate this change.
	26	*Chassé*, step; *assemblé*	The first half of this bar is a repetition of the second half of the previous bar.
	27–29	12 walking steps, 4 per bar	During these three bars the two men circle each other using ordinary walking steps (although they are undoubtedly more of a stagger than a walk); the floor patterns nearly collide between the second and third frames of bar 29. Dancer 2, bar 27, frame 1: a "d" has been erased.
81	30	*Demi-coupé*; 360° *pirouette* on one foot *en dedans*	The tie connecting the two frames of the first dancer's part seems to indicate that the two steps are to be thought of as one continuous motion, a reading also suggested by the unusual placement of the music: beats three and four seem to be aligned with the tie, and there is no separate metrical pulse corresponding to the *pirouette* step symbol in the second frame. Dancer 2, frame 1: a "g" behind the body symbol has been erased.
	31	*Chassé*, step to side, free leg gestures in front, step; jump to fourth position twice, changing feet	The first frame of this bar is identical to the third frame of bar 2; as was the case there, this step may also be interpreted as a *jeté*.
	32	Jump to first position; *demi-contretemps*	
	33	*Demi-contretemps*; *rond de jambe* ending in second position	In the second frame of both parts a turn sign, probably continuing in the direction of the previous turn, is missing. In the third frame a vertical line indicating a wide step is missing in the second dancer's part. The *rond de jambe* is probably performed prior to the change of weight.
	34	*Entrechat à quatre* from second position, landing in wide second position; two hops, the free leg in front	
	35	*Chassé*, the free leg swinging wide behind, three hops moving sideways upstage, free leg in front	
	36	*Jeté*, step, step	

Step vocabulary

The dryness of the preceding step descriptions unfortunately obscures the hilarious pantomimic quality implicit in the dance notation. Almost every bar offers some subtle or not-so-subtle joke at the expense of the "noble style." Although only a live performance can really do justice to this remarkable choreography, some of the more striking step-units are mentioned below. In bars 1–2 the cross-rhythm between the step-units and the music may be intended to suggest men who can't quite keep the beat. The mock bravura sequence of backward and forward jumps in bar 6 is also found in the Harlequin choreographies. The *pirouettes* in bar 23 offer another opportunity for drunken pantomime; the dancers are undoubtedly reeling dizzily as they try to work out the direction in which they want to head. Perhaps the funniest passage occurs in bars 27–9, where the two drunks circle each other using ordinary walking steps. The humor in this passage can be appreciated at two levels: as slapstick comedy, in which the two drunks stagger around in circles, trying to focus on something and nearly running into each other; and as a sendup of the *entrée grave*, the conventions of which barely allowed one unadorned walking step, let alone twelve. In the first half of bar 31 the speed of the steps as well as the manner in which they are executed suggest a humorous rather than a serious reading; in fact, throughout the dance the sudden and inappropriate contrasts between slow and fast steps suggest that consistency of movement is completely beyond the control of the dancers. The *entrechat à quatre* has already been mentioned; two bars from the end of the dance the drunks somehow manage to summon their remaining strength to perform one last display of bravura. Even the final bar contains a joke: each of the last two steps is performed with a 90° turn in the wrong direction, so that the men are in effect falling over their own feet as they struggle to reach their closing positions at upstage center, facing the audience.

Floor patterns

The floor patterns also contribute to the pantomime implicit in the step vocabulary. In addition to the passage described above in which the two men stagger around each other, there are several occurrences of sudden and awkward changes of direction, movements consistent with the efforts of a drunk trying to coordinate legs and brain. The floor patterns also reflect the men's struggles to orient themselves spatially, either by determinedly keeping each other in view or by turning away and attempting to use the two lines of the oboe band as a frame of reference.

Dance/music relationships

The music serves as a foil to the dance by sounding as if it were accompanying gods when it is used to accompany drunks. Although the phrasing of the dance does not contradict the musical phrasing, it is clear that the choreographic interest lies elsewhere.

VII. RIGAUDON

The drunk dance is followed immediately by a rigaudon for the four female wedding guests and the bridegroom, a charming choreography that contains several unique features. Perhaps its most remarkable aspect is that it is a combination of two separate choreographies: one for the four women who perform as a group, and one for La Couture, who for much of the dance has a separate step vocabulary and floor pattern, both of which contrast with those of the women. In addition, the unusual hey figure in the final section of the dance is unique among notated choreographies.

The dance may also have a dramatic function, depicting La Couture's last fling as a bachelor. Taking advantage of the drunken state of the male wedding guests, he attempts to seduce the female wedding guests. Seemingly oblivious to his presence at the beginning of the dance, by the end they have fallen meekly in line behind him.

Ex. 6.7

Music

Another binary dance form, the music is played once through (AABB) for the notated choreography, then is repeated for La Couture's unnotated solo. For the latter, the manuscript specifies that the music should be played one time ("une fois l'air"): although this annotation does not specify whether the music is to be played with or without repeats of its two sections (i.e., AABB or AB), the former is much more likely given the pattern of repeats required by a substantial number of choreographies in Feuillet notation.[12]

The key has returned to G major and the melody again uses the triadic outlines that are characteristic of so many of the dances in the mascarade. Rhythmic gestures in the melody link it firmly to other contemporary rigaudons; these include the quarter-note upbeat, the gradual acceleration from the opening half notes to quarter notes and then eighth notes in bar four, and the arrangement of these eighth notes as a melodic turn.

Casting and staging

There is no heading above the dance notation, and none of the five roles is identified in the manuscript or distinguished by the type of body symbol. In the music section of the manuscript this dance is entitled "Rigaudon pour les filles de la noce"; given the number of dancers required it appears that the term *filles de la noce* is used here in a more general sense to include not only the two *filles* who performed in dances IV and V, but the two *Dames Gigognes* as well (see chapter 3 for further discussion of ambiguities in regard to the casting). Even this extension only accounts for four of the five required dancers, but the choreography itself resolves the ambiguity. There is a clear distinction in step vocabulary and floor pattern between the dancers notated on the upper four staves and those of the fifth dancer that suggests differentiation on the basis of gender. The four similar parts are obviously intended for the four women; the fifth dancer's identity is revealed at the end of the choreography (p. 88), where an annotation calls for an unnotated solo to be performed by La Couture.

Key for dance VII: 1 = b; 2 = a; 3 = c; 4 = d; 5 = X (La Couture)

The dance begins with the four women standing in a rectangular shape in the upper third of the performing area with La Couture in the center:

```
        b           a
              X
        c           d
```

To reach their starting positions the women need only move slightly towards center stage

---

[12] For a discussion of this issue see Little, "Problems of repetition and continuity."

The dances 155

from their home positions where they presumably remained during the commedia scene, while La Couture moves downstage from the back of the performing area. The dance ends upstage in a semi-circular formation:

$$X_d \quad _c \quad b \quad ^a$$

List of step-units

The notation for this dance contains a number of errors, inconsistencies, and omissions that present certain problems in its reconstruction. In the following discussion we will first identify what appear to be faulty readings in the notation, and then discuss the effect that these readings have on the identification of the steps and step-units.

The manuscript at this point seems to have been prepared in two layers, judging by the clear differences in size and thickness between the step symbols in the various dancers' parts. For example, beginning with the fourth frame on p. 83 the step symbols for the top three women are smaller than the same symbols for the fourth woman, the latter matching those of La Couture in terms of size and thickness of stroke. Only on the last two pages of the dance (pp. 87 and 88) do the step symbols all appear to be the same size. In general the smaller symbols present more accurate readings than do the larger ones, suggesting that the former were added at a later stage in the preparation of the manuscript.

However, in spite of these corrections the choreography remains incomplete. Step symbols for all five dancers are given on the first page of the dance, but after this page the step symbols appear only haphazardly as follows: for dancers 1, 4, and 5 on p. 84 and the first system of p. 85; for dancers 1 and 4 on the second system of that page; for dancers 4 and 5 on the first system of p. 86. For the final figure, which starts on p. 87, the notation is more consistent, step symbols being provided for each dancer as he or she enters; however, even in this section there are some omissions.

Another type of error occurs on p. 85, where the notation staves for the third and fourth women have been switched. This can easily be demonstrated by comparing the positions of the two dancers at the end of the previous page – dancer 3 is at stage right, dancer 4 at stage left – with their reversed positions in the first frame of p. 85. It is clear from the choreography that they could not have traveled this distance in one step. The notations for the two roles remain switched for the remainder of the dance.

More problematic is the use of inconsistent step notations in the four women's parts. In most instances we are inclined to label these inconsistencies as errors, based on the high level of error already evident in this dance, and on the paradigm of consistency which can be observed in the other group dances in the mascarade. On the other hand, it is remotely conceivable that Favier was deliberately violating this paradigm in the rigaudon, and this possibility should not be ruled out completely.

One such example occurs in the first bar of the dance (frames 2 and 3 on p. 83) in which all five dancers have step symbols in the larger notation style. In each of the two frames the first and second women perform a *chassé*, the free foot moving to the front; the third and fourth women have similar notation, but without the leap, resulting in a *chassé sans sauter*. Two aspects of this bar are troubling: first, except for a problematic passage on p. 85 nowhere else in the dance do the women perform simultaneously two different versions of the same step, and since in other respects their movements are identical, there seems no choreographic or dramatic reason for them to do so here. Second, for much of the first part of this dance there seems to be a deliberate contrast between the leaps of La Couture and the gentler rises of the women; thus it would make more sense for all four women to begin the dance with the *sans sauter* version of the step.

Another kind of inconsistency occurs on p. 85 – the page with the greatest number of errors and/or problematic readings – where some of the step symbols appear to have been misplaced. For example, from the third to the eighth frames the symbols for the fourth [*recte* third] woman are displaced by one frame, relative to the first woman, resulting in a sequence of two *fleurets*, each beginning on the second quarter note of the bar and performed in a SLS rhythm. Since the step symbols for the first woman are consistent with the choreographic style, and since all four women are moving in symmetrical figures at this point (the other two women are lacking step symbols of any kind) it seems clear that the reading of the first woman is correct. Since La Couture's steps follow those of the fourth woman, they are probably also in error; it would seem that the scribe simply copied the symbols from the fourth stave, since the step symbols for La Couture break off after the first frame of the second system.

In spite of these difficulties the dance can still be reconstructed with confidence. The list of step-units presents the most plausible reading, one that follows the smaller or "corrected" notation and that preserves consistency in the step-units among the dancers. In bars 14 and 15, the displaced symbols of the fourth woman and La Couture are given in square brackets.

Page	Bar no.	Step-unit or description (women)	Step-unit or description (La Couture)	Comments
83	0	Preparatory position	No preparatory position shown	The starting position of the third woman should be the same as the second woman, i.e., with the weight on the left foot.
	1	First and second women: two *chassés* in place; third and fourth women perform the same steps *sans sauter*	*Jeté, jeté*	The reading for the third and fourth women is probably correct; see previous discussion.
	2	*Coupé* to first position	Leap to second position (weight on both feet), step	In bars 1–4 and bar 6 the women's steps are similar to La Couture's, but the vigorous hops and leaps of the male role are replaced by the women's gentler *élevés* which remain on the ground. Fourth woman, frame 2: missing dot.
	3	*Contretemps balonné sans sauter*	*Contretemps balonné*	
	4	*Contretemps sans sauter*	*Contretemps*	In the first frame women 1 and 3 should have a symbol for an *élevé* rather than a *saut*.
	5	*Coupé, coupé*	*Contretemps balonné*	In frame 3 of the fourth woman's part the *demi-coupé* should be to the side rather than forward. A step and body symbols have been erased in the second frame of La Couture's part.

The dances 157

Page	Bar no.	Step-unit or description (women)	Step-unit or description (La Couture)	Comments
84	6	*Assemblé sans sauter*	*Assemblé*	
	7	*Coupé, coupé*	*Contretemps balonné*	In La Couture's opening hop the free leg moves behind the body rather than to the front or side, the normal positions for the *contretemps balonné*. In the second frame of his part a half-note rest has been corrected to a quarter-note rest.
	8	*Assemblé sans sauter*	*Assemblé*	Second woman: missing dot.
	9	Bend/rise on supporting leg while free leg is in the air to the side, first element of Favier step	*Contretemps balonné*	Bars 9 and 10 in the women's parts comprise an unnamed step-unit, in the middle part of which occurs the Favier step, crossing the bar line.
	10	Second element of Favier step, *demi-coupé*	*Contretemps balonné*	
	11	Same as bar 9	*Jeté, jeté*	Third and fourth women cross over to the opposite sides of the stage; first and second women remain on their original sides.
	12	Same as bar 10	*Assemblé*	La Couture has a half-note rest in the second frame of this bar.
85	13	*Demi-coupé*	Step	Notation for dancers 3 and 4 has been switched.
	14	*Fleuret* [fourth woman; *demi-coupé, coupé*]	*Fleuret?* [Step, *coupé*]	See discussion preceding the list of step-units. It seems likely that La Couture's step-units in this and the following bar should match those of the first woman. The literal reading is given in brackets. The dot in the first frame of this bar (missing in the third woman's part) probably indicates a beat.
	15	*Fleuret* [fourth woman: step, *coupé*]	*Fleuret?* [Step, *coupé*]	

Page	Bar no.	Step-unit or description (women)	Step-unit or description (La Couture)	Comments
85	16	Step	Step	No step symbol is shown in the first woman's part; both the fourth woman and La Couture have a plain walking step, but since their previous bars are corrupt it is possible that a more climactic step was intended in order to match the musical cadence.
	17	*Demi-contretemps sans sauter*	Same as women?	Step symbols for La Couture are missing for the rest of this page, but begin again on p. 86.
	18	*Fleuret*	*Coupé*, pivot with free leg moving in front of body?	This *fleuret* and those in bars 20 and 23 begin with a variant *demi-coupé*. A correction has been made in the third frame of La Couture's part, but the step-unit and the transition to the following bar still seem awkward.
86	19	*Demi-contretemps sans sauter*	Same as women?	
	20	*Fleuret*	Same as women	In the third frame a dot appears in the third and fourth women's parts but not in the first and second women's parts.
	21	Step/rise (no bend), *demi-coupé*	*Coupé à deux mouvements*	The step/rise in the women's part (first frame) can also be found as the second half of the Favier step (bars 10 and 12); in each case the step is taken to fourth position behind.
	22	*Demi-coupé, rond de jambe*	Bend/rise on supporting foot (no weight change)	La Couture's foot sign may have been changed from a "g" to a "d," presumably so that the subsequent *fleuret* can begin with the left foot. However, this change precludes the forward traveling indicated by the notation, suggesting that the reading is still corrupt.

The dances 159

Page	Bar no.	Step-unit or description (women)	Step-unit or description (La Couture)	Comments
86	23	Fleuret	Same as women	Second woman, frame 1: missing dot. In bars 23 and 24 of the second woman's part the body symbols were originally further downstage.
	24	Step	Demi-coupé	All five dancers form a column in the center of the performing area, facing the audience; La Couture is in the front.
	25	—	Fleuret	The women remain in place while La Couture begins weaving through them; they join in the weaving figure one by one. The choice of feet for each of the dancers in the hey figure does not follow any discernible pattern, and may be in error.
87	26–7	Two *fleurets*, fourth woman	Two *fleurets*	The fourth woman follows behind La Couture.
	28–9	Two *fleurets*, third and fourth women	Two *fleurets*	The third woman joins the line. La Couture's symbols (bottom stave of p. 87) were erroneously copied onto the next higher stave (third woman) and then erased.
	30–1	Two *fleurets*, first, third and fourth women	Two *fleurets*	The first woman joins the line. In frames 2 and 3 of bar 30 the fourth woman (third stave) has two consecutive steps on the left foot.
88				Step symbols for the women are missing in the first two frames of p. 88. Also on this page freeze-frame notation for the oboes appears to have been added below the dance notation and then erased.
	32	*Fleuret*, all women	Fleuret	The second woman joins the line.

Page	Bar no.	Step-unit or description (women)	Step-unit or description (La Couture)	Comments
88	33–[64]	—	An unnotated solo performed by La Couture	"la coutur dence / soeulle une fois / lere" [*La Couture danse seul une fois l'air*. La Couture dances alone one time through the music.]

Step vocabulary

The contrast between La Couture's step-units and those of the women, notational ambiguities notwithstanding, may well be intended to differentiate the two choreographies on the basis of gender, particularly in the first twelve bars of the dance. For example, the bridegroom's vigorous *contretemps*, *contretemps balonnés*, and *assemblés* are replaced in the women's parts by versions of these steps performed *sans sauter*, i.e., without leaps. As the dance continues the contrast between La Couture's step vocabulary and that of the women diminishes. Both genders perform the same step-units in the majority of bars 13–24, La Couture having adopted the gentler style of the women when his more vigorous posturing proved unsuccessful in attracting their attention. The repetition of eight *fleurets* in the final section of the dance is in striking contrast to the variety of step-units found in the rest of the choreography. In this passage the floor pattern and dramatic content clearly take precedence over the steps.

In the following lists the frequency of each step-unit is given only for the first 24 bars of the dance. The contrast between the two sets of step-units in terms of quality of motion – smooth vs. springing – can be seen clearly: eleven of La Couture's step-units contain at least one *saut*, whereas none of the women's does.

Women		*La Couture*	
fleuret	5	*contretemps balonné*	5
assemblé sans sauter	2	*fleuret*	5
demi-coupé	2	*assemblé*	3
Favier step	2	*demi-contretemps sans sauter*	2
demi-contretemps sans sauter	2	*jeté* (2 per bar)	2
coupé (2 per bar)	2	walking step	2
(1 per bar)	1	*contretemps*	1
walking step	2	*coupé*	1
chassé sans sauter (2 per bar)	1	*demi-coupé*	1
contretemps sans sauter	1	other	2
contretemps balonné sans sauter	1		
other	1		

Floor patterns

In terms of its floor pattern this is surely the most interesting choreography in the mascarade. The dance exhibits considerable spatial variety, ingenious interactions among the performers, and floor patterns susceptible to a narrative interpretation.

The two independent floor patterns that occur simultaneously during the first twenty-four bars of this dance can be read as a reflection of the genders of the performers. The women's patterns are characterized by curved shapes and graceful interactions; La

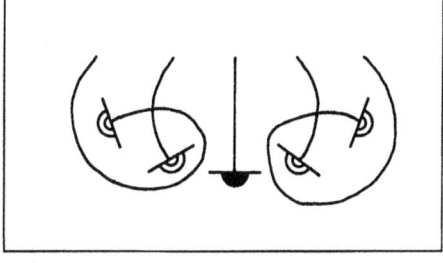

Ill. 6.7

Couture, on the other hand, moves forward and back on a line that defines the axis of symmetry of the women's patterns. Although his movement also incorporates some turns, the essential nature of his floor pattern is straight and direct. If he is indeed trying to attract the attention of the village women by his more vigorous steps, he initially fails in his quest; the women proceed to dance with each other, seemingly oblivious to La Couture except for a brief moment in bar 8 when all five dancers are lined up across the stage (ill. 6.7). When, beginning at bar 13, La Couture adopts the gentler step vocabulary of the women they seem more receptive to his advances and retreats. As a result of this amorous by-play at the end of bar 24 the women have fallen into a column behind him in preparation for the final "follow-the-leader" figure.

The closing figure of the dance is completely different not only from previous figures in the mascarade but also from other notated Baroque dances. Favier's inspiration for this weaving or hey pattern may have been the English country dance, which had been introduced with great success to the French court in 1684. However, the hey is by no means unique to this genre; it appears in sixteenth-century French and Italian dances, and its roots are undoubtedly even earlier. In any case, its use here seems to evoke the idea of a rustic style of dance, appropriate to a village wedding. La Couture, at the head of the column, begins weaving through the women who are standing behind him. As he passes each one, she peels off and joins the weaving figure, until suddenly the column has dissolved into a semi-circular formation (see chapter 3, ill. 3.6a/b). The simple, uniform step allows all interest to be concentrated on the figure, which reinforces the idea that La Couture has indeed overcome the resistance of the village girls. Both the hey figure and the line dance are choreographic motives that are developed further in the next two dances.

Dance/music relationships

The dance exhibits a close correspondence between the choreography and the musical structure. Except for the final bar, the dotted-half-note cadence at the end of each eight-bar strain is reinforced in the dance by the use of a single step, rather than a step-unit, taken on the first beat of the bar. These points of repose also serve to articulate the changes in the choreographic figures. On a more detailed level there is some evidence of two-bar and four-bar phrasing of step-units, either by direct repetition of a step-unit or by repeating a two-bar step sequence, but this is not consistent throughout the dance.

VIII. PASSEPIED

The passepied shares certain characteristics with the opening dance of the mascarade. Perhaps the most significant one is that both are group dances in which the oboes play a prominent role, participating in the action as the dance band for the wedding festivities. In the processional the oboes lead the other characters into the performing area, and then occupy the center of this space during the second part of the dance. In the first part of the passepied the oboes likewise occupy the center of the performing area, in this instance as the focus of the choreographic figure; and toward the end of the dance they interact with the dancers in a striking manner. Another point of similarity between the two choreographies is that both take as their point of departure Renaissance group dances – the pavane and the branle – that emphasize communality rather than virtuosity. A third point of comparison is that both dances have two choreographic sections, the first of which is in freeze-frame notation while the second is in standard Favier score notation; this notational change is reflected in our subdivisions (IA/IB and VIIIA/VIIIB). However, the visual contrast in the manuscript between these two sections is somewhat misleading, particularly in the case of the passepied. Favier clearly conceived of this dance as a single organic choreography; he deemphasized the change to score notation by placing it five bars after the repeat of the passepied music, rather than at the beginning of the repeat; furthermore, he provided continuity between the two parts of the dance by the use of similar choreographic motifs – circles, serpentine lines, and straight lines.

The freeze-frame portion of the passepied is, however, more elaborate than that of the opening processional, not only in terms of the floor patterns but also because the dancers, led by La Couture, are performing a menuet step traveling sideways to the left, rather than the simple walking step of the opening dance. No parallels to this line dance exist in the repertoire of notated Baroque dances. The choreography is of particular interest because of its apparent links to earlier line dances: the Renaissance branle and the medieval *carole*.[13] According to Arbeau the passepied had its origin as a branle; thus it is possible that Philidor's choice of the passepied was a conscious attempt to evoke the rustic setting with which this dance had been originally associated.

In VIIIB the eight dancers divide according to gender into two groups of four; each group performs a short passage alone before joining together for the final segment in which they weave through the columns formed by the oboe band. This unexpected figure provides a fitting climax to what must rank as the most unusual dance in the mascarade, and makes explicit the integration of the instrumentalists into the dramatic action. In addition to its links to the opening pavane this choreography also demonstrates connections to the preceding rigaudon (VII), both because of the presence of La Couture in the first part of the dance and the weaving patterns in the second part.

Ex. 6.8

Music

As was the case in dance V the transcription of the music given here has been barred in 6/4 to match the menuet step, each of which requires six quarter-note beats or two bars of 3/4 music. In the manuscript score the music is barred in 3/4 with a mensuration sign of 3.[14] Another of the binary dances, the passepied music is performed in its entirety twice (AABBAABB), for a total of forty bars of music. The A strain consists of two 2-bar phrases, the second of which is a variation of the first. The phrasing of the B strain is less

---

[13] See Heartz, "Branle"; and John Stevens, "Carole," *New Grove Dictionary of Music and Musicians* III, p. 814. Both articles include illustrations of a line dance.

[14] The music for Baroque passepieds is usually notated in 3/8 or 6/8, an indication that it was faster than the menuet.

regular; the cadence on the second half of bar 10 is preceded by a hemiola across the bar line, creating a counter-rhythm with the step, a characteristic also found in many Baroque passepieds in Feuillet notation. The melody, which moves in step-wise fashion with many repeated notes and ornamental eighth-note turn figures, has a simple folk-like quality. It is interesting to note the similarity of the melody of the passepied A strain to the B strain melody of the preceding rigaudon. Since the two dances are performed consecutively a kind of *Tanz/Nachtanz* relationship is suggested.

Casting and staging

In this choreography movement is notated for oboes as well as dancers; the notation for the oboes is not continuous, indicating that during portions of the dance they remain stationary. None of the dancers is identified by role or gender at the beginning of VIIIA. However, when La Couture is identified later in the choreography – by means of the rubric "la couture va au fond" ("La Couture goes to the back," p. 90, fifth system, second frame) – it becomes clear that he has been the leader of the line dance, and was standing at the left of the semi-circle of dancers at the beginning of the dance. The exact order of dancers in the rest of the line is impossible to determine with certainty. However, our proposed solution is based upon the principle of economy of movement from the preceding dance and upon the observation that iconographic representations of line dances generally show men and women in alternation within the line.

At the end of the rigaudon (VII) La Couture and the four women are standing in a semi-circle. The transition to the passepied, which apparently follows without a break, is easily made if La Couture and the four women remain in their formation, and the four men simply slip in between them to create a semi-circular line that alternates men and women. If we assume that men A and B performed the drunk dance, and are therefore closer to center stage than are C and D, who have not danced since the "Allons" chorus (II), the arrangement of the dancers will be as follows:

Beginning of VIIIA: X d C c A b B a D[15]

In the second half of VIIIA the oboes – having previously formed a circle in the center – move upstage; at the same time La Couture peels off and the remaining eight dancers break into two groups of four, ending in the following position:

Ending of VIIIA: d   D
                          C   a
                          c   B
                          A   b
                        [oboes]
                            X

It will be observed that this formation does not position the dancers in mirror image by gender, as might have been expected on the model of the dancers' positions in the menuet (V). However, in order to arrive at mirror-image symmetry at this point in the dance, it would have been necessary to place dancers of the same gender next to each other at the start of the line dance (for example: X d C A c b B D a). In this instance the alternation of men and women seems more desirable than the preservation of mirror-image symmetry.

The second part of the passepied (VIIIB) begins with a short four-bar passage for the four women alone. The notation depicts them in a rectangular formation, but their positions relative to the men are not indicated, and must be inferred from the closing formation of VIIIA. By the end of their four-bar segment this rectangle has rotated 90°

---

[15] If C and D were closer than A and B to the center the following pattern would result: X d A c C b D a B. If this or any other formation were used it would also affect our proposed casting for VIIIB, the second part of the dance, and the subsequent dances as well.

clockwise, and each woman is standing next to a different man. Once again the notation does not show the relative positions of the men and women, but a comparison of the last frame of the women's section with the first frame of the men's section seems to indicate that mirror-image symmetry has been reestablished, as the following diagram illustrates. The oboes remain in their circle upstage from the dancers.

```
     Beginning of VIIIB:      End of bar 4: women have
                                rotated 90° clockwise

          d    D                   C    D
          C    a                   c    d

          c    B                   b    a
          A    b                   A    B
```

Key: 1 = d; 2 = c; 3 = a; 4 = b

The men's section of the dance, set to the first repetition of the B music, also involves a 90° clockwise rotation. The rectangular formation is retained, and each man ends on the upstage side of the woman next to whom he was standing at the beginning of VIIIB. In the last two bars of the men's section movement notation for the oboes reappears, indicating that the circle has started to break up. Taking two walking steps per 6/4 bar of music the oboes move into two lines facing each other across the stage.

```
   Beginning of men's section:    End of men's section: men have
                                    rotated 90° clockwise

          C    D                       c         d
          c    d                       A         C

          b    a                       b         a
          A    B                       B         D

                                       o         o
                                       b         b
                                       o         o
                                       e         e
                                       s         s
```

Key: 1 = C; 2 = A; 3 = B; 4 = D

The final section of the dance, for all eight dancers, begins from this formation and ends with the dancers in a semi-circle upstage, a formation similar to the one that began section VIIIA. During the last two bars of the dance the oboes return to their home positions along the sides.

Key for dance a8: 1 = c; 2 = d; 3 = A; 4 = C; 5 = b; 6 = a; 7 = B; 8 = D
Ending of VIIIB: c A b B D a C d

List of step-units

For VIIIA the dance notation portion of the manuscript provides only the first strain of the tune, after which the dance notation continues without music; brackets have been placed around bar numbers for which music is lacking in the dance notation. On p. 90 two more bars of music are provided, but they appear to have been misplaced. Hence there is a certain amount of ambiguity about the exact amount of music required. This problem is discussed more extensively in the section on dance/music relationships.

Page	Bar no.	Step-unit or description	Comments
		VIIIA. [Line dance, 8 dancers and La Couture]	
89	0	[Starting position of performers shown]	"lon comance le passe pied en cette figure setenent les mains / autour" [*L'on commence le passepied en cette figure se tenant les mains autour*. One begins the passepied in this formation holding hands along the line.] Above first frame of dance notation: "sytuation" [*situation*, i.e., the positions of the dancers].
	1	*Pas de menuet*	Symbols for the *pas de menuet* are given in this bar only, although as in the menuet (dance V), the step-unit is presumably meant to be repeated throughout the dance. The dancers travel sideways to their own left, and small letters adjacent to the leader of the line (La Couture) show how the menuet step adapts to this sideways motion: steps onto the right foot are taken in front of the body, steps onto the left foot are made to the side. At the same time the two columns of oboes move towards each other into a circular shape in the center of the performing area.
	2		At the beginning of this bar each oboe player turns to form an outward-facing circle. Above third frame: "les aubois demeurent / dans la mesme figure" [*les hautbois demeurent dans la même figure*]. The oboes remain in this position until the middle of the next page; they are not depicted in the notation again until they begin their next move.
	[5]		The music notation stops for the next 56 frames; it begins again with the last bar of the B strain in the middle of the next page.
	[last system, frames 3–8]		In the fifth frame of this system the line of dancers doubles back on itself and begins to circle the oboes again, moving counter-clockwise. The position of the oboes is shown by small dots in the last three frames on this page.
90	[fourth and fifth systems]		Two bars of music appear: the last bar of the B strain followed by the first bar of the A strain. In the second frame of the fifth system there is an extra *g'* quarter-note. Fourth system, sixth frame: "les aubois dessende" [*les hautbois descendent*]; the oboes, still in their outward-facing circle, move upstage for the next three bars.

Page	Bar no.	Step-unit or description	Comments
90			Fifth system, second frame: "la couture va au fonds" [*La Couture va au fond*]; La Couture, who has been leading the line dance, breaks off from the line and moves toward upstage center; the remaining eight dancers split into two groups of four, also moving upstage in semi-circular shapes. Small foot signs ("d" and "g") appear in frames 3–5 of the fifth system, showing how the menuet step is to be adapted to the mirror-image pattern.
			A collette has been pasted in at the bottom of the page; above it appears the text "lon se tien les mains" [*l'on se tient les mains*]. No previous instructions to drop hands were given. In the fourth frame of this collette an erasure has deleted the oboes who were erroneously depicted as being downstage of the dancers.
91			
	[24]		Last frame, line dance: the oboes are in the same position that they occupied at the end of the previous page.

VIIIB: [Notated passepied for the eight dancers][16]

Page	Bar no.	Step-unit or description	Comments
	5	*Contretemps de menuet*	The third element in this bar and the next is a variant *demi-coupé*. "les 4 fa. dence" [*les 4 femmes dansent*]. The rhythm of the step-unit has changed from the menuet pattern used in the line dance (SL LS) to a new rhythm (LS LS) that is used for the remainder of the choreography.
	6	*Contretemps de menuet*	Dancer 4, frame 3: the letter "g" is an error. The step-unit ends with a step to first position, allowing for a change to mirror-image symmetry in the next bar.
92			
	7	*Contretemps de menuet*	Dancers 1 and 3 move in mirror-image symmetry to dancers 2 and 4 in this bar and the next. Dancer 2, frame 1: turn sign to the left rather than to the right.
	8	*Coupé, assemblé*	The three step-units that end with an *assemblé* (see bars 14 and 20) correspond to the final bars of the three strains of music. This step-unit was used in a similar context in the menuet (V).

---

[16] Dance VIIIB starts at the repeat of the first strain of music; the bars have been numbered accordingly, beginning with bar 5.

The dances 167

Page	Bar no.	Step-unit or description	Comments
92			A blank frame is headed "les 4 hom. dence" [*les 4 hommes dansent*], and is followed by yet another frame showing the starting positions for the four men, corresponding to the last quarter-note of bar 8.
	9	*Contretemps de menuet*	This step-unit differs from the one performed by the women in that the third element is a *jeté* rather than a *demi-coupé*. It appears again in bars 10, 13, 15, 18, and 19.
93	10	*Contretemps de menuet*	In the fourth frame, all but the third dancer step left to fifth position behind; he steps right to fourth position front, bringing him parallel to the fourth dancer. The change to mirror-image symmetry is completed at the end of this bar.
	11	*Contretemps de menuet*	An extra step is added in the second half of this step-unit; in effect the *coupé* becomes a *fleuret*, and the rhythm of the complete step-unit is LS SSS. There is mirror-image symmetry between dancers 1 and 2 and dancers 3 and 4.
	12	*Contretemps de menuet*	Same step-unit as bar 11. Dancer 1, frame 3: an extra dot appears to the left of the "g." In the fifth frame dancers 3 and 4 avoid changing weight by stepping to fifth position front.
94	13	*Contretemps de menuet*	In left margin: "aubois." The oboes, who have remained upstage in a circular formation since the end of VIIIA, now begin moving towards their home positions. For the next two bars (13 and 14) they take two steps per bar. Turning downstage and toward the center, they form into two lines and start backing up towards the sides.
	14	*Jeté*, step, *assemblé*	This is a sprung version of the cadential step-unit performed by the four women in bar 8, the *coupé* of the latter being replaced here by a *jeté*, step. The last frame of this bar shows the starting positions of all eight dancers for the final six bars of the dance. The oboes remain in the positions they reached at the end of bar 14, in preparation for the dancers who will weave through them.
95			
	15	*Contretemps de menuet*	See comment to bar 9. Mirror-image symmetry continues through the rest of the dance, both for the group as a whole (odd-numbered dancers start with the opposite foot from the even-numbered dancers) and within each pair of dancers: 1 and 2, 3 and 4, etc.

Page	Bar no.	Step-unit or description	Comments
95	16	*Demi-contretemps; demi-contretemps*	This step-unit is similar to the *contretemps de menuet* in the previous bar, except that the third element, a *jeté*, has been replaced by a hop.
96	17	*Jeté*, step, *demi-contretemps*	Although this step-unit begins with a leap rather than a hop, it is clearly related to the *contretemps de menuet* family; if the first and third elements are reversed it is identical to the step-unit in bar 9. The eighth-note *e"* in the second frame of the music should be a quarter note. The two lines of dancers begin moving through the oboes.
	18	*Contretemps de menuet*	Dancer 1, last frame: the body symbol should be rotated counter-clockwise, in mirror-image to dancer 2.
97	19	*Contretemps de menuet*	The oboes begin moving once again, taking two steps backwards per bar of music and also closing the gaps left open for the dancers; the two files start on opposite feet. Dancer 5, frames 3 and 4: feet should be the same as the other odd-numbered dancers; dancer 6, frame 3: missing dot; dancer 7, last frame: crossed-out "d" to the right of the body symbol.
98	20	*Demi-contretemps, assemblé*	This version of the cadence step substitutes a hop for the *demi-coupé*.

Step vocabulary

The two sections of the passepied offer a striking contrast to each other with respect to the choice of step-units. VIIIA uses only the *pas de menuet*, performed in the same rhythm as in dance V (SL LS), whereas VIIIB eschews the menuet step entirely in favor primarily of the more energetic *contretemps de menuet*. Furthermore, the latter step-units are performed in a new rhythm, LS LS. The replacement of the opening iambic SL by a trochaic LS lends rhythmic emphasis to the first element of the step-unit and also underlines the vigor of the step vocabulary.

Like the line dance, dance VIIIB also has a limited step vocabulary, using only three different step-units in sixteen bars: 12 *contretemps de menuet*; three step-units ending with an *assemblé*, all of which function cadentially; and one pair of *demi-contretemps*. However, as the list of step-units makes clear, the *contretemps de menuet* appears in a variety of guises.

The choice of step-units in VIIIB seems to have been made in such a way as to suggest gender differentiations. As in the rigaudon (VII), the men's step-units make more use of hops and leaps, whereas the women's step-units tend to remain on the ground. When the women dance alone they perform the regular, less vigorous, version of the *contretemps de menuet*, containing only one sprung element, and their cadential step-unit has only one sprung element. In the dance for four men the cadential step-unit and several of the *contretemps de menuet* include two sprung elements. In the final strain for all eight dancers the men's versions of these two step-units predominate.

Floor patterns

The floor patterns in both parts of the passepied are dominated by circles, lines, and a serpentine flow of movement which pervades the entire dance. One of the delights of this choreography is the constant metamorphosis of these shapes – circles into lines and lines into circles.

In the line dance (VIIIA) La Couture and his companions trace a floor pattern that is quite easy to follow in the manuscript; the movements of the oboe band at the beginning of the choreography are carefully notated along with those of the dancers. From their home positions along the sides of the performing area the instrumentalists move toward the center of the stage; by the end of bar 2 they have formed an outward-facing circle, around which La Couture and the dancers move, traveling clockwise and moving to their own left, so that they face the oboes as they circumnavigate their circle. The pattern is then reversed: the dancers travel counter-clockwise, still moving to their left and circling the oboes, but now facing outward. Following this figure the oboes begin to move upstage along with La Couture, while the line of dancers divides into two groups of four, each of which also moves upstage, forming lines on either side of the performing area. During the final segment of VIIIA (top of p. 91) the two lines of dancers essentially mark time, moving sideways downstage, backing away from each other, and then moving sideways upstage, downstage, and upstage.

Dance VIIIB begins with a short choreographic segment for the four women. Although there is no frame showing their preparatory position, the women apparently start from a rectangular formation, each one facing across the rectangle. On the first step each woman turns to her own left to face outward and continues by traveling sideways to her own right, so that during the next two bars the women's rectangle rotates clockwise 90°. As the women move to their new positions they also turn clockwise along the path of travel; the entire effect is that of rotating bodies in orbit around an imaginary sun. Having reached their new positions, the women continue the turning motive, each one circling more or less in place, but now in mirror-image symmetry, moving slightly further to the sides as they do so. They end facing each other, close to the men, who now take their turn.

The men's dance is slightly longer (six bars as opposed to four) and slightly more complicated than the women's, in that two separate patterns are being traced simultaneously during the first three bars of the choreography. Dancers C and B (the first and third dancers in the notation) move in rotational symmetry, each to his own right, along the sides of the stage for one bar, after which each travels on a short circular path away from and back to place. At the same time, dancers A and D (second and fourth dancers in the notation) move across the stage, also in rotational symmetry, each to his own right; ill. 6.8 shows the patterns of dancers A and B. At this point mirror-image symmetry takes effect on both a horizontal and vertical axis; dancers C and A change sides, as do dancers B and D. As in the women's segment, the men end facing each other across the stage. It should be noted that these two sequences have been carefully planned to take place downstage so as not to interfere with the oboes, who until bar 13 of VIIIB were still occupying the upper half of the stage. At this point the oboe circle breaks into two lines – parallel to the sides of the stage – which separate and move slightly upstage.

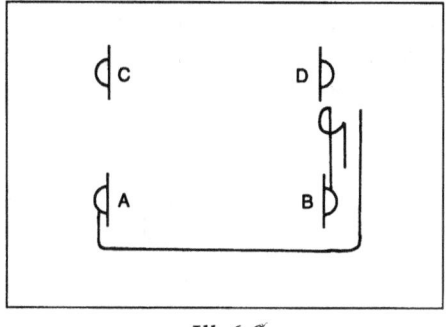

Ill. 6.8

The final segment of VIIIB begins with the men and women dancing in couple formation, but the interaction within each pair found in other couple-oriented dances in the mascarade – holding hands, circling each other – is missing. Instead, the choreographic pattern is a line dance for two groups of four dancers, moving in mirror-image symmetry reminiscent of the second half of dance VIIIA, after the line had divided into two groups. The two lines of dancers weave through the oboes in "S" and reverse "S" patterns, ending in a semi-circular formation similar to that of the opening of VIIIA (see chapter 3, ill. 3.7). This figure combines the hey motif from the rigaudon with the serpentine shapes from the first part of the passepied. As the dancers finish their figure the oboes move slightly downstage and then back up to their home positions along the sides of the stage.

Dance/music relationships

In the first section of the passepied (VIIIA) there are some significant difficulties in trying to determine the precise relationship between the music and the dance, since the notation of both music and dance steps in this section is incomplete. Because of the repetition of the step-unit, the notator apparently felt that it was necessary to provide only the opening bar of step notation, and the musical notation also breaks off after a few bars, even though blank music staves have been provided for the remainder of the dance. Only the freeze-frame notation of the dance figure continues throughout. Thus it is not immediately obvious from the dance notation either what repeat scheme is needed for the music or exactly how the music and choreography fit together at specific points. However, a fragment of music appears on p. 90 which shows that the music starts again after finishing the B section.

In VIIIB, on the other hand, the notation of the steps, the music, and the figures are all complete, and from this we can establish that this section requires one repetition of the first strain of music and two repetitions of the second strain, or ABB. Thus it appears likely that the repeat scheme of the music for the two sections together must be AABBAABB, the typical repeat scheme for passepieds in Feuillet notation. The problem remains of how to match the steps and figures of VIIIA to the music.

Two discrepancies confuse the matching of steps and music: (1) if the relationship set up at the beginning between music and dance step – four frames of dance notation to six quarter notes of music – remains in effect throughout the dance, there should be ninety-six frames of dance notation in VIIIA when in fact there are ninety-nine; (2) assuming that the music/dance ratio remains constant, the fragment of music on p. 90 signalling the second repetition of the AABB structure occurs eight frames too soon; but since the placement of this fragment of music coincides with an important structural point in the choreography – it is here that La Couture breaks off from the line of dancers, who themselves break into two groups – it certainly seems plausible that Favier intended this choreographic change to be signalled by the repetition of the music.

If, on the other hand, we conclude that the freeze-frame notation was intended to show the floor pattern and the approximate rate of travel rather than a more precise correlation between the number of frames of dance notation and number of bars of music, it becomes possible to preserve the correspondence Favier appears to have intended between a significant choreographic moment and a structural point in the music.[17] This explanation would allow a slight stretching of the choreography on pp. 89–90 to preserve this correspondence; it would also allow a compression of the top two systems of dance notation on p. 91, improving what otherwise seems to be an uncharacteristically repetitive and pointless passage.[18]

---

[17] This hypothesis also makes practical sense; it is more difficult to control the spacing of a line dance – and thus more problematic to notate it – than it is for individual dancers to make small adjustments as they travel.

[18] One other hint that the end of the line dance may be corrupt: there is a collette at the bottom of p. 90 that replaces 4½ frames of dance notation. Perhaps corrections were also intended for the top of the next page, but were never inserted.

IX. CHŒUR "PASSONS TOUJOURS LA VIE"

The danced chorus "Passons," like "Allons," involves all eight dancers, who appear to function at least in part as surrogates for the singers; the last eight bars also include movement notation for the oboes and singers. However, the fifty-six-bar "Passons" is much more substantial than the earlier eleven-bar chorus, and here the sung and danced sections alternate until the last strain, which is performed by both groups. The character of the choreography in the two choruses is also quite different: whereas "Allons" involves almost pure pantomime for dancers who function as a crowd, the notated portions of "Passons" reintroduce the couple formations and courtship motives of the menuet (V) that are perhaps intended to suggest that the "pleasure" referred to by the chorus is the pleasure of love. The idyllic, romantic side of the rustic wedding *topos* – established in the menuet and continued in the rigaudon and the passepied – now resumes until the final strain of the chorus.[19] In this segment, which is both sung and danced, the reentrance of the commedia characters returns us to the burlesque world of Cathos and La Couture.

Music

The entire piece comprises seven 8-bar sections in an arch form with rondeau elements: ABCB'DBA. Sections A, C, and D (bars 1–8, 17–24, and 33–40) are performed by the singers and the oboe band; they are joined by the dancers in the final A section (bars 49–56). The three B sections (bars 9–16, 25–32, and 41–8) are danced but not sung; they are identical except that the middle section (B') is transposed to the dominant. The first two are danced by the wedding guests; the third is a solo for one of the men, and no dance notation is provided. Only the music for the danced sections (B, B', and the final A section) is included here. In the final section of choreography the texted bass line of the chorus, rather than the oboe melody, appears above the dance notation. (See the discussion for the other danced chorus (II) where the same practice occurs.)

---

[19] It is, of course, possible that these courtship dances were performed in a burlesque fashion; however, there are no hints in the notation that comic intent is present.

Casting and staging

The position of this piece within the mascarade is open to question (see chapter 3), and this uncertainty also affects the casting. Our casting diagrams are based on the conclusion that the dance follows the passepied (VIII), as its position in the dance section of the manuscript would indicate; in this case the arrangement of the dancers would presumably remain unchanged from the ending of VIII to the beginning of IX, as we have indicated below. If, on the other hand, "Passons" precedes the drunk dance (VI), as it does in the music section of the manuscript, a somewhat different arrangement of dancers would be required.

At the beginning of the dance all eight dancers are arranged in a line at the back of the performing area but in front of the chorus, presumably in the order in which they ended the passepied: c A b B D a C d. They wait while the chorus sings the first eight-bar phrase; during the subsequent instrumental strain four dancers, unidentified in the manuscript, move forwards, ending about two-thirds of the way downstage. After the next sung section there is again a danced instrumental interlude for the four dancers who remained upstage; since these four are identified as the four *paysans* (male peasants) we can deduce that the first group of four dancers must have been the four women.[20] This parallels the situation in dance VIIIB, where the four women perform as a group, followed by the four men, each group in turn moving forward downstage. However, in dance IX the men's choreography lasts for only two bars, during which they move forward to join their partners in the same formation as at the beginning of the dance.[21] There is an unnotated solo for one of the men during the next interlude; presumably he begins and ends from the same position. In any case, the dancers end in the same relative positions in which they begin, although slightly further upstage. During the last strain both the oboes and the singers shift their positions further upstage, along with the dancers.

Key for four women (p. 99): 1 = c; 2 = d; 3 = b; 4 = a
Key for four men (p. 100): 1 = A; 2 = C; 3 = B; 4 = D
Key for all eight dancers (p. 101): 1 = c; 2 = d; 3 = A; 4 = C; 5 = b; 6 = a; 7 = B; 8 = D.

Adjacent dancers take inside hands, forming couples as follows: c–A, b–B, D–a, C–d. As in the menuet, mirror-image symmetry takes precedence over social convention: in both left-hand couples the woman is on her partner's left. The dance ends in the same formation.

List of step-units

Page	Bar no.	Step-unit or description	Comments
99	1–8	[Chorus]	No movement notation; dancers remain in opening formation while chorus sings. The last quarter note of bar 8 shows the preparatory position of the dancers.
	9	*Fleuret*	Bars 9–16 are danced by the four women.

---

[20] It is possible that the masculine plural noun *paysans* refers not to the four men but to two mixed couples, presumably the two peasants and the two Dames Gigognes, C–c and D–d; by extension this would mean that the first section of the dance was performed not by the four women but by the two *garçons* and *filles de la noce*, A–a and B–b. However, this arrangement seems less likely, given the division of the group by gender that Favier already used in the passepied; moreover, it creates a number of difficulties in the overall casting of the dance.

[21] The notation is somewhat ambiguous; the assignment of roles in the dance for eight is based on a comparison of the ending positions of the two groups; for example, the first woman appears to be further to the left of the frame in bar 16 than the first man does in bar 26. Thus, she will be to his left in bar 27 and is therefore the first dancer. Other arrangements of dancers are possible; however, this one preserves the mirror-image symmetry with respect to the entire group as well as the couple formation implied by the choreography.

Page	Bar no.	Step-unit or description	Comments
99	10	*Coupé à deux mouvements*	
	11	*Fleuret*	
	12	*Coupé à deux mouvements*	
	13–14	*Pas balancé*	Performed in mirror-image symmetry by each pair of women.
	15	*Fleuret*	
100	16	*Demi-coupé*	
	17–24	[Chorus]	No movement notation; dancers remain stationary while chorus sings. Last quarter note of bar 24 (bottom of p. 100): "les 4 payisans." The starting positions of the four men are shown.
	25	*Fleuret*	The first two bars of this eight-bar strain are performed by the four men only, the women remaining in place.
	26	[*Fleuret*]	The step symbols below the music staves indicate a *fleuret*. However, in the third frame of this bar only the first dancer has a body symbol and a foot sign, the frames for the other three dancers remaining blank. The symbol for the first dancer has been altered and is difficult to decipher; a possible reading is a step forward on the left foot. A fourth frame for this bar appears on p. 101; it includes at the top of the page the two eighth notes of music that had originally appeared at the end of the previous frame. However, this frame is not part of the step-unit (no step symbol appears at the bottom, or it may have been erased); it is included to show the position of all eight dancers prior to their performance a8. In any case, the foot positions of the men as shown in this frame confirm that the step-unit for all four men in bar 26 is a *fleuret*.
101	27–9	Three *demi-contretemps*	Above the first frame of the first and third dancers' parts respectively appear the following instructions: "la m.d. a la 3es" [*la main droite à la troisième personne*], "la m.g. ala pr." [*la main gauche à la première personne*]. These two dancers are standing next to each other and take inside hands, performing as a couple for the remainder of the dance. Although none of the other couples is instructed to take hands, the choreography for all four couples is identical and it seems reasonable to assume that the remaining three couples would follow suit. During the next four bars each man circles his partner, pulling her with him as he goes.

Page	Bar no.	Step-unit or description	Comments
102	30	*Demi-contretemps*	Dancer 1, frame 1: error has been crossed out below body symbol. Dancer 2, frame 1: the notator erroneously entered the third dancer's symbols; these have been partially erased, the correct symbols appearing on the right-hand side of the frame.
	31	*Fleuret*	
	32	*Demi-coupé*	Below the dance notation in the left margin appears the rubric "un paysant / dence soeulle" [*un paysan danse seul*; one of the peasants, i.e., a male dancer, performs alone].
	33–40	[Chorus]	No movement notation; dancers remain in their positions while the chorus sings.
	41–8	[Solo dance, unnotated]	The solo peasant dance probably takes place during this instrumental interlude, rather than during the preceding chorus, in accordance with the pattern of alternating chorus and dance established in the first five sections of the piece.
103	49	*Contretemps balonné*	As was the case in the other danced chorus, the music at the top of the page is now from the bass line of the chorus rather than the melody line of the oboes. As in bar 27, the first and third dancers have rubrics in the first frame regarding the taking of hands: "donne la m.d. ala 3es pers." [*donne la main droite à la troisième personne*]; "donne la m.g. ala pre. et / la d. ala 5esme" [*donne la main gauche à la première personne et la main droite à la cinquième personne*; the first dancer gives his right hand to the third dancer, etc.]. None of the other dancers is instructed to take hands. An additional symbol, a small letter "b" (for "bras"? = arms) also appears in the first frame, upper left-hand corner of dancer 1, and lower right-hand corner of dancers 5 and 7. In addition, it appears that at least four "b"s have been erased from the first dancer's part in bars 49–51. (See further discussion below.) In the second frame, turn signs for dancers 5–8 are missing.

Page	Bar no.	Step-unit or description	Comments
103			Movement notation for the oboes and singers appears on two separate staves at the bottom of the page. Although neither group is identified, it is clear from their previous positions that the oboes occupy the upper stave, the singers the lower. The singers do not move until the following bar. The oboes, traveling sideways, move upstage taking one step per bar of music as follows: those on stage left step to second position with their right foot, in the next bar to fourth position behind with their left foot, and so on, while those on stage right perform the mirror-image of this sequence.
	50	*Contretemps balonné*	Frame 1, dancer 5: "b" in upper right-hand corner. The singers move backwards upstage for two bars, taking two steps per bar of music instead of the usual one. Those to the left of center stage start with the right foot, while those on stage right start with the left foot.
	51	*Contretemps balonné*	Frame 2, dancer 1: "b" in upper right-hand corner.
104	52	*Contretemps balonné*	In this and the subsequent three bars there are minor differences in the direction of the second element of the *contretemps balonné*, necessitated by the floor pattern. For example, in this bar dancers 7 and 8, who form the bottom of the "V," leap forward rather than backward. The oboes continue to move upstage. Although the singers have no step symbols or foot signs in this bar, in the second frame their position relative to the music staff has changed suggesting that they continue to travel.
	53	*Contretemps balonné*	The oboes continue as before; the center singer (unidentified, but undoubtedly La Couture) disengages himself from the others and begins moving downstage, taking one step per bar of music starting with the right foot.
	54	*Contretemps balonné*	
105	55	*Contretemps balonné*	The oboes remain in the positions reached in the previous bar. La Couture apparently continues his movement downstage, although step symbols are missing in both this and the following bar.
	56	*Coupé* to first position	

Step vocabulary

Like the other choreographies in the mascarade that are performed by the full complement of dancers, "Passons toujours" uses a relatively limited and straightforward step vocabulary.

contretemps balonné	7
fleuret	6
demi-contretemps	4
coupé	3
demi-coupé	2
pas balancé	1

Although there appears to be an almost even division between the *contretemps* family and the contrasting *à terre* step-units, the characteristic alternation of the two types – see dances IB and XB, for example – does not occur. Instead, the *contretemps* step-units appear in two isolated groups: a sequence of four *demi-contretemps* in the middle of the dance and a sequence of seven *contretemps balonnés* at the end. Repetitive passages of this sort are rare both in the mascarade and in dances in Feuillet notation; they usually are an indication that some aspect of the choreography other than the step vocabulary has become prominent.

Floor patterns

The first danced strain is for the women alone, who progress slowly downstage, turning towards and away from each other as they move forward. This passage is reminiscent of the openings of the other two dances for four women: the rigaudon (VII) and the passepied (VIIIB). The mirror-image *pas balancé* in bars 13–14, in which the two pairs of women turn towards each other and then away, is a nice preparation for the full circle each one traces in the following two bars.

After the eight intervening bars of chorus the men are clearly eager to catch up with their partners. Moving purposefully forward, they cover the same distance in two bars that the women took eight bars to traverse. As the couples take inside hands each man begins to circle his partner, the woman turning as well, but in a smaller radius in response to her partner's lead. The circling pattern flows into a wide "V"-shaped figure, and the dancers move upstage in this formation for the last two bars of the strain, leaving the center of the stage clear for the subsequent solo passage. No choreographic notation is provided for this solo, nor is there any indication as to which of the male dancers performs the solo.

The final strain appears to be little more than an extended choreographic retreat. Turning to face the audience, the dancers move backwards and at the same time flatten the "V" into a straight line. Since the singers are standing behind the dancers, they too must back up, as the notation shows them doing in bars 50–1. During the last four bars of the piece the center singer (undoubtedly La Couture, whose air follows) moves downstage. The oboes move sideways upstage along the sides. The last frame on p. 105 of the facsimile shows the positions of the oboes and singers at the end of bar 56; the dancers are in a line in front of the singers at the back of the performing area.

The contrast between the varied figures and step-units of the first two sections of this dance and the monochromatic final strain is puzzling. One could perhaps argue that this extended eight-bar coda balances the leisurely opening figure danced by the four women, or that it is merely an expanded version of the upstage retreating patterns found at the end of some of the other group dances. However, some tiny clues – a number of small "b"s that appear in various positions on several of the staves on p. 103 – hint at the possibility that some additional action is taking place. Six of these "b"s are clearly legible; others appear to have been erased. Although no explanation for this symbol is offered in the manuscript, the "b" seems to stand for *bras* or arm. If we consider the positions of the "b"s – they appear both above and below the frames of dance notation as well as on the right and left sides – a possible explanation comes to mind: the dancers – who are already holding hands – are raising and lowering their joined arms along the line, apparently at random.

This explanation leads to a further, more speculative, hypothesis: that Harlequin and Mezzetin, who had remained concealed onstage since the spoken scene, now reappear and move through the arches (see chapter 3, ill. 3.8). While this scenario presents certain technical difficulties for the dancers, it is an attractive theory for several reasons: it helps to explain the asymmetrical arch formations, which occur only in the stage-left arm of the "V"; it turns a relatively uninspired eight-bar choreographic passage into a surprising and amusing finale; and it provides an imaginative way of reintroducing the two commedia characters prior to the *charivari*, in which they undoubtedly participated.

Why, one might ask, did Favier not notate the movements of the two Italians, when he was so meticulous about notating every other aspect of the production? Here again we can only speculate, but it is not unreasonable to assume that the movements and actions of the two comedians were intended to be improvised.

Dance/music relationships

The rondo-like characteristics of the musical form are reinforced by the alternation of sung and danced sections. Furthermore, each danced segment is performed by a different group: a section for the four women; a section beginning with the four men and continuing with all four couples; a solo section; and the final section for all eight dancers. In the first two eight-bar segments the regular musical phrasing is matched by regular groupings of dance steps.

X. LA PAVANE

The final dance of the mascarade is essentially a choreographic and musical reprise of the opening march, but with the significant difference that its ultimate goal is to clear the stage of performers, rather than fill it. Like the opening march it has more than one choreographic section, but in this dance there is a more continuous flow between the three sections than is the case in the initial dance. The dance begins with a recessional march for the entire cast (XA), similar to the processional in IA; it is interrupted before anyone actually leaves the performing area by a dance for the eight dancers (XB) that closely resembles much of dance IB; finally, the recessional march (XC) resumes, continuing until everyone is off stage. As in the opening dance of the mascarade, a plain walking step and freeze-frame notation are used for the recessional march sections. The choreography for the eight dancers (XB) uses standard Favier score notation, while the movements of the singers and oboes continue to be represented by freeze-frame notation.

Music

The music for the recessional is identical to that of the opening dance, and, as in the processional, it is repeated several times. In this dance, however, the recessional march (XA) is interrupted after the music has been played only once; the eight dancers perform during the second time through the music (XB); when the music begins a third time the recessional is resumed by the entire cast (XC), and the music continues until everyone has left the performing area.[22]

---

[22] An additional repeat of the music may be necessary depending on the size of the performing space.

Casting and staging

The recessional is preceded by the *charivari*, for which no movement notation is provided (although three blank pages appear in the manuscript at this point in the mascarade). However, it seems likely that the dancers in particular, and perhaps the entire cast, would have participated in some sort of movement, and that this would have provided an opportunity for the cast to move into position for the final dance.

The freeze-frame notation of XA resembles that of IA in that the performers are shown "emerging" one couple at a time, from an undefined area. In dance IA this was clearly another room, the performers entering through a doorway on stage right. In XA, although the notation would seem to suggest that the performers again make an entrance, this time from upstage left, this clearly cannot be the case; instead, it is likely that they are waiting in column formation along the back of the performing area.

The manuscript is silent as to the identities of the performers; however, from the choreography as well as marginal annotations in the next section (XB) it is clear that the column begins with the nine instrumentalists, followed by the eight dancers, and ending with the nine singers. Thus the performers exit in the same order in which they entered in the processional. Unlike the latter, where the oboes entered three abreast, in XA they march two abreast, with one person leading the column.[23] In the notated dance for the eight dancers (XB) there are again no clues as to the identities of the individual dancers; but since much of this choreography is identical to the opening dance for the same eight dancers, it seems reasonable to assume that the roles did not change. Thus the order of dancers and key is the same as for dance IB: 1 = A; 2 = a; 3 = B; 4 = b; 5 = C; 6 = c; 7 = D; 8 = d.

Beginning position	*Ending position* [last frame, p. 115]	
A a	d D	c C
B b		
C c	a A	b B
D d		

In addition to the twenty-six performers already accounted for, two additional performers, standing side-by-side behind the singers, are notated for the first time in dance XB, the first frame of bar 2. Although they are not identified by name either here or later in the manuscript, their body symbols are distinguished from those of the singers by the use of a dot, and it is clear that they can only be the commedia characters, Harlequin and Mezzetin, from scene 2. This differentiation of body symbols is extended to all of the performers in dance XC (p. 116): the oboes are indicated by a vertical line through the center of the body sign and the singers by filled-in body symbols; the body symbols for the dancers remain unfilled.

List of step-units

Page	Bar no.	Step-unit or description	Comments
		[XA: Recessional march for the entire cast]	
106	1–24	Step [walking step]	The performers take one step per bar of music, beginning with the right foot. By bar 14 the oboes have broken off from the rest of the performers, who remain stationary in their column at stage left. During the next ten bars the oboes travel downstage, across the front of the performing area and then upstage on stage right.

---

[23] It is tempting to speculate that the leader of the recessional was Philidor himself, perhaps keeping time with his drum.

The dances 179

Page	Bar no.	Step-unit or description	Comments
106			Only the first twelve bars of music have been copied into the manuscript and bar 6 has been omitted; no further music is provided for the rest of this section, or for the other two sections of the dance, although a blank staff has been left for this purpose.

[*XB: March for the 8 dancers*] The step sequences for dances IB and XB are identical until bar 17, enabling us to match step-units to music even though the music is missing.

Page	Bar no.	Step-unit or description	Comments
107	0	[Preparatory position for dancers]	The positions of the oboes and the singers are shown below the dance notation; a walking step has been notated and crossed out.
	1	*Contretemps balonné*	In the first frame of this bar the oboes are shown advancing upstage, taking one step per bar of music. This movement continues until bar 7.
	2	*Contretemps balonné*	In the first frame the singers are shown advancing downstage; at the back of their column are shown the two commedia characters – the first time they have been notated in the manuscript. Below them is written: "les musissiens / sa reste" [*les musiciens s'arrêtent*]. The singers remain in this position until the third section of the dance (XC).
108	3	*Pas de bourrée*	
	4	*Pas de bourrée*	Dancer 5, frames 1–3: dancer 4's symbols were erroneously copied and have been crossed out.
	5	*Contretemps balonné*	Dancer 7, frame 2: the "d" below the body symbol has been partially erased.
109	6	*Contretemps balonné*	
	7	*Pas de bourrée*	The oboes make a quarter turn to their right to face the center of the stage.
110	8	*Assemblé*, step	Only one step-symbol for the *assemblé* is provided, even though dancers 1 and 2 are on opposite feet from the other six dancers. Dancer 2, frame 1: the turn sign below the body symbol has been crossed out. Above bottom stave: "les autbois et les musissiens / demeurent dans cette sytuation" [*les hautbois et les musiciens demeurent dans cette situation*; the oboes and singers remain in this position]. The oboes have made another quarter turn to the right to face the audience; in this frame only they are notated with filled-in body symbols. Neither the oboes nor the singers are depicted again in the dance score until the end of dance XB.

Page	Bar no.	Step-unit or description	Comments
110	9	*Assemblé*, step, step	As in the previous bar, dancers 1 and 2 should have a separate step symbol to indicate that they are on opposite feet from the other dancers.
111	10	*Contretemps balonné*	Bars 10–17 repeat the step-units of bars 1–8.
	11	*Contretemps balonné*	
	12	*Pas de bourrée*	
112	13	*Pas de bourrée*	Dancer 2, frame 3: the "d" has been crossed out, although it is correct.
	14	*Contretemps balonné*	All of the dancers perform the hop with the free leg to the side; however, the leap that follows is performed in three different directions: back, side, and front.
113	15	*Contretemps balonné*	
	16	*Pas de bourré*	
	17	*Assemblé*, step	See comment to bar 9.
114	18	*Assemblé*, step, step	See comment to bar 9.
	19	*Contretemps*	
115	20	*Fleuret*	
	21	*Assemblé*	It is not clear how the last three frames of dance notation on p. 115 fit to the music; we are assuming that each frame is set to a bar of music, so that bar 24, the last bar of the march, coincides with the resumption of the recessional on p. 116.
	22(?)	*Coupé*. Dancers 1, 3, 5, and 7 travel sideways to the right, closing in first position. Dancers 2 and 4 travel forward and to the left, closing in first position. Dancers 6 and 8 travel backwards upstage.	In bars 22 and 23 the dancers move from two single columns on either side of the stage to couple formation, in two double columns. They accomplish this as follows: the men (odd-numbered dancers) shift sideways to stage right, while the women (even-numbered dancers) move upstage or downstage as necessary to join their partners.
			The step symbols in bars 22 and 33 appear to be a telescoped version of the standard *coupé* notation; that is, the two elements of the *coupé*, each of which would normally be placed in a separate frame, are compressed into a single frame.
	23(?)	*Coupé*. As in bar 22.	The rubrics in the last frame of this page indicate the order in which each pair of dancers is to join the recessional column; first dancer: "ces 2 por. les 4es [*ces deux partent les quatrièmes*; these two (i.e., dancers 1 and 2) leave last]; third dancer: "ces 2 porttes les premiers" [*ces deux partent les premiers*]; fifth dancer: "ces 2 portes les sagonde" [*ces deux partent les secondes*];

Page	Bar no.	Step-unit or description	Comments
115			seventh dancer: "ces 2 por. les 3es" [*ces deux partent les troisièmes*]. These instructions result in the following order: couple 1 = dancers 3 and 4; couple 2 = dancers 5 and 6; couple 3 = dancers 7 and 8; couple 4 = dancers 1 and 2. As the dancers fall in behind the oboes in the first four frames of p. 116 the notation indicates which feet they should use; each couple starts on the right foot, but since the entrances are one bar (i.e., one step) apart, successive couples will be on opposite feet for the remainder of the procession. The oboes are depicted again, this time turned towards the center of the stage.

[XC: Final section of recessional march]

Page	Bar no.	Step-unit or description	Comments
116	1–12?	Step	There are 12 frames of dance notation, each of which shows one walking step; presumably the music and the recessional continue until all the characters have exited upstage right. Above fourth frame: "les musissiens ne parte qui cy." At end of last frame: "tout le[s] acteurs [restent] en set sy[tuation] jusqu a ce [qu'ils] ne soient p[lus] dans la s[alle]" [*tous les acteurs restent en cette situation jusqu'à ce qu'ils ne soient plus dans la salle*; all the performers remain in this formation until they are no longer in the room].

Step vocabulary

In both XA and XC only plain walking steps are used, one per bar of music. The step vocabulary of dance XB is very similar to that of IB, and like the former is quite restricted.

contretemps balonné	8
pas de bourrée/fleuret	7
assemblé	5
coupé	2
contretemps	1

The alternation of the lively *contretemps balonné* with the more flowing *pas de bourrée*, a characteristic of dance IB, is preserved in this dance as well. The *assemblé*, sometimes followed by one or more steps, is again used prominently in the latter section of the dance.

Floor patterns

The floor pattern of the first part of the recessional (XA) is to some extent a mirror image of the opening processional (IA): in the closing dance the column of performers moves in a clockwise direction around the performing area starting from the upstage left corner, but with the oboes now aligned in twos rather than threes, with a single instrumentalist at the head. However, unlike the opening march, in which the eight dancers perform at the end of the processional, in the concluding march the eight dancers interrupt the recessional to reprise their opening choreography, after which the column reforms and the recessional continues. These differences obviously have an effect on the floor patterns of the dancers as well as on the movements of the other cast members.

The movements of the oboes show the greatest contrast. Although they lead the processional column in both dances I and X, in the latter they remain at the side of the performing area rather than participating – at least visually – in the choreography for the eight dancers. During the first six bars of XB they continue to move upstage in their column, turning toward the center of the stage in bar 7 and then toward the audience in bar 8, remaining in this position until the end of XB.

In spite of the absence of the oboes at center stage, the floor pattern of XB is almost identical to that of IB until bar 12, and the two patterns are very similar for several bars after that. Dance XB begins further downstage than does IB, allowing the dancers to remain clear of the other performers. The final six bars of XB differ considerably from IB, since the dancers, rather than retreating to a symmetrical formation upstage center as at the end of IB, must reorganize into a column downstage in preparation for the continuation of the recessional. This figure begins in bar 18 where the couples, who had been facing each other, turn around each other until all end facing downstage in bar 21. During the next two bars the couples move so that partners are standing side by side, but with the woman on the left of the man (ill. 6.9). The two couples on stage left are lined up in front of the column of singers and the two couples on stage right are likewise positioned in front of the oboes.

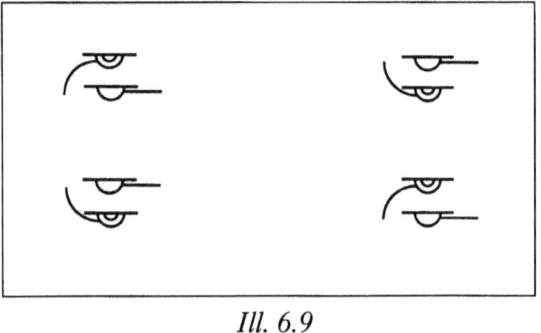

Ill. 6.9

Section XC, the continuation of the recessional march, begins on p. 116, coinciding with the return of freeze-frame notation and the march step, one per bar. However, the absence of music at this point in the manuscript makes the precise moment difficult to pinpoint, and in fact there is a certain amount of choreographic overlap between the end of XB and the beginning of XC that serves to blur the division between the two sections, thus creating a more unified finale. The oboes, who have already started their about-face in the last frame of p. 115, resume their forward motion traveling upstage in the second frame of p. 116, and six frames later the leader has exited. Meanwhile, the dancers are reforming the recessional column, "peeling off" one couple at a time, as is indicated both by the rubrics in the last frame on p. 115 and by the diagrams on p. 116. The freeze-frame notation on this page may once again be schematic rather than literal, since it shows couple 3 crossing the stage in four steps, rather than the twelve or so steps allotted for the same distance in IA. The singers do not begin moving forward again until the fifth frame of p. 116. They and the comedians who are behind them follow the column of oboes and dancers until all have exited.

Dance/music relationships

Music notation for dance XA breaks off after the first twelve bars, and no music has been provided for dances XB or XC, even though blank music staves are provided throughout.

However, because dances I and X use the same music, and because their choreographies are similar, the absence of music does not pose major problems. In dance XA it is clear from the first twelve bars that one frame of notation equals one bar of music; thus the total dance, consisting of twenty-four frames of notation, requires the music to be played once. Since the step symbols of dances IB and XB are almost identical through bar 17 there is no difficulty fitting the dance to the music up to this point. The next nine frames of dance notation (beginning on p. 114 in the manuscript) can be divided into three 3-element step-units on the basis of the patterns of steps; all three would presumably be performed in the SSL rhythm established for such step-units earlier in the dance. If this is the case, the three step-units would comprise bars 18–20 of music. The next frame, an *assemblé*, probably takes an entire bar of music, and is thus bar 21. If the analysis in the list of step-units is correct, the last two frames on p. 115 correspond to bars 22 and 23, and the final bar of the march music coincides with the first frame of p. 116. In any case the precise correspondence of music and dance at this point is not crucial to the staging, since the march repeats for the third time and continues until all the participants have left the room.

7

The sources

The manuscript of *Le Mariage de la Grosse Cathos* reproduced here is part of the Philidor Collection, formerly housed in the Paris Conservatoire de Musique, now in the Music Department of the Bibliothèque Nationale. The two superscript letters of its call number, Rés. F. 534[a–b], reflect the two parts of the volume: the first contains the text and music of the mascarade, the second the choreographic notation. The two parts are now bound together but the binding is not original; at some time, probably when the volume acquired its current leather binding, the right-hand side of each leaf was trimmed, resulting in the loss of a small amount of dance notation and of verbal instructions on a few pages. The volume is in folio format, the paper of which now measures 28.7 cm by 43.4 cm; its gathering structure is irregular. It lacks Philidor's *ex libris*,[1] but is known to have been part of the royal library in the eighteenth century.[2]

Three different original hands are evident in the manuscript, two in the first part and one in the second. The music is in the characteristic hand of Philidor himself, with the text and headings for the music copied by a different, unidentified scribe. In the second part of the volume, the melody line notated across the top of the page, the choreographic notation, and the verbal instructions all appear to have been copied in the same ink and in the same hand, probably that of Favier. Aside from the likelihood that no one besides their inventor would have been capable of accurately transcribing the unusual notational symbols, there are several surviving examples of Favier's signature on legal documents. The very plain hand that he used to sign his name resembles the one used to write the instructions in the choreographic manuscript.

The first part of the volume contains two unnumbered preliminary pages – the title page and a cast list – followed by the pages of the score numbered 1–40. The pagination in this part of the volume is original, in the hand of the scribe who wrote the headings. The second part of the manuscript contains seventy-nine pages, seven of which are blank. Its first page consists of the first page of dance notation, there being no separate title page or other preliminary material in this part of the manuscript. Four of the blank pages are due to the fact that the choreography for a new dance always begins on the recto side of the leaf; there are also three unnumbered, blank sides between pp. 105 and 106. The pagination of the second section has been made continuous with that of the first (numbered pp. 41–116) but the numbering is not original; it may well have been added when the volume was rebound. Faint traces of an earlier set of page numbers are visible on some pages; these are forty-seven numbers higher than the current page numbers, thus suggesting that the dance notation may have been part of a larger volume of unknown contents before it was bound as it is now. Faint numbers appear in the musical score at

---

[1] Many of the volumes that belonged to the royal collection during Philidor's tenure as music librarian have the following printed *ex libris* glued onto an early page: "Ce livre appartient à Philidor l'aîné, Ordinaire de la Musique du Roy, & Garde de tous les Livres de sa Bibliothèque de Musique, l'an 1702." The *ex libris* is generally followed by Philidor's paraph, the manuscript flourish by which he indicated that he himself had checked the book in question.

[2] The work is listed in a 1765 inventory of the music library at the château of Versailles (Tessier, "Un catalogue," p. 116).

three places;³ these were added as place markers by the twentieth-century copyist who prepared the Library of Congress transcription discussed below.

Although the two parts of the manuscript were copied separately, they were probably completed at around the same time. The title page of the musical portion of the manuscript is dated 1688; documents in the French National Archives reveal that Philidor was paid for copying this work that very year.⁴ Given the probability that the work was put on only once, it seems unlikely that much time could have elapsed between the performance and the notating of its dances. Moreover, the paper used in both parts of the manuscript is very similar; it comes from several different lots, but some of the same watermarks are found in both. Many of these watermarks coincide with ones found in French manuscripts of harpsichord music dating from the same period.⁵

In both parts of the manuscript the pages were prepared for the notation by using a rastrum to draw five-line staves across the paper. In the musical score each page has sixteen staves, although on pp. 5 and 31 a seventeenth stave has been added by hand at the bottom of the page. In the pages of dance notation the paper uses two different formats. Most of the dances are notated on paper prepared with twelve five-line staves. In dances IA (pp. 41–2), III–VIIIA (pp. 61–91), and IX (pp. 99–105) there are no alterations to the original staves, but in dances IB (pp. 43–51), VIIIB (pp. 91–8), and XA (p. 106), either one or two lines were carefully added by hand in ink, giving each stave either six or seven lines (see, for example, pp. 92 and 107). These additions were made where needed in order to accommodate the movements of the dancers relative to the dancing space. A second format is used for dances II (pp. 53–9) and XB (pp. 107–15). These pages have a total of eleven staves, the top of which, intended for the music, has five lines, while the remaining ten were drawn with a six-line rastrum. In dance XB a seventh line was added by hand to the top of each stave. In addition, the staves have sometimes been extended by hand into the right margin, particularly in the dance portion of the manuscript (see, for example, p. 13 in the music, pp. 89 and 105 in the dance notation). As with the vertical extensions, these additions were made by the notator when they were necessary. On p. 116 some of the material extended into the right margin was lost when the pages of the volume were trimmed.

In its format and layout the musical portion of the manuscript closely resembles its companion volumes in the Philidor Collection, many of which contain ballets by Lully that Philidor copied in 1689 and 1690 as presentation volumes for the king. The full score includes all instrumental and vocal parts as well as the complete text of the spoken scene, the title page, and a list of characters that provides the names of most of the singers. Such a full and carefully copied text was clearly destined for a library, not for the performers, for whom Philidor or his assistants would have copied separate parts. Meticulous corrections in both the music and the dance portions of the manuscript – few of them visible in the facsimile – indicate the care that was taken in its preparation.

Given the history of the Philidor Collection during the nineteenth century, the survival of this volume is truly fortuitous. Of the fifty-nine volumes inventoried as being in the collection of the Conservatoire de Musique by the Abbé Nicolas Roze, its librarian from 1807 to 1819, almost half have disappeared. In 1820 seven volumes were plundered for their bindings, and the contents destroyed. The destroyer's choice was not random: Lully's works were spared, but several of Philidor's and his family members' were lost, including

---

[3] See the number 18 next to the second system of p. 8, the number 32 at the end of the second system on p. 16, and the number 63 in the middle of the second system on p. 29. The twentieth-century copyist may have added more numbers that were later erased.

[4] F-Pan KK214, fol. 27: "Autre chapitre de despence extraordinaire a cause de plusieurs petits divertissemens de musique faicts a Versailles pendant lad[ite] année 1688...A André Danican Filidor, pour avoir faict copier la musique de la mascarade du *Mariage de la Cousture* [:] 100 lt" (cited in Benoit, *Musiques de cour*, p. 115). This record could conceivably refer to the parts that must have been copied for the performers of the mascarade, in addition to (or rather than) the score.

[5] For example, various configurations of grapes, a circle with the word "Colombier" around the perimeter, a bar with hearts and letters (see Gustafson, *French Harpsichord Music* I, pp. 171–223). The current state of knowledge does not permit dating to a specific year on the basis of the watermark alone.

three volumes of ballets and two anthologies of dance music in which Philidor's compositions were prominently featured. By 1856 another seventeen volumes had disappeared, probably the victims of theft. Later in the century a few volumes were restored to the collection while still others were lost. Volumes 52, *La Princesse de Crète*, and 53, *L'Amant Guéri*, two other theatrical works by Philidor, have never been found; volume 54, *Le Mariage de la Grosse Cathos*, numbered among those few that miraculously returned to the library.[6]

A second score of this mascarade, also in Philidor's hand, is located at the Bibliothèque de l'Arsenal in Paris, with a call number of Ms. 3239. It is in small, oblong format, and is less complete than the Bibliothèque Nationale score in that it is missing the inner instrumental parts in the choruses;[7] it lacks the choreographic notation, but includes the text of the spoken scene. The title of the work as given in this manuscript places the dramatic focus on the bridegroom rather than the bride: *Le Mariage de la Couture | avec La grosse Cathos | Mascarade | Representée devant Monseigneur et mise en musique | par Philidor l'aisné ordinaire de la musique du Roy | 1688*. Most of the differences in music and text between this score and the more complete one in the Bibliothèque Nationale are minor, consisting primarily of spelling variants, ornaments, or a few rhythmic variants in the recitatives, but in two cases the Arsenal score provides correct readings for places that are in error in the F-Pn score. In one case it has the correct title for one of the dances (see the discussion below; the error may be seen on p. 18 of the facsimile). In the other it supplies a transitional measure missing from the end of the *charivari* (facsimile, p. 39; see the discussion in chapter 4, p. 77).

In addition to the above scores, a diplomatic transcription of the entire Philidor collection, copied during the early part of this century, is located in Washington, D.C. in the Library of Congress (M 2 .P45 Case). Volume 54, *Le Mariage de la Grosse Cathos*, includes not only the music but also the dance notation, painstakingly copied, although not entirely without errors.[8] Users of this transcription should not view it as a primary source.

To date no separate copy of the libretto has been located, although one seems to have been in the royal library in the eighteenth century. A manuscript catalogue in the collection of the Bibliothèque Nationale gives a partial list of contents for several volumes of texts for seventeenth- and early eighteenth-century ballets that were once in the king's music library. The twelfth and last volume of these "Livres de Paroles" contained twenty-one divertissements, mostly by members of the Philidor family, including *Le Mariage de la Grosse Cathos*.[9] This volume, alas, has disappeared.

The first five dances notated in the second part of the manuscript have a heading for the dance at the top of each page, and two of them, dances I and III, identify the performers (see pp. 43 and 61). Starting on p. 77 with the dance for two drunks, the dances lack headings; thereafter the tune, notated at the top of each page, must be used to identify the dance. The dance notation is supplemented throughout by a few verbal explanations for the dancers, on the order of "lon commance le passe pied en cette figure

---

[6] The information in this paragraph is taken from Fellowes, "The Philidor manuscripts."

[7] The omission of the inner instrumental parts in the choruses may be due to the format of the volume which has only six staves per page; since the voice parts require four staves, only two remain for the instruments.

[8] This assessment is based on a comparison of the original dance notation with the corresponding pages of the Library of Congress copy. Facsimiles of the first two pages of the Library of Congress copy are reproduced in Orlan Earl Thomas, "Music for double-reed ensembles from the seventeenth and eighteenth centuries: 'Collection Philidor'" (unpublished DMA thesis, Eastman School of Music of the University of Rochester, 1974), pp. 115–17.

[9] F-Pn (Manuscrits) Ms. fr. 24.357, fol. 139. The entry here appears to have been copied from a catalogue of the king's music library: "Dans le catalogue general de tous les livres de plainchant, et Livres de Musique tant pour le Spirituel que pour le profane qui sont dans la bibliothèque de musique du Roy[:] Recueil de Livres de Paroles . . ." Some of the "Livres de Paroles" are described as printed, but no such indication is given for volume 12. Other librettos listed as being in the same volume, for example the Philidor mascarades from 1700, were published at the time of the work's performance, and copies of the publications survive, but whether the copies in the lost volume were prints or manuscripts is unknown. Works apparently included in the volume date from between 1688 and 1704.

se tenant les mains autour" ("the passepied is begun in this formation with everyone holding hands"). Because these annotations are not always easy to read, and because the scribe's spelling is quite primitive, even by the relaxed standards of the day, this verbal text has been transcribed into modern French in chapter 6 as part of the narrative account of each dance.

There are are five discrepancies between the music and dance portions of the manuscript. The first has to do with the the cast of the mascarade. Although the singing roles given in the cast list following the title page correspond to the singing parts in the score itself as well as to the number of singers shown in the dance notation, the dancing roles from the same list do not entirely correspond to the dancing roles as notated in the second part of the manuscript. The cast list seems to call for ten dancers: *une Dame Ragonde dansante* and *six voisins et voisines dansants*, plus three *garçons de la noce* who are not singers and therefore presumably dance. None of the dancers' names is given in this list. Marginal indications in the dance notation (pp. 43 and 61), on the other hand, call for two *garçons de la noce*, two *filles de la noce*, two male peasants, and two Dames Gigognes, for a total of eight dancers, five of whom are identified as to the person playing the role. Since the notation itself clearly requires eight dancers in four couples, it would appear that the cast list in the musical score is inaccurate in regard to the dancers.[10]

The second discrepancy concerns the time signatures of the dance pieces. Favier gave the duple-meter dances either a time signature of 2 (dances I, III, VI, and X) or no time signature at all (dances VII and IX); he also omitted the time signature in the passepied (VIII). Philidor, however, used ₵ for most of the duple dances (I, III, VII, and X), 2 only for dances VI and IX. He also supplied a time signature of 3 for the passepied. These discrepancies between the music and dance scores seem to reflect indifference or carelessness on Favier's part rather than meaningful differences in interpretation regarding meter and tempo between the composer and the choreographer.

The third discrepancy is due to an error in the musical score. The first dance on p. 18 of the score reproduced here is entitled "I^e Entrée. 2 Filles De La Nopce", but in the choreographic notation (p. 61) it is designated for "Deux Garçons de la Nopce" and the names given are of performers who had danced men's roles earlier in the ballet. The Bibliothèque de l'Arsenal score confirms the designation of this dance for two men: there it is labelled "Premiere Entrée. Pour 2 Païsant." The unknown scribe who wrote the headings into the Bibliothèque Nationale score probably confused this dance with the one immediately following, a gigue, which is the one intended for the two "filles de la nopce."

In one place, the musical and dance scores disagree as to the order of the pieces. In the musical score the chorus "Passons toujours la vie" precedes a group of three dances – the "Air des ivrognes," rigaudon, and passepied – but follows them in the dance notation. The implications of this discrepancy for performance are discussed in chapter 3, p. 54.

The fifth discrepancy concerns the music for the passepied. This dance is choreographed twice, the first time as a line dance (see pp. 89–91). Since both the dance step and the music repeat, only the floor pattern is notated after the beginning of the dance, and as a result the correspondence between music and dance is not entirely clear. This problem is discussed in chapter 6, p. 170.

The discrepancies mentioned raise questions for the reconstruction of this work, but are all amenable to solution. Considering that this manuscript is the only one known (or perhaps even the only one ever to have existed) from this period that attempted to record both the music and the dance for a complete work, the level of agreement between dance and music notation and the overall accuracy are remarkably high.

---

[10] Discrepancies between lists of performers that appear at the beginning of a libretto or score and the information from within the musical or literary texts themselves are unfortunately not uncommon for works from this period. The list of the performers in the libretto for Lully's opera *Proserpine*, for example, includes nine roles that are not mentioned anywhere else in either the libretto or the score; they probably were singers who performed in the vocal ensembles of the closing scene of the opera.

Facsimile of
Le Mariage de la Grosse Cathos
(F-Pn Rés. F. 534ᵃ⁻ᵇ)

In the dance section of the manuscript each new dance begins on a recto, with the result that verso pages 52, 60, 68, and 82 contain staff lines but no musical or choreographic notation. This layout has been preserved in the facsimile, blank pages having been inserted for the pages listed above. Between pages 105 and 106 the manuscript includes three pages containing staff lines but no musical or choreographic notation. In the facsimile a single blank page has been inserted at this point, so that the arrangement of rectos and versos in the remainder of the facsimile (pp. 106–16) preserves that of the manuscript, with even-numbered pages as rectos and odd numbered pages as versos. Page 117 of the manuscript also contains staff lines but no notation.

Le Mariage de La Grosse Cathos

Mascarade

Mise en Musique

Par Philidor l'ainé Ordinaire de la Musique du Roy.

1688.

Acteurs.

La Couture, Epoux de la Grosse Cathos .... Mr. Philbert

La Grosse Cathos, Epouse de la Couture .... Mr. guilligon

Mr. Du Pont, Bourgeois de Paris .... Mr. Mirebel

Made. DuPont, sa femme Maitresse de la Grosse Cathos.. Mr. Le Roy

L'Abbé du Plessis, Oncle de la Couture .... Mr. Morck

Gripetout, Ecornifleur .... Mr. Gingint

Harlequin, Fourbe se disant Mere Nourrice de la Couture

Mezetin, Fourbe se disant Pere Nourricier de la Couture

Mr. Simon, Suisse amy de la Grosse Cathos .... Mr.

Dame Ragonde, Parente de la grosse Cathos .... Mr. Jonquet

Une Dame Ragonde Dansant

6. Voisins, et Voisines dansants

Trois Garçons de la Nopce

Un Garçon de la Nopce, chantant à la Serenade de la mariée. Mr.

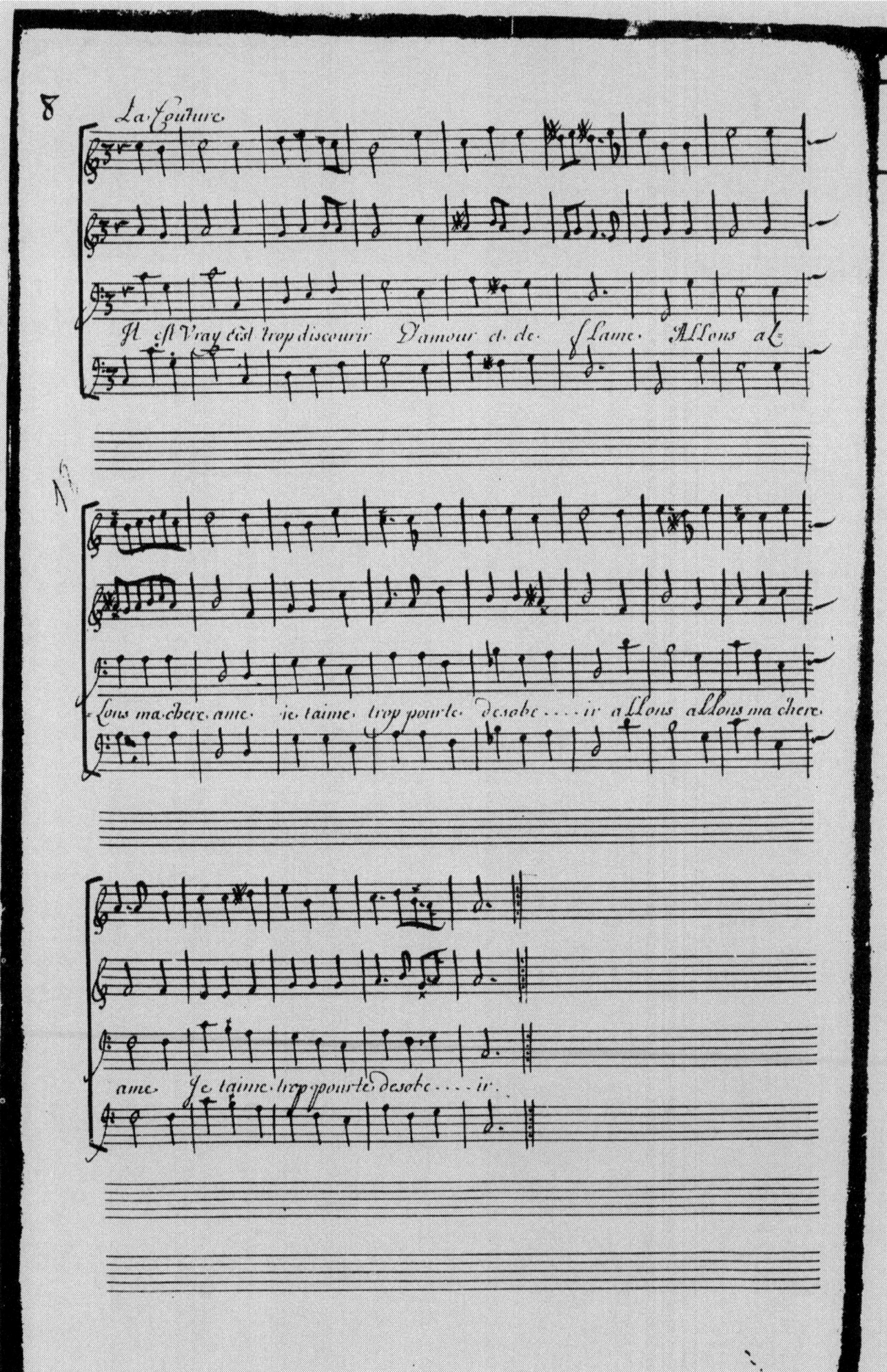

Scene Seconde.   9

Harlequin, Mezetin, La Couture.

Mezetin.

Auant que d'aller plus loin, dy-moy, as-tu fait vne serieuse reflexion sur ton entreprise? N'aprehende-tu pas, qu'vn orage de coups de batons ne soit la recompense de notre fourberie, si l'on vient à la decouurir?

Harlequin.

Tu t'allarmes de peu de choses. Je te donne le sieur de la Couture pour vne piece d'homme des plus stupides du Royaume. C'est vn Animal d'vne espece toute particuliere, et qui croira Ingenûment tout ce que nous luy dirons. Le V'oicy. Je vais l'aborder, et sois assuré que nous-nous diuertirons comme il faut à ses dépens, pourueu que tu Jouë bien ton rôle.

Mezetin.

Ce n'est pas ce qui m'Embarasse.

Harlequin

Ah! Mon cher Nourriçon quelle Joye pour moy de vous voir le Mary d'vne femme qui vaut son pesant d'or, d'vne femme qui est la pudeur et la modestie mesme. Je sens mon coeur qui palpite. J'en ay vne Joye Inconceuable, et Je ne puis m'empecher de vous Embrasser.

Mezetin.

Tout beau n'allez pas si vite, c'est à moy à qui cet honneur est deu.

Harlequin

Que veut donc dire ce vieux grenard!

Mezetin

Je dy que je le baiseray le premier, malgré toy, et malgré tes dents.

Harlequin.

Voyez qu'un peu ce gros butor, comme il se jette à corps perdu sur ce pauvre petit mouton. Cela me fait saigner le coeur... quoy, encore ! Ah ! c'en est trop. Je veux en avoir ma part. Reçoy, Mon cher fils ces tendres baisers que mon amour...

La Couture.

Que diable me veulent ces gens là. Je croy qu'ils ont envies de m'étrangler.

Mezetin.

Est-ce la l'accüeil que vous me faits ?

Harlequin.

Est-ce ainsi que vous receuez d'une personne que vous deuriez regarder comme votre mere ? Ouurez les yeux, et reconnoissez....

La Couture.

Ah ! que de préambule, laissez-moy de repos.

Harlequin

Votre Ingratitude va-t-elle Jusqu'au point d'auoir du mépris pour nous ?

La Couture.

Le diable emporte si je vous connois.

Harlequin.

Hebien, aprends, coeur de roche, que je suis ta mere Nourrice, et que celuy que tu vois est ton pere, Nourricier. Si tu n'auois pas succé le laict de ces chastes Sein, auvois-tu eu l'Industrie de t'ériger en Prince des petites maisons ? Auvois-tu qu te rendre si recommandable dans tous les Cabarets de Paris ? Va tu ne merite pas les tendresses que l'on a pour toy.

La Couture.

Quoy c'est vous qui estes ma Mere Nourrice! Parbleu. Je ne l'aurois jamais creu si vous ne me l'eussiez dit. Demeurez. Je vous prie pour honnorer mes nopces de votre presence.

Harlequin.

Ne te l'avois-je pas bien dit? est-ce que je me suis trompé?

Mezetin.

Cela va le mieux du monde.

La Couture.

Prenez place tous deux, Je serois bien aise de m'entretenir avec vous de beaucoup de particularitez qui me concernent, et vous prier de me dire ce qu'est devenu mon pere, Vous sçavez que Je l'ay perdu que je n'avois encore que quatre ans.

Mezetin.

Ah! l'honneste homme de pere que vous aviez! Nous estions tous deux les meilleurs amis du monde. Plus je vous regarde, et plus je voy que vous luy ressemblez. Vous avez tous les traits de son visage, et toutes ses manieres d'agir! C'estoit un de ces grands hommes qui ne s'apliquent qu'aux actions heroiques. Il ne trouvoit rien d'Impossible dans tout ce qu'il entreprenoit. Mais son merite estant trop grand pour demeurer dans le lieu de sa naissance où Il avoit aquis tant de reputation, on l'en retira malgré luy, pour l'Envoyer à Marseille sur les Galleres.

La Couture.

Sur les Galeres!

Mezetin.

Ouy sur les Galeres, et ce fut la où Il finit glorieusement ses jours au service du Roy.

Harlequin.

Donnez luy un coup à boire, Je voy bien que la voix luy manque à ce recit funeste, et ne m'oubliez pas.... Pour moy Je suspens mon déplaisir vous féliciter sur le beau choix que vous avez fait; et que je ne puis assez admirer. En effect la Grosse Cathos qui vous est tombée en partage, se peut dire la perle, et la cresme de toutes les personnes de son sexe. Elle l'emporte autant sur toutes les autres femmes, que le Vin de Champagne, l'emporte sur le Vin de Bretigny. Jamais plus de beauté ne fut joint a plus de merite. Son tein n'est pas de ces teins fades qui ont recours au fard. C'est un tein d'un cramoisy merveilleux. Elle a le nez le plus mignon du monde. Sa bouche quoy que grande est d'un azur ébloüissant, et sa taille rondelette, témoigne assez la beauté de son Embonpoint. Ouy quand on la voit auprès de vous, on est forcé de dire.

Elle est digne de luy, comme il est digne d'elle.

Ah! que nous verrons naitre de petits La Couturiaux d'un mariage si bien assorty. Je voudrois de tout mon coeur vous en voir déja une douzaine.

La Couture.

La peste, pour une Paysanne, elle a le caquet bien affilé, N'y auroit il point quelque chose de caché la dessous? Voyons.

Mezetin.

Si vostre pere estoit encore au monde, qu'il auroit de Joye de vous voir dans le rang Illustre où vous estes aujourd'huy!

La Couture.

Puisque vous le connoissiez si bien, de quel pays estoit-il?

Mezetin.

Il estoit Gascon.

La Couture.

Vous en avez menty, mon pere estoit natif de Caen en Normandie.

Harlequin.

Le Païs ne fait rien à l'affaire.

La Couture.

Vous avez bien la mine d'estre tous deux des fourbes, et des Ecornifleurs, qui n'estes venu Icy que pour attraper une franche lipée, Ecoutez, ma bile commence, a s'échauffer Je vous conseille en amy de décamper, si vous ne voulez estre asommez dans un moment.

Harlequin

Quoy, nous traiter ainsi? nous qui sommes de si honnestes gens!

Mezetin.

Tire me le paysan, gros cheval de _____

La Couture.

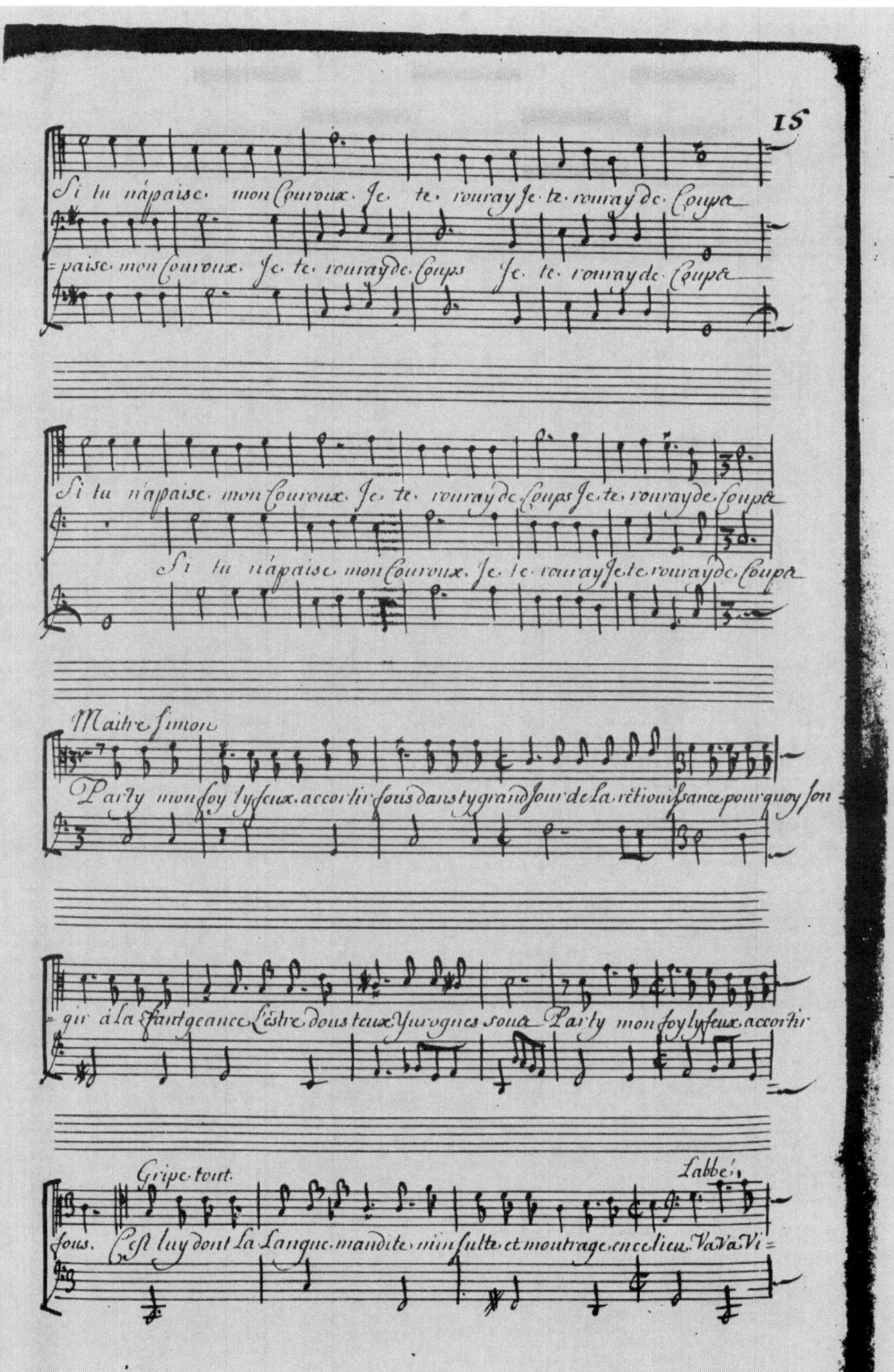

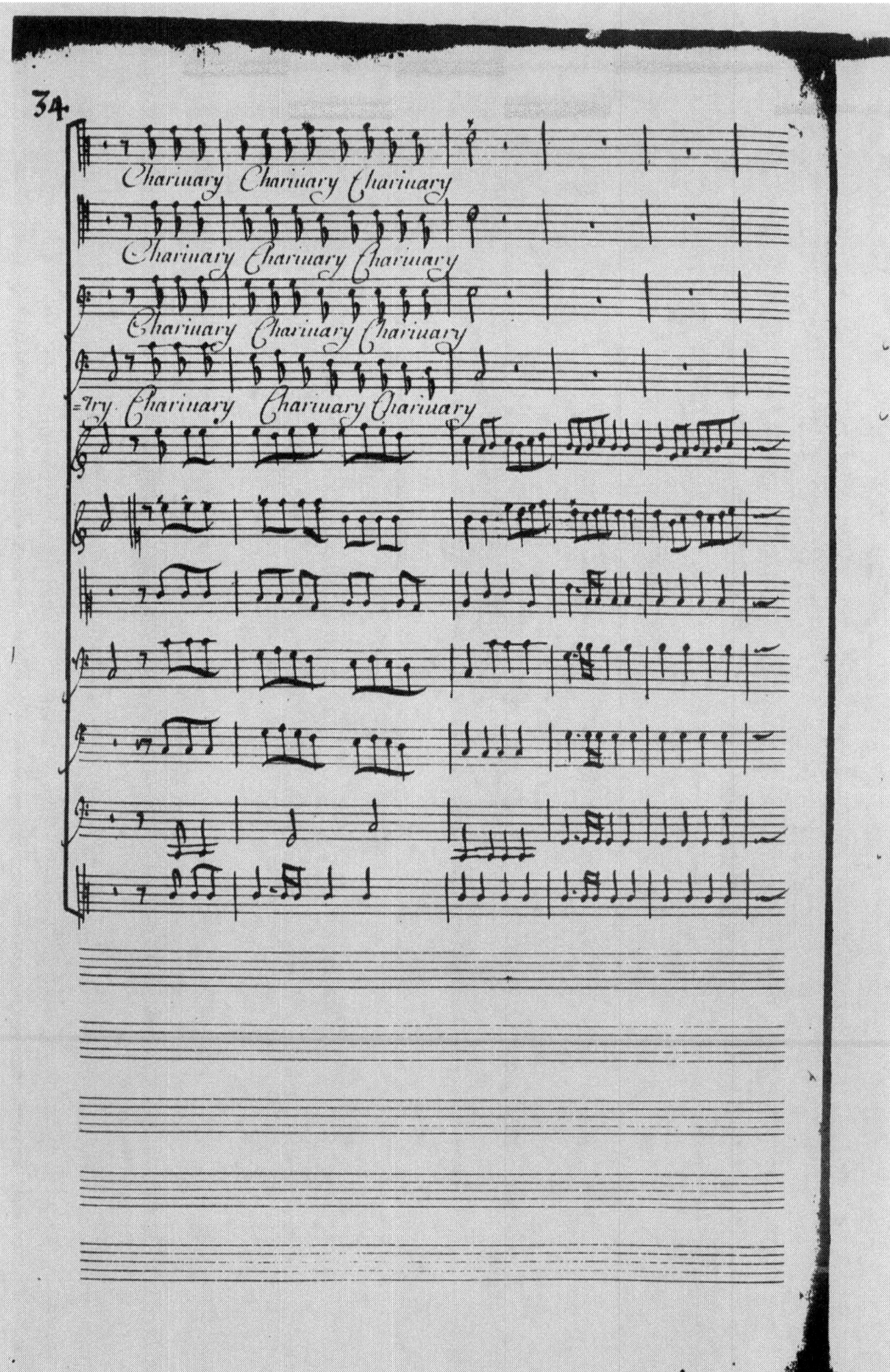

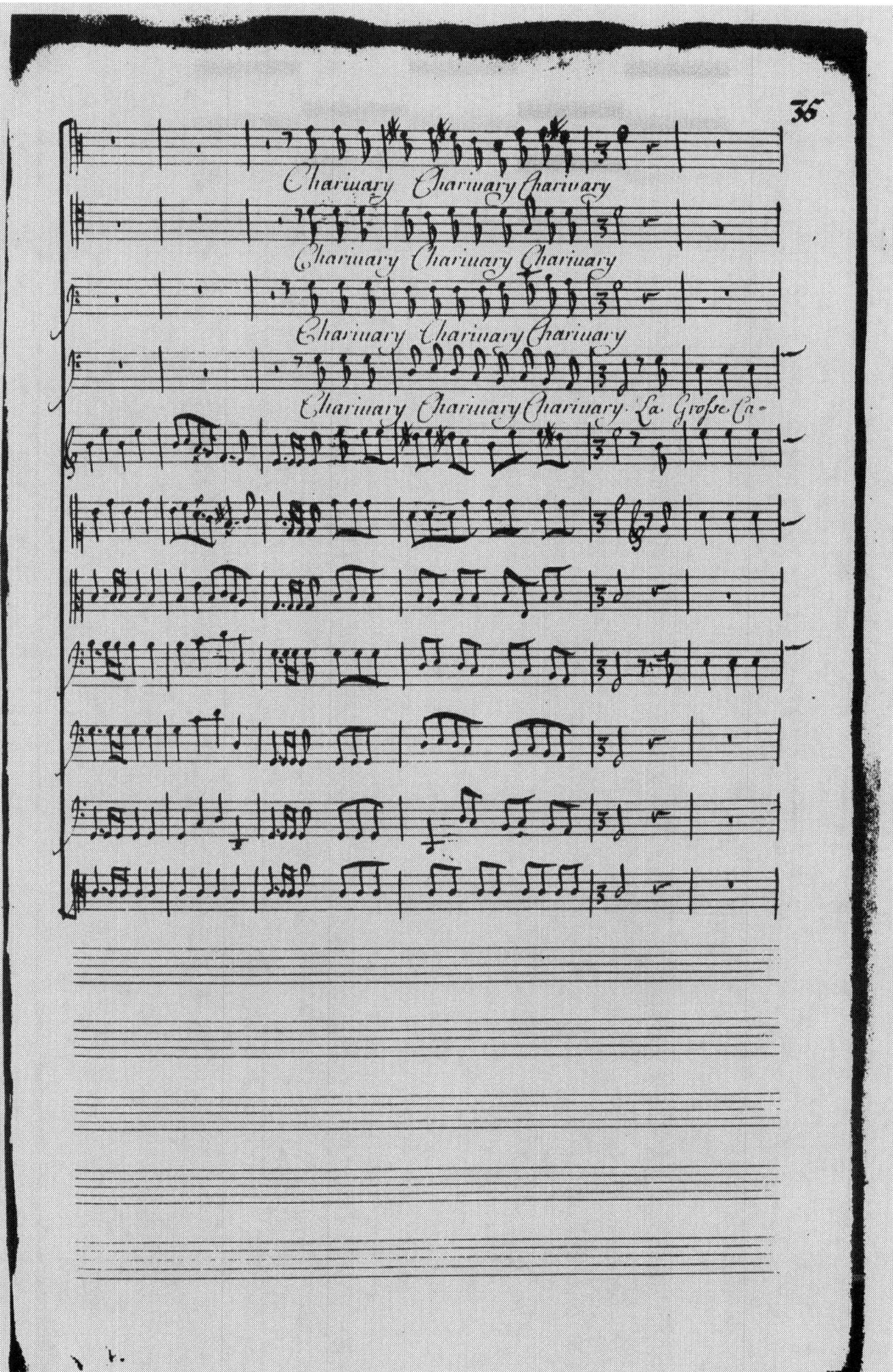

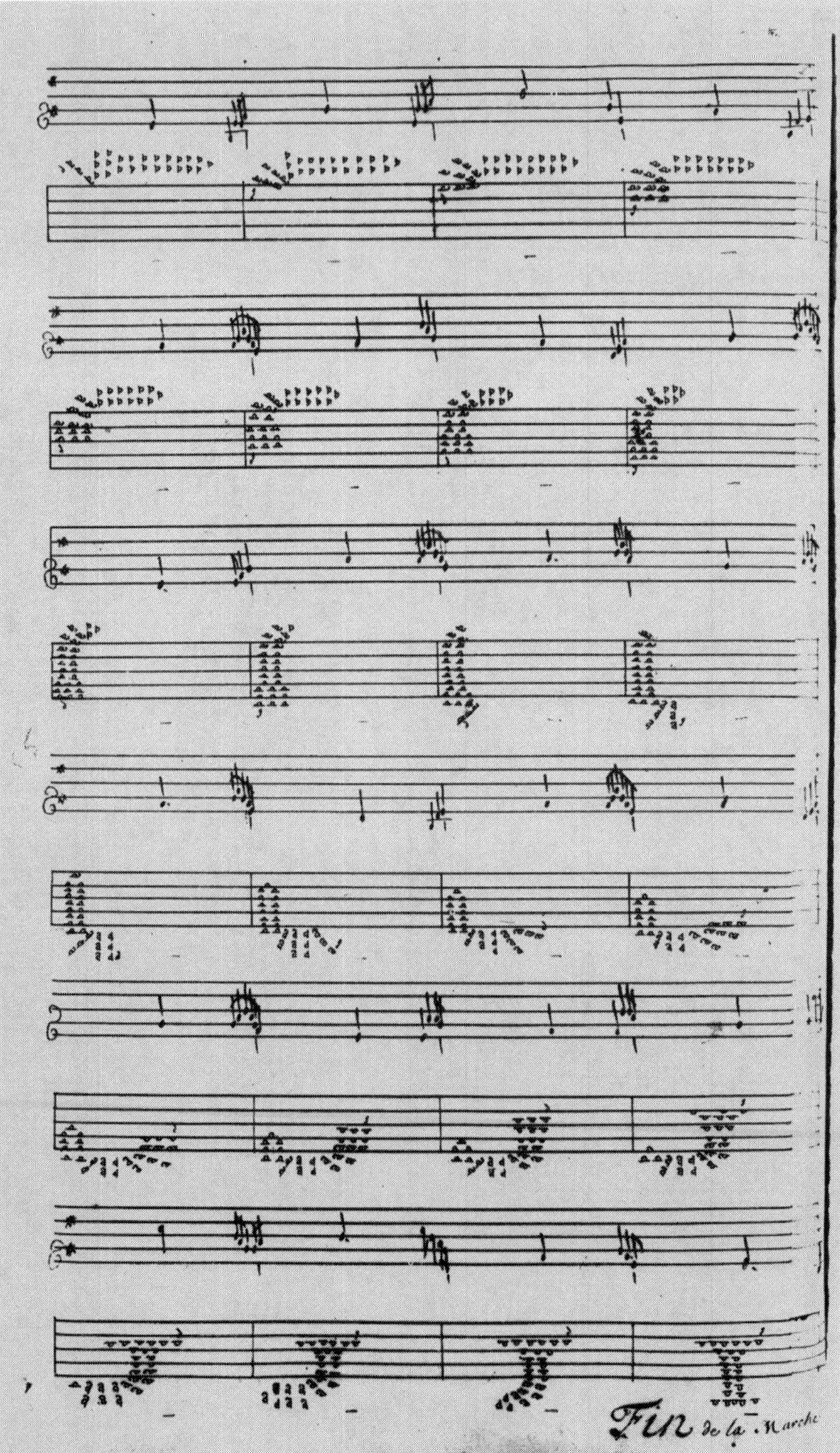

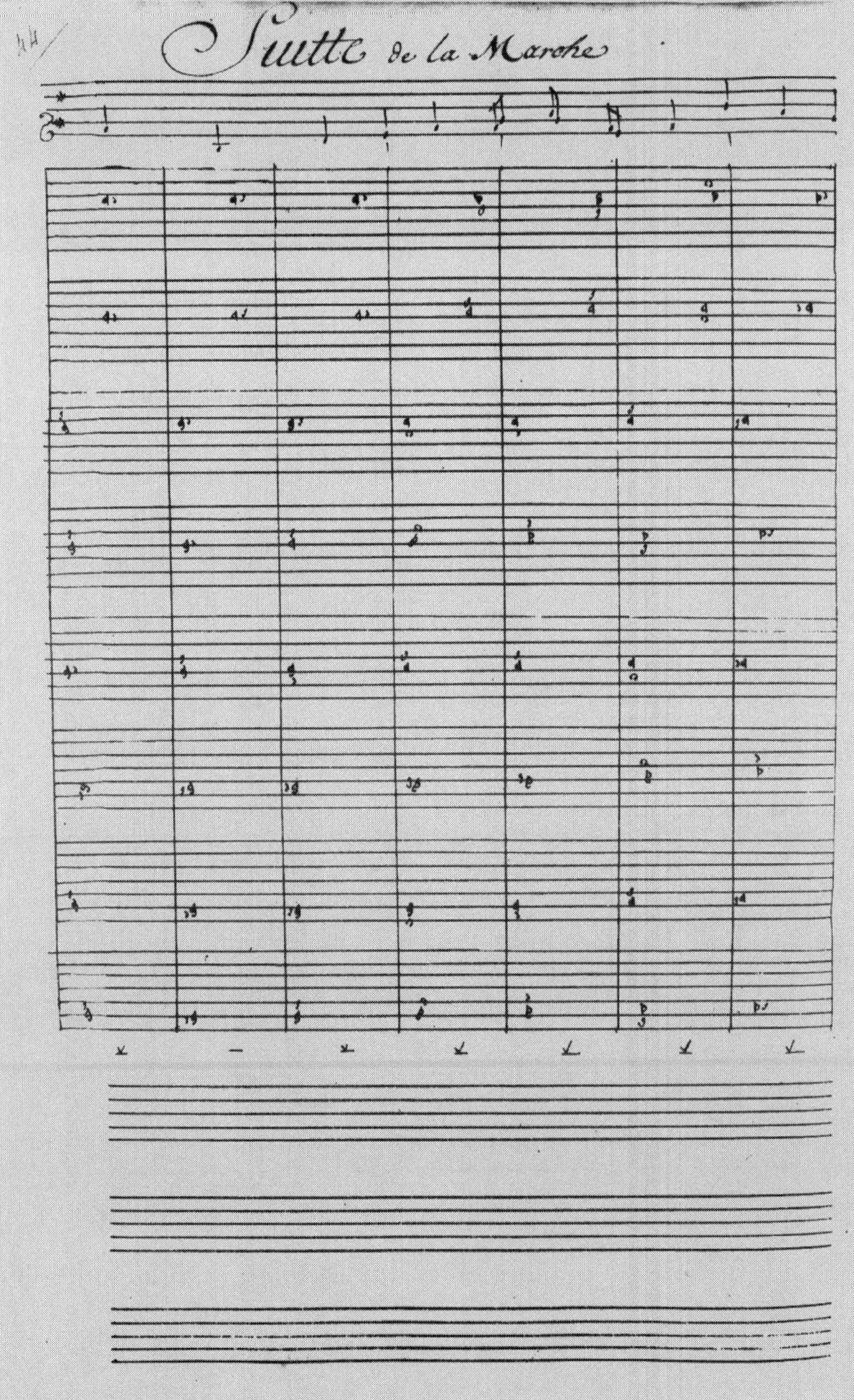

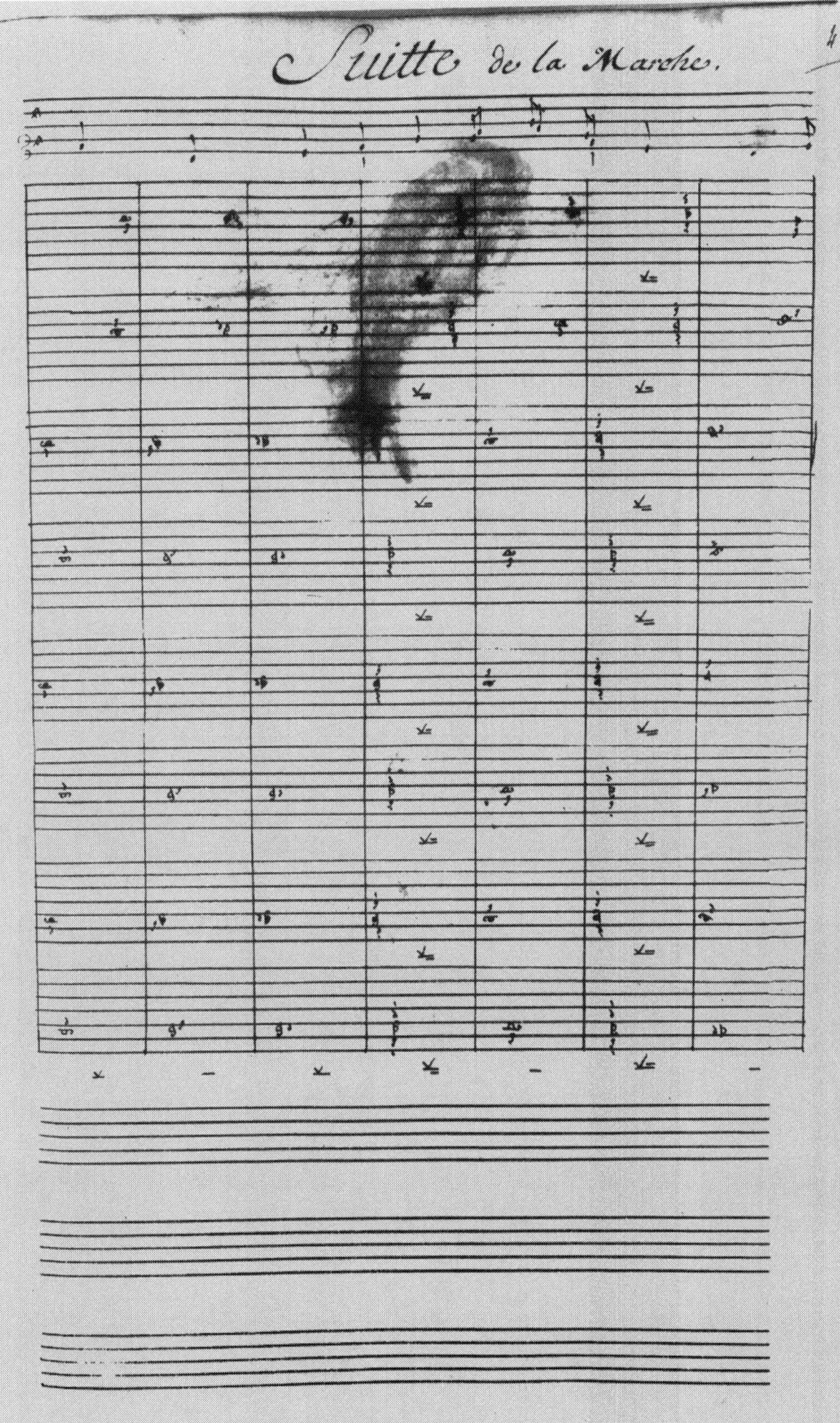

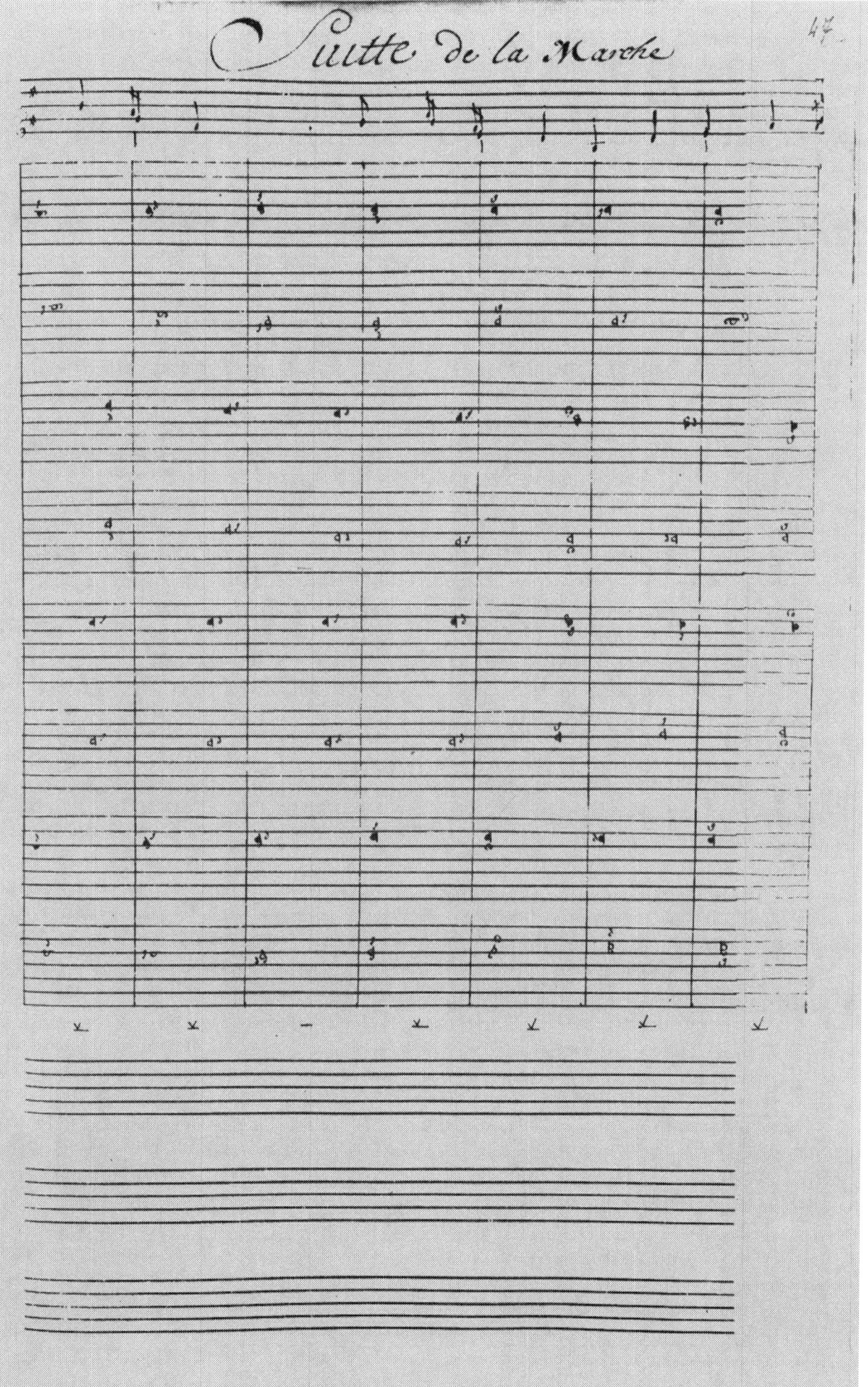

Suitte de la Marche

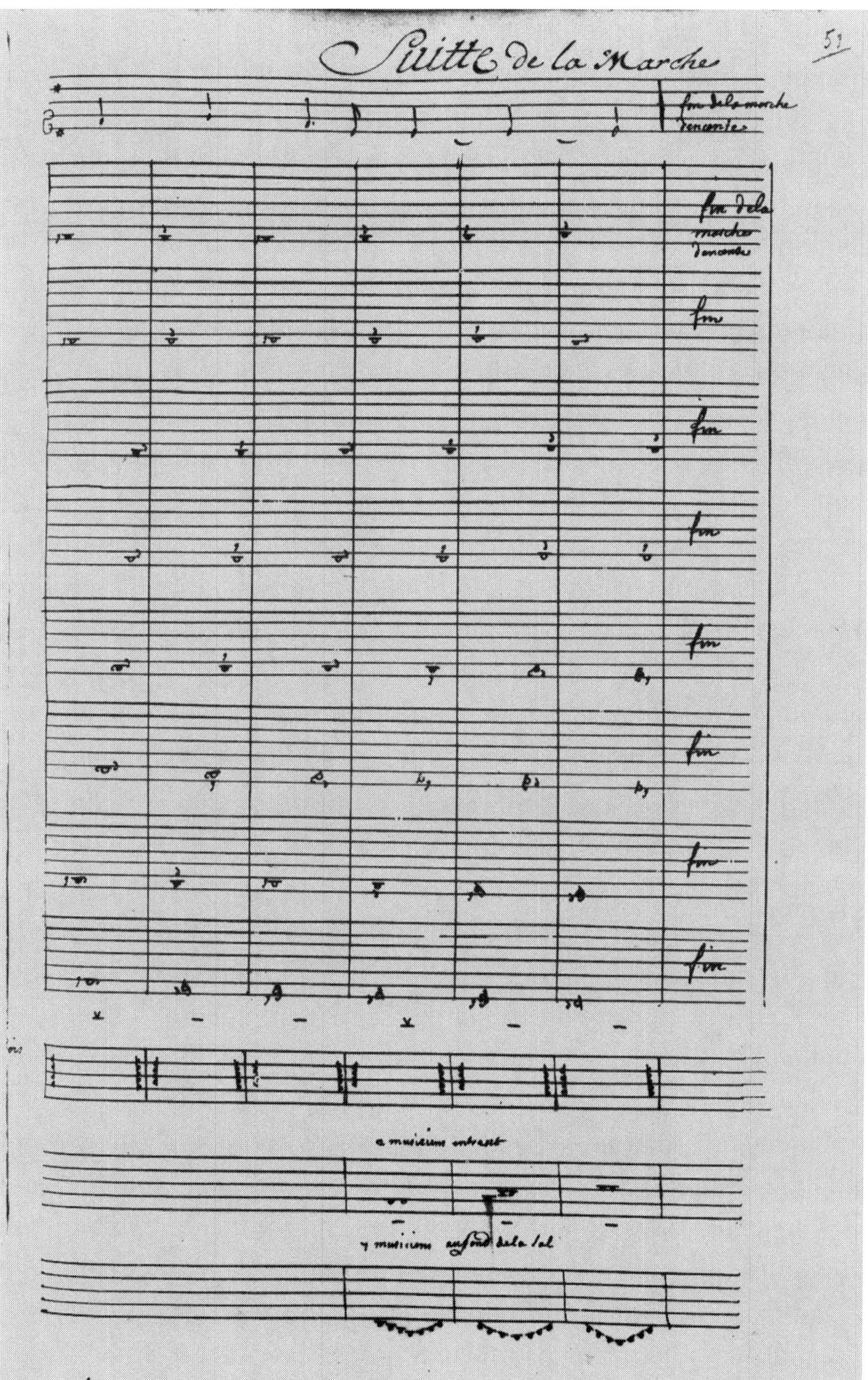

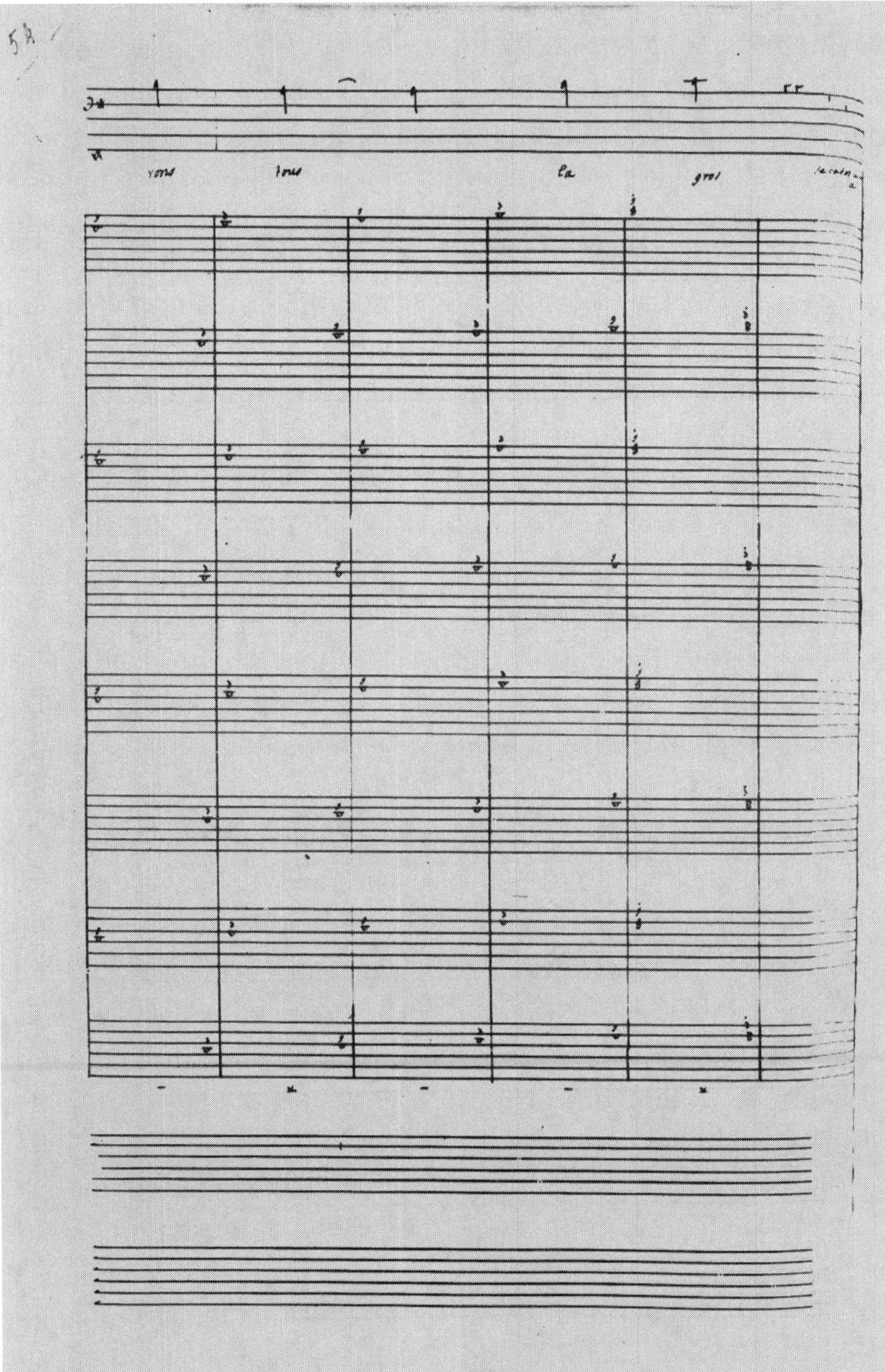

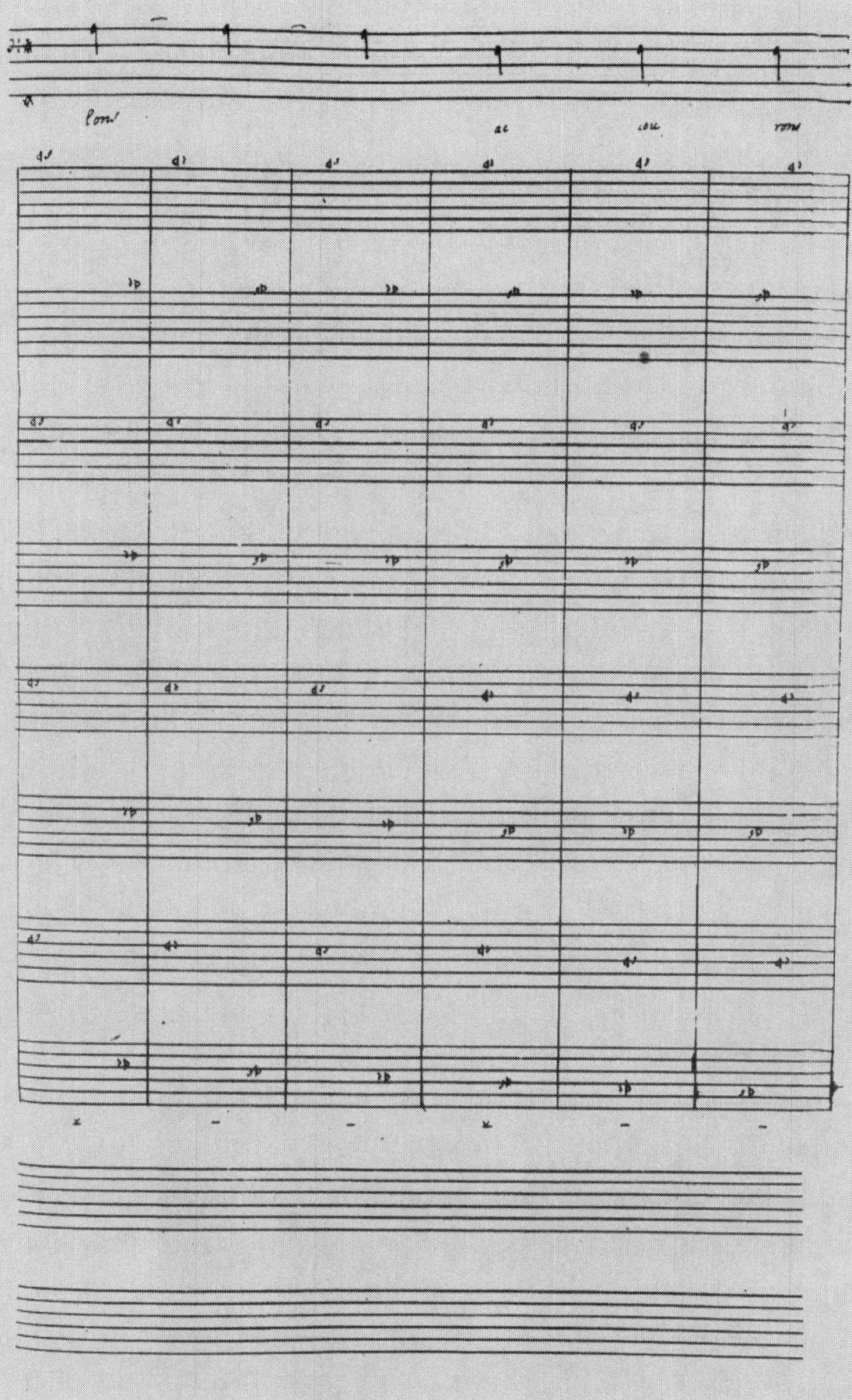

56,

tous　　　　　la　　　　grrr　　le calot lumoie　　Pomo

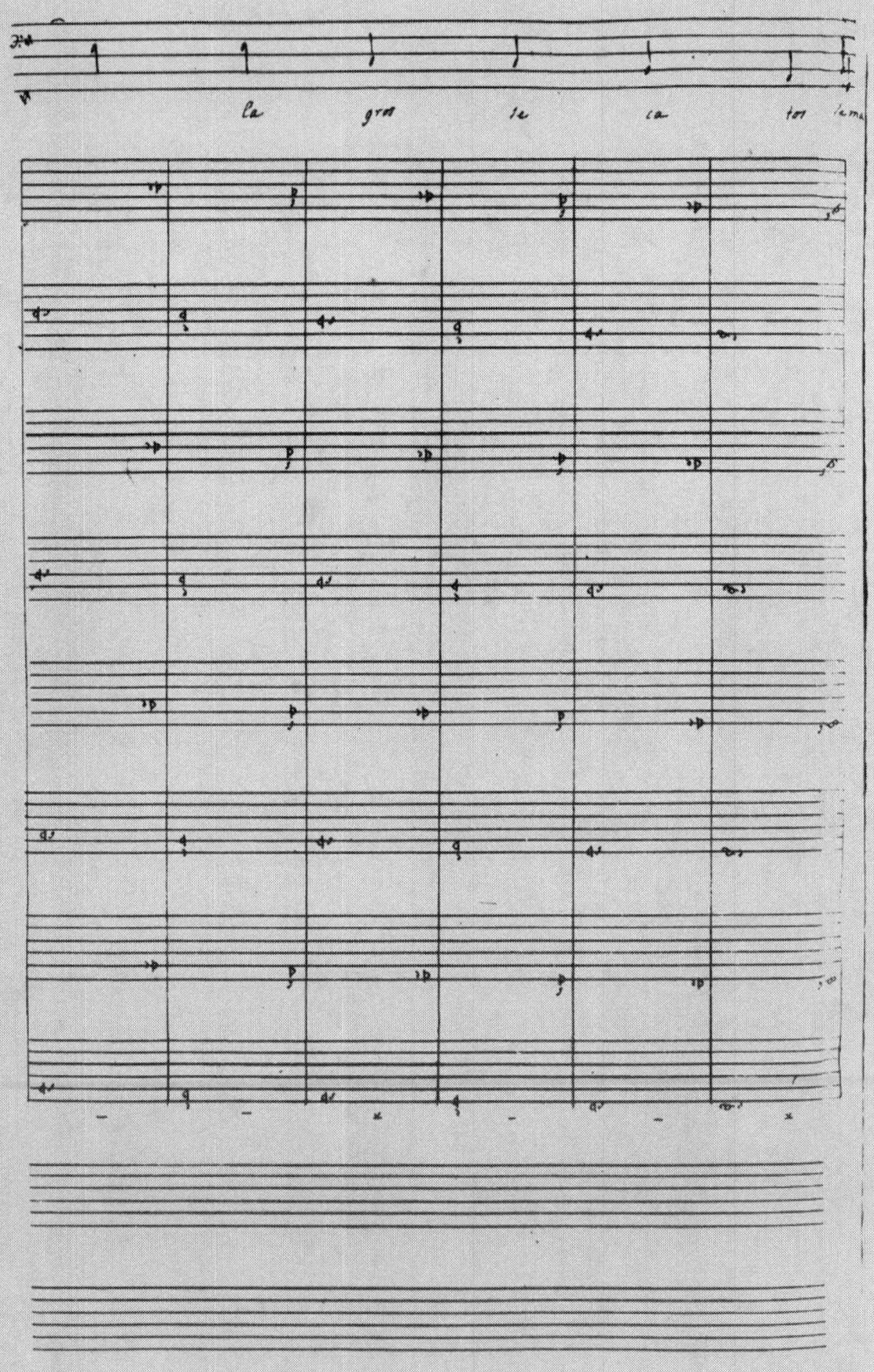

Entrée de deux Garçons de la Nopce

Suitte de l'Entrée des filles de la Nopce.

Entrée des 2. Garçons, et des 2. filles de la Nopce.

Suitte de l'Entrée des Garçons, et Filles de la Nopces

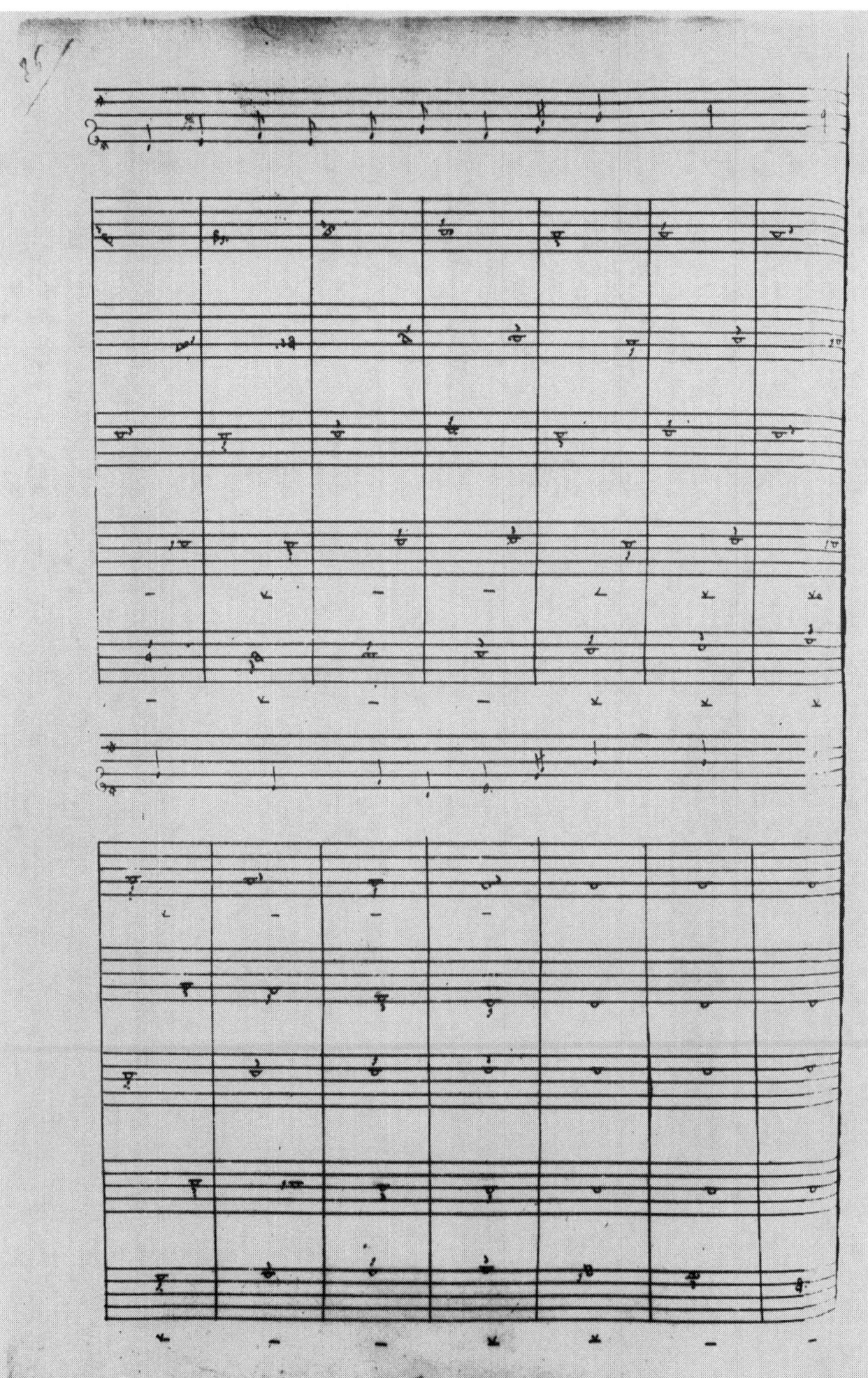

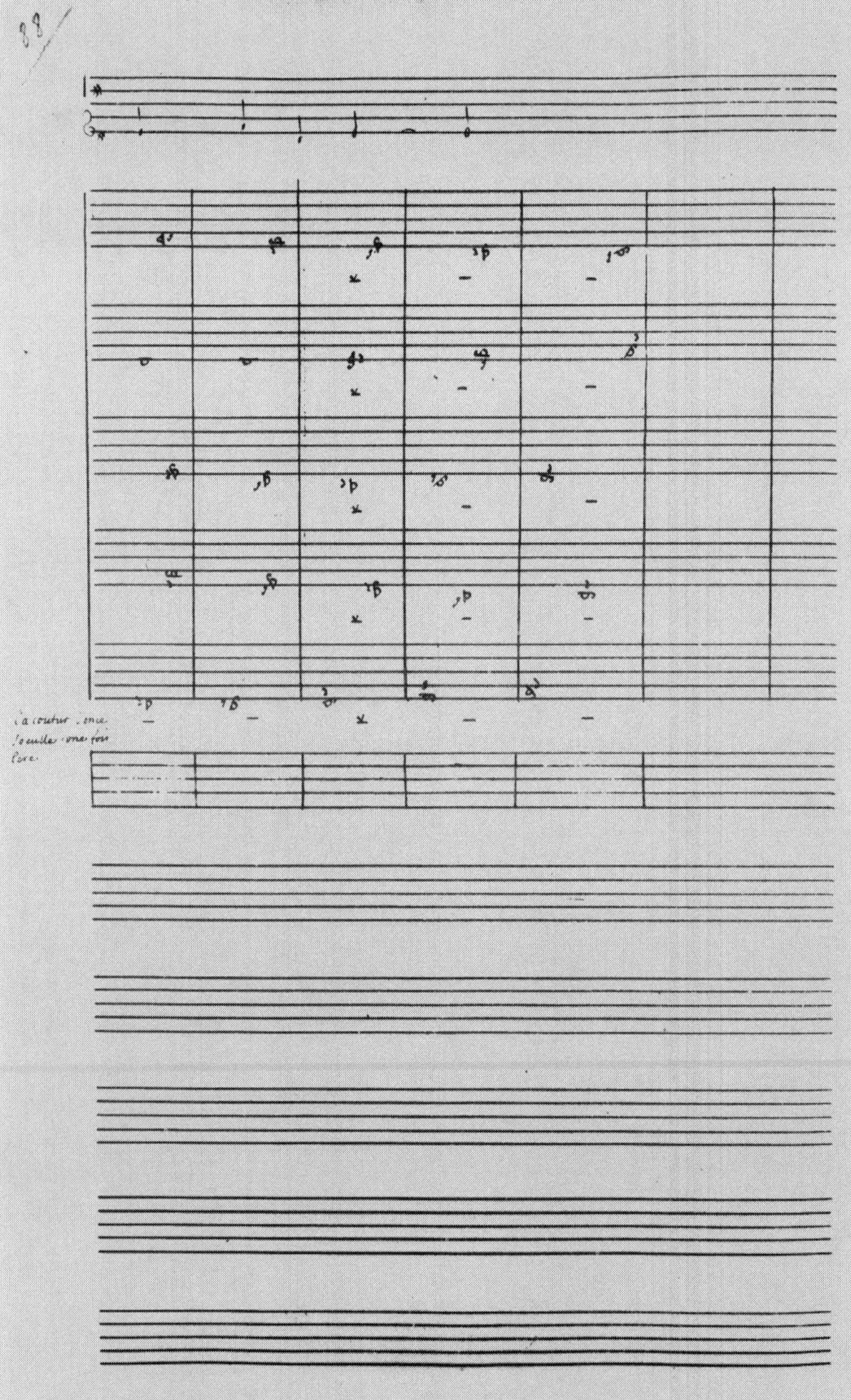

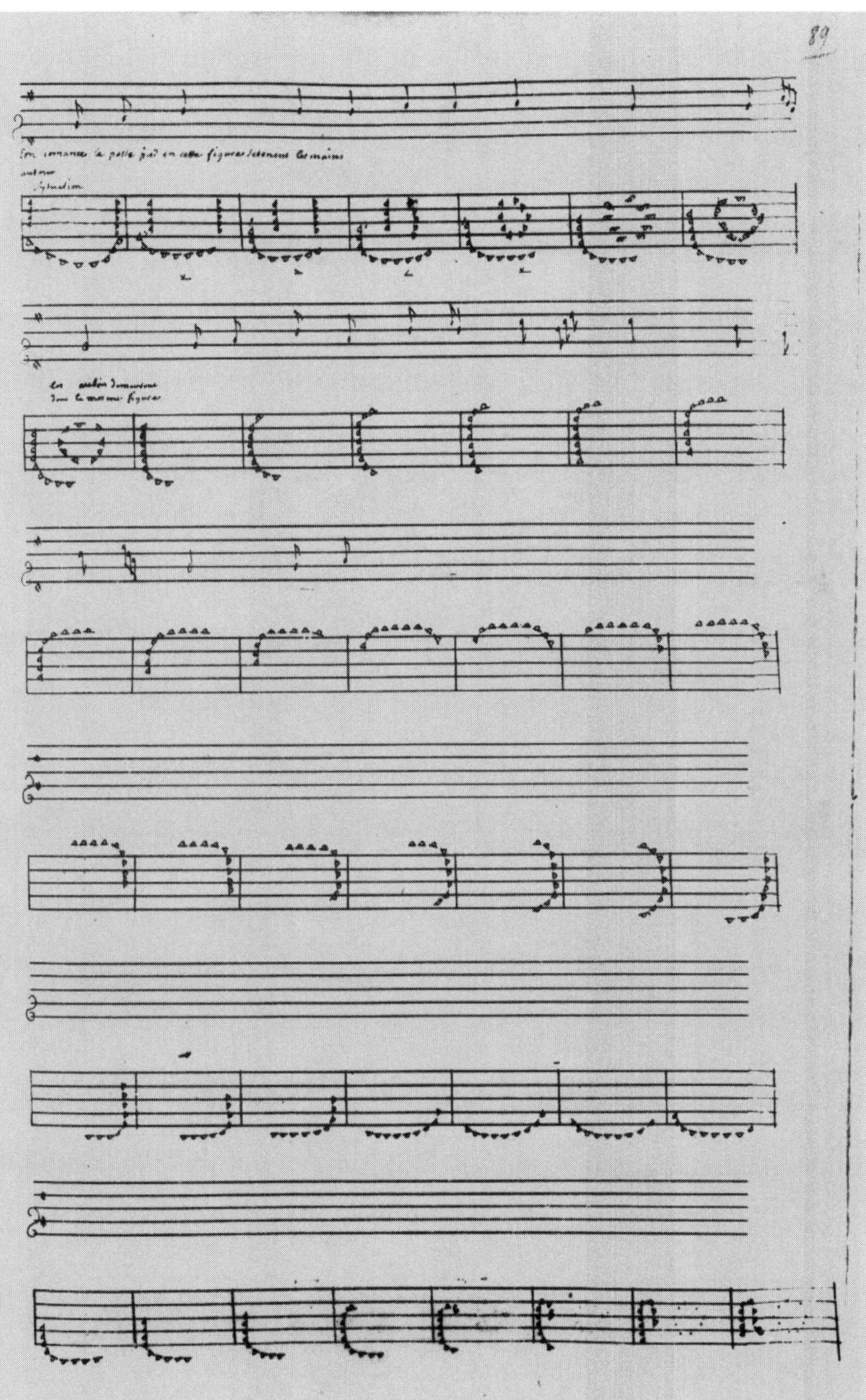

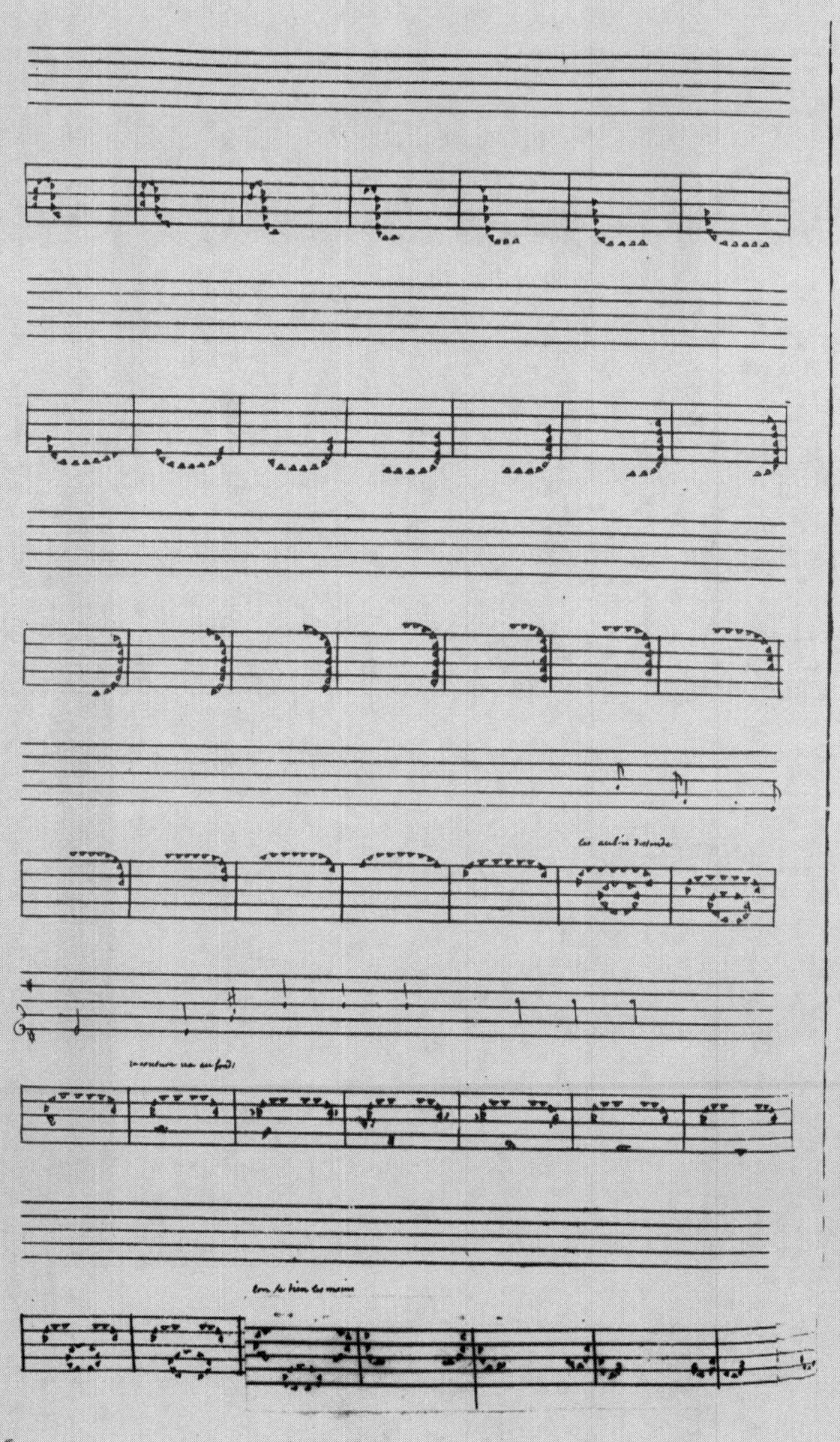

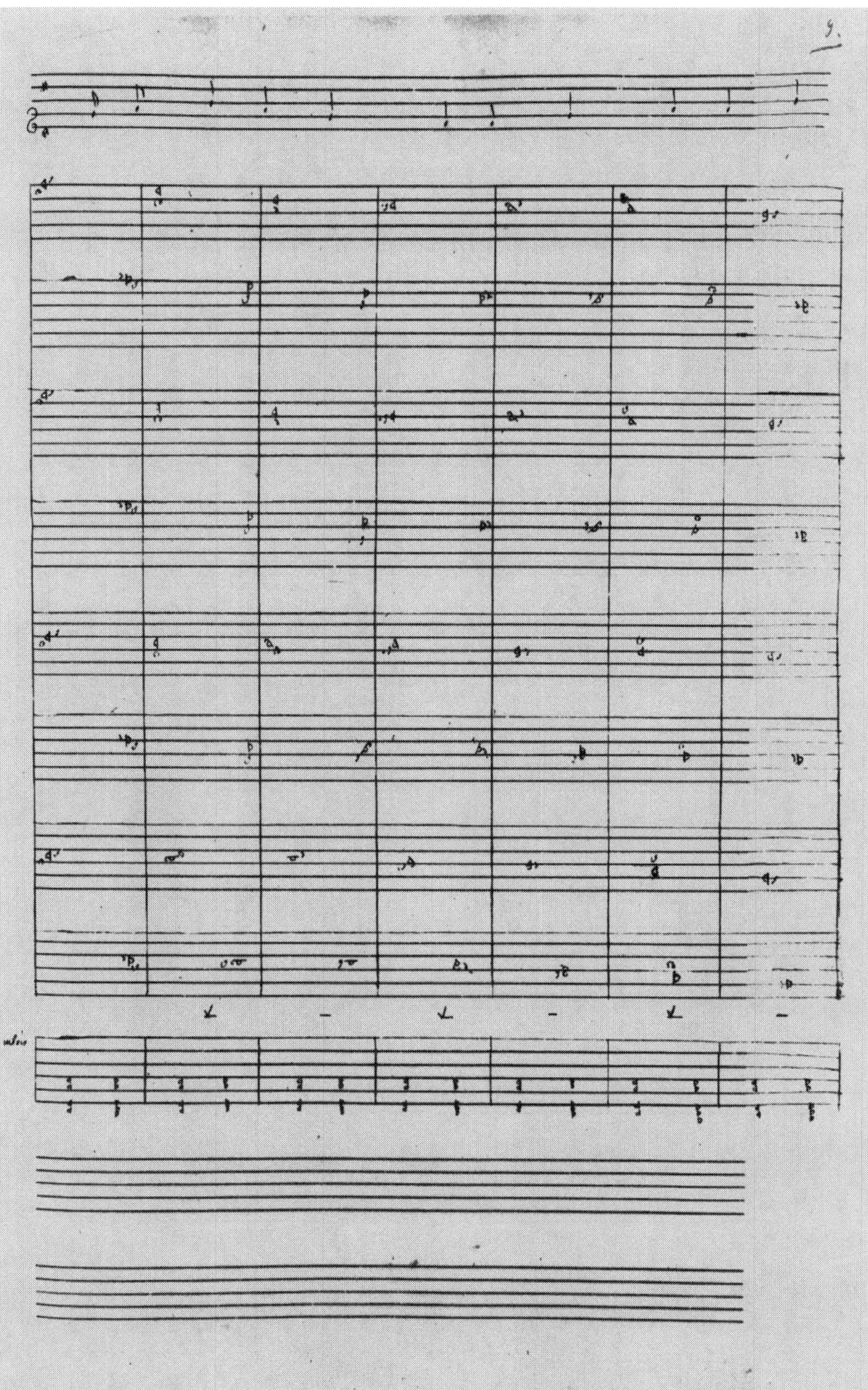

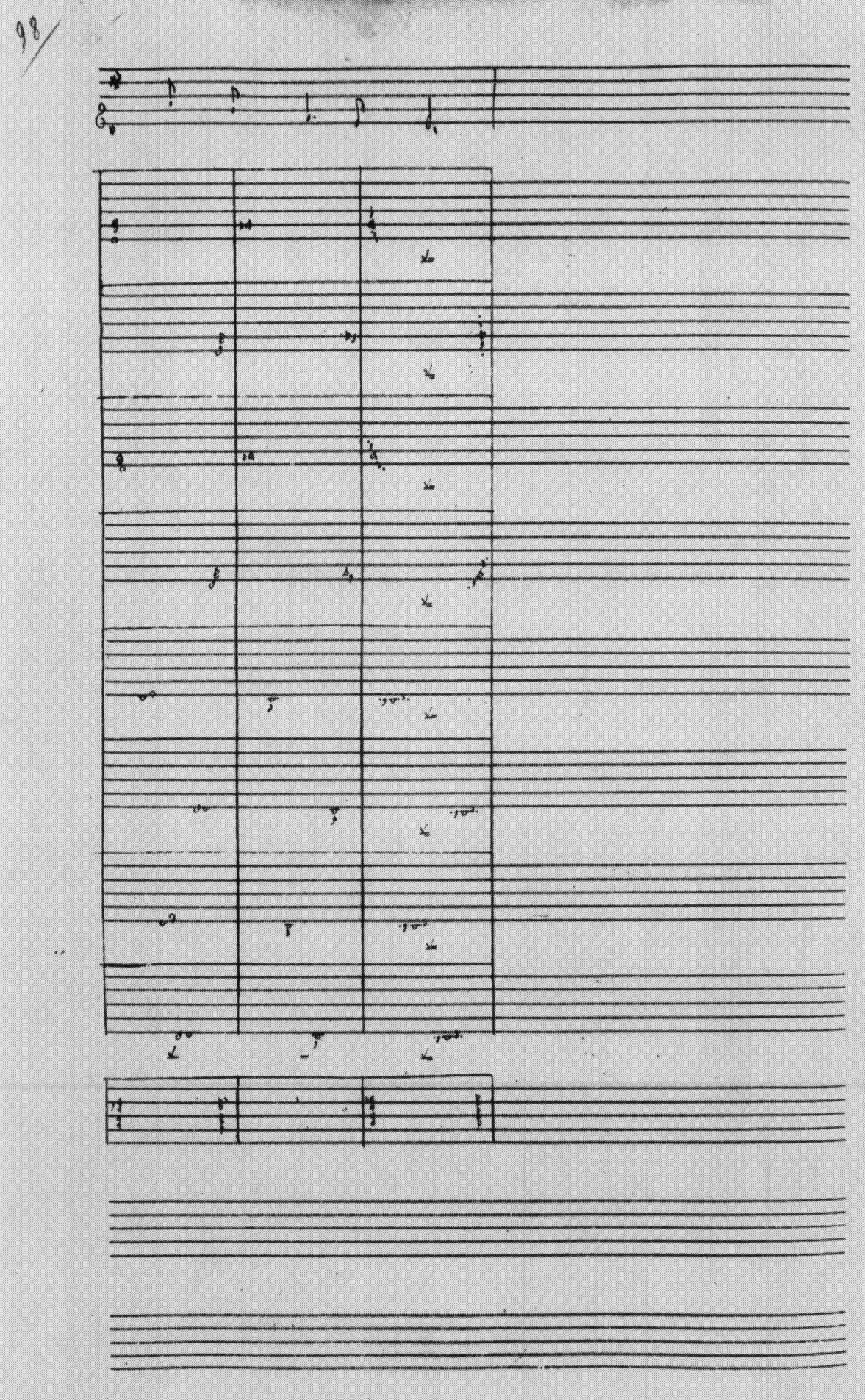

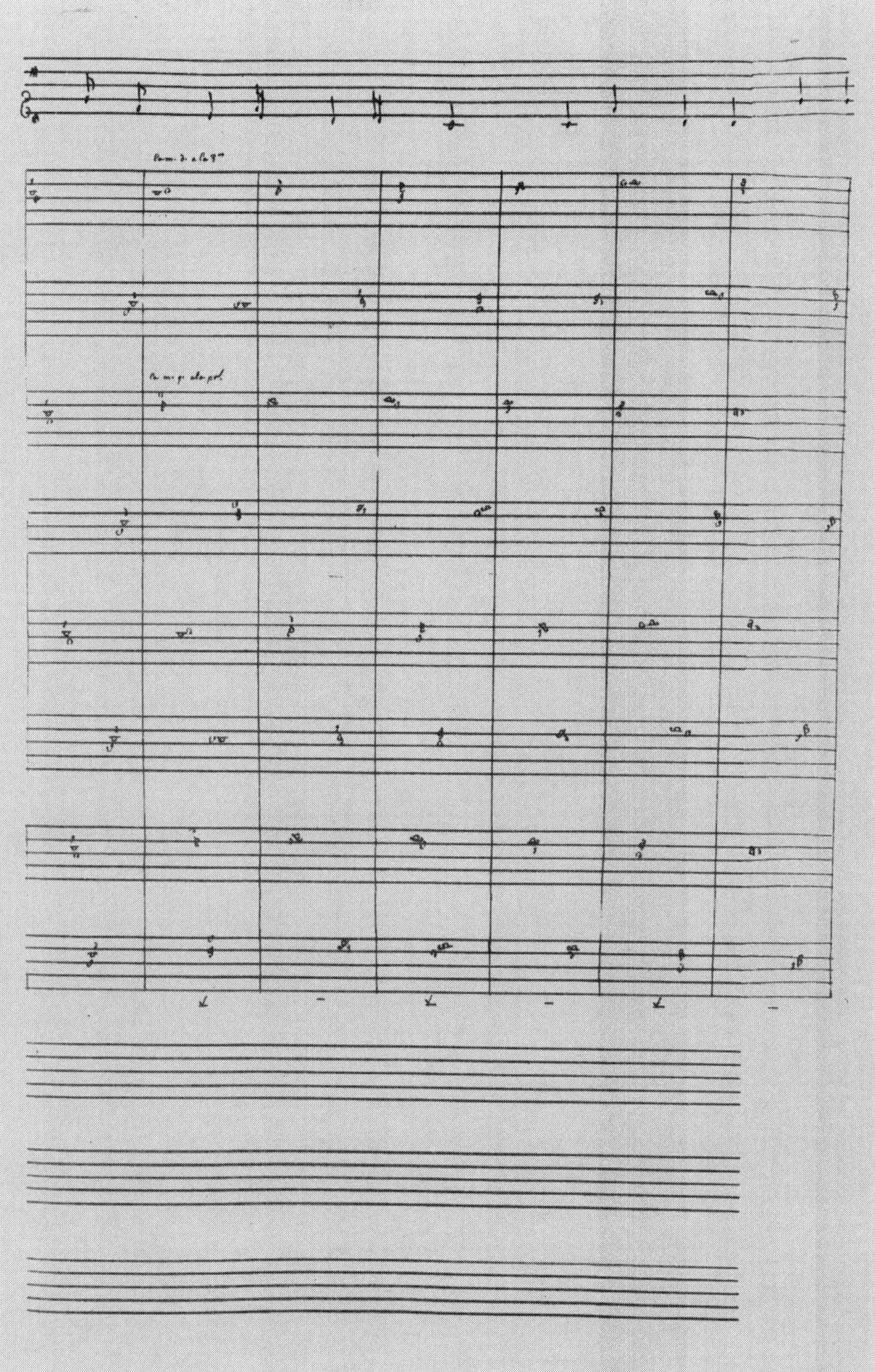

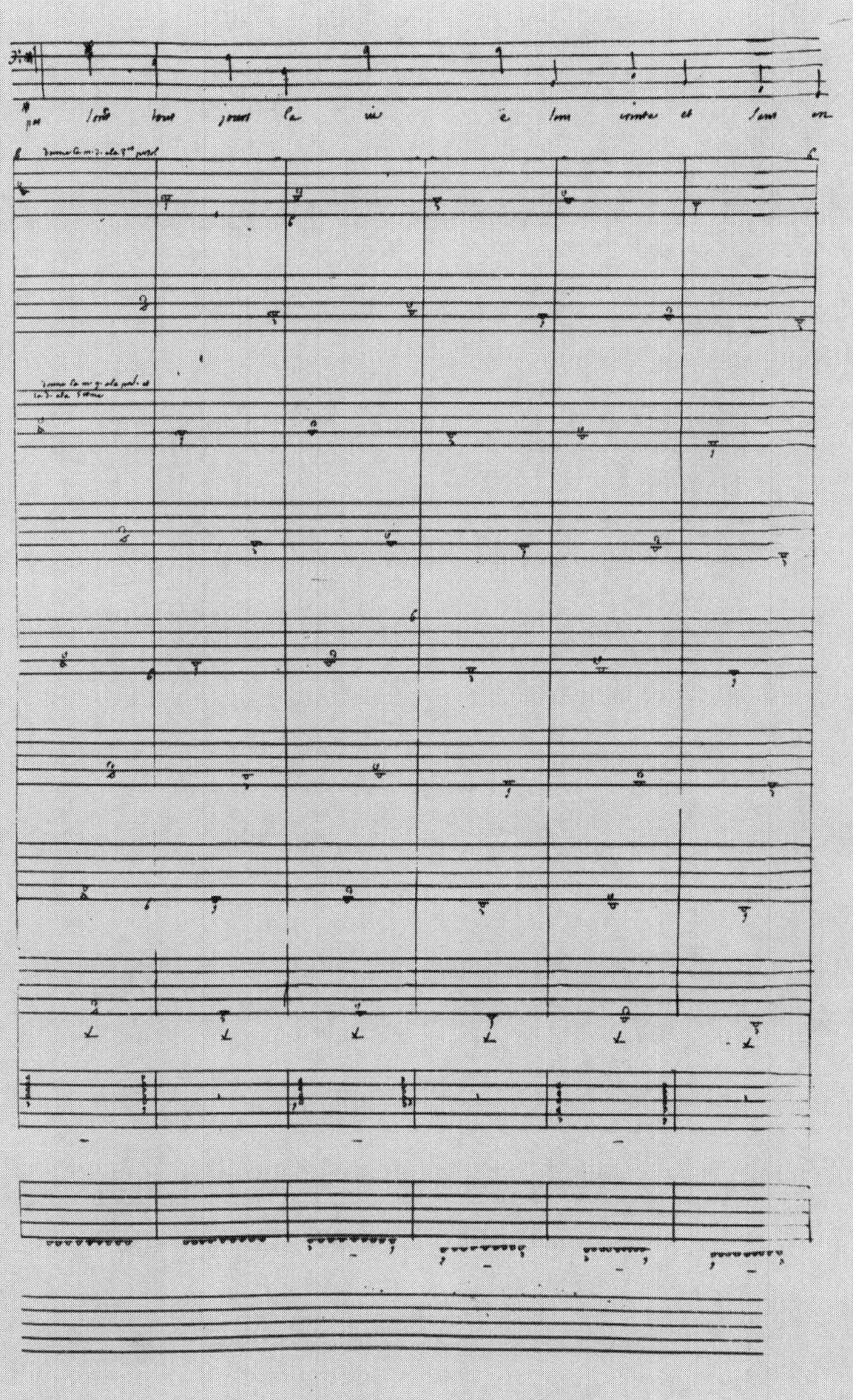

Between pages 105 and 106 of the manuscript there are three pages containing staff lines but no musical or choreographic notation.

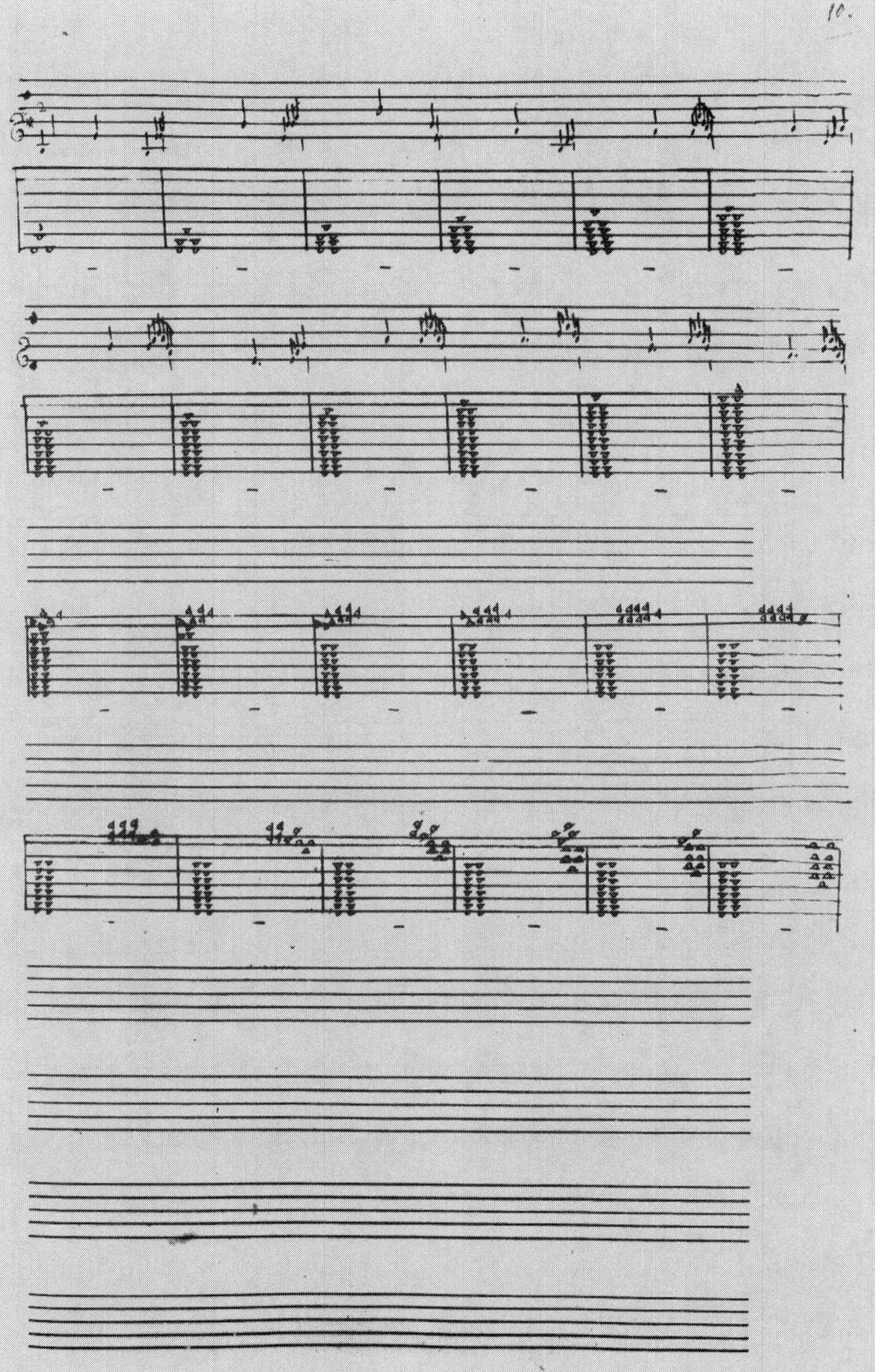

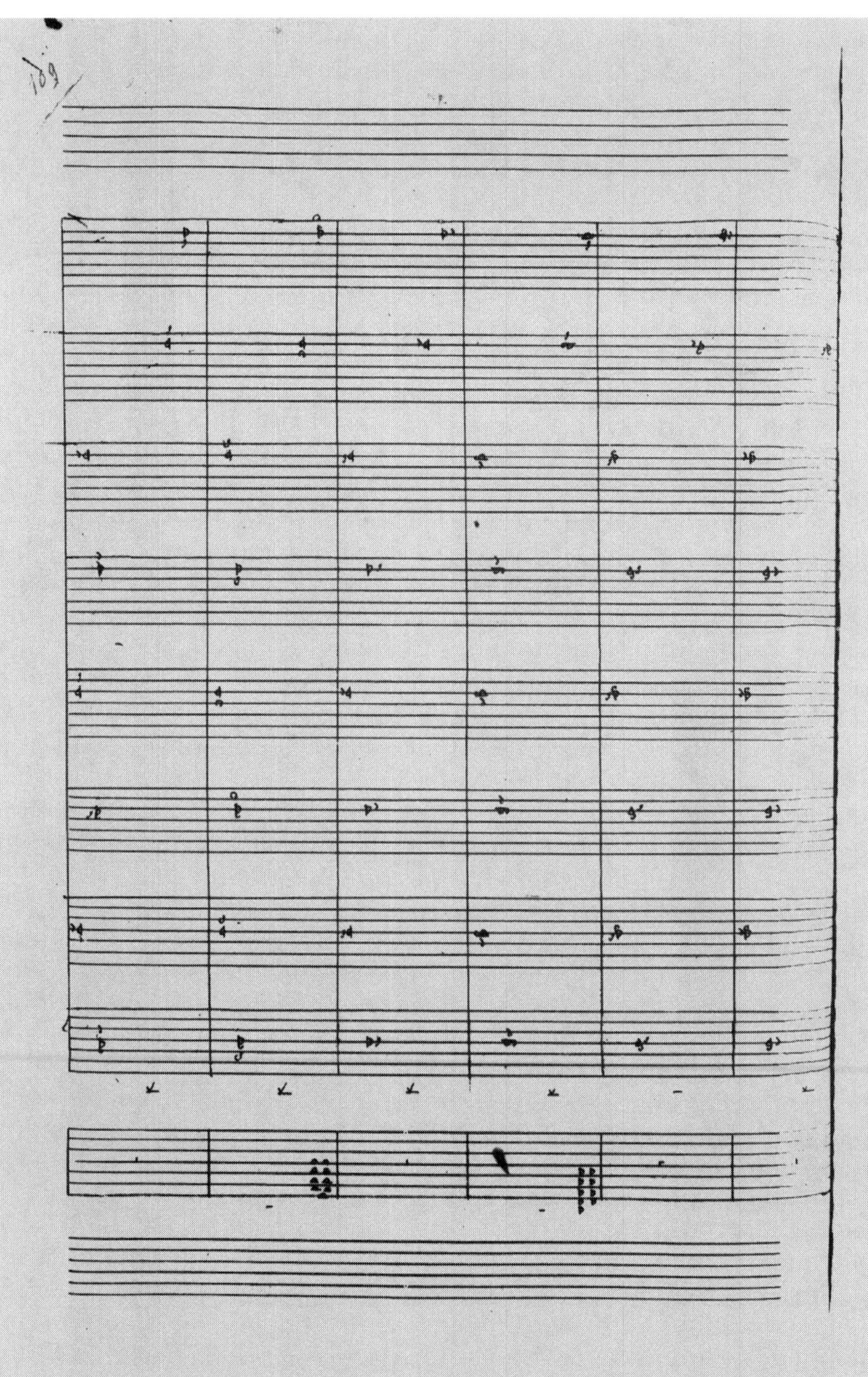

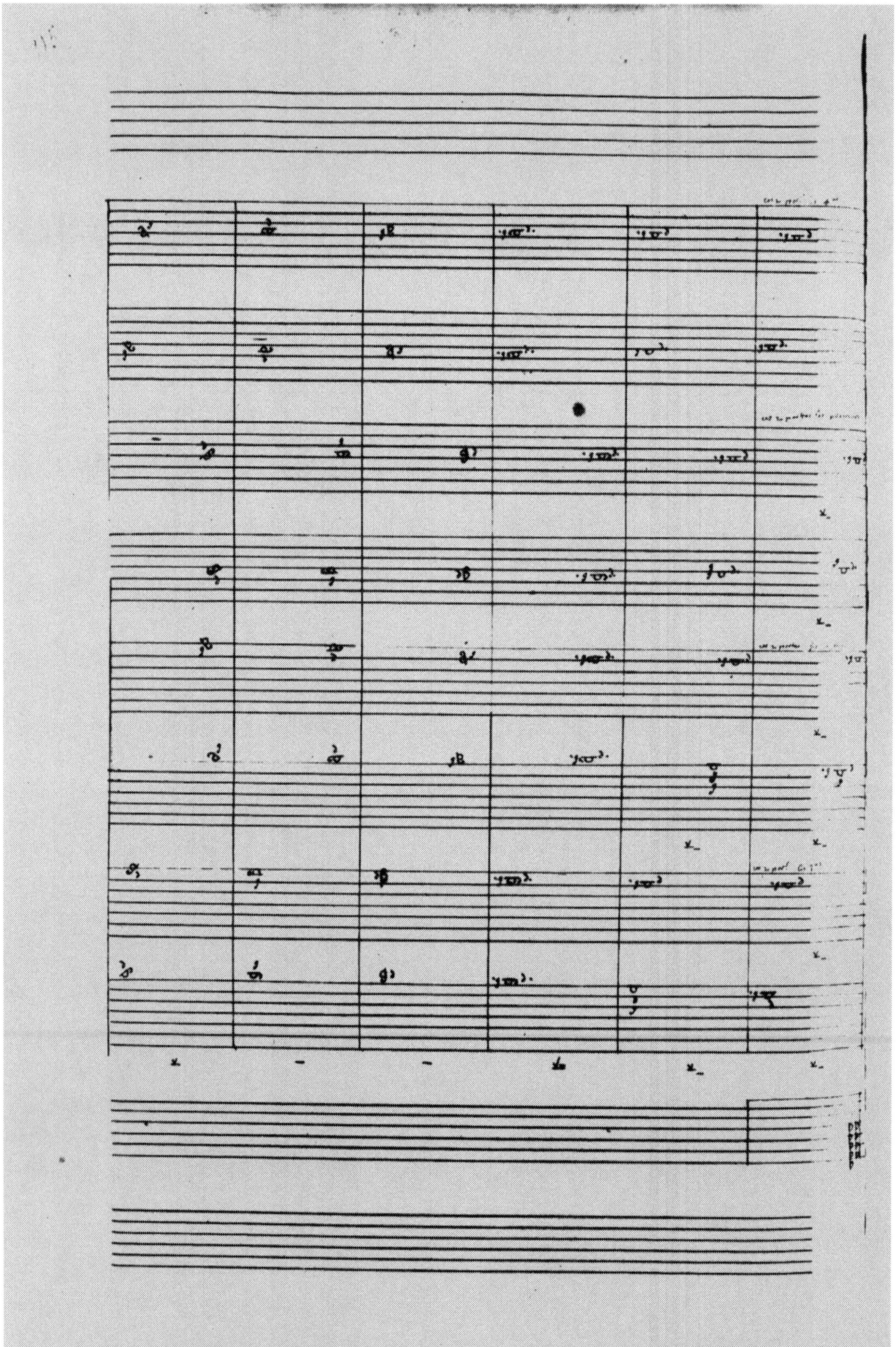

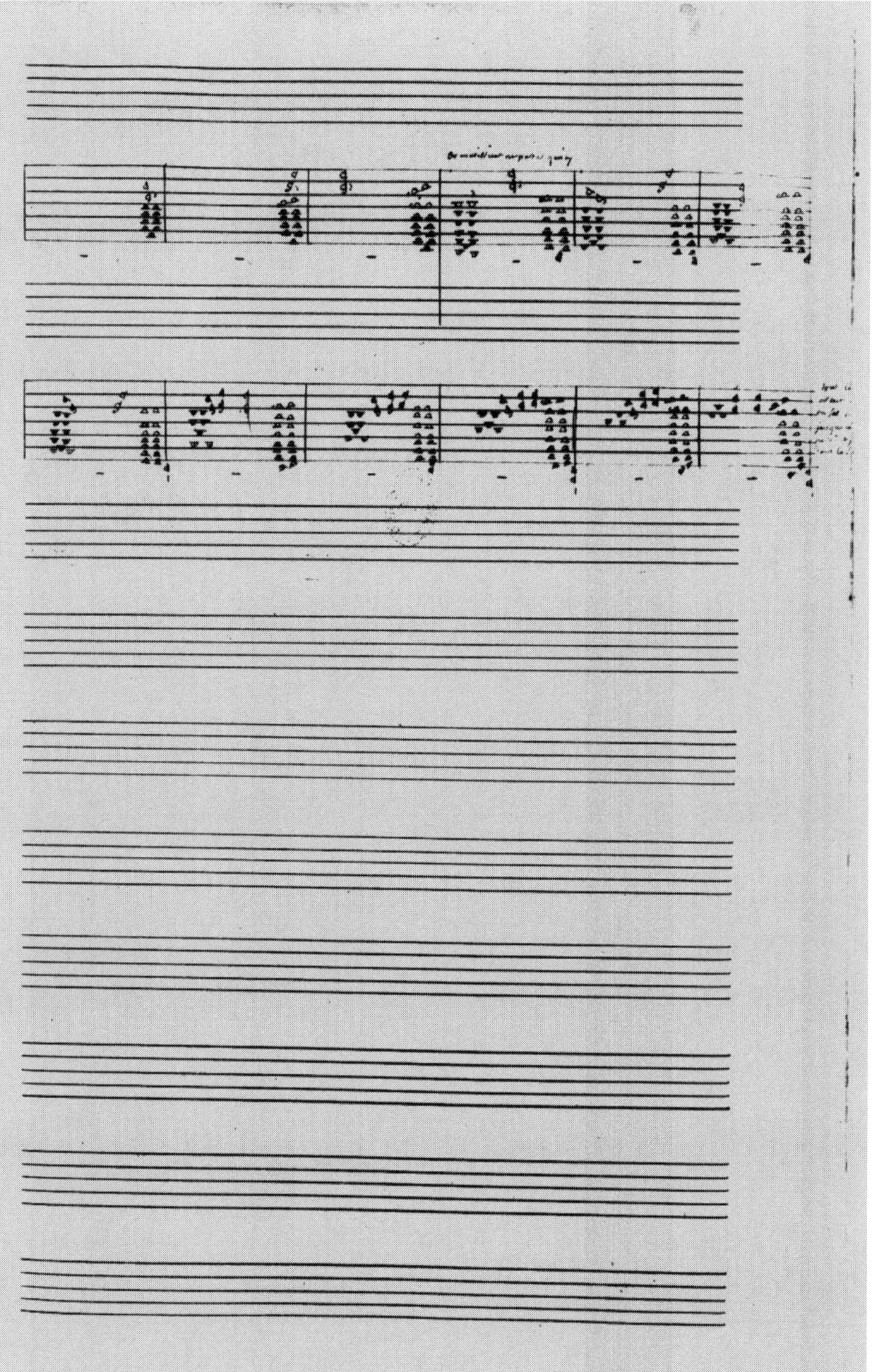

Appendix A

Libretto

Since no copy of the libretto for this mascarade is known, the text given here has been extracted from the score and is delineated according to the poetic structure. Abbreviations have been fully written out, spelling has been modernized, and some punctuation added. The bracketed numbers refer to the dance pieces. The translation aims for intelligibility rather than elegance and cannot serve as a substitute for the French text in performance. Anyone wishing to present the spoken scene in English should feel free to take liberties with the text and or even to make it the basis for improvisation, as the Italian comedians would have done.

Le Mariage de la Grosse Cathos
Mascarade mise en musique par
Philidor l'aîné, ordinaire de la musique du roi
1688

Acteurs (Singers)

La Couture époux de la Grosse Cathos (husband of Grosse Cathos)	Mr Philbert
La Grosse Cathos épouse de La Couture (wife of La Couture)	Mr Guillegau
Mr Dupont bourgeois de Paris (a Parisian bourgeois)	Mr Miracle
Mme Dupont sa femme, maîtresse de la Grosse Cathos (his wife, Grosse Cathos's mistress)	M^r Le Roy
L'Abbé du Plessis oncle de La Couture (La Couture's uncle)	Mr Morel
Gripetout écornifleur (scrounger)	Mr Gingant
Harlequin fourbe se disant mère nourrice de La Couture (scoundrel pretending to be La Couture's wet nurse)	
Mezzetin fourbe se disant père nourricier de La Couture (scoundrel pretending to be La Couture's foster father)	
Maître Simon suisse ami de la Grosse Cathos (Swiss friend of Grosse Cathos)	M^r [blank]
Dame Ragonde parente de la Grosse Cathos (relative of Grosse Cathos)	Mr Jonquet
Un garçon de la noce chantant à la sérénade de la mariée (a male wedding guest who sings in the serenade for the bride)	M^r [blank]

[Danseurs[1]] (Dancers)

Garçons de la noce (male wedding guests)	Mrs Dumirail et Favier l'aîné
Filles de la noce (female wedding guests)	Mrs Germain et Richer
Paysans (peasants)	Mrs Barazé et [blank]
Dames Gigognes	M^rs [blank]

[Scène Première] / [Scene One]

La Pavane:
[1A.] Marche pour neuf hautbois, huit danseurs, et neuf musiciens
[1B.] Marche dansante pour les huit danseurs

The Pavane:
[1A.] March for nine oboes, eight dancers, and nine singers
[1B.] Danced march for the eight dancers

Mme Dupont:
Allons mes enfants, venez tous,
La Grosse Cathos se marie.

Mme Dupont:
Come on, my children, everybody come,
Grosse Cathos is getting married.

Mr Dupont:
La Couture est son digne époux,
Tout comble aujourd'hui son envie.

Mr Dupont:
La Couture is her worthy husband,
Today all her desires are fulfilled.

Abbé du Plessis:
Ah! le beau choix.

Abbé du Plessis:
Oh, what a wonderful choice!

Gripetout:
        Qu'il fera de jaloux.
Le ciel doit prendre soin d'une si belle vie.

Gripetout:
        He will make many men jealous.
Heaven must be watching over such a beautiful life.

Maître Simon:

Jy trouve moy sty menage pien toux,
La Couture est pon troste[2] et son fâme est jolie.
[= Je trouve moi ce ménage bien doux,
La Couture est bon ?? et sa femme est jolie.]

Maître Simon: [in pidgin French throughout]
I find this household very nice
La Couture is [??] and his wife is pretty.

Mr et Mme Dupont:
Allons mes enfants, venez tous,
La Grosse Cathos se marie.

Mr and Mme Dupont:
Come on, my children, everybody come,
Grosse Cathos is getting married.

[11.] *Chœur*:
Allons, accourons tous,
La Grosse Cathos se marie.

[11.] *Chorus*:
Come on, let's all hasten,
Grosse Cathos is getting married.

Gripetout:
Elle obtient l'objet de ses feux,
Que son sort est heureux.

Gripetout:
She has obtained the object of her desire
How happy is her lot!

---

[1] The dancing roles are listed here as they appear in the dance notation; in the cast list following the title page of the musical score, the dancers are identified as follows (performers' names are not given): "une Dame Ragonde dansante, six voisins et voisines dansants, trois garçons de la noce." For a discussion of the differences between these two lists, see chapter 7, p. 187.

[2] At its first appearance on p. 3 of the F-Pn score this word has an acute accent at the end ("trosté"), but the accent is lacking at its repetition and also in the F-Pa score. The reading without the accent is undoubtedly correct, since by the rules of French prosody a mute syllable is required at the caesura of an alexandrine in which the second hemistiche starts with a vowel, as is the case here.

Abbé du Plessis:
La Couture souffrait une peine cruelle
Pour la beauté dont son cœur est épris.
Mais la Grosse Cathos est le prix
De son amour fidèle.

Chœur:
Chantons le choix charmant
De cet heureux amant.³

Grosse Cathos:
Morbleu! vous me rompez la tête.
Que de raisons, que de façons pour former une fête.
Je n'ai que faire d'opéra
Dans le temps que la faim m'accable.
Ah! chantez tant qu'il vous plaira,
Pour nous, mon cœur, allons nous mettre à table.

La Couture:
Il est vrai c'est trop discourir
D'amour et de flamme.
Allons, ma chère âme,
Je t'aime trop pour te désobéir.

Scène Seconde
Harlequin, Mezzetin, La Couture

Mezzetin:
Avant que d'aller plus loin, dis-moi? As-tu fait une sérieuse réflexion sur ton entreprise? N'appréhendes-tu pas qu'un orage de coups de bâtons ne soit la récompense de notre fourberie, si l'on vient à la découvrir?

Harlequin:
Tu t'alarmes de peu de choses. Je te donne le sieur de La Couture pour une pièce d'homme des plus stupides du royaume. C'est un animal d'une espèce toute particulière, et qui croira ingénument tout ce que nous lui dirons. Le voici. Je vais l'aborder, et sois assuré que nous nous divertirons comme il faut à ses dépens, pourvu que tu joues bien ton rôle.

Mezzetin:
Ce n'est pas ce qui m'embarrasse.

Abbé du Plessis:
La Couture was suffering a cruel pain
For the beauty of whom he is enamored.
But Grosse Cathos is the reward
For his faithful love.

Chorus:
Let us sing of the charming choice
Of this fortunate lover.

Grosse Cathos:
Zounds! You are breaking my head.
What pretexts, what a fuss, for putting together a party.
I couldn't care less about opera
When hunger overcomes me.
Oh, sing as much as you like,
As for us, dear heart, let's go eat.

La Couture:
It's true, it's a bit much carrying on
About love and desire.
Let's go, my beloved,
I love you too much to disobey.

Scene Two
Harlequin, Mezzetin, La Couture

Mezzetin:
Before going any farther, tell me. Have you given serious thought to your enterprise? Aren't you afraid that a storm of blows will be the reward for our skulduggery if it is discovered?

Harlequin:
You're worrying over nothing. I offer you Monsieur de La Couture as a man as stupid as they come in the kingdom. He is an animal of a very special type, and will naively believe anything we tell him. Here he is. I'll approach him, and rest assured that we'll have a good time at his expense, provided you play your role well.

Mezzetin:
That's not what worries me.

---

³ The F-Pn score has "ces" instead of "cet," but no corresponding plural ending on "amant." The F-Pa score shows both readings of the adjective, also with "amant" in the singular. Given the rhyme scheme and the singular noun, the singular form of the adjective seems more likely.

Harlequin:
Ah! mon cher nourrisson! Quelle joie pour moi de vous voir le mari d'une femme qui vaut son pesant d'or, d'une femme qui est la pudeur et la modestie même. Je sens mon cœur qui palpite. J'en ai une joie inconcevable, et je ne puis m'empêcher de vous embrasser.

Mezzetin:
Tout beau, n'allez pas si vite, c'est à moi à qui cet honneur est dû.

Harlequin:
Que veut donc dire ce vieux pénard?

Mezzetin:
Je dis que je le baiserai le premier, malgré toi, et malgré tes dents.

Harlequin:
Voyez un peu ce gros butor, comme il se jette à corps perdu sur ce pauvre petit mouton. Cela me fait saigner le cœur... quoi, encore? Ah! c'en est trop. Je veux en avoir ma part. Reçois, mon cher fils, ces tendres baisers que mon amour...

La Couture:
Que diable me veulent ces gens-là? Je crois qu'ils ont envie de m'étrangler.

Mezzetin:
Est-ce là l'accueil que vous me faites?

Harlequin:
Est-ce ainsi que vous recevez une personne que vous devriez regarder comme votre mère? Ouvrez les yeux, et reconnaissez...

La Couture:
Ah! que de préambule, laissez-moi de repos.

Harlequin:
Votre ingratitude va-t-elle jusqu'au point d'avoir du mépris pour nous?

La Couture:
Le diable emporte si je vous connais.

Harlequin:
Hé bien, apprends, cœur de roche, que je suis ta mère nourrice, et que celui que tu vois est ton père nourricier. Si tu n'avais pas sucé le lait de ce chaste sein, aurais-tu eu l'industrie de t'ériger en prince des petites maisons? Aurais-tu pu te rendre si recommandable dans tous les cabarets de Paris? Va, tu ne mérites pas les tendresses que l'on a pour toi. [Allons-nous en.][4]

Harlequin:
Ah! My dear nursling! What joy for me to see you the husband of a woman who is worth her weight in gold, of a woman who is propriety and modesty incarnate. I feel my heart pounding. My joy is inconceivable and I can't refrain from kissing you.

Mezzetin:
Easy does it, don't go so fast. That honor should be mine.

Harlequin:
What does this old idiot mean?

Mezzetin:
I say that I will kiss him first, in spite of you and in spite of your teeth.

Harlequin:
Take a look at this big brute, how he throws himself headlong at this poor little lamb. It makes my heart bleed. What? Still more? Oh, this is too much! I want to have my part. Accept, my dear son, these tender kisses that my love...

La Couture:
What the devil do these people want of me? I think they'd like to strangle me.

Mezzetin:
Is that the welcome you give me?

Harlequin:
Is this the way you receive someone that you should see as your mother? Open your eyes and recognize...

La Couture:
Ah! What a preamble! Give me some peace.

Harlequin:
Does your ingratitude go so far as to disdain us?

La Couture:
The devil take me if I know you.

Harlequin:
Well, let me tell you, heart of stone, that I am your foster mother and the person you see there is your foster father. If you hadn't suckled the milk from my chaste breast would you have had the industry to set yourself up as the prince of the brothels? Could you have made yourself so welcome in all the cabarets in Paris? Bah, you don't deserve the tenderness we have for you. [Let's go.]

---

[4] The text in brackets is found only in the F-Pa score.

La Couture:
Quoi, c'est vous qui êtes ma mère nourrice? Parbleu, je ne l'aurais jamais cru si vous ne me l'eussiez dit. Demeurez, je vous prie pour honorer mes noces de votre présence.

Harlequin:
Ne te l'avais-je pas bien dit? Est-ce que je me suis trompé?

Mezzetin:
Cela va le mieux du monde.

La Couture:
Prenez place tous deux, je serais bien aise de m'entretenir avec vous de beaucoup de particularités qui me concernent, et vous prier de me dire ce qu'est devenu mon père. Vous savez que je l'ai perdu que je n'avais encore que quatre ans.

Mezzetin:
Ah! l'honnête homme de père que vous aviez! Nous étions tous deux les meilleurs amis du monde. Plus je vous regarde, et plus je vois que vous lui ressemblez! Vous avez tous les traits de son visage, et toutes ses manières d'agir! C'était un de ces grands hommes qui ne s'appliquent qu'aux actions héroïques. Il ne trouvait rien d'impossible dans tout ce qu'il entreprenait. Mais son mérite étant trop grand pour demeurer dans le lieu de sa naissance où il avait acquis tant de réputation, on l'en retira malgré lui pour l'envoyer à Marseille sur les galères.

La Couture:
Sur les galères?

Mezzetin:
Oui, sur les galères, et ce fut là où il finit glorieusement ses jours au service du roi.

Harlequin:
Donnez-lui un coup à boire. Je vois bien que la voix lui manque à ce récit funeste, et ne m'oubliez pas . . . Pour moi, je suspens mon déplaisir, pour vous féliciter sur le beau choix que vous avez fait, et que je ne puis assez admirer. En effet, la Grosse Cathos qui vous est tombée en partage, se peut dire la perle, et la crème de toutes les personnes de son sexe. Elle l'emporte autant sur toutes les autres femmes, que le vin de Champagne l'emporte sur le vin de Brétigny. Jamais plus de beauté ne fut joint à plus de mérite. Son teint n'est pas de ces teints fades qui ont recours au fard. C'est

La Couture:
What! *You* are my foster mother? I never would have believed it if you hadn't told me. Stay, I pray you to honor my wedding with your presence.

Harlequin [to Mezzetin]:
What did I tell you! Was I wrong?

Mezzetin [to Harlequin]:
It couldn't be going better.

La Couture:
Please sit down, both of you. It would give me great satisfaction to chat with you about several items which concern me, and to beg you to tell me what became of my father. You know that I lost him before I was even four years old.

Mezzetin:
Ah, such a worthy father you had! He and I were the best friends in the world. The more I look at you, the more I see how much you look like him. You have all his features and all his mannerisms. He was one of those men who engage only in heroic deeds. He succeeded in everything he undertook. But his merit was too great for him to remain in his birthplace where he had acquired such a reputation, and he was withdrawn in spite of himself and sent to Marseilles to the galleys.

La Couture:
To the galleys?

Mezzetin:
Yes, to the galleys. And it was there that he gloriously ended his days in the service of the king.

Harlequin:
Give him a drink. I can see that this sad story has taken away his voice. And don't forget me . . . As for me, I suspend my displeasure in order to congratulate you on the happy choice you have made, which I cannot admire enough. Yes, Grosse Cathos who has fallen to your lot may be said to be the pearl, nay, the cream of her sex. She surpasses all other women just as champagne surpasses the wine of Brétigny. Never was so much beauty joined to such merit. Her complexion is not one of those flat complexions that need to resort to make-up. Her complexion is a lovely shade

un teint d'un cramoisi merveilleux. Elle a le nez le plus mignon du monde. Sa bouche, quoi que grande, est d'un azur éblouissant, et sa taille rondelette témoigne assez la beauté de son embonpoint. Oui, quand on la voit auprès de vous, on est forcé de dire:
"Elle est digne de lui, comme il est digne d'elle."
Ah! que nous verrons naître de petits La Couturiaux d'un mariage si bien assorti. Je voudrais de tout mon cœur en voir déjà une douzaine.

La Couture:
La peste, pour une paysanne, elle a le caquet bien affilé. N'y aurait-il point quelque chose de caché là-dessous? Voyons.

Mezzetin:
Si votre père était encore au monde, qu'il aurait de joie de vous voir dans le rang illustre où vous êtes aujourd'hui.

La Couture:
Puisque vous le connaissiez si bien, de quel pays était-il?

Mezzetin:
Il était Gascon.

La Couture:
Vous en avez menti, mon père était natif de Caen en Normandie.

Harlequin:
Le pays ne fait rien à l'affaire.

La Couture:
Vous avez bien la mine d'être tous deux des fourbes, et des écornifleurs, qui n'êtes venu ici que pour attraper une franche lippée. Écoutez, ma bile commence à s'échauffer et je vous conseille en ami de décamper, si vous ne voulez être assommés dans un moment.

Harlequin:
Quoi, nous traiter ainsi? Nous qui sommes de si honnêtes gens!

Mezzetin:
Tu me le payeras, gros cheval de carosse.

La Couture:
Maître Simon, et vous, mon oncle, obligez-moi de chasser d'ici tous ceux qui pourraient nous incommoder.

of crimson. She has the daintiest nose in the world. Her mouth, although somewhat large, is a ravishing shade of blue, and her plump little middle bears witness to the beauty of her embonpoint. Yes, when when we see her at your side, we are obliged to say:
"She is worthy of him, just as he is worthy of her."
Ah! And to think that we will someday see the birth of little La Couturettes from such a well-arranged match. I wish with all my heart that there were already a dozen of them.

La Couture:
Good grief! For a peasant she has a sharp tongue! Is it possible that she's hiding something underneath here? Let's take a look.

Mezzetin:
If your father were still among the living, how happy he would be to see you at the illustrious rank you hold today.

La Couture:
Since you knew him so well, where did he come from?

Mezzetin:
He was Gascon.

La Couture:
You're lying. My father was a native of Caen in Normandy.

Harlequin:
The place has nothing to do with it.

La Couture:
The two of you look to me like a pair of scoundrels and ne'er-do-wells who only showed up here to get a free drink. Listen, my temper is warming up and I offer you my friendly advice to clear out, if you don't want to see stars in a minute.

Harlequin:
What? You are treating us like this? We who are such worthy people!

Mezzetin [to Harlequin]:
You'll pay for this, you fathead!

La Couture:
Master Simon, and you, Uncle! Help me get rid of all those who could disturb us.

[Scene Troisième]	*[Scene Three]*

Abbé du Plessis:
Il faut rendre la place nette.
Ton minois me déplaît, et je prétends enfin
Que tu déloges sans trompette.[5]

Gripetout:
Quel est le soin qui t'inquiète,
Ne suis-je pas de ce festin?

Abbé du Plessis:
Ecornifleur insigne,
Non, non, tu n'es pas digne
De goûter notre vin.

Gripetout:
Que dit donc ce faquin hérissé de latin?

Abbé du Plessis:
Il faut rendre la place nette.
Ton minois me déplaît, et je prétends enfin
Que tu déloges sans trompette.

Gripetout:
Méchant railleur ridicule pédant.

Abbé du Plessis:
Gazetier insolent.

Gripetout:
Tais-toi, l'on sait fort bien que ton âme fantasque
Tourne souvent casaque.

Abbé du Plessis:
Lâche usurier.

Gripetout:
Vilain gibier.

Abbé du Plessis:
Grosse pécore.

Gripetout:
Oses-tu raisonner encore?

Tous Deux:
Si tu n'apaises mon courroux
Je te rouerai de coups.

Abbé du Plessis:
We must clear the place out.
I don't like your looks, and I intend
You to scram without ceremony.

Gripetout:
What's bothering you?
Am I not one of the party?

Abbé du Plessis:
Notorious scrounger,
No, no, you are not worthy
Of tasting our wine.

Gripetout:
What on earth is this latinizing cad talking about?

Abbé du Plessis:
We must clear the place out.
I don't like your looks and I intend
You to scram without ceremony.

Gripetout:
Nasty nattering ridiculous pedant!

Abbé du Plessis:
Insolent blabbermouth!

Gripetout:
Shut up! Everyone knows that your capricious soul
Often turns coat.

Abbé du Plessis:
Cowardly usurer!

Gripetout:
Ugly gallows-bird!

Abbé du Plessis:
Fat hayseed!

Gripetout:
Do you still dare open your mouth?

Both:
If you don't calm my wrath
I'll beat you till you're black and blue.

---

[5] Written "trompettes" in the plural here, but singular upon repetition below. From the rhyme with "nette" it is clear that the singular reading is the correct one.

Maître Simon:
Party mon foy ly feux accortir fous

Dans ty grand jour de la retiouissance
Pour quoy songir à la fantgeance
L'estre dous teux yvroynes sous
Party mon foy ly feux accortir fous.

[= Pardi, ma foi, je veux vous accorder.
Dans ce grand jour de la réjouissance
Pourquoi songer à la vengeance?
Vous êtes tous deux ivrognes saoûls.
Pardi, ma foi, je veux vous accorder.]

Gripetout:
C'est lui dont la langue maudite
M'insulte et m'outrage en ce lieu.

Abbé du Plessis:
Va, va, vilain fesse-matthieu.
Tu n'en es pas encore quitte.

Tous Deux:
Si tu n'apaises mon courroux
Je te rouerai de coups.

Maître Simon:
Party mon foy ly feux accortir fous.

Dame Ragonde:
Ah! messieurs, quelle cohue,
Quel désordre, quel fracas.
Sortez, allez dans la rue,
Terminez tous vos débats.
Vous méritez que l'on vous chasse.
Fi! doit-on quereller ainsi?
Sans raisonner faites-nous place,
Nous prétendons danser ici.

[III.] Entrée de deux garçons de la noce

[IV.] Entrée de deux filles de la noce (Gigue)

[V.] Entrée des deux garçons et des deux filles de la noce (Menuet)

Chœur:
Dans ce grand jour unissons-nous
Pour partager des jeux si doux.

Grosse Cathos et La Couture:
J'aime la panse,
J'aime la danse.
Et toujours le bon vin
Dissipe mon chagrin.

Maître Simon:
For heaven's sake, I'd like to get you to agree.
On this great day of rejoicing
Why are you thinking about vengeance?
You are both drunk.
For heaven's sake, I'd like to get you to agree.

Gripetout:
He's the one whose cursed tongue
Insults and offends me.

Abbé du Plessis:
Come on, you old skinflint,
You're not out of this yet.

Both:
If you don't calm my wrath
I'll beat you till you're black and blue.

Maître Simon:
For heaven's sake, I'd like to get you to agree.

Dame Ragonde:
Ah, gentlemen, what a jumble,
What disorder, what a racket!
Leave, go into the street,
Put an end to your disputes.
You deserve to be run out of here.
Fie! Must you quarrel like this?
Don't argue, just make room for us.
We want to dance here.

[III.] Entrée for two male wedding guests

[IV.] Entrée for two female wedding guests (Gigue)

[V.] Entrée for the two male and two female wedding guests (Menuet)

Chorus:
On this wonderful day let us join together
To share these sweet pastimes.

Grosse Cathos and La Couture:
I love my belly,
I love dancing.
And good wine always
Dispels my ill-humor.

Maître Simon:
Pour moy qui n'aure point d'amour,
Prendre plaisir a poire tout le jour.

[= Pour moi qui n'ai point d'amour
Je prends plaisir à boire tout le jour.]⁶

[VI.] Air des ivrognes

[VII.] Rigaudon pour les filles de la noce [et La Couture]

[VIII.] Passepied

[IX] *Chœur*:
Passons toujours la vie
Sans trouble⁷ et sans envie.
Les plaisirs sont faits
Pour nous tout exprès.

La Couture:
Ma foi, c'est assez rire.
Que chacun se retire
Sans tumulte et sans bruit.
L'amour me transporte,
Je veux qu'on m'apporte
Mon bonnet de nuit.

Chœur:
Charivari, charivari, charivari!

Un Garçon de la Noce:
Dans cette nuit obscure
Troublons le repos si chéri
De Cathos et de La Couture.
Leur tendre amour sera bientôt flétri.

Chœur:
Charivari, charivari, charivari!

Un Garçon de la Noce:
La Grosse Cathos fait paraître
Beaucoup d'ardeur pour son nouveau mari.

Mais dans deux jours, peut-être,
Cherchera-t-elle un favori.

Chœur:
Charivari, charivari, charivari!

[XA. & XB.] La Pavane

Maître Simon:
I who have no one to love,
Take pleasure in drinking all day long.

[VI.] Drunk dance

[VII.] Rigaudon for the female wedding guests [and La Couture]

[VIII.] Passepied

[IX.] *Chorus*:
Let us always spend our lives
Without trouble and without envy.
The pleasures of life have been made
Expressly for us.

La Couture:
Well, that's enough laughing.
Let everyone retire
Without commotion or noise.
Love carries me away,
I want someone to bring me
My nightcap.

Chorus:
Charivari, charivari, charivari!

A Male Wedding Guest:
On this dark night
Let's disturb the precious slumber
Of Cathos and La Couture.
Their tender love will soon wither.

Chorus:
Charivari, charivari, charivari!

A Male Wedding Guest:
Grosse Cathos demonstrates
A good deal of ardor towards her new husband.

But in a couple of days, perhaps,
She'll be on the lookout for a sweetheart.

Chorus:
Charivari, charivari, charivari!

[XA. & XB.] The Pavane

---

⁶ The order of the next four pieces follows the sequence in the dance notation rather than the score (see chapter 3, p. 54), that is, the chorus "Passons toujours la vie" follows the three dances rather than preceding them.

⁷ The dance notation (facsimile, p. 103) has "crinte" (i.e., *crainte*) rather than "trouble."

Appendix B

Facsimile of the article "Chorégraphie" by Louis-Jacques Goussier in volume 3 of the *Encyclopédie ou dictionnaire raisonné des sciences, des arts et des métiers*, ed. Diderot and d'Alembert (Paris, 1753), pp. 367–73; and of the two plates accompanying the article published in volume 3 of the plates (Paris, 1762).

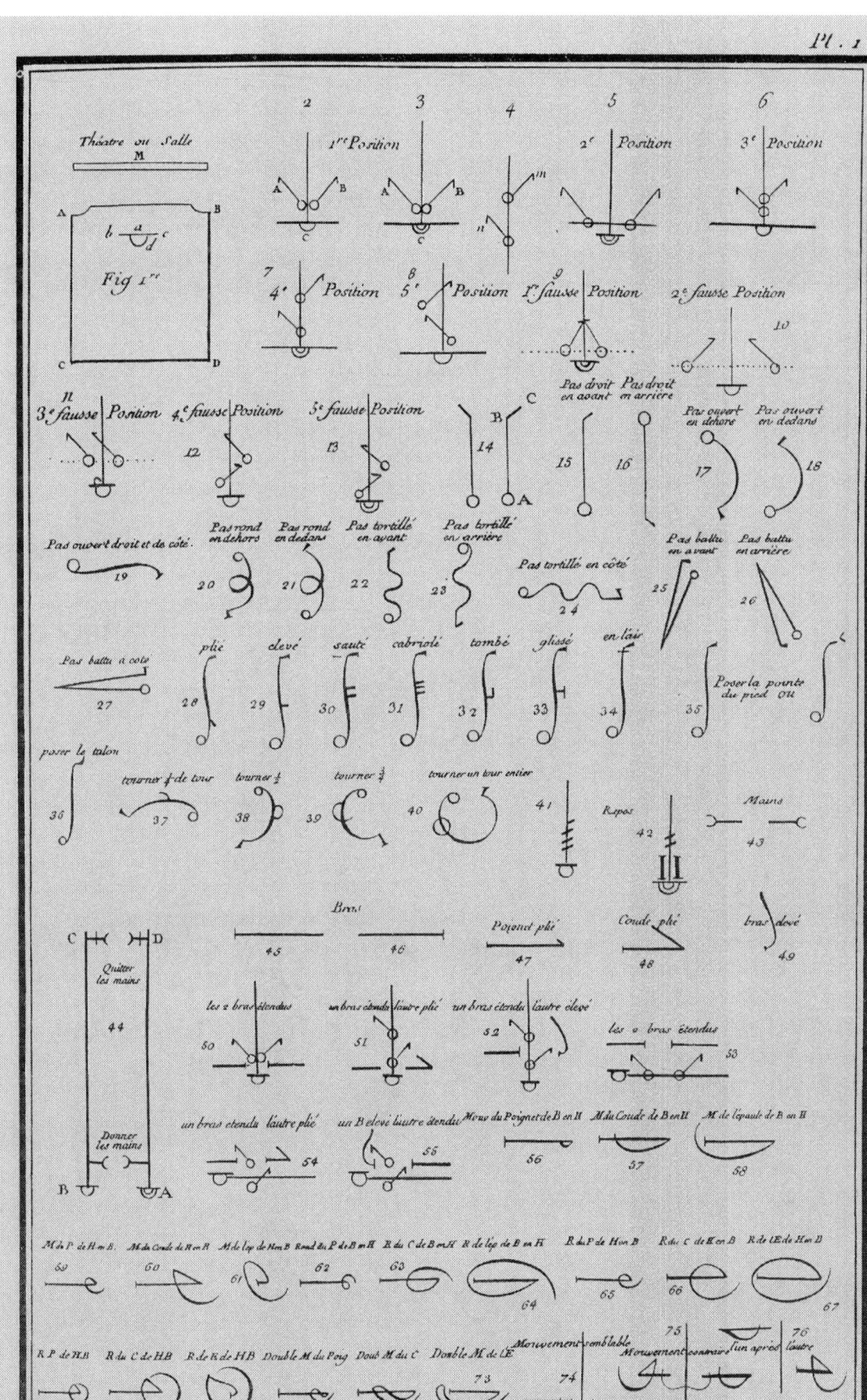

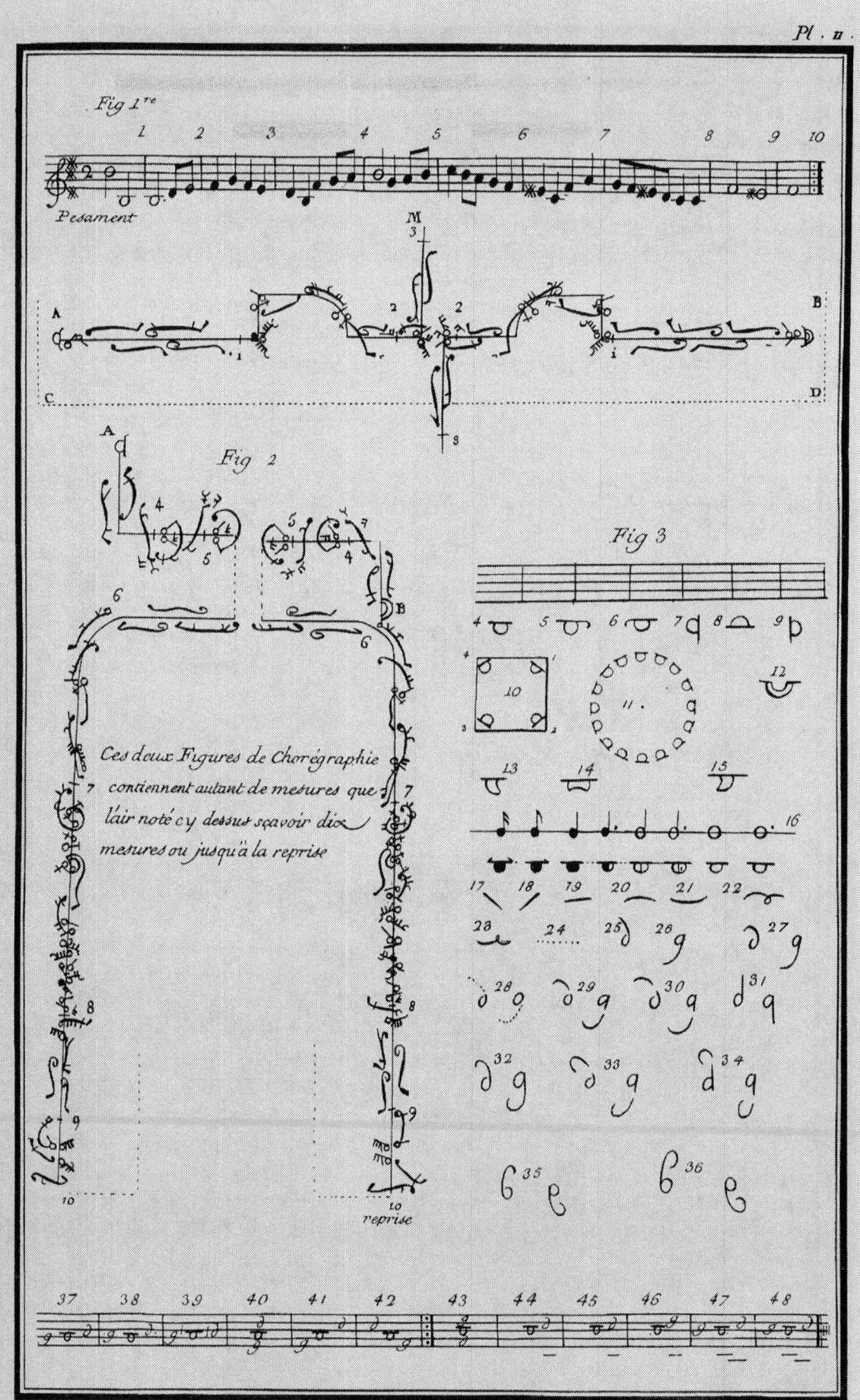

CHO

CHOPPER, v. n. (*Maréchall.*) c'est heurter du pié contre terre. Le cheval a ce défaut, lorsque dans ses différentes allures il ne leve pas les piés assez haut. *Voyez* CHEVAL.

CHOQUARD, *voyez* CHOUCAS ROUGE.

CHOQUE *ou* CHOC, s. m. est un outil dont les *Chapeliers* se servent pour donner au feutre la forme de chapeau, & pour faire descendre également la ficelle jusqu'au lien, c'est-à-dire jusqu'à l'endroit où les bords du chapeau se terminent & touchent au commencement de la tête. On ne se sert de cet outil qu'après que la ficelle a été descendue jusqu'au bas de la forme, par le moyen d'un autre outil qu'on appelle *avaloire*.

Le *choque* est fait de cuivre & de figure presque quarrée, mais un peu tourné en rond afin de mieux embrasser la forme du chapeau. Il a deux ou trois lignes d'épaisseur, cinq pouces de hauteur, & un peu plus de largeur; le haut qui lui tient lieu de poignée, est fait du même morceau de cuivre roulé à jour, & d'environ un pouce de diametre. Le chapelier tient cet instrument de la main droite; & en le pressant fortement sur la ficelle par sa partie inférieure, il la fait descendre également jusqu'au lien, & répete cette opération tout autour du chapeau. *Voyez la fig. 13. Pl. du Chapelier.*

L'ouvrier doit avoir soin quand il donne cette façon au chapeau, que la forme soit posée horisontalement & de niveau sur une plaque de fer, afin que le lien du chapeau soit égal par-tout, & que la forme ne soit pas plus haute d'un côté que de l'autre. *Voyez l'article* CHAPEAU.

CHOQUER LA TOURNEVIRE, (*Marine.*) c'est rehausser la tournevire sur le cabestan, afin d'empêcher qu'elle ne se croise ou qu'elle ne s'embarrasse lorsqu'on la vire. *Voyez à l'article* CABESTAN, l'incommodité de cette manœuvre, & les meilleurs ouvrages que nous ayons sur ce sujet. (*Z*)

CHORÉE, s. m. (*Belles-Lettr.*) c'est, dans l'ancienne poésie Greque & Latine, un pié ou une mesure de vers composée d'une longue & d'une breve, comme ārmă. On l'appelle plus ordinairement *trochée. Voyez* TROCHÉE. (*G*)

* CHORAGES, s. m. (*Hist. anc.*) partie des théatres anciens : c'en étoit comme le fond des coulisses ; c'est-là qu'on disposoit quelquefois des chœurs de musique, & qu'on gardoit les habits & les instrumens de la scene ; c'est de là que l'on tiroit tout ce qui paroissoit aux yeux : d'où l'on voit que ces endroits devoient être assez spacieux. *V.* THÉATRE.

* CHORAULE, s. m. (*Hist. anc.*) on donnoit ce nom chez les Grecs & chez les Romains, à celui qui présidoit sur les chœurs. Celui qu'on voit dans les antiquités du P. Montfaucon, *tom. III. Planche CXC*. est revêtu d'une tunique, & tient de chaque main une flûte dont le petit bout est appuyé sur sa poitrine.

CHORDAPSUS, s. m. est le nom Latin d'une colique qu'on appelle autrement *volvulus*, passion iliaque, ou colique de *miserere*; quoique d'autres prétendent que c'est une espece particuliere de colique de *miserere*. Voyez MISERERE & ILIAQUE.

Ce mot est ordinairement Grec, χορδαψός, composé de χορδὴ, *boyau*, & ἅπτειν, *nouer*.

Galien la définit une tumeur ou enflûre des intestins gresles, qui les fait paroître pleins & tendus comme une corde. Archigene la distingue du *miserere*, & la fait consister en une tumeur à un certain endroit des intestins gresles, laquelle s'affaisse & cede lorsqu'on la presse avec la main : il ajoute qu'elle est extrèmement dangereuse, & que souvent elle fait mourir le malade en trois ou quatre heures, à moins qu'elle ne vienne à suppuration ; ce qui même ne fait pas encore cesser tout-à-fait le danger. Il est cependant probable que le *chordapsus* n'est rien autre chose que le *miserere*. Celse n'en faisoit pas non plus deux maladies distinctes. *Voyez* COLIQUE DE *MISERERE*.

CHOREGE, s. f. m. c'étoit chez les Grecs le directeur de leurs spectacles ; il en regloit les dépenses, soit que le spectacle se donnât à ses frais, soit qu'il se donnât aux frais du public. Ainsi la fonction du *chorege* d'Athenes étoit la même que celle de notre directeur d'opéra.

CHORÉGRAPHIE, s. f. ou *l'art d'écrire la danse* comme le chant, à l'aide de caracteres & de figures démonstratives : c'est un de ceux que les anciens ont ignorés, ou qui n'a pas été transmis jusqu'à nous. Aucun auteur connu n'en fait mention avant le dictionnaire de Furetiere : il y est parlé d'un traité curieux fait par Thoinet Arbeau, imprimé à Langres en 1588, intitulé *Orchésographie*. Thoinet Arbeau est le premier & peut-être le seul qui ait pensé à transmettre les pas de la danse avec les notes du chant : mais il n'a pas été fort loin. Son idée est la chose qui mérite le plus d'éloge. Il portoit l'air sur des lignes de musique à l'ordinaire, & il écrivoit au-dessus de chaque note les pas qu'il croyoit qu'on devoit exécuter : quant au chemin qu'il convenoit de suivre, & sur lequel ces pas devoient être exécutés successivement, ou il n'en dit rien, ou il l'explique à-peu-près en discours. Il ne lui vint point en pensée d'en faire la figure avec des lignes, de diviser ces lignes par des portions égales correspondantes aux mesures, aux tems, aux notes de chaque tems ; de donner des caracteres distinctifs à chaque mouvement, & de placer ces caracteres sur chaque division correspondante des lignes du chemin, comme on a fait depuis.

L'ordre que nous suivrons dans cet article est donc déterminé par l'exposition même de l'art. Il faut commencer par l'énumération des mouvemens, passer à la connoissance des caracteres qui désignent ces mouvemens, & finir par l'emploi de ces caracteres, relatif au but qu'on se propose, la conservation de la danse.

Dans la danse on se sert de pas, de pliés, d'élevés, de sauts, de cabrioles, de tombés, de glissés, de tournemens de corps, de cadences, de figures, &c.

La position est ce qui marque les différentes situations des piés posés à terre.

Le pas est le mouvement d'un pié d'un lieu à un autre.

Le plié est l'inflexion des genoux.

L'élevé est l'extension des genoux pliés ; ces deux mouvemens doivent toûjours être précédés l'un de l'autre.

Le sauté est l'action de s'élancer en l'air, ensorte que les deux piés quittent la terre : on commence par un plié, on étend ensuite avec vitesse les deux jambes ; ce qui fait élever le corps qui entraîne après lui les jambes.

La cabriole est le battement des jambes que l'on fait en sautant, lorsque le corps est en l'air.

Le tombé est la chûte du corps, forcée par son propre poids.

Le glissé est l'action de mouvoir le pié à terre sans la quitter.

Le tourné est l'action de mouvoir le corps d'un côté ou d'un autre.

La cadence est la connoissance des différentes mesures & des endroits de mouvement le plus marqués dans les airs.

La figure est le chemin que l'on suit en dansant.

La salle ou le théatre est le lieu où l'on danse : il est ordinairement quarré ou parallélogramme, comme on voit en *ABCD*, *figure prem.* de *Chorégraphie*. *AB* est le devant ou le vis-à-vis des spectateurs placés en M; BD, le côté droit; & AC, le côté gauche: CD est le fond du théâtre ou le bas de la salle.

La présence du corps, qui a quatre combinaisons différentes par rapport aux quatre côtés de la salle, est désignée dans la *Chorégraphie* par les caracteres qu'on voit dans la même figure; *a* est le devant du corps, *d* le dos, *c* le bras droit, & *b* le bras gauche. Dans la premiere de ces quatre sortes de présence, le corps est vis-à-vis le haut AB de la salle; dans la seconde, il regarde le bas CD; dans la troisieme, il est tourné du côté droit BD; & dans la quatrieme, il regarde le côté gauche AC.

Le chemin est la ligne qu'on suit: cette ligne peut être droite, courbe, & doit prendre toutes les inflexions imaginables & correspondantes aux différens desseins d'un compositeur de ballet.

Des positions. Il y a dix sortes de positions en usage; on les divise en bonnes & en fausses. Dans les bonnes positions qui sont au nombre de cinq, les deux piés sont placés régulierement, c'est-à-dire que les pointes des piés soient tournées en-dehors.

Les mauvaises se divisent en régulieres & en irrégulieres; elles different des bonnes en ce que les pointes des piés sont ou toutes deux en-dedans; ou que s'il y en a une en-dehors, l'autre est toûjours en-dedans.

Cette figure ' marquera celle du pié.

La partie faite comme un o représente le talon; le commencement de la queue joignant le zéro, la cheville; & son extrémité, la pointe du pié.

Dans la premiere des bonnes positions, les deux piés sont joints ensemble les deux talons l'un contre l'autre. *Voyez la fig. 2. & 3.* A est le pié gauche, B le pié droit; on connoîtra ce pié par le petit crochet *m*, fig. 4. qui est tourné à droite; & l'autre, par un petit crochet semblable *n*, qui est tourné à gauche: c'est la position de l'homme. La position de la femme s'en distinguera par un autre demi-cercle concentrique au premier, comme on le voit *fig. 3.*

Dans la deuxieme, les deux piés sont ouverts sur une même ligne; ensorte que la distance entre les deux talons est de la longueur d'un pié. *Voyez fig. 5.*

Dans la troisieme, le talon d'un pié est contre la cheville de l'autre. *Voyez fig. 6.*

Dans la quatrieme, les deux piés sont l'un devant l'autre, éloignés de la distance du pié entre les deux talons qui sont sur une même ligne. *Voyez fig. 7.*

Dans la cinquieme, les deux piés sont croisés l'un devant l'autre; ensorte que le talon d'un pié est directement vis-à-vis la pointe de l'autre. *Voy. fig. 8.*

Dans la premiere des fausses positions, qui sont de même au nombre de cinq, les deux pointes des piés se touchent, & les talons sont ouverts sur une même ligne. *Voyez fig. 9.*

Dans la seconde, les piés sont ouverts de la distance de lalongueur du pié entre les deux pointes qui sont toutes deux tournées en-dedans, & les deux talons sont ouverts sur une même ligne. *Voy. fig. 10.*

Dans la troisieme, la pointe d'un pié est tournée en-dehors & l'autre en-dedans; ensorte que les deux piés soient paralleles l'un à l'autre. *Voyez fig. 11.*

Dans la quatrieme, les deux pointes des piés sont tournées en-dedans; mais la pointe d'un pié est proche de la cheville de l'autre. *Voyez fig. 12.*

Dans la cinquieme, les deux pointes des piés sont tournées en-dedans; mais le talon d'un pié est vis-à-vis la pointe de l'autre. *Voyez fig. 13.*

Du pas. Quoique le nombre des pas dont on se sert dans la danse soit presque infini, on les réduit néanmoins à cinq, qui peuvent démontrer toutes les différentes figures que la jambe peut faire en marchant; ces cinq pas sont le pas droit, le pas ouvert, le pas rond, le pas tortillé, & le pas battu.

Les traits de la *figure 14.* désigneront le pas; la tête A indiquera où est le pié avant que de marcher; la ligne AB, la grandeur & la figure du pas; & la ligne BC, la position du pié à la fin du pas: on distinguera qu'il s'agit du pié droit ou du pié gauche, selon que la ligne BC sera inclinée à droite ou à gauche de la ligne du chemin.

On connoîtra à la tête A du pas sa durée: si elle est blanche, elle équivaudra à une blanche de l'air sur lequel on danse; si elle est noire, elle équivaudra à une noire du même air; si c'est une croche, la tête ne sera tracée qu'à moitié en forme de *c*.

Dans le pas droit, le pié marche sur une ligne droite: il y en a de deux sortes, l'un en avant, l'autre en arriere. *Voyez fig. 15. & 16.*

Dans le pas ouvert, la jambe s'ouvre: il y en a de trois sortes, l'un en-dehors, l'autre en-dedans en arc de cercle, & le troisieme à côté qu'on peut appeler *pas droit*, parce que sa figure est droite. *Voyez les fig. 17. 18. 19.*

Dans le pas rond, le pié en marchant fait une figure ronde: il y en a de deux sortes, l'un en-dehors, l'autre en-dedans. *Voyez les fig. 20. & 21.*

Dans le pas tortillé, le pié en marchant se tourne en-dedans & en-dehors alternativement: il y en a de trois sortes, l'un en avant, l'autre en arriere, le troisieme à côté. *Voyez les fig. 22. 23. 24.*

Dans le pas battu, la jambe ou le pié vient battre contre l'autre: il y en a de trois sortes, l'un en avant, l'autre en arriere, & le troisieme de côté. *Voyez les fig. 25. 26. 27.*

On pratique en faisant les pas plusieurs agrémens, comme *plié, élevé, sauté, cabriolé, tombé, glissé, avoir le pié en l'air, poser la pointe du pié, poser le talon, tourner un quart de tour, tourner un demi-tour, tourner trois quarts de tour, tourner le tour en entier,* &c.

Le plier se marque sur le pas par petit tiret panché du côté de la tête du pas, comme on voit *fig. 28.*

L'élever se marque sur le pas par un petit tiret perpendiculaire. *Voyez la figure 29.*

Le sauter, par deux tirets perpendiculaires. *Voy. la fig. 30.*

Le cabrioler, par trois. *Voyez la fig. 31.*

Le tomber, par un autre tiret placé au bout du premier, parallele à la direction du pas, & tourné vers la pointe du pié. *Voyez la fig. 32.*

Le glisser, par une petite ligne parallele à la direction du pas, & coupée par le tiret en deux parties, dont l'une va vers la tête & l'autre vers le pié. *fig. 33.*

Dans le pié en l'air, le pas est tranché comme dans la *fig. 34.*

Dans le poser la pointe du pié sans que le corps y soit porté, il y a un point directement au bout de la ligne qui représente le pié comme dans la *fig. 35.*

Dans le poser le talon sans que le corps y soit porté, il y a un point directement derriere, ce qui représente le talon. *Voyez la fig. 36.*

Le tourner un quart de tour, se marque par un quart de cercle. *Voyez la fig. 37.*

Le tourner un demi-tour, par un demi-cercle. *Voyez fig. 38.*

Le tourner trois quarts de tour, par les trois quarts de la circonférence d'un cercle. *Voyez fig. 39.*

Le tourner un tour entier, par un cercle entier. *Voyez fig. 40.*

Lorsqu'il y a plusieurs signes sur un pas, on exécute les mouvemens qu'ils représentent les uns après les autres, dans le même ordre où ils sont placés, à commencer par ceux qui sont les plus près de la tête du pas, qu'il faut considérer divisés en trois parties ou tems. On fait dans le premier tems les mouvemens qui sont marqués sur la premiere partie du pas: dans le second, ceux qui sont placés sur le milieu: & dans le troisieme, ceux qui sont placés à la fin.

fin. Ainsi quand il y a un signe plié au commencement du pas, il signifie qu'il faut *plier* avant de marcher. De même des autres.

Les sauts se peuvent exécuter en deux manieres; ou l'on saute des deux piés à la fois, ou l'on saute en marchant d'un pié seulement. Les sauts qui se font des deux piés à la fois, seront marqués sur les positions, comme il sera démontré dans l'exemple ci-après; au lieu que les sauts qui se font en marchant, se marquent sur les pas.

Le pas sauté se fait de deux manieres; ou l'on saute & retombe sur la jambe qui marche, ou l'on saute & retombe sur l'autre jambe.

S'il y a un signe sauté sur un pas, & point de signe en l'air après, c'est une marque que le saut se fait sur la jambe même qui marche; s'il y a un signe en l'air, c'est une marque que le saut se fait sur l'autre jambe que celle qui marche.

La danse, de même que la musique, est sans agrément si la mesure n'est rigoureusement observée.

Les mesures sont marquées dans la danse par de petites lignes qui coupent le chemin; les intervalles du chemin compris entre ces lignes, sont occupés par les pas, dont la durée se connoît par les têtes blanches, noires, croches, &c. qui montrent que les pas doivent durer autant de tems que les notes de la musique placées au-dessus de la figure de la danse. *Voy. l'exemple*. Ainsi un pas dont la tête est blanche, doit durer autant qu'une blanche de l'air sur lequel on danse; & un pas dont la tête est noire, doit durer autant qu'une noire du même air. Les positions marquent de même par leurs têtes, les tems qu'elles doivent tenir.

Il y a trois sortes de mesures dans la danse; la mesure à deux tems, la mesure à trois tems, & la mesure à quatre tems.

La mesure à deux tems comprend les airs de gavotte, gaillarde, bourrée, rigaudon, gigue, canarie, &c.

La mesure à trois tems comprend les airs de courante, sarabande, passacaille, chacone, menuet, passe-pié, &c.

La mesure à quatre tems comprend les airs lents, comme par exemple l'entrée d'Apollon, de l'opéra du Triomphe de l'amour, & les airs de Loure.

Quand il faudra laisser passer quelques mesures de l'air sans danser, soit au commencement ou au milieu d'une danse, on les marquera par une petite ligne qui coupera le chemin obliquement: il y aura autant de ces petites lignes que de mesures; une demi-mesure sera marquée par une demi-ligne oblique; ainsi le repos marqué *fig. 41*. est de trois mesures & demie. Lorsqu'on aura un plus grand nombre de mesures de repos, comme par exemple dix, on les désignera par des bâtons qui en vaudront chacun quatre. *Voyez la fig. 42*. Les tems, demi-tems & quarts de tems, se marqueront par un soûpir, un demi-soûpir, & un quart de soûpir, comme dans la musique.

Aux airs qui ne commencent pas en frappant, c'est-à-dire où il y a des notes dans la premiere mesure sur lesquelles on ne danse point ordinairement, comme aux airs de gavotte, chacone, gigue, loure, bourrée, &c. on marquera la valeur de ces notes au commencement. *Voyez l'explication de l'exemple ci-après*.

Les figures des danses se divisent naturellement en deux especes, que les maîtres appellent *régulieres* & *irrégulieres*.

Les figures régulieres sont celles où les chemins des deux danseurs font symmétrie ensemble; & les irrégulieres, sont celles où ces mêmes chemins ne font pas de symmétrie.

Il y a encore dans la danse des mouvemens des bras & des mains, ménagés avec art.

Tome III.

Les mains sont marquées par ces caracteres représentés *fig. 43*. le premier est pour la main gauche, & le second pour la main droite; on place celui qui représente la main droite, à droite du chemin, & le second à gauche. On observera, quand on aura donné une main ou les deux, de ne point quitter qu'on ne trouve les mêmes signes tranchés. *Voyez la fig. 44*. *A* représente la femme, *B* l'homme auquel la femme *A* donne la main gauche, qu'il reçoit dans sa droite: ils marchent ensemble tout le chemin *A D B C*, à la fin duquel ils se quittent; ce qui est marqué par les mains qui sont tranchées.

Les différens ports des bras & leurs mouvemens, sont marqués par les signes suivans. *A, B, C, fig. 45*. marque le bras droit; le même signe, *fig. 46*. tourné de l'autre côté, marque le bras gauche. *A* marque l'épaule, *B* le coude, & *C* le poignet. Pour placer les bras sur le chemin, on distinguera les endroits où on va en avant & en arriere, de ceux où l'on va de côté; à ceux où on va en avant & en arriere, on marquera les bras aux deux côtés du chemin, le bras droit du côté droit, & le bras gauche du côté gauche; à ceux où l'on va de côté, on les marquera dessus & dessous, observant toûjours que celui qui est à droite est le bras droit, & celui qui est à gauche est le bras gauche.

Exemples des différentes attitudes des bras.

45 & 46, le bras étendu.
47, le poignet plié.
48, le bras plié.
49, le bras devant soi en hauteur.
50, les deux bras ouverts.
51, le bras gauche ouvert, & le droit plié au coude.
52, le bras gauche ouvert, & le droit tout-à-fait fermé.
53, les deux bras ouverts.
54, le bras gauche ouvert, & le droit fermé du coude.
55, le bras droit ouvert, & le gauche tout-à-fait fermé.

Exemples des mouvemens de bras.

56, mouvement du poignet de bas en-haut.
57, mouvement du coude de bas en-haut.
58, mouvement de l'épaule de bas en-haut.
59, mouvement du poignet de haut en-bas.
60, mouvement du coude de haut en-bas.
61, mouvement de l'épaule de haut en-bas.
62, rond du poignet de bas en-haut.
63, rond du coude de bas en-haut.
64, rond de l'épaule de bas en-haut.
65, rond du poignet de haut en-bas.
66, rond du coude de haut en-bas.
67, rond de l'épaule de haut en-bas.
68, rond du poignet de bas en-haut.
69, rond du coude de bas en-haut.
70, rond de l'épaule de bas en-haut.
71, double mouvement du poignet de bas en-haut, & de haut en-bas.
72, double mouvement du coude.
73, double mouvement de l'épaule.

Les bras peuvent agir tous deux en même tems ou l'un après l'autre. On connoîtra quand les deux bras agissent tous deux en même tems par une liaison allant de l'un à l'autre. *Voy. la fig. 74*. qui marque que les deux bras agissent en même tems, & par mouvement semblable; la *fig. 75*. marque aussi que les deux bras agissent en même tems, mais par mouvement contraire.

Si les deux bras n'ont pas de liaison, c'est une marque qu'ils doivent agir l'un après l'autre. Le premier est celui qui précede: ainsi dans l'exemple *fig. 76.* le bras droit, qui est le plus près de la position, agit le premier.

Explication des cinq premieres mesures du Pas de deux lutteurs, dansé par MM. Dupré & Javiliers dans l'opéra des fêtes Greques & Romaines, représentées dans la derniere Planche de Chorégraphie.

On a observé dans cet exemple la valeur des tems que les pas tiennent; cette valeur est marquée par les têtes des mêmes pas, ainsi qu'il est expliqué ci-dessus: on y a joint la tablature de l'air sur lequel ce pas de deux a été exécuté: on a marqué les mesures par les chiffres 1, 2, 3, *&c.* afin de pouvoir les désigner plus facilement. Celles de la *Chorégraphie* sont de même marquées par des chiffres placés vis-à-vis des lignes qui séparent les mesures; ainsi depuis 0 jusqu'au chiffre 1, c'est la premiere mesure; depuis le chiffre 1 jusqu'au chiffre 2, c'est la seconde; ainsi des autres.

Il faut aussi observer que, dans l'exemple proposé, les chemins des deux danseurs font symmétrie dans plusieurs parties; ainsi ayant expliqué pour un, ce sera dans les parties comme si on l'avoit fait pour tous les deux. Dans les autres parties où les chemins des deux danseurs ne font point symmétrie, & où leurs mouvemens ne font point semblables & coexistans, nous les expliquerons séparément, désignant l'un des danseurs par la lettre *A*, & l'autre par la lettre *B*.

Avant toute chose il faut expliquer par un exemple ce que nous entendons par des *chemins symmétriques*. Soient donc les deux lettres *p p*, elles sont semblables, mais elles ne font point symmétrie; retournons une de ces lettres en cette sorte *q p* ou *p q*, elles feront symmétrie: ainsi la symmétrie est une ressemblance de figure & une dissemblance de position. B Σ Γ est semblable à B Σ Γ, mais symmétrique avec Γ Σ B; il suffit de les mettre vis-à-vis l'un de l'autre B Σ Γ Γ Σ B pour s'en appercevoir. Enfin, si on souhaite un autre exemple, la contre-épreuve d'une estampe, ou la planche qui a servi à l'imprimer, font symmétrie ensemble; ainsi que la forme de caracteres qui a servi à imprimer cette feuille, faisoit symmétrie avec la feuille que le lecteur a présentement sous les yeux. Ceci bien entendu, il est facile de comprendre que si le danseur *A*, *Planc. II. fig. prem.* placé vis-à-vis de celui qui est en *B*, part du pié gauche, ce dernier doit partir du pié droit: c'est en effet ce que l'on observe dans cet exemple. Ainsi comme nous n'expliquerons pour les parties symmétriques que la tablature du danseur *A*, il faudra pour avoir celle du danseur *B* changer les mots *droit* en *gauche* & *gauche* en *droit*.

Les deux danseurs commencent par la quatrieme position; le danseur *A* fait du pié gauche un pas droit en avant: ce pas doit durer une noire ou quart de mesure; il est suivi d'un semblable pas fait par le pié droit, qui vaut aussi une noire, comme on le connoît par sa tête qui est noire; le troisieme pas est du pié gauche, & dure seulement une croche, ainsi qu'on le connoît par sa tête crochue: il est chargé de deux signes, le plié au commencement du pas, & l'élevé à la fin; le quatrieme qui est du pié droit, vaut aussi une croche, & le suivant une noire: ce qui fait en tout quatre noires, & épuise la premiere mesure de l'air à deux tems notés au-dessus. Tous les pas de cette mesure sont des pas droits en avant.

La seconde mesure 1, 2, est occupée dans l'air par les notes *re fa* ✶ *sol*; la premiere est une blanche pointée, & les deux dernieres des croches; & dans la danse elle est occupée par des positions & des pas. La premiere position où on arrive à la fin de la premiere mesure, est la troisieme; elle est affectée des signes plié & cabriolé, & de celui de tourner un quart de tour, ce qui met la présence du corps vis-à-vis le haut de la salle de cette position qui vaut une noire: on retombe à la quatrieme, le pié droit en l'air; ce pié fait ensuite un pas ouvert de côté qui dure aussi une noire: le pas suivant qui est du pié gauche, dure une croche; il est affecté du signe plié au commencement, & du signe en l'air, suivi de celui de tourner un quart de tour à gauche, qui remet la présence du corps comme elle étoit au commencement; & ensuite du sauté, à la fin duquel on retombe à la quatrieme position, le pié droit en l'air, qui fait un pas ouvert de côté, lequel n'est point compté dans la mesure, parce que sa tête se confond avec celle de la position, & qu'il n'est qu'une suite du sauté. Le pié restant en l'air ainsi, le corps est porté sur l'autre jambe: elle ne pourra marcher que le premier ne soit posé à terre en tout ou en partie, c'est-à-dire seulement sur le talon ou la pointe du pié; dans la *figure*, c'est la pointe du pié qui porte à terre. Le pié gauche fait un pas droit en avant, lequel vaut une croche; il est suivi du signe de repos ou quart de soûpir, qui avec les pas que nous avons expliqués, acheve de remplir la mesure.

La mesure suivante 2, 3, est remplie par trois pas qui valent chacun une noire. Le premier qui est du pié droit, a le signe en l'air au commencement; il est suivi de la premiere position affectée du signe plié & sauté sur le pié gauche, pour marquer que le saut se fait sur cette jambe, l'autre étant en l'air; ensuite est un soûpir qui vaut une noire de repos, après lequel est un pas ouvert de côté fait par le pié gauche: ce pas est chargé de deux signes qui marquent, le premier qu'il faut plier au commencement du pas, & le second qu'il faut élever à la fin. Le pas suivant qui est du pié droit, est un pas droit du même sens, qui ramene la jambe droite près de la gauche.

Il faut remarquer qu'après le soûpir de cette mesure, les chemins des danseurs cessent de faire symmétrie; car l'un s'avance vers le haut de la salle, & l'autre s'en éloigne: cette diversité de mouvement continue jusqu'au troisieme tems de la mesure suivante.

Le premier pas de la mesure 3, 4, est un pas ouvert de côté du pié droit, avec les signes plié & élevé, le premier au commencement du pas, & le second à la fin; il est suivi d'un pas ouvert de côté fait par le pié gauche, à la fin duquel le pié reste en l'air pendant un quart de mesure. Le pas suivant qui est un pas ouvert de côté, est affecté du signe de tourner un quart de tour: on voit auprès de ce pas la main droite que le danseur *A* donne à la main gauche de l'autre danseur, faisant l'effort simulé que deux lutteurs font pour renverser leur adversaire.

Au commencement de la mesure suivante, les danseurs sont revenus à la premiere position, où ils restent pendant une demi-mesure; ce que l'on connoît par la tête noire de la position, & le soûpir qui la suit. Le premier pas suivant est un pas ouvert en-dedans, qui dure une noire: on voit au commencement de ce pas le signe en l'air, suivi de celui de tourner un quart de tour; ce qui fait connoître que ce pas doit être fait sans que le pié pose à terre: il est fait par le pié droit, qui revient se placer à la position. Le pas suivant est encore affecté du signe de tourner un quart de tour, ce qui remet les danseurs vis-à-vis l'un de l'autre: on y trouve aussi le signe des mains tranché, ce qui fait connoître qu'à la fin de ce pas les danseurs doivent se quitter.

Ce que nous avons dit jusqu'à présent, suffit pour entendre comment on déchiffre les danses écrites. Nous laissons au lecteur muni des principes établis ci-devant, les cinq dernieres mesures de l'exemple pour s'exercer, en l'avertissant cependant d'une chose essentielle à savoir, c'est que lorsque l'on trouve plusieurs positions de suite, comme dans la mesure 7, 8, les mouvemens que les positions représentent se font tous en la même place ; il n'y a que les pas qui transportent le corps du danseur d'un lieu en un autre, & que la durée de la somme de ces mouvemens qui doit être renfermée dans celle du pas précédent.

Si la tête d'une position est noire, ou si elle est blanche, & qu'il sorte de sa tête un pas, alors on compte le tems qu'elle marque. Il y a un exemple de l'un & de l'autre dans la mesure 7, 8 : le reste est sans difficulté.

Un manuscrit du sieur Favier m'étant tombé entre les mains, j'ai cru faire plaisir au public de lui expliquer le système de cet auteur, d'autant plus que son livre ne sera probablement jamais imprimé. Mais avant toutes choses, je vais rapporter son jugement sur les méthodes de *Chorégraphie*, sur lesquelles il prétend que la sienne doit prévaloir : ce que nous discuterons dans la suite.

« Les uns, dit-il, prétendent écrire la danse en se
» servant des lettres de l'alphabet, ayant réduit, à
» ce qu'ils disent, tous les pas qui se peuvent faire
» au nombre de vingt-quatre, qui est le même que
» celui des lettres : d'autres ont ajouté des chiffres à
» cette invention littérale, & donnent pour marque à
» chaque pas la premiere lettre du nom qu'il porte,
» comme à celui de bourrée un *B*, à celui de me-
» nuet un *M*, à celui de gaillarde un *G*, &c. Ces
» deux manieres sont à la vérité très-frivoles ; mais
» il y en a une troisieme (celle du sieur Feuillet que
» nous avons suivie ci-devant en y faisant quelques
» améliorations) qui paroît avoir plus de solidité :
» elle se fait par des lignes qui montrent la figure ou
» le chemin que suit celui qui danse, sur lesquelles
» lignes on ajoûte tout ce que les deux piés peu-
» vent figurer, &c. mais quelque succès qu'elle puis-
» se avoir, je ne laisserai pas de proposer ce que j'ai
» trouvé sur le même sujet, & peut-être que mon
» travail sera aussi favorablement reçû que le sien,
» sans pourtant rien diminuer de la gloire que ce fa-
» meux génie s'est acquise par les belles choses qu'il
» nous a données ».

Cet auteur représente la salle où l'on danse par des divisions faites sur les cinq lignes d'une portée de musique (*Voyez la fig. 3.*) les côtés portent le même nom que dans la *fig. 1. Pl. I. de Chorégr.* qui représente le théatre ; chaque séparation de ces cinq portées représente la salle, quelque largeur qu'elle ait : c'est dans ces salles que l'on place les caracteres qui représentent tout ce que l'on peut faire dans la danse, soit du corps, des genoux, ou des piés.

Le caractere de présence du corps est le même dans les deux *Chorégraphies* (*Voyez la fig. 4.*) ; mais celle-ci marque sur les présences du corps le côté où il doit tourner : ainsi la *fig. 5.* fait voir que le corps doit tourner du côté droit, & la suivante qu'il doit tourner du côté gauche. Par ces deux sortes de mouvement le corps ayant divers aspects, c'est-à-dire étant tourné vers les différens côtés de la salle, on peut les marquer par les *fig. 4. 7. 8. 9.* la premiere (4.) représente le corps tourné du côté des spectateurs, ou vers le haut de la salle ; la seconde (7) représente le corps tourné ensorte que le côté gauche est vers les spectateurs ; la troisieme (8), que le dos est tourné vers les spectateurs ; & la quatrieme (9), que le côté droit les regarde. Mais comme la salle a quatre angles, & que le corps peut être tourné vers les quatre coins, on en marque la position en cette maniere (*Voyez la fig. 10.*) ; le coin 1 à gauche des spectateurs s'appelle le *premier coin* ; les second, troisieme, quatrieme, sont où l'on a placé les nombres 2, 3, 4.

Tome III.

Outre ces huit aspects, on en peut encore imaginer huit autres entre ceux-ci, comme la *fig. 11.* le fait voir.

Ces seize aspects sont les principales marques dont on se sert ; elles se rapportent toutes au corps : mais comme il faut marquer tous les mouvemens que l'on peut faire dans une entrée de ballet composée de plusieurs danseurs, soit qu'elle fût de belle danse ou de posture, comme sont les entrées de gladiateurs, de devins, d'arlequin, soit que les mouvemens soient semblables ou différens, soit que quelques-uns des danseurs demeurent en une même place pendant que les autres avancent ; ces différens états seront marqués par les caracteres suivans : la *fig. 4.* représente le corps droit & debout ; la *fig. 12.* le corps panché en avant comme dans la révérence à la maniere de l'homme, ce que l'on connoît par la ligne qui représente le devant du corps qui est concave ; la suivante (*13.*) représente le corps panché du côté droit, ce que l'on connoît par la ligne de ce côté qui est concave ; la *fig. 14.* fait voir que le corps panche en arriere, ce que l'on connoît par la ligne du dos qui est concave ; enfin la *fig. 15.* fait voir que le corps panche du côté gauche.

L'idée de marquer les tems des pas par la forme ou couleur de leur tête étoit venue à cet auteur ; mais elle nous avoit été communiquée par M. Dupré, & nous l'avons introduite dans la *Chorégraphie* du sieur Feuillet où elle manque : la différence principale de ces deux manieres, est que dans celle-ci on marque la valeur des pas sur les caracteres des présences. *Voyez la fig. 16.* qui fait voir les différentes formes du caractere de présence, & leur valeur au-dessus marquée par des notes de musique.

Ces marques à la vérité seroient d'une grande utilité ; mais cependant l'auteur ne conseille pas de s'en servir qu'on ne soit très-habile dans la *Chorégraphie* & la Musique.

La *fig. 17.* qui est une ligne inclinée de gauche à droite, marque qu'il faut plier les genoux.

La *fig. 18.* marque au contraire qu'il faut les élever.

La ligne horisontale (*fig. 19.*) marque qu'il faut marcher.

La *fig. 20.* qui est une ligne courbe convexe en-dessus, marque qu'il faut marcher en avançant d'abord le pié dans le commencement du pas, & continuer en ligne courbe jusqu'à la fin de son action.

La *fig. 21.* qui est la même ligne courbe convexe en-dessous, marque qu'il faut marcher en reculant d'abord le pié dans le commencement du pas, & continuer en ligne courbe jusqu'à la fin de son action.

La *fig. 22.* marque le mouvement qu'on appelle *tour de jambe en-dehors*.

La *fig. 23.* marque le mouvement qu'on appelle *tour de jambe en-dedans*.

La *fig. 24.* qui est une ligne ponctuée en cette sorte . . . . marque que le pié fait quelque mouvement, sans sortir cependant du lieu qu'il occupe.

La *fig. 25.* qui est un *d*, indique le pié droit.

La suivante (*26.*), qui est un *g*, indique le pié gauche.

Ces deux mêmes lettres (*fig. 27.*) dont la queue est un peu courbe, signifient qu'il faut poser la pointe des piés, & laisser ensuite tomber le talon à terre.

Les deux mêmes lettres *d g* (*fig. 28.*), dont la queue est ponctuée, signifient qu'il faut poser les piés sur la pointe sans appuyer le talon.

Les deux mêmes lettres (*fig. 29.*), dont la queue est séparée de la tête, signifient qu'il faut poser le talon, & appuyer ensuite la pointe du pié à terre.

Les deux mêmes lettres (*fig. 30.*), dont la queue est discontinuée dans le milieu, marquent qu'il faut poser les piés sur le talon, sans appuyer la pointe à terre.

Les deux mêmes lettres (*fig. 31.*), dont les queues font droites comme celles du *d* & du *q*, marquent qu'il faut poser le talon & la pointe du pié en même tems, ce qu'on appelle *poser à plat*.

Après les marques qui font voir toutes les différentes manieres de poser les piés à terre, nous allons exposer celles qui les représentent en l'air.

La *fig. 32.* signifie que les piés sont en l'air, ce que l'on connoît par leur queue qui est recourbée du côté de la tête.

Les deux mêmes lettres (*fig. 33.*) dont la queue est discontinuée dans le milieu & recourbée vers la tête, marquent que les piés sont en l'air la pointe haute.

Ces deux mêmes lettres (*fig. 34.*), dont la queue est discontinuée & recourbée vers la tête comme dans les précédentes, & la partie de la queue depuis la tête jusqu'à la rupture élevée perpendiculairement comme à la *fig. 31.* marquent que la pointe & le talon sont également éloignés de terre.

Dans tout ce que nous venons de dire on doit entendre que les piés sont tournés en-dehors, comme dans les cinq bonnes positions expliquées ci-devant. Il faut présentement expliquer les marques qui font connoître qu'ils sont tournés en-dedans, comme dans les cinq fausses positions. C'est encore les deux mêmes lettres *g d* (*fig. 35.*), mais retournées en cette sorte *8 p*.

On peut donner à ces deux dernieres lettres toutes les variétés que nous avons montrées ci-devant, & faire autant de situations des piés en-dedans comme nous en avons fait voir en-dehors, soit à terre, soit en l'air. L'exemple suivant (*fig. 36.*) fait voir que les piés sont tournés en-dedans & en l'air, ce qu'on connoît par le *d* & le *g* retournés, & par leurs queues qui regardent la tête de ces lettres.

Ces différentes sortes de positions des piés étant quelquefois de distances que l'auteur appelle *naturelles*, c'est-à-dire éloignés l'un de l'autre de la distance d'un des piés, ou ensemble, comme lorsqu'ils se touchent, ou écartés, lorsque la distance d'un pié à l'autre est plus grande que celle d'un pié. Il marque la premiere par les lettres *d g* jointes au caractere de présence, sans y rien ajoûter (*V.* la figure *37.*): pour la seconde il met un point, ensorte que la lettre du pié soit entre le caractere de présence & le point (*Voyez la fig. 38.*): & pour la troisieme, une petite ligne verticale placée entre le caractere du pié & celui de présence. *Voyez la fig. 39.*

La *fig. 40.* qui est un *o*, indique qu'il faut pirouetter.

Le saut se connoît lorsque la ligne *élevé* placée sur la ligne *marché*, est plus grande que la ligne *plié* placée sur la même ligne *marché* : on connoît aussi à quelle partie du pas les agrémens doivent être faits, par le lieu que les signes de ces agrémens occupent sur la ligne *marché* : si ces signes sont au commencement de la ligne *marché*, c'est au commencement du pas ; s'ils sont au milieu, ce sera au milieu du pas qu'on doit les exécuter ; ou si ils sont à la fin de la ligne, ce ne doit être qu'à la fin du pas qu'on doit les exécuter.

« Voilà tous les différens caracteres avec lesquels on peut décrire les mouvemens, actions, positions, que l'on peut faire dans la danse : il ne reste plus qu'à les assembler ; mais c'est ce qui se fait en tant de manieres, que si je puis y réussir, comme je l'espere, j'aurai lieu d'être satisfait de mes réflexions, dit l'auteur ».

Nous allons voir comment l'auteur y réussit.

Ces deux lignes ——— indiquent que le pié droit commence & acheve son mouvement, & que le pié gauche commence & finit le sien après ; ce qui est marqué par la ligne de dessus qui est pour le pié droit, laquelle précede l'autre selon notre maniere d'écrire de gauche à droite : la ligne de dessous est pour le pié gauche ; elle n'est tracée qu'après l'autre ; ce qui fait connoître que le pié qu'elle représente ne doit marcher qu'après que l'autre a fini son mouvement.

Ces deux autres lignes ——— font connoître que le pié gauche commence & finit son mouvement, & que le pié droit commence & acheve le sien après.

Ces deux autres lignes ——— indiquent que le pié droit commence son mouvement, & que dans le milieu de celui-ci le pié gauche commence le sien, qu'ils continuent ensemble, que le pié droit finit le premier, & que le pié gauche acheve après.

Ces deux lignes ——— font connoître que le pié droit & le pié gauche commencent ensemble, & que le pié droit finit son mouvement après celui du pié gauche.

Ces deux autres lignes ——— font connoître que le pié droit commence le premier son mouvement, & que le pié gauche commence après, qu'ils continuent ensemble, & finissent en même tems.

Ces deux autres lignes ——— font connoître que le pié droit & le pié gauche commencent & finissent leurs mouvemens ensemble.

Ainsi de toutes les combinaisons possibles deux à deux des lignes représentées *fig. 19. 20. 21. 22. 23. 24.* dont il seroit trop long de faire l'énumération.

Les *fig. 37. 38. 39.* ont déjà fait connoître trois situations ; les trois suivantes en représentent encore d'autres : ainsi par la *fig. 40.* on verra le pié droit devant le corps, & le pié gauche derriere.

Par la *fig. 41.* on verra le pié droit devant & de côté, & par conséquent le pié gauche derriere & de côté.

Par la *fig. 42.* on verra la situation qu'on appelle *croisée*, le pié droit devant la partie gauche du corps, & le pié gauche derriere la partie droite ; & *vice versa* de toutes les combinaisons dont ces arrangemens sont susceptibles.

Ces trois derniers exemples qui montrent les situations ou positions naturelles, peuvent encore être ensemble ou écartés, en y ajoûtant le point ou la petite ligne.

Toutes ces situations pourront être un pié en l'air, en donnant à la lettre qui représente ce pié la marque de cette circonstance qui a été ci-devant expliquée. Nous allons passer aux exemples de l'emploi de la ligne *marché*.

La *fig. 43.* représente la situation ou position qui est le pié gauche à terre devant, & le pié droit en l'air derriere. On connoîtra la position en ce qu'elle sera toûjours la premiere de chaque danse, & qu'il n'y aura point au-dessous de ligne *marché* ; les différentes positions des piés qui pourroient y être étant assez démontrées précédemment pour les connoître. Cette position tient dans la danse lieu de clé, dont l'usage en Musique est de faire connoître le ton & le mode de chaque air, & le premier son par lequel il commence ; de même celle-ci montre le lieu de la salle où la danse doit commencer, en se la représentant toûjours comme renfermée dans les rectangles formés par les lignes verticales, & les portées de musique sur lesquelles on écrit la danse.

De cette situation on passera à la seconde (*figure 44.*), où on remarquera qu'il faut marcher ce qui est marqué par la ligne qui représente ce mouvement, laquelle est décrite au-dessous de la figure qui représente la salle. Mais comme cette ligne *marché* suppose que l'un des deux piés doit faire un mouvement, on connoîtra que c'est le pié droit, puisque la lettre *d* est seule dans la salle, & est au côté droit du corps. Mais comme cette lettre est décrite la queue retournée à la tête, le pié droit se portera en l'air, & cette situation de pié finira cette premiere action, & servira de position pour passer à la suivante.

La *fig.* 45. représente qu'il faut marcher le pié droit à terre de côté : après ce mouvement on sortira de terre le pié gauche, qui doit rester en l'air au-dessus de l'endroit où il étoit posé. On ne marque rien pour cette action du pié gauche, parce qu'elle est nécessaire pour achever le pas. Lorsque les mouvemens qui se suivent se font par des piés différens, la fin de cette action est une situation naturelle ; celle des piés ensemble ou écartés, sera marquée par un caractere particulier.

La figure suivante (46.) représente qu'il faut marcher le pié gauche croisé devant sortant de terre, le pié droit joignant au derriere du talon du pié gauche. Cette situation ensemble étant marquée par un point qui est au derriere du corps, ce point se place à côté du corps si on finit cette action les piés ensemble de côté.

La *fig.* 47. représente qu'il faut marcher le pié droit à terre de côté, & que le pié gauche sortira de terre & se portera écarté en l'air au côté gauche du corps : cette derniere circonstance est marquée par la lettre *g* séparée du corps par une petite ligne verticale, qui signifie, ainsi qu'il a été dit, que le pié est éloigné du corps.

La *fig.* 48. que l'on ne regardera que comme l'explication de la 47. représentera par conséquent la même chose ; elle indiquera de plus par les deux lignes qui y sont décrites, que le pié droit marchera le premier, & que le pié gauche marchera ensuite ; la ligne de dessous, ainsi qu'il a été dit, étant pour celui-ci, & étant postérieure par rapport à celle de l'autre pié.

Après avoir donné ces exemples pour la ligne *marché* sur laquelle on place les signes des agrémens, comme plié, élevé, sauté, cabriolé, *&c.* il est bon d'examiner ces mêmes marques, pour connoître toutes les places que le corps peut occuper sur la ligne de front.

Par la *fig.* 43. on verra que le corps est posé au milieu du côté gauche de la salle ; c'est la position dans laquelle la *figure* 43. le représente au même lieu, puisque l'action qui y est marquée n'oblige point le corps à faire aucun changement ; le pié en l'air qui est derriere la position le porte en l'air de côté à la *fig.* 44. laissant toûjours le poids du corps sur le pié gauche : les *fig.* 44. 45. 46. 47. le représentent un peu éloigné de ce pié ; ce qui se peut encore en autant d'autres places que l'on jugera à propos, selon le nombre de pas qui peuvent être faits en la largeur d'une salle ; les situations sur la longueur sont marquées par les lignes des portées & les intervalles des mêmes lignes.

En donnant à toutes les places les seize aspects dont il est parlé ci-dessus, & qui sont représentés *fig.* 11. il est certain qu'il n'y a pas un seul endroit d'une salle où l'on ne puisse marquer telle position des piés & situation du corps que l'on voudra ; ce qui est tout ce que l'on se propose de faire quand on veut écrire une danse sur le papier.

On écrit aussi dans ce nouveau systême l'air au-dessus de la danse, & le tout sur du papier de musique ordinaire, ensorte qu'au premier coup d'œil une danse écrite en cette maniere paroît un *duo* ou un *trio*, *&c.* si deux ou plusieurs danseurs dansent ensemble.

Nous avons promis de comparer ensemble ces deux manieres, nous tenons parole : nous croyons, quoique l'invention de cet auteur soit ingénieuse, que l'on doit cependant s'en tenir à celle du sieur Feuillet, où la figure des chemins est représentée, sur-tout depuis que nous y avons fait le changement communiqué par M. Dupré, au moyen duquel on connoît la valeur des pas par la couleur de leur tête, ainsi qu'il a été expliqué dans la premiere partie de cet article. L'inconvénient de ne point marquer les chemins est bien plus important, que celui qui résulte de ne point écrire la musique sur les lignes & dans les intervalles, comme quelques auteurs l'avoient proposé. *Voyez l'article* MUSIQUE, où ces choses sont discutées. (*D*)

CHOREN, (*Géog.*) petite ville d'Allemagne dans la Misnie, proche d'Astembourg.

* CHORÉVÊQUES, sub. m. (*Théol.*) celui qui exerçoit quelques fonctions épiscopales dans les bourgades & les villages. On l'appelloit le *vicaire de l'évêque*. Il n'est pas question dans l'église de cette fonction avant le iv. siecle. Le concile d'Antioche tenu en 340 marque ses limites. Armentarius fut réduit à la qualité de *chorévêque* en 439 par le concile de Riez, le 1er de ceux d'Occident où il soit parlé de cette dignité. Le pape Léon III. l'eût abolie, s'il n'en eût été empêché par le concile de Ratisbonne. Le *chorévêque*, au-dessus des autres prêtres, gouvernoit sous l'évêque dans les villages. Il n'étoit point ordonné évêque ; il avoit rang dans les conciles après les évêques en exercice, & parmi les évêques qui n'exerçoient pas ; il ordonnoit seul des clercs mineurs & des soûdiacres, & des diacres & des prêtres sous l'évêque. Ceux d'Occident porterent l'extension de leurs priviléges presqu'à toutes les fonctions épiscopales ; mais cette entreprise ne fut pas tolérée. Les *chorévêques* cesserent presque entierement au x. siecle, tant en Orient qu'en Occident, où il paroît qu'ils ont eu pour successeurs les archiprêtres & les doyens ruraux. *Voyez* ARCHIPRÊTRES *&* DOYENS. Il y a cependant des dignitaires encore plus voisins des anciens *chorévêques* ; ce sont les grands-vicaires, tels que celui de Pontoise, auxquels les évêques ou archevêques ont confié les fonctions épiscopales sur une portion d'un diocese trop étendu pour être administré par un seul supérieur. Le premier des soûdiacres de S. Martin d'Utrecht, & le premier chantre des collégiales de Cologne, ont titre de *chorévêque*, & fonction de doyens ruraux. L'église de Treves a aussi des *chorévêques*. Ce nom vient de χορος, *lieu*, & de επισκοπος, *évêque*, évêque d'un lieu particulier. *Voy.* EVÊQUE, ARCHEVÊQUE, *&c.*

CHORGES, (*Géog.*) petite ville de France en Dauphiné. *Long.* 24. *lat.* 44. 35.

CHORGO, (*Géog.*) petite ville de la basse Hongrie, près d'Albe royale.

CHORIAMBE, s. m. (*Belles-Lett.*) dans l'ancienne Poésie, pié ou mesure de vers composée d'un chorée ou trochée & d'un iambe, c'est-à-dire de deux breves entre deux longues, comme *hĭstŏrĭās*. (*G*)

CHORION, s. m. (*Anat.*) est la membrane extérieure qui enveloppe le fœtus dans la matrice. *Voyez* FŒTUS. Ce mot vient du Grec χοριον, *contenir*.

Elle est épaisse & forte, polie en-dedans, par où elle s'unit à une autre membrane appellée *amnios*, mais rude & inégale en-dehors, parsemée d'un grand nombre de vaisseaux, & attachée à la matrice par le moyen du *placenta* qui y est fort adhérent. *Voyez* AMNIOS, PLACENTA.

Cette membrane se trouve dans tous les animaux.

Le *chorion*, avec l'*amnios* & le *placenta*, forme ce qu'on appelle les *secondines* ou l'*arriere-faix*. *Voyez* SECONDINES. (*L*)

CHORISTE, s. m. chanteur qui chante dans les chœurs de l'opéra ou dans ceux des motets au concert spirituel, & dans les églises. *Voyez* CHANTEUR *&* CHANTRE ; *voyez aussi* CHŒUR. (*B*)

Bibliography

Choreographic sources cited

The following does not provide a complete list of sources for Baroque dance, but merely mentions those choreographic sources to which reference is made in this book. For a fuller list of the dance manuals important for an understanding of French Baroque dance, see the bibliography in Hilton, *Dance of Court and Theater*; for a full list of the choreographies in Feuillet notation, see Little and Marsh, *La Danse Noble*; for primary source writings about French dance, see Schwartz and Schlundt, *French Court Dance and Dance Music*.

Arbeau, Thoinot. *Orchesographie*. Lengres, 1589; trans. Mary Stewart Evans, reprinted with a new introduction and notes by Julia Sutton. New York: Dover, 1967.

Behr, Samuel Rudolph. *Anderer Theil der Tantz-Kunst*. Leipzig, 1703.

Caroso, Fabritio. *Il ballarino*. Venice, 1581; reprint New York: Broude Bros., 1967.

Nobiltà di dame. Venice, 1600; trans. Julia Sutton. Oxford University Press, 1986.

Feuillet, Raoul Auger. *Chorégraphie, ou l'art de décrire la dance*. Published with *Recueil de dances, composées par M. Feuillet* and *Recüeil de dances, composées par M. Pecour*. Paris, 1700; reprint New York: Broude Bros., 1968.

Recueil de contredanses. Paris, 1706; reprint New York: Broude Bros., 1968.

"Traité de la cadence" in *Recüeil de dances, contenant un tres grand nombres, des meillieures entrées de ballet de M^r. Pecour*. Paris, 1704; trans. John Weaver as *A Small Treatise of Time and Cadence in Dancing*. London, 1706.

Gaudrau, Michel. *Nouveau recüeil de dance de bal et celle de ballet . . . de la composition de M^r. Pecour*. Paris, [1713].

[Goussier, Louis-Jacques.] "Chorégraphie." *Encyclopédie ou dictionnaire raisonné des sciences, des arts et des métiers*. Ed. Diderot and d'Alembert. Vol. 3. Paris, 1753; plates published in vol. 3 of the plates, Paris, 1762.

Lambranzi, Gregorio. *Neue und curieuse theatralische Tantz-Schul*. Nuremberg, 1716; reprint Leipzig: Peters, 1975 and New York: Dance Horizons, 1972; trans. F. Derra de Moroda as *New and Curious School of Theatrical Dancing*. London: Imperial Society of Teachers of Dancing, 1928; reprint New York: Dance Horizons, 1966.

Lorin, André. *Livre de contredance présenté au Roy* [c. 1685], F-Pn (Manuscrits) Ms. fr. 1697; and *Livre de la contredance du Roy* (1688), F-Pn (Manuscrits) Ms. fr. 1698.

Negri, Cesare. *Le gratie d'amore*. Milan, 1602; reprint New York: Broude Bros., 1969.

[Pasch, Johannes.] *Maître de Danse, oder Tantz-Meister*. [Glückstadt & Leipzig, 1705.]

Pemberton, E[dmund]. *An Essay for the Further Improvement of Dancing*. London, 1711; reprint Farnborough: Gregg International, 1970.

Rameau, Pierre. *Abrégé de la nouvelle méthode dans l'art d'écrire toutes sortes de danses de ville*. Paris, [1725]; reprint Farnborough: Gregg International, 1972.

Le maître à danser. Paris, 1725; reprint New York: Broude Bros., 1967; trans. Cyril W. Beaumont as *The Dancing Master*. London, 1931; reprint New York: Dance Horizons, 1970.

Siris, P. *The Art of Dancing*. London, 1706.

Taubert, Gottfried. *Rechtschaffener Tantzmeister*. Leipzig, 1717; reprint Munich: Heimeran Verlag, 1976.

Tomlinson, Kellom. *A Work Book by Kellom Tomlinson: Commonplace Book of an Eighteenth-*

Century English Dancing Master, A Facsimile Edition. Ed. J. Shennan. Dance & Music No. 6. Stuyvesant, NY: Pendragon Press, 1992.

The Art of Dancing. London, 1735; reprint Farnborough: Gregg International, 1970.

Weaver, John. *A Small Treatise of Time and Cadence in Dancing*. London, 1706; reprinted with Weaver, *Orchesography*, Farnborough: Gregg International, 1971.

Orchesography or the Art of Dancing. London, 1706; reprint Farnborough: Gregg International, 1971.

Books and articles

The following list includes published books and articles consulted in the course of this study. Manuscript documents are cited in footnotes to the relevant chapters.

Anthony, James R. *French Baroque Music from Beaujoyeulx to Rameau*. 2nd edn. New York: W. W. Norton & Co., 1978.

"Lully's airs—French or Italian?" *The Musical Times* 128 (March, 1987), 126–9.

"The musical structure of Lully's operatic airs." Jean-Baptiste Lully: *Actes du Colloque/Kongreßbericht, Saint-Germain-en-Laye–Heidelberg 1987*. Ed. Jérôme de La Gorce and Herbert Schneider. Laaber: Laaber Verlag, 1990, 65–76.

Astier, Régine. "Pierre Beauchamps and the ballets de collège." *Dance Chronicle* 6 (1983), 138–63.

"La vie quotidienne." *Les goûts réunis*, numéro spécial: La danse baroque (1982), 30–9.

"When fiddlers danced to their own tunes." *The Marriage of Music and Dance*, papers from a conference held at The Guildhall School of Music and Drama, 9–11 August 1991. London: National Early Music Association, 1992.

For other works by this author, see also Kunzle, Régine.

Baines, Anthony. "James Talbot's manuscript, I. Wind instruments." *Galpin Society Journal* 1 (1948), 9–26.

Woodwind Instruments and their History. 3rd edn. London: Faber and Faber, 1967.

Banducci, Antonia. "Staging a *tragédie lyrique*: a 1748 promptbook of Campra's *Tancrède*." *Early Music* 21 (1993), 180–90.

Barnett, Dene. *The Art of Gesture: The Practices and Principles of Eighteenth-Century Acting*. Heidelberg: C. Winter, 1987.

"The performance practice of acting." *Theatre Research International* 2/3 (May, 1977), 157–86; 3/1 (October, 1977), 1–19; 3/2 (February, 1978), 79–93; 5/1 (Winter, 1979–80), 1–36; 6/1 (Winter 1980–81), 1–32.

Bate, Philip. *The Oboe*. London: Ernest Benn Limited and New York: W. W. Norton, 1975.

"Oboe." *New Grove Dictionary of Music and Musicians*. London: Macmillan, 1980.

Benoit, Marcelle. *Musiques de cour: chapelle, chambre, écurie, 1661–1733*. Paris: Editions A. & J. Picard, 1971.

Versailles et les musiciens du roi, 1661–1733. Paris: Editions A. & J. Picard, 1971.

Bowers, Jane. "The Hotteterre family of woodwind instrument makers." *Concerning the Flute*. Ed. Rien de Reede. Amsterdam: Broekmans & Van Poppel B. V., 1984, 33–54.

"New light on the development of the transverse flute between 1650 and about 1770." *Journal of the American Musical Instrument Society* 3 (1977), 5–56.

Brenner, Clarence D. *A Bibliographical List of Plays in the French Language 1700–1789*. Berkeley: [no publisher], 1947; reprinted, with an index of composers by Michael A. Keller and Neal Zaslaw. New York: AMS Press, 1979.

Brossard, Yolande de. *Musiciens de Paris, 1535–1792: Actes d'état civil d'après le Fichier Laborde de la Bibliothèque Nationale*. Paris: Editions A. & J. Picard, 1965.

Christout, Marie-Françoise. *Le ballet de cour de Louis XIV: 1643–1672*. Paris: Editions A. & J. Picard, 1967.

Cobau, Judith. "The preferred *pas de menuet*." *Dance Research Journal* 16 (1984), 13–17.

Coeyman, Barbara. "Theaters for opera and ballet during the reigns of Louis XIV and Louis XV." *Early Music* 18 (1990), 22–37.

"The stage works of Michel-Richard Delalande in the musical-cultural context of the French court, 1680–1726." Unpublished Ph.D. dissertation, City University of New York, 1987.

Danchin, Pierre. "The foundation of the Royal Academy of Music in 1674 and Pierre Perrin's *Ariane*." *Theatre Survey* 25 (1984), 55–67.

[Dangeau, Philippe de Courcillon de.] *Journal du Marquis de Dangeau avec les additions inédites du Duc de Saint-Simon*. Ed. E. Soulié et al. 19 vols. Paris: Firmin Didot, 1854.

Derra de Moroda, Friderica. "Chorégraphie: the dance notation of the eighteenth century: Beauchamp or Feuillet?" *The Book Collector* (1967), 450–76.

Dubos, Jean-Baptiste. *Réflexions critiques sur la poésie et sur la peinture*. Paris, 1719; trans. Th. Nugent. *Critical Reflections on Poetry, Painting, and Music*. 5th edn. London, 1748.

Dufourcq, Norbert and Marcelle Benoit. "Les musiciens de Versailles à travers les minutes notariales de Lamy conservées aux Archives départementales de Seine-et-Oise." *Recherches sur la musique française classique* 3 (1963), 189–206.

"Les musiciens de Versailles à travers les minutes du baillage de Versailles conservées aux Archives départementales de Seine-et-Oise." *Recherches sur la musique française classique* 6 (1966), 197–226.

"Les musiciens de Versailles à travers les minutes notariales de M. Gayot conservées aux Archives départementales des Yvelines (1661–1733)." *Recherches sur la musique française classique* 15 (1975), 155–90.

Dulac, Georges. "Louis-Jacques Goussier, encyclopédiste." *Recherches nouvelles sur quelques écrivains des Lumières*. Ed. Jacques Proust. Geneva: Droz, 1972, 63–110.

Du Pradel, Abraham [Nicolas du Blegny]. *Le livre commode des adresses de Paris*. Paris, 1692.

Ecorcheville, Jules. "Quelques documents sur la musique de la Grande Ecurie du Roi." *Sammelbände der Internationalen Musikgesellschaft* 2 (1900–01), 608–42.

Vingt suites d'orchestre du XVIIe siècle français. Berlin: L. Lipmannssohn and Paris: Fortin & Cie., 1906; reprint New York: Broude Bros., 1970.

Ellis, Helen Meredith. "The dances of J. B. Lully (1632–1687)." Unpublished Ph.D. dissertation, Stanford University, 1967.

"Inventory of the dances of Jean-Baptiste Lully." *Recherches sur la musique française classique* 9 (1969), 21–55.

For other works by this author, see also Little, Meredith Ellis.

Eppelsheim, Jürgen. *Das Orchester in den Werken Jean-Baptiste Lullys*. Tutzing: Hans Schneider Verlag, 1961.

Fellowes, E. H. "The Philidor manuscripts: Paris, Versailles, Tenbury." *Music and Letters* 12/2 (1931), 116–29.

Fleurot, François. *Le hautbois dans la musique française, 1650–1800*. Paris: Picard, 1984.

Flood, W. H. Grattan. "Quelques précisions nouvelles sur Cambert et Grabu à Londres." *Revue musicale* 9 (1928), 351–61.

Fournel, Victor. "Théâtre de la cour (ballets et mascarades)." *Les contemporains de Molière*, vol. II, 171–666. Paris: Firmin Didot, 1866.

Fürstenau, Moritz. *Zur Geschichte der Musik und des Theaters am Hofe zu Dresden*. 2 vols. Dresden: Rudolf Kunze, 1861–62; reprint Leipzig: Edition Peters, 1971.

[Gherardi, Evaristo.] *Le theâtre italien de Gherardi*. 6 vols. Amsterdam: Adrian Braakman, 1701 (reprint of the Paris, 1700 edition).

Grobe, Edwin P. "S. Bre., French librettist at the court of Charles II." *Theatre Notebook* 9 (1954–55), 20–1.

Grout, Donald Jay. "The music of the Italian theatre at Paris, 1682–97." *Papers of the American Musicological Society* (1941), 158–70.

"Seventeenth-century parodies of French opera." *Musical Quarterly* 27 (1941), 211–19 and 514–26.

Guest, Ann Hutchinson. *Dance Notation: The Process of Recording Movement on Paper*. New York: Dance Horizons, 1984.

Guilcher, Jean-Michel. "André Lorin et l'invention de l'écriture chorégraphique." *Revue d'histoire du théâtre* 21 (1969), 256–64.

La contredanse et les renouvellements de la danse française. Paris: Mouton, 1969.

Gustafson, Bruce. *French Harpsichord Music of the 17th Century: A Thematic Catalog of the Sources with Commentary*. 3 vols. Ann Arbor: UMI Research Press, 1979.

Halfpenny, Eric. "A seventeenth-century oboe consort." *Galpin Society Journal* 7 (1954), 60–2.

"The English 2- and 3-keyed hautboy." *Galpin Society Journal* 2 (1949), 10–26.

"The French hautboy: a technical survey, Part I." *Galpin Society Journal* 6 (1953), 23–34.

"The 'Tenner Hoboy.'" *Galpin Society Journal* 5 (1952), 17–27.

Hansell, Kathleen. "Opera and ballet at the Regio ducal teatro of Milan, 1771–1776." Unpublished Ph.D. dissertation, University of California at Berkeley, 1980.

Harris-Warrick, Rebecca. "Ballroom dancing at the court of Louis XIV." *Early Music* 14 (1986), 41–9.

"Contexts for choreographies: notated dances set to the music of Jean-Baptiste Lully." *Jean-Baptiste Lully: Actes du Colloque/Kongreßbericht, Saint-Germain-en-Laye–Heidelberg 1987*. Ed. Jérôme de La Gorce and Herbert Schneider. Laaber: Laaber Verlag, 1990, 433–55.

"A few thoughts on Lully's *hautbois*." *Early Music* 18 (1990), 97–106.

"Interpreting pendulum markings for French Baroque dances." *Historical Performance* 6/1 (1993), 9–22.

"La Mariée: the history of a French court dance." *Jean-Baptiste Lully and the Music of the French Baroque: Essays in Honor of James R. Anthony*. Ed. John Hajdu Heyer. Cambridge University Press, 1989, 239–58.

Haynes, Bruce. "Johann Sebastian Bach's pitch standards: the woodwind perspective." *Journal of the American Musical Instrument Society* 11 (1985), 55–114.

"Lully and the rise of the oboe as seen in works of art." *Early Music* 16 (1988), 324–38.

Heck, Thomas F. *Commedia dell'Arte: A Guide to the Primary and Secondary Literature*. New York and London: Garland Publishing, 1988.

Hilton, Wendy. *Dance of Court and Theater: The French Noble Style 1690–1725*. Princeton: Princeton Book Company, 1981.

Isherwood, Robert M. *Music in the Service of the King: France in the Seventeenth Century*. Ithaca: Cornell University Press, 1973.

Jeschke, Claudia. *Tanzschriften, Ihre Geschichte und Methode: Die Illustrierte Darstellung eines Phänomens von den Anfängen bis zur Gegenwart*. Bad Reichenhall: Comes, 1983.

Jurgens, Madeleine. *Documents du Minutier Central concernant l'histoire de la musique (1600–1650)*. Vol. I, Paris: S.E.V.P.E.N., 1967; vol. II, Paris: La Documentation Française, 1974.

Jurgens, Madeleine and Marie-Antoinette Fleury. *Documents du Minutier Central concernant l'histoire littéraire (1650–1700)*. Paris: Presses Universitaires de France, 1960.

Jurgens, Madeleine and Elizabeth Maxfield-Miller. *Cent ans de recherches sur Molière, sur sa famille et sur les comédiens de sa troupe*. Paris: S.E.V.P.E.N., 1963.

Kougioumtzoglou-Roucher, Eugénia. "Aux origines de la danse classique: le vocabulaire de la belle danse (1661–1701)." 2 vols. Unpublished doctoral thesis, Université de Paris XIII, 1991.

Kunzle, Régine. "In search of L'Académie Royale de Danse." *York Dance Review* 7 (1978), 3–15.

"The illustrious unknown choreographer, Pierre Beauchamps." *Dance Scope* 8/2 (1974), 32–42 and 9/1 (1975), 30–45.

For other works by this author, see also Astier, Régine.

La Gorce, Jérôme de. "L'Académie Royale de Musique en 1704, d'après des documents inédits conservés dans les archives notariales." *Revue de musicologie* 64 (1979), 160–91.

Berain, dessinateur du Roi Soleil. Paris: Editions Herscher, 1986.

"Guillaume-Louis Pecour: a biographical essay." *Dance Research* 8/2 (1990), 3–26.

"L'opéra français à la cour de Louis XIV." *Revue d'histoire du théâtre* 35 (1983), 387–401.

"Some notes on Lully's orchestra." *Jean-Baptiste Lully and the Music of the French Baroque: Essays in honor of James R. Anthony*. Ed. John Hajdu Heyer. Cambridge University Press, 1989, 99–112.

Lagrave, Henri. *Le théâtre et le public à Paris de 1715 à 1750*. Paris: Librairie C. Klincksieck, 1972.

Lancelot, Francine. "Ecriture de la danse: le système Feuillet." *Revue de la Société d'Ethnographie Française* 1 (1971), 29–50.

"Les ornements dans la danse baroque." *Les goûts réunis*, numéro spécial: La danse baroque (1982), 72–8.

Lesure, François. "Concerts de hautbois et musettes au milieu du XVIIe s." *Revue de musicologie* 37 (1955), 83–4.

L'opéra classique français. Geneva: Editions Minkoff, 1972.

Little, Meredith Ellis. "French court dance in Germany at the time of Johann Sebastian Bach: *La Bourgogne* in Paris and Leipzig." *International Musicological Society: Report of the*

Twelfth Congress, Berkeley 1977. Ed. Daniel Heartz and Bonnie Wade. Kassel: Bärenreiter, 1981, 730–4.

"Problems of repetition and continuity in the dance music of Lully's 'Ballet des Arts.'" *Jean-Baptiste Lully: Actes du Colloque/Kongreßbericht, Saint-Germain-en-Laye–Heidelberg 1987.* Ed. Jérôme de La Gorce and Herbert Schneider. Laaber: Laaber Verlag, 1990, 423–32.

For other works by this author, see also Ellis, Helen Meredith.

Little, Meredith Ellis and Carol G. Marsh. *La Danse Noble: An Inventory of Dances and Sources.* Williamstown, New York, Nabburg: Broude Brothers Ltd., 1992.

Loubet de Sceaury, Paul. *Musiciens et facteurs d'instruments de musique sous l'ancien régime: statuts corporatifs.* Paris: Editions A. Pedone, 1949.

Lully, Jean-Baptiste. *Oeuvres complètes.* Ed. Henry Prunières. Paris: Editions de la Revue Musicale, 1930–9.

McBride, Robert. "Ballet: a neglected key to Molière's theatre." *Dance Research* 2 (1984), 3–18.

McGowan, Margaret. *L'art du ballet de cour en France (1581–1643).* Paris: Editions du C.N.R.S., 1963.

Marie, Alfred and Jeanne. *Mansart à Versailles.* 2 vols. Paris: Editions Jacques Fréal, 1972.

Marsh, Carol G. (ed.). *Anthony L'Abbé, A New Collection of Dances,* facsimile edition with introduction. In Series D of Music for London Entertainment. London: Stainer & Bell, 1991.

Marsh, Carol. "French court dance in England, 1706–1740: a study of the sources." Unpublished Ph.D. dissertation, City University of New York, 1985.

Marsh, Carol G. and Rebecca Harris-Warrick. "A new source for seventeenth-century ballet: *Le Mariage de la Grosse Cathos.*" *Dance Chronicle* 11 (1988), 398–428.

Marx, Joseph. "The tone of the Baroque oboe: an interpretation of the history of double-reed instruments." *Galpin Society Journal* 4 (1951), 3–19.

Massip, Catherine. "La collection musicale Toulouse-Philidor à la Bibliothèque nationale." *Fontes Artis Musicae* 30/4 (1983), 184–207.

La vie des musiciens de Paris au temps de Mazarin (1643–1661). Paris: Editions A. & J. Picard, 1976.

Mather, Betty Bang with the assistance of Dean M. Karns. *Dance Rhythms of the French Baroque: A Handbook for Performance.* Bloomington and Indianapolis: Indiana University Press, 1987.

Mélèse, Pierre. *Le théâtre et le public à Paris sous Louis XIV: 1659–1715.* Paris: E. Droz, 1934.

[Ménestrier, Claude-François.] *Des ballets anciens et modernes selon les règles du théâtre.* Paris: R. Guignard, 1682.

Mongrédien, Georges. *Dictionnaire biographique des comédiens français du 17e siècle.* 3rd edn. Paris: Editions du C.N.R.S., 1981.

Moureau, François. "Les comédiens italiens et la cour de France (1664–1697)." *XVIIe Siècle* 33 (1981), 63–81.

"Lully en visite chez Arlequin: parodies italiennes avant 1697." *Jean-Baptiste Lully: Actes du Colloque/Kongreßbericht, Saint-Germain-en-Laye–Heidelberg 1987.* Ed. Jérôme de La Gorce and Herbert Schneider. Laaber: Laaber Verlag, 1990, 235–50.

[Parfaict, François and Claude.] *Histoire de l'ancien théâtre italien, depuis son origine en France jusqu'à sa suppression en l'année 1697.* Paris: Rozet, 1767; reprint New York: AMS Press, 1978.

Petre, Robert. "Six new dances by Kellom Tomlinson: a recently discovered manuscript." *Early Music* 18 (1990), 381–90.

Pierce, Ken. "Saut what? (Sauts in early eighteenth-century dance)." *Proceedings of the Eleventh Annual Conference of the Society of Dance History Scholars* (1988), 68–95.

Pougin, Arthur. "La troupe de Lully." *Le Ménestrel* 61 (1895), 299–300, 316–17, 323–4, 332–3, 339–40, 347–8.

Powell, John Scott. "Music in the theater of Molière." Unpublished Ph.D. dissertation, University of Washington, 1982.

Prunières, Henry. *Le ballet de cour en France avant Benserade et Lully.* Paris: Henri Laurens, 1914.

[Pure, Michel de.] *Idées des spectacles anciens et nouveaux.* Paris: M. Brunet, 1668.

Ralph, Richard. *The Life and Works of John Weaver*. New York: Dance Horizons, 1985.

Rebman, Elisabeth Huttig. "*Chorégraphie*: an annotated bibliography of eighteenth-century printed instruction books." Unpublished M.A. thesis, Stanford University, 1981.

Rice, Paul F. *The Performing Arts at Fontainebleau from Louis XIV to Louis XVI*. Ann Arbor: UMI Research Press, 1988.

Richardson, Philip J. S. "The Beauchamp mystery: some fresh light on an old problem." *Dancing Times* 438 (March, 1947), 299–302; 439 (April, 1947), 351–7.

Rosow, Lois. "French Baroque recitative as an expression of tragic declamation." *Early Music* 11 (1983), 468–79.

"Lully." *New Grove Dictionary of Opera*. London: Macmillan Publishers Limited, 1992.

"Lully's 'Armide' at the Paris Opera: a performance history: 1686–1766." Unpublished Ph.D. dissertation, Brandeis University, 1981.

"The metrical notation of Lully's recitative." *Jean-Baptiste Lully: Actes du Colloque/ Kongreßbericht, Saint-Germain-en-Laye–Heidelberg 1987*. Ed. Jérôme de La Gorce and Herbert Schneider. Laaber: Laaber Verlag, 1990, 405–22.

"Performing a choral dialogue by Lully." *Early Music* 15 (1987), 325–35.

Sadler, Graham. "The role of the keyboard continuo in French opera 1673–1776." *Early Music* 8 (1980), 148–57.

[Saint-Simon, Louis de Rouvroy, Duc de]. *Mémoires de Saint-Simon*. Ed. A. de Boislisle. 41 vols. Paris: Librairie Hachette, 1879–1928.

Sandman, Susan G. "Indications of snare-drum technique in Philidor Collection Ms. 1163." *Galpin Society Journal* 30 (1977), 70–5.

"Wind band music under Louis XIV: the Philidor Collection, music for the military and the court." Unpublished Ph.D. dissertation, Stanford University, 1974.

Sawkins, Lionel. "For and against the order of nature: who sang the soprano?" *Early Music* 15 (1987), 315–24.

Schmidt, Carl B. "Berkeley Ms. 454: Philidor *l'aîné*'s 'Enigma Variations.'" *Journal of Musicology* 10 (1992), 362–404.

Catalogue Raisonné of the Literary Sources for the Tragédies Lyriques of Jean-Baptiste Lully: Lully Livret Catalogue (LLC). New York: Broude Brothers, in press.

Schneider, Herbert. *Chronologisch-Thematisches Verzeichnis Sämtlicher Werke von Jean-Baptiste Lully (LWV)*. Tutzing: Hans Schneider Verlag, 1981.

Schwartz, Judith L. and Christena L. Schlundt. *French Court Dance and Dance Music: A Guide to Primary Source Writings, 1643–1789*. Stuyvesant, NY: Pendragon Press, 1987.

Scott, Virginia. *The Commedia dell'Arte in Paris, 1644–1697*. Charlottesville: University Press of Virginia, 1990.

Semmens, Richard Templar. "Woodwind treatment in the early ballets of Jean-Baptiste Lully." Unpublished Master's thesis, University of British Columbia, 1975.

Silin, Charles I. *Benserade and his Ballets de Cour*. Baltimore: The Johns Hopkins Press, 1940; reprint New York: AMS Press, 1978.

Sourches, Louis-François de Bouchet de. *Mémoires sur le règne de Louis XIV*. Ed. G.-J. de Cosnac and A. Bertrand. 13 vols. Paris: Librairie Hachette, 1882–93.

Sutton, Julia. "The minuet: an elegant phoenix." *Dance Chronicle* 8 (1985), 119–52.

Tessier, André. "Un catalogue de la bibliothèque de la musique du roi au château de Versailles." *Revue de musicologie* 15 (1931), 106–17 and 172–89.

Thoinan, Ernest [Roquet, Antoine Ernest]. *Les Hotteterre et les Chédeville*. Paris: Edmont Sagot, 1894.

"Les Philidor." *La France musicale*, 22 Dec. 1867, 397–9; 29 Dec. 1867, 405–7; 5 Jan. 1868, 1–3; and 12 Jan. 1868, 9–11.

"Philidor (Danican-)." *Supplément* (Arthur Pougin, ed.), vol. 2 of F.-J. Fétis, *Biographie universelle des musiciens et bibliographie générale de la musique*. Paris: Firmin-Didot et Cie, 1881, 332–7.

Waquet, Françoise. "'Philidor l'aîné, ordinaire de la musique du roy et garde de tous les livres de sa bibliothèque de musique': un essai de biographie d'après des documents inédits." *Revue de musicologie* 66 (1980), 203–16.

Ward, John. "Newly devis'd measures for Jacobean masques." *Acta Musicologica* 60 (1988), 111–42.

Wiel, Taddeo. *I teatri musicali veneziani del settecento*. Venice: Fratelli Visentini, 1897.

Winter, Marian Hannah. *The Pre-Romantic Ballet*. London: Pitman Publishing, 1974.

Witherell, Anne L. *Louis Pécour's 1700* Recueil de Danses. Ann Arbor: UMI Research Press, 1983.
Zaslaw, Neal. "The enigma of the haute-contre." *The Musical Times* 115 (November 1974), 939–41.
   "Lully's orchestra." *Jean-Baptiste Lully: Actes du Colloque/Kongreßbericht, Saint-Germain-en-Laye–Heidelberg 1987*. Ed. Jérôme de La Gorce and Herbert Schneider. Laaber: Laaber Verlag, 1990, 539–79.
   "When is an orchestra not an orchestra?" *Early Music* 16 (1988), 483–95.

Index

Académie Royale de Danse, 9, 24n, 25n, 26, 32–3, 87
Académie Royale de Musique (Opéra), 1, 3, 7, 9, 10, 11, 14n, 22, 23, 26, 32–3, 35, 43, 69, 71, 83, 84, 88n
Acis et Galatée (Lully), 29
air (vocal), 4, 9, 43, 47–8, 62, 63, 67, 72, 73, 74–6, 81
"Air des ivrognes" (drunk dance; dance VI), 47n, 48, 54–5, 61, 62, 64, 78, 79, 80, 103, 105, 108, 109, 110, 111, 112–13, 115, 125, 135, 149–53, 172, 187
Alceste (Lully), 23, 64
d'Alembert, Jean le Rond, 87
"Allons, accourons tous" (chorus, dance II), 45, 47, 52, 60, 64, 76–7, 78, 81, 113–14, 132–5, 171
Amadis (Lully), 35n
Amant Guéri, L', see *Travaux d'Hercule, Les*
Amants Magnifiques, Les (Lully), 10
Amazones, Les (Anne Danican Philidor), 21, 43n, 73
Amour Malade, L' (Lully), 69
Amours de Ragonde, Les (Mouret), 43n
Amour Vainqueur, L' (Anne Danican Philidor), 20
d'Anglebert, Jean-Henry, 7
Arbeau, Thoinot, 49, 83, 86n
Ariane (Cambert), 23
arm and hand gestures, 58, 62n, 88, 91n, 104, 142–3, 145–6, 176
assemblé, 107, 110, 112, 113, 118n, 131, 132, 134, 143, 144, 160, 168, 181, 183
Atys (Lully), 3–4, 23, 30, 33, 43, 62

balancé, pas, 107, 109, 115, 147, 176
ballet de cour, 1–4, 8–10, 17, 35, 60, 61, 65, 67, 68, 81, 83, 84, 186
  performers in, 5, 6, 7, 8, 14n, 15, 16, 22, 24, 29, 31
Ballet de Flore (Lully), 22n
Ballet de la Nuit, 35n
Ballet de l'Impatience (Lully), 22
Ballet de M. de Vendosme, 84n
"Ballet de neuf danseurs" (Feuillet), 65, 97, 126n
Ballet des Amours Déguisés (Lully), 22
Ballet des Arts (Lully), 2n, 35n
Ballet des Ballets (Lully), 3
Ballet des Muses (Lully), 22, 30
Ballet des Plaisirs (Lully), 3
Ballet des Saisons (Lully), 1, 2
Ballet et musique, 28
balls, 2–3, 5, 6, 7, 10, 16, 24, 25, 30n, 35, 37, 41, 56, 72
Barazé, 32, 33, 41, 124
basse danse, 83
bassoon, see oboe
Beauchamps, Pierre
  as choreographer, 3, 9, 23, 32, 84
  as composer, 9, 20, 23n
  as dancer, 10, 33–4, 35
  as inventor of dance notation, xi, 23, 83–7, 88, 91, 102
Behr, Samuel Rudolph, 86
Bellérophon (Lully), 8, 76
Benserade, Isaac de, 1, 14n
Berain, Jean, 8n, 18, 37n, 39, 40n, 42, 45, 58n
Biancolelli, Giuseppe Domenico (Dominique), 11–13, 33–4
Blamont, Collin de, 89
Borel, Jean (Miracle), 29–30, 40
Bourgeois Gentilhomme, Le (Lully/Molière), 3, 6n, 13, 15, 26n, 28, 30, 32, 33
Bourgogne, Duchesse de, 15, 24n, 30n, 85n
bourrée, pas de, 91, 93, 107, 110, 111, 113, 131, 143, 181
branle, 56, 57n, 80n, 162
Brémond, Sébastien, 28
Brionne, Comte de, 10, 24, 26n, 36n, 42
Brossard, Sébastien de, 85
Brunet, Jean, 30–1
Brunet, Jean-Louis, 31

cabriole, 105, 107–8, 139, 140
Cadmus et Hermione (Lully), 63, 80
Cambert, Robert, 23, 28, 29, 33
Campra, André, 80
Canal de Versailles, Le (Philidor l'aîné), 18, 29, 30, 69, 73
Carnaval, Le (Lully, 1668), 2n, 7
Carnaval Mascarade, Le (Lully, 1675), 3, 8, 28
carnival, entertainments for, 2–3, 4, 24, 35, 36n, 59, 72, 73
Caroso, Fabritio, 83, 92–3
Cassandre, 2n, 10
Cavalli, Francesco, 6
Caverley, Thomas, 81

Cercle d'Anet, Le (Philidor l'aîné), 20
chaconne, 10, 26n, 84, 86
Chambonnières, Jacques Champion de, 7
chambre (musicians of the), 4–5, 7–8, 16, 29–31
Champmeslé, Charles Chevillet de and Marie, 25–6
chapelle (musicians of the), 4–5, 16, 29–30, 68
charivari, 46, 48, 58–9, 61, 64, 68, 71, 72, 76, 77, 78, 81, 177–8, 186
Charles II of England, 23, 28
chassé, 108, 112, 120, 155, 160
Chorégraphie, ou l'art de décrire la danse (Feuillet), 53n, 83–5, 88–9, 91n, 92, 93, 94, 96, 102, 106, 110, 111, 115, 118n, 119
choreographies, see dances
choruses
  dancing in, 47, 49, 52, 57–8, 60–1, 63–4, 171
  structures of, 76–8
  see also "Allons, accourons tous" and "Passons toujours la vie"
comedy-ballet, 1, 3, 4, 14n, 22, 26, 35, 68
comédie française, 3, 10, 25–6, 36, 41
comédie italienne, xi, 3, 10–13, 26, 33–4, 36, 40–1, 43, 46
commedia dell'arte, 10; see also *comédie italienne*
Compan, Charles, 87n
Constantini, Angelo, 11–13, 34
Conti, Princesse de (Marie Anne de Bourbon), 3, 10, 10n, 24, 26n, 36–7, 38, 39, 42, 49
continuo, 7, 68, 72–3
contredanse, 29, 54n, 85, 86, 87, 93n, 106, 122, 147–8
contretemps, 107, 108, 111, 112, 113–14, 131, 139–40, 143, 144, 160, 176, 181
  à deux mouvements, 108, 117n, 120n
contretemps balonné, 58n, 108, 113–14, 131, 160, 176, 181
contretemps de menuet, 106, 107, 109, 112, 113–16, 119, 147, 148, 168
Corneille, Pierre, 74
country dance, 56, 57n, 85, 161
coupé, 94, 109, 112, 113–14, 125, 143, 144, 160, 176, 181
courante, 24, 28
Couture-Boussey, La, 43

cromornes et trompettes marines, les, 5–6, 15–16

Danaë (Anne Danican Philidor), 21
dance music, collections of, 29, 30n, 73n, 82n, 186
dance notation, invention of, xi–xii(n), 23, 83–7, 91–2
dancers
  amateur, 3, 10, 24, 26n, 35, 37, 41
  professional, 3, 9–10, 22–3, 26n, 35–6, 41
  training of, 10, 22n
dances
  as entr'actes, 3, 10, 26n, 35–6
  ballroom, 2–3, 10, 24, 28–9, 95, 143
  comic, xii, 46, 53n, 55, 67, 80, 135, 139–40, 149, 153
  construction of, 49–59, 63–6
  dating of, 82–3
  within ballets, 2, 9, 10, 24, 64–5
  within operas, 3–4, 63–6
  see also choruses, dancing in; Favier, principles of choreography; Feuillet notation, dances in
dancing masters, 9–10, 22, 24–5, 32, 82–3, 84
Dangeau, Marquis de, *Journal*, 3, 26n, 32, 35–7, 85
danses à deux, see dances, ballroom
Dauphin, *see* Louis de Bourbon
Dauphine, *see* Marie-Anne Christine-Victoire de la Bavière
De La Haise (dancing master), 86–7, 91
demi-contretemps, 96, 106, 108, 109–10, 113–14, 119, 125, 143, 144, 160, 168, 176
demi-coupé, 94, 103, 106–11 *passim*, 114, 117, 118–20, 140, 143, 160, 176
demi-jeté, 107n, 120n
Descouteaux, François Pignon, 7, 30, 31
Désolation des Deux Comédies, La, 41
Diane et Endymion (Anne Danican Philidor), 20
Diderot, Denis, 87
Dido and Aeneas (Purcell), 80
divertissement, 14n, 24, 35, 36, 186
  within an opera, 3–4, 54, 63
  within *Le Mariage de la Grosse Cathos*, 4, 46, 53, 61, 147
Dominique, *see* Biancolelli, Giuseppe Domenico
douze grands hautbois, les, see *joueurs de violons*; see also oboes, ensembles of
drum, 59, 67, 71–2, 73, 77
drunk dance, *see* "Air des Ivrognes"
Duchesse de Bourbon (Madame la), 10, 36n
Dumirail, Romain, 3, 23, 32–3, 41, 124, 136, 149–50
Dumoulin (dancer), 22n, 43, 45, 58n
Dupré (dancer), 88–9, 90, 92

échappé, pas, 100, 110
écurie, grande
  music for, 16–17, 69, 70, 71, 79
  musicians of the, 4–7, 15–17, 30–1

Eglogue de Marly, L' (Pierre Danican Philidor), 20
Encyclopédie ou dictionnaire raisonné, xiii, xiv, 86, 87–92, 97, 99, 104
entrechat, 110, 112, 115, 149, 153
"Entrée de deux filles de la noce" (gigue; dance IV), 47, 53, 78, 79, 103, 108, 109, 110, 112, 113, 114, 140–4, 187
"Entrée de deux filles et deux garçons de la noce" (menuet; dance V), 43, 47, 50n, 53–5, 57, 60–1, 78, 79, 94, 103, 109, 112–14, 144–8, 162, 163, 171, 172
"Entrée de deux garçons de la noce" (dance III), 47, 50n, 53, 78, 79, 80, 102, 103, 108, 110, 111, 113, 114, 116, 135–40, 187
entrée grave, 55, 80, 149, 153

Facheux, Les (Beauchamps), 9, 23n
false positions of feet, 102, 136, 139–40
Faure (dancer), 23
Fausse Prude, La, 11n
Favier, Bernard Henri, 22, 26n
Favier family, 7, 9, 21–2, 25, 26, 27
Favier, Jacques, 21–2, 23
Favier, Jean (II), 24, 25, 26–7, 34, 88n
Favier, Jean Jacques, 22, 26n
Favier *l'aîné*, Jean
  as choreographer and notator, xiii, 23, 24, 26n, 27–9, 48–50, 56, 57, 58, 59, 62, 63–6, 78, 82–3, 86, 88–94, 121–2, 184, 187
  as composer, 23, 27
  as dancer, xiii, 3, 9–10, 13, 22–3, 26, 32, 36, 37, 41, 124, 136, 149–50
  as dancing master, xiii, 24–5, 37
  biography of, 21–7
  principles of choreography, xii, 53, 63–6, 125, 131, 134–5, 139–40, 143, 144, 147–8, 153, 160–1, 162, 163–4, 168–70, 176, 181–3
  works by, 23, 27–9
Favier *le cadet*, 22, 25n, 26n
Favier notation, xi–xiii, 48–9, 50n, 56, 58, 82–3, 86–94, 97–9, 99–105, 106–12, 117–22
  applied to movements of instrumentalists, xi, 9, 48–52, 62–3
  applied to movements of singers, xi, 48–9, 51, 61–2
  timings of steps, 88–9, 96, 104, 113–16, 145, 156, 168, 183
Favier step, 106, 110–11, 112, 113, 140, 143, 160
Fête d'Arcueil, La (Philidor *l'aîné*), 15, 19
Fêtes de l'Amour et de Bacchus, Les (Lully), 69
Fêtes Grecques et Romaines, Les (Blamont), 89
Feuillet notation, xi–xiii, 53, 82, 83–5, 87–97, 98–112 *passim*, 115–22 *passim*, 125, 126
  dances in, xii, 24n, 28–9, 50, 52, 54, 55n, 56n, 62, 65, 80, 82, 87, 95, 117n, 121n, 135n, 140, 143–4, 145, 147, 154, 163, 170, 176

Feuillet, Raoul Auger, xi, 29, 53, 65, 82–7, 88, 91, 92, 93–4
  see also *Chorégraphie*
fleuret, 98, 107, 109–14 *passim*, 117, 120, 131, 134, 139, 143, 160, 176, 181
floor patterns, 49, 50–9, 62, 65, 85, 126, 131–2, 134–5, 140, 144, 147–8, 153, 160–1, 169–70, 176–7, 181–2
flute
  development of, 31
  ensembles of, 8, 15
  performers on, 6n, 7–8, 15, 31–2
Fossard, François, 16

gaillarde, pas de, 91, 93, 103, 110–11
Galanterie du Temps, La (Lully), 2n
Gaudrau, Michel, 84
Georges Dandin (Molière), 30
Germain (Antoine or Louis), 32, 41, 124, 141
Gherardi, Evaristo, 12, 34, 46n
Gigogne, Dame, 41, 43, 123–4, 154, 172n, 187
  see also Dame Ragonde
gigue, see "Entrée de deux filles de la noce"
gigue, music, 79, 140
Gingant, Louis, 13, 30, 40
glissé, 96, 105, 109, 119
Goussier, Louis–Jacques, xiv, 87–94
grand ballet, 2, 59
grande bande, la, see *grands violons, les*
grands hautbois, les, see *joueurs de violons*; see also oboes, ensembles of
grands violons, les, 7, 8, 9, 21, 22, 23, 71
Grotte de Versailles, La (Lully), 10n
Guillegau (Guillegault), André, 30, 40

Harlequin, 11–13, 33–4, 40–1, 46–7, 53, 58, 59, 104, 110, 153, 177–8
  see also Biancolelli
hautbois des mousquetaires, les, 6
hautbois et musettes de Poitou, les, 5–6, 8n, 30
Hotteterre family, 43

Idylle sur la Paix, L' (Lully), 10n
instrumentalists on stage, xii–xiii, 7, 8–9, 14n, 15, 32, 46, 49–52, 55–9, 60, 62–3, 71–2, 73, 127–32, 161–2, 163–70, 176, 178–82
Intermèdes de la Comédie des Fées (Lalande), 26
Isaac (dancer), 85n
Isis (Lully), 8, 22, 62, 64

Javiliers (dancer), 89
jeté, 107–9, 111, 117, 119–20, 125, 160
Jeu d'Echecs, Le (Pierre Danican Philidor), 20
Jonquet (Jean or Pierre), 30, 40
joueurs de fifres et tambours, 5, 15–16
joueurs de violons, hautbois, sacquebouttes et cornets, les (*les douze grands hautbois*), 5, 16–17, 68

Index

La Grange, Charles Varlet, Sieur de, 26n, 41n
Lalande, Michel Richard de, 17, 26, 80
Lambranzi, Gregorio, 135n
La Vallière, Louise de, 10n, 37
Lendemain de la Noce de Village, Le (Anne Danican Philidor), 18, 21, 43n, 63, 72n
Le Noble, *see* Schwartzenberg, Jean-Louis
Le Roy, Fursy (or Philippe Le Roy de Beaumont), 13, 30, 40
Lesczinski, Stanislas, 27
Létang (Lestang), 10, 23, 36
Lorin, André, 83–7, 91, 93, 94, 106, 107, 122
Louis XIII, 14, 15n, 84n
Louis XIV, 1, 2, 6n, 10, 11, 15n, 16, 22, 24, 25n, 31, 32, 33–4, 35, 36, 83–5, 185
Louis XV, 27, 85n
Louis de Bourbon (the Dauphin; Monseigneur), 3, 4n, 6n, 10, 10n, 24, 32n, 36–7, 42
Lully, Jean-Baptiste, 1–4, 7, 8–9, 16, 17, 22–3, 25, 33, 60, 61, 62, 63, 64, 65, 67–8, 69, 70, 72, 73, 74–6, 79, 80, 81, 83
works by, xii, 2–4, 6, 7, 8–9, 10n, 11n, 15, 16, 17n, 22–4, 26, 28, 29–30, 31n, 32–3, 35, 41, 43, 45, 54, 55, 62, 63, 64, 68, 69, 76, 80, 84, 86, 185, 187n

Magny, Claude Marc, 23, 88
Maintenon, Madame de, 11n
Marais, Marin, 7
"Marche pour neuf hautbois, huit danseurs, et neuf musiciens" ("La pavane"; dance I), 46, 49–52, 63, 64, 78, 79, 80, 126–32, 177–8, 181–3
see also "Pavane, La" (dance X)
march, 59, 69, 80
Mariage de la Grosse Cathos, Le
cast of, xii, 6–7, 12–13, 14, 29–34, 40–1, 43, 186–7
genre of, xi, 2, 4
Italian comedians in, xii, 12, 26, 33–4, 36, 40–1
music of, 17, 18, 74–81, 127, 133, 136, 140–1, 145, 149, 154, 162, 171
performance of, xi, 19, 35–7
scores of, xi, 47n, 54n, 77, 184–7
scoring of, 67–73, 76
staging of, xii–xiii, 2, 8–9, 48–66, 127–9, 133, 136, 141, 145, 149–50, 154–5, 163–4, 172, 178
synopsis of, 45–8
see also divertissement within *Le Mariage*
Mariage de Ragonde, Le (Mouret), 41
Marie-Anne Christine-Victoire de la Bavière (the Dauphine), xiii, 24, 25, 28, 42
mascarade, 24, 35, 36, 37, 40–1, 48, 59, 67, 72, 80
as a genre, xi, 2–4
examples of, 2, 2n, 4, 19–21

Mascarade du Capitaine, La, 2n
Mazarin, Cardinal, 2
Mazuel, Jean, 21
"Menuet" (dance V), *see* "Entrée de deux filles et deux garçons de la noce"
menuet
dance type, 53, 96, 116, 147
music, 80, 145
menuet, pas de, 53, 57, 80, 91, 93–4, 96, 111–12, 113–16, 147, 168
timing of, 113–16
meter, 24n, 74–5, 77, 78, 79–80, 162n, 187
Mezzetin, 11–12, 33–4, 40–1, 46–7, 53, 58–9, 177–8
see also Constantini
Miracle, *see* Borel, Jean
Mithridate (Racine), 3
Molière, Jean-Baptiste Poquelin, 3, 9, 10, 25–6, 74
Monseigneur, *see* Louis de Bourbon
Monsieur de Pourceaugnac (Lully/Molière), 28, 33, 68
Montespan, Madame de, 10n
Morel (Maurel), Antoine, 13, 30, 40
Mouret, Jean-Joseph, 41

Naissance de Vénus, La (Lully), 22
Negri, Cesare, 83, 92–3
Noce de Village, La (Philidor *l'aîné*), 17, 18, 19, 43n, 72n, 79
Nopces de Village, Les (Lully), 2, 8–9, 28, 69

oboes
development of, 69–70
ensembles of, xiii, 5–7, 15–16, 40–1, 43, 68–73, 76, 77
sizes of, 68, 70–2, 76
see also instrumentalists on stage
opera, 1–4, 8, 11n, 17, 35, 43, 60, 61, 63, 64, 67, 74–5, 76, 80, 81, 84
performers in, 5, 14n, 15, 22, 26, 29–33
Opéra, *see* Académie Royale de Musique
Orontée (Lorenzoni), 32n

pantomime, 52, 55, 59, 61, 64, 132, 153, 171
Pasch, Johannes, 86n
"Passepied" (dance VIII), 48–9, 52–4, 56–7, 60, 62, 63, 64–5, 78, 79, 94, 109–10, 112–15, 121, 123, 161–72, 176, 187
passepied
dance type, 147n, 162
music, 17, 28, 79–80, 162–3
"Passons toujours la vie" (chorus, dance IX), 43, 47, 52, 54, 56–7, 60, 63–5, 78, 81, 103, 104, 107, 109, 110, 113, 133, 171–7
Pastorale (Pierre Danican Philidor), 20
"Pavane, La" (recessional; dance X), 48, 49, 50n, 53, 58–9, 63–4, 78, 113, 124, 177–83
see also "Marche pour neuf hautbois"
pavane, dance type, 24n, 28, 49, 78, 108, 113–14, 121, 127, 162, 177

Pécour (Pécourt), Guillaume, 3, 10, 23, 24n, 26n, 36, 53, 82n, 84, 93, 94
Pemberton, Edmund, 97n
performance spaces, 8, 10–11, 36, 37, 48, 49, 60, 71, 72
petits violons, les, 7, 8, 16, 37, 71
Perrin, Pierre, 29
Persée (Lully), 35
Phaéton (Lully), 84, 86
Philbert (Philibert Rebillé), 8, 13, 18, 30–2, 40, 56, 65
Philidor, André Danican (Philidor *l'aîné*)
as composer, xi, xiii, 8, 14, 17, 18, 30, 62, 65–6, 67–8, 71, 72, 73, 75–81, 116, 126, 127, 162, 187
as music copyist and librarian, xi, 16–17, 18, 29, 35, 54, 69, 71, 73n, 77, 78, 80n, 83, 184–7
as performer, xiii, 5–6, 7n, 13, 15–16, 25n, 178n
biography of, 14–17, 43
works by, 4, 6, 17–21, 26, 29, 40n, 41, 43, 72n, 73, 185–6
Philidor, Anne Danican, 17, 18n, 20–1, 63
Philidor Collection, 16n, 18–20, 184–6
Philidor family, 5, 14–15, 17–18, 20–1, 185–6
Philidor, François André, 17
Philidor, Jacques (Philidor *le cadet*), 6, 15, 17
Philidor *le père*, see Philidor *l'aîné*, André Danican
Philidor, Pierre Danican, 17, 20
pirouette, 100, 110, 112, 153
Plessis, du (oboist), 43
Pomone (Cambert), 23
Princesse de Crète, La (Philidor *l'aîné*), 18, 29, 30, 36, 186
Proserpine (Lully), 8, 32n, 187n
Psyché (Lully), 15, 29, 32, 45, 64
Purcell, Henry, 80

Quinault, Philippe, 3, 74

Racine, Jean, 3, 74
Ragonde, Dame, 41, 43–4, 46, 53, 67, 75, 136, 187
see also Dame Gigogne
Rameau, Jean-Philippe, 80
Rameau, Pierre, 9n, 23, 32, 88, 89n, 93–4, 109–11, 115, 116
Rassicod, Genevieve, 21n, 25–6
Raynal, Guillaume, 24
recessional, *see* "La Pavane" (dance X)
récit, 2, 4
recitative, xiii, 4, 43–4, 47–8, 62, 67, 72, 73, 74–5, 81
Revente des Habits, La (Lully), 55
Richer, 32, 33, 41, 124, 141
"Rigaudon" (*pour les filles de la noce*; dance VII), 43, 48, 54, 55–7, 58, 64–5, 78, 79, 108, 110, 112, 113, 125, 153–63, 168, 170, 171, 176, 187
rigaudon
dance type, 23n, 29, 78
music, 17, 28, 79, 154
rigaudon, pas de, 97, 108, 112–13, 143

Roland (Lully), 35n, 41, 69
Rousseau, Jean-Jacques, 87, 90n
Roy de la Chine, Le (Philidor *l'aîné*), 6, 18, 19, 30, 43n, 72n, 73

Saint-Simon, Duc de, 25, 36n
sarabande, 24n, 28
saut, 98, 106–7, 117–20
Savoyards, Les (Philidor *l'aîné*), 19, 41, 43n
Schwartzenberg, Jean-Louis, 17
Siris, P., 84
sissonne, pas de, 107, 112–13, 143–4
staging practices, see *Mariage de la Grosse Cathos, Le*, staging of
step rhythms, *see* Favier notation, timing of steps

strings, ensembles of, 68–9
symmetry (choreographic), xii, 50, 53, 60, 62, 65, 126, 131, 140, 147–8, 161, 163–4, 169–70, 172

Taubert, Gottfried, 93n
Temple de la Paix, Le (Lully), 24
temps de courante, 109, 119, 143
Thésée (Lully), 8n, 23, 33, 62
tombé, 96, 100, 110
Tomlinson, Kellom, 81n, 93n, 115, 122
tortillé, pas, 104
tragédie en musique, see opera
"Traité de la cadence," 115, 121
Travaux d'Hercule ou l'Amant Guéri, Les (Philidor *l'aîné*), 19–20, 186

Triomphe de Bacchus, Le (Favier), 23, 27
Triomphe de l'Amour, Le (Lully), 4, 7, 10n, 24, 30, 33, 80

Vaisseau Marchand, Le (Philidor *l'aîné*), 6, 18, 19, 43n, 72n
Vendôme, Duchesse de, 17, 20
versification, French, 74–5
vingt-quatre violons du roi, les, see *grands violons, les*
violinists as dancing masters, 9, 21–2
violons du cabinet, see *petits violons, les*

Xerxès (Cavalli/Lully), 6, 8, 22

For EU product safety concerns, contact us at Calle de José Abascal, 56–1°, 28003 Madrid, Spain or eugpsr@cambridge.org.

www.ingramcontent.com/pod-product-compliance
Lightning Source LLC
LaVergne TN
LVHW082244060526
838200LV00046B/2047